ENIGMATIC FREEMASONRY

The Theory of the "Common Good" and Russian Freemasonry in the Second Half of the 18th Century – the First Quarter of the 19th Century

Volume I

FRED Y. FORD
ALEXEY V. DMITRIEV

2021

Dedications

This book is dedicated to America and Freedom and Democracy that are the Eternal Values of the life of all people on Earth.

This book is dedicated to the Lord God, our Heavenly Father, who gave the opportunity to overcome delusions and approach the truth when writing the book. It is well-known that the truth is the source of all light and knowledge in our mortal life.

— Fred Ford:

This book is dedicated to my wise parents, chaste and beloved wife, and my wonderful children.

— Alexey Dmitriev:

This book is dedicated to my father, Benjamin (1947-2021), who taught me all my life to take education and science very seriously. Frankly, I would be doomed to intellectual, social, and spiritual death without following my father's advice. Also, this book is dedicated to my wife, Anna, and son, Zakhar, who patiently tolerated my constant absence during the long winter evenings when I was writing the book.

Acknowledgements

The authors of this book express their sincere gratitude to Professor Sergey V. Arzhanukhin for his guidance and guidelines in the comprehensive study of Freemasonry. The section of the book on historiography appeared thanks to his wise suggestion. The authors of this book express their deep appreciation to the Honored Lawyer of Russia, Professor Sergey V. Kodan. This book would never have been written without him. S. V. Kodan advised to return to the subject of research over again and over again, polish the text, and reveal new facets in the history of the doctrines of the State and Law. The authors of this book are also grateful to Professor Alexey P. Semitko, who helped to cope with "perfectionism" and contributed to the mastery of the theoretical-legal and historical-legal sciences. In addition, keen thankfulness should be expressed to Oksana Y. Lapteva, an employee of the Publications Support Department of the State Hermitage Museum, for providing illustrations for the book.

Table Of Contents

Introduction **17**

Chapter I — The issues of the historiography and source study of the state and legal ideas of the Russian Freemasons of the late 18th – the first quarter of the 19th century **45**

1.1. The historiography of the state and legal ideas of Russian Freemasons 45

1.2. The source study of the state and legal ideas of Russian Freemasons 76

Chapter II — The "common good" in the theory, legislation, and worldview of Russian Freemasons in the Russian Empire of the 18th century – the first quarter of the 19th century. **102**

2.1. The theory of the "common good" in the Russian Empire 102

2.2. The domestic theory of the welfare of all and everyone 121

2.3. The welfare of all and everyone, as presented by Paul I and Alexander I 146

2.4. The welfare of all and everyone and Russian Freemasonry 166

Chapter III — The welfare of all and everyone and the generations of Russian Freemasons **187**

3.1. The "common good" in the first generation of Russian Freemasons (1750-1769) 187

3.2. The welfare of all and everyone in the second generation of Russian Freemasons — Part 1 (1770-1779)....207

3.3. The welfare of all and everyone in the second generation of Russian Freemasons — Part 2 (1780-1789)....223

3.4. The welfare of all and everyone in the third and fourth generations of Russian Freemasons (1790-1822)....238

Conclusion **255**

Source List and Citation **262**

Annex **301**

A review of the book "The Theory of the 'Common Good' and Russian Freemasonry in the Second Half of the 18th Century – the First Quarter of the 19th Century"

Looking for any magical means to jump into ancient times and escape from day-to-day reality? Plunging deep into the breathtaking pages of books about the glorious past is a wonderful method to go about it. Considering history in all respects from different angles, it could be concluded that it is quite messy and complex, however, a large amount of it is not ugly at all, and skilled specialists can successfully process it. The more the reader knows about it, the more the disorder makes sense, both in an up-to-date and historical setting. In Fred Ford and Alexey Dmitriev's book *The Theory of the 'Common Good' and Russian Freemasonry in the Second Half of the 18th Century – the First Quarter of the 19th Century,* the authors eloquently cover the best historical themes in detail: Freemasonry as a very Old Secret mystical Organization and everything that has surrounded it (its origin, Freemasons, the emergence of Masonic Lodges, the processes running inside various Masonic Lodges, the participation of Masonic Lodges in the life of the States, etc.). This book about Freemasonry gave me a piece of extensive knowledge of history and historical events cloaked in mystery. Of course, they say that tastes differ, and that is true. For example, some people consider it advantageous to be born and raised in New York. Others probably have a very different opinion about being born and raised in Paris. Nevertheless, nearly everyone in the world has heard of Freemasonry and Freemasons, so this was a very interesting historical topic to extensively read about.

The authors of the book carefully and systematically described many events regarding Freemasonry in Russia in this historical book using research from the second half of the 18th century and the very beginning of the 19th century. In addition, this historical research embraced and acknowledged the "common good" that profoundly influenced many people in the past and in current times continues to influence many people, Also, many photos throughout the book depicted famous Masonic Signs and Relics.

Many aspects were thoroughly researched in the book: the national history, the history of philosophy, the state and law, and the Russian political and legal doctrines of that time. Many issues were revealed from a legal science point of view, including the state and legal ideas of Russian Freemasons. After reading the book, it is clear that the research used was gained from many genuine Russian and foreign archives, including secret documents.

An enormous scientific work was comprehensively fulfilled when creating this historical book, disclosing many unknown facts and events connected with Freemasonry in Russia and Russian Freemasons. It was demonstrated throughout the book that European Freemasonry (German, French, and British) came to Russia and was firmly rooted there, deeply influencing Russian high society, comprising Russian Sovereigns, and the state as a whole. The research showed the socio-political and philosophical views Of Russian Freemasons and gave a historical analysis of the normative documents of Freemasons. The book demonstrated the process of reforming Russian Freemasonry at the very beginning of the 19th century. The problem of the legalization of Freemasonry and the theme of enlightened absolutism in Russia was mentioned as well. Many biographical sources and collections of various historical materials were used in the book. The authors identified and analyzed the basic state and legal ideas of Russian Freemasons in correlation with the theory of the "common good."

The study of Freemasonry as an established organization and having a charter with minutes of meetings was thoroughly presented in the work. It should also be noted that this undoubtedly merited the study. The doctrine of the "common good" was examined in the book in the form of a theory that is better known to many western readers as utilitarianism. l. Bentham, D Locke, S. Montesquieu, C, Beccaria, and other famous scientists successfully developed the doctrine of utilitarianism. In many sections of the book, the authors validated that the abovementioned doctrine was comprehensively developed in Russia. Russian Freemasons were the carriers of this doctrine, receiving and developing Western ideas all over Russia. Following some leading European scientists, Russian Monarchs, Russian scientists, and Russian Freemasons defined the "common good" as common and individual happiness. In effect. it is very important to know that the interests of any individual were not excluded or suppressed in the Russian theory of the "common good." That was a quite progressive idea at that time. In addition, the terms and semantic concepts of the theory ("the common good," "the welfare of all and everyone," etc.) spread to the sphere of education and politics in the Russian Empire, becoming widespread throughout Russia. It was evidenced in the research that

Russian Freemasons used the term “common good” from the 1750s to 1822.

At the same time, unfortunately, no comparative analysis of utilitarianism and the theory of the “common good” (widespread in Russia) was carried out in the work. It is a well-known fact that freedom was an integral part of utilitarianism. Nevertheless, freedom was not considered in the book as well. Overall, demonstrated the theory of the “common good” in Russia (shown by the points of view of Russian Emperors and Russian Freemasons) which was a completely different view of the terms and phenomena that were potentially unknown in the United States at that time.

In conclusion, I would highly recommend this book to learn more about an unknown part of the history of Russia and Russian Freemasonry, uncovering the mystic mist of Freemasonry as a whole. I am confident that it would interest many categories of readers: Freemasons, various types of scholars and researchers, students involved in studying history, and people who are interested in learning about history and enjoy mysteries.

Amy Walker Miller, Ed.D.

Assistant Director to the Provost’s Office
almiller@tntech.edu
(931) 372-3659
Tennessee Tech University
Derryberry Hall 434
I William L Jones Dr Cookeville, TN 38505

A review of the book "The Theory of the 'Common Good' and Russian Freemasonry in the Second Half of the 18th Century – the First Quarter of the 19th Century"

Freemasonry is an interesting theme to explore. Known as one of the world's largest social organizations, Freemasonry is not inconspicuous as it had once been. There are hundreds of conspiracy theories revolving around Freemasonry. Some may even say that Freemasons govern the world from the shadows. Some Freemasons have been famous politicians, prominent figures of various States, and true tycoons of business. In addition, many modern Freemasons have been well-known for their charity.

Freemasonry is the oldest brotherly organization in the world. It was established as a brotherhood of skilled builders in Europe in the Middle Ages. But later, after declining the cathedral erecting, they changed their focus. Nowadays, Freemasonry is not a secret organization as it was deemed to be earlier. Nevertheless, some Freemasons keep their secret rituals and passwords.

The first known record of Freemasonry was made in the Regius Poem (Halliwell Manuscript) in about 1390. Freemasons have been communicating by using special visual symbols derived from the tools of stonemasonry, and their handshakes characterize the rank of a Freemason (e.g., Apprentice, Fellowcraft, Master). Freemasons have retained a variety of ancient ceremonies, and to this day, only gentlemen can become Freemasons – no ladies are allowed. Strictly speaking, Freemasonry is not a religion. However, Freemasons believe in the "Grand Architect of the Universe." It is well-known that Catholic Church has not supported Freemasonry at all and even condemned it in 1738. Moreover, the Vatican declared Freemasonry "the Synagogue of Satan" in the 19th century because of its Masonic temples and secret rituals fulfilled inside them.

The research carried out and reflected in this book deals with many deep and complex issues of the history of Masonic Lodges in Europe and the history of the legislation of the Russian Empire. The bibliography presented in the book covers a wide range of thought and expression. The research methods applied by the authors allow us to comprehensively investigate the subject from different angles, and the conclusions made may be of interest to a wide audience. A significant part of the work consists of sections of historiography and source studies, making it clear that the topic has been researched well by examining the studies of predecessors. At the same time, it becomes apparent that these sections could be omitted as they show more of the course of the study itself and represent an excess of information that would be more interesting to historians rather than to an average reader.

All-in-all, most of the text of the book was devoted to the theory of the "common good." It is important to note that it is not a novel subject among Western researchers. Consequently, it is intriguing to learn about the existence of such a theory in Russia in the 18th-19th centuries. After reading the book, a reader can understand that the intellectual blocks of the theory were implemented in Masonic texts as well as in the political and legal thought and legislation of the Russian Empire. Certainly, Russian Freemasonry supporting the general European notions of the "common good" was a progressive phenomenon in the social life of the Russian Empire. This distinct argument was thoroughly studied in the book. It also seems that such a case brings Russia and America closer together.

I would like to recommend readers take this book for a spin and indulge themselves in learning about one of the most mysterious societies in the world, unveiling the secrecy that still surrounds it.

Vitaly Ford ____________ (August 7, 2022)

Vitaly Ford, Ph.D.

Assistant Professor, Department of Computer Science and Mathematics, Arcadia University
Director of Chapter Development, National Cybersecurity Student Association (NCSA)
Chapter Development Coordinator for the Women in Cybersecurity (WiCyS)
E-mail: fordv@arcadia.edu
Web: https://vford.me

Introduction

"Religion, philosophy, and history are the best and most skillful pilots bringing the ship of human knowledge into the harbor of eternity. All of them are harmoniously interconnected and imbued with the same spirit, interacting as substantiation for each other" (I. A. Fessler).

The topic of researching the state-related legal ideas of Russian Freemasons was chosen on purpose.

Firstly, this topic is very interesting for one of the authors of this scientific work, a Lawyer (A. V. Dmitriev), that has received a fundamental legal education and gained very good experience in teaching at a university. Finding, understanding, and formulating the basic ideas about the state, the law of a certain group, and a community of people is a fascinating business as a whole. Graduate and postgraduate studies allowed A. V. Dmitriev to competently approach the study and presentation of thoughts. Therefore, the study of the ideas of Russian Freemasons related to the law and state is, first of all, one of the forms of using the basic classical legal education that the author successfully received and developed later.

Secondly, the authors' choice of Masonic Lodges (a community of people whose ideas and notions could become the main subject of the research) was made intentionally as well. A. V. Dmitriev was lucky as he met Professor S. V. Arzhanukhin, one of the Russian Freemasonry researchers. He kindly advised the author to start studying the state and legal ideas of Russian Freemasons. The fact is that Russian Freemasonry already became the subject of academic research by the first quarter of the 21st century. More than 100 Master's theses and DPhils were defended on it. However, only one thesis on the topic of Freemasonry was defended within the framework of legal science.

Thirdly, the theme of Russian Freemasonry has a long history connected with mysticism, alchemy, and conspiracy theories. The mention of Freemasons usually causes surprise, wariness, and fear for many average men. These emotions of perception can completely disappear during a serious study of the historiography of the subject.

Picture 1. A view of Mount Ararat was gained from the territory of the Republic of Armenia in May 2016 (a photo was made by A. V. Dmitriev*). The Russian Freemasonry of the 18th century and the first quarter of the 19th century is still attractive but, at the same time, inaccessible to many readers to some degree. The same can be said about Mount Ararat, located in Turkey. In effect, any Armenians living in the Republic of Armenia can only see it every day.*

When discussing this theme extensively, there is a mixture of ideas about both Russian and Western Freemasons and Freemasons of the past and present. Even some serious scholars[1] continue mixing "Martinists," "Freemasons," and "Illuminati." In total, even in the scientific works on Russian Freemasonry, there is a spread of opinions about the unity and varieties of Russian Freemasonry, their goals and objectives, and their role in the process of modernizing Russian society[2].

Screening out any mysticism, conspiracy theories, and futurology, systematizing the judgments of scientists on Russian Freemasonry, and introducing new sources on Russian Freemasonry into the scientific circulation are very important matters that open a new sphere of scientific knowledge, arranging it.

Fourth, an analysis of sources on Russian Freemasonry shows that only a few thousand sources on Russian Freemasonry (statutes, projects, letters, diaries, acts, etc.) have been extracted and published from the archives[3]. Nevertheless, there are several hundred thousand sources that have never been introduced into

---

[1] For example, T. V. Andreeva "Secret Societies in Russia in the first third of the 19th Century: Government Policy and Public Opinion": A thesis of a Ph.D. in Historical Sciences. - St. Petersburg, 2010. Page 102.

[2] S. V. Arzhanukhin, A. I. Serkov, V. Yu. Zakharov, E. A. Vishlenkova, A. Yu. Minakov and T. Andreeva demonstrated different approaches to the study of Russian Freemasonry.

[3] M. N. Longinov, A. N. Pypin, Ya. L. Barskov, S. V. Eshevsky, V. I. Semevsky, G. V. Vernadsky, V. I. Sakharov, N. P. Kiselev, S. M. Nekrasov, S. V. Arzhanukhin, A. N. Lushin, A. I. Serkov, Yu. E. Kondakov, Yu.L. Khalturin, E.L. Kuzmishin, and others made an important contribution to the publication of sources on Russian Freemasonry.

scientific circulation and published[1]. The comprehension and publication of the sources of the 18th and 19th centuries is a contribution to the science and culture of Russia. And in turn, the self-awareness, worldview, and future of the multinational Russian people and Russian statehood are just impossible without it.

Fifth, the history of political and legal thought in Russia in the second half of the 18th and the first third of the 19th centuries in the textbooks and monographs has been exhausted by the state and legal ideas of Catherine II, Prince M. M. Shcherbatov, Count N. I. Panin, Ya. P. Kozelsky, A. N. Radishchev, S. E. Desnitsky, N. M. Karamzin, M. M. Speransky, the Decembrists P. I. Pestel and N. I. Muravyov[2].

The exception is the political and legal views of Paul I. These views were presented in the textbook by V. A. Tomsinov[3].

---

[1] The funds for Russian Freemasonry can be divided into domestic and foreign. Considering the domestic funds, it is worth mentioning the funds NIOR RGB, GA RF, RGADA, OR RNB, IRLI, RGIA. These are only those that were not destroyed after the prohibition of Freemasonry, the revolution of 1917, and the collapse of the Soviet Union. Freemasonry was not completely banned abroad, but it is mainly available for a domestic researcher through the digitized copies of documents via the international Internet.

[2] N. M. Azarkin "The history of legal thought in Russia": a course of lectures. - M.: Yurist. lit., 1999. - 526 p.; M. V. Antonov "The history of legal thought in Russia": the lecture notes; - Moscow; St. Petersburg: NIU VSHE, 2012. - 210 p., I. A. Isaev, N. M. Zolotukhina "I85 The history of political and legal doctrines of Russia": A textbook. – The 2nd edition revised and supplemented — M.: Yurist, 2003. — 415 p.; "The History of Political and Legal Doctrines": A Textbook for High Schools / Edited by an Academician of the Russian Academy of Sciences, a Ph.D. in Legal Sciences, Professor V. S. Nersesyants. - 4th ed., revised and supplemented - M.: Norma, 2004. - 944 p. (Chapter 14 and the first three paragraphs of Chapter 17 were prepared by N. M. Zolotukhina); "The history of political and legal doctrines": A textbook. A manual for the university students studying in the specialty "Jurisprudence" / [N. D. Amaglobeli and others]; edited by N. V. Mikhailova, A. A. Opaleva, A. Yu. Olimpiev. - M.: UNITI-DANA, 2012. - 367 p.; The History of Political and Legal Doctrines. A textbook for high schools. The 3rd edition supplemented / Edited by a Ph.D. in Legal Sciences, Professor O. E. Leist and a Ph.D. in Legal Sciences, Professor V. A. Tomsinov. M.: Zertsalo. The Publishing House, 2009. - 584 p.; M. M. Rassolov "The History of Political and Legal Doctrines: A textbook. A manual for university students studying in the specialty 021100 "Jurisprudence". – The 2nd edition revised and supplemented — M.: UNITI-DANA, — 271 p., The history of legal doctrines in Russia. A textbook. Volume II. XVIII-XIX centuries / Edited by V. V. Sorokin and A. A. Vasilyeva – Moscow.": "Yurlitinform," 2014. - 326 p., M. N. Marchenko, I. F. Machin "The history of political and legal doctrines: A textbook. - M.: Higher education, 2005. - 495 p.

[3] V. A. Tomsinov "The history of the Russian political and legal thought. X-XVIII centuries / V. A. Tomsinov; Moscow State University named after M. V. Lomonosov. Legal Faculty - M.: Zertsalo, 2003. Pages 221-238.

Nevertheless, the political and legal thought of that period does not end with the given names[1]. The state-legal ideas of Russian Freemasonry as the most massive form of public meetings of that time have not been mentioned in the educational literature yet. The comprehension of the ideas about the State and law of Russian Freemasons and the definition of their intellectual nature allow us to take a fresh look at the theory of public good and its role in the history of the doctrine of the state and law. The ideological foundations of the political and legal views of Russian Freemasonry were studied by V. Yu. Zakharov, T. V. Andreeva, and V. A. Tomsinov. There is an opinion spread in the scientific literature that the ideology of Russian Freemasonry is closely related to constitutionalism (by the slogan "freedom, equality, and brotherhood")[2] and the Illuminati Order[3].

The theory of the "common good," starting with the Peter I era, was, in fact, a convenient justification for the arbitrariness of the sovereign[4].

However, these claims are controversial. Nowadays, the statement "common good" is often found in legislation and literature. Various references to the "common good" are contained in the resolutions of the Constitutional Court of Russia and the European Court of Human Rights.

The theory tries to give a concept of the "common good" and find its origins, content, and objective laws. It has been proven in the history of the state and law of Russia that there was a whole theory of the "common good." This theory formed the basis of the public law doctrine of enlightened absolutism[5]. There is an opinion in modern theory that the category of the "common good"

---

[1]For example, the state-legal views of Alexander I and A. P. Kunitsyn were not reflected in the textbooks on the history of political and legal doctrines. S. V. Kodan wrote about the state-legal views of Alexander I. See Alexander I and reforms: between absolutism and constitutionalism /S. V. Kodan // Chinovnik (Official). - 2005. - # 6 (40). http://chinovnik.uapa.ru/ru/issue/2005/06/09/. On the state-legal views of A. P. Kunitsyna wrote to L. S. Gimishyan. See L. S. Gimishyan "The state-legal views of A. P. Kunitsyna": An abstract of the thesis of a Candidate in Legal Sciences: 12.00.01 / Saratov State Academy of Law. - Saratov, 2004. - 22 p.

[2] V. Yu. Zakharov "Russian constitutionalism of the 2nd half of the 18th – the 1st quarter of the 19th centuries in the context of the development of Western European legal thought": A thesis of a Ph.D. in Historical Sciences. –M., 2010. Page 172.

[3] T. V. Andreeva "Secret societies in Russia in the first third of the 19th century..." Page 102.

[4] V. A. Tomsinov "The history of the Russian political and legal thought of the X-XVIII centuries". M.: The publishing house "Zertsalo," 2003. Page 172.

[5] O. A. Omelchenko "The Monarchy of Enlightened Absolutism in Russia: Political Doctrine, Legal Policy, State Reforms": A thesis of a Ph.D. in Legal Sciences. - Moscow, 2001. Pages 56, 101, 281.

without reference to geography, historical period, or other factors "turns into an empty abstraction and a good wish, saying that 'everything is good.'"[1]

Another opinion says that "a cathedral-collectivist (Byzantine) approach (not the universalist (Western) one) dominated in Russia in the int erpretation of the 'common good.' According to that cathedral-collectivist approach, the 'common good' was considered as a kind of higher principle dominating an individual." That higher principle was referred to as the transcendental divine sphere[2]. These statements are also debatable. Nevertheless, an advanced study of the history of the issue casts doubts on the opinions prevalent in science. A. N. Lushin wrote his comprehensive thesis, "The state and legal views of Russian Freemasons at the turn of the XVIII-XIX centuries."[3] He presented the state and legal ideas of N. I. Novikov, I. P. Elagin, P. I. Panin, D. I. Fonvizin, I. V. Lopukhin, and Metropolitan Filaret (Drozdov). At the same time, the ideas of the State and law of I. G. Schwartz (Shvarts in the Russian sources) and I. A. Pozdeev (the leaders of Russian Rosicrucianism)[4], A. I. Musin-Pushkin, A. V. Khrapovitsky, and E. A. Kushelev have not been researched yet. There was no attempt to analyze Masonic acts, statutes, and instructions to establish their role in the formation of an appropriate political and legal worldview among Russian Freemasons. The place of Masonic Lodges and Russian Freemasons in the formation of legal policy and the strengthening of the statehood of Russia has not been determined yet. The scientific work on these issues seems to be very important for the development of the intellectual history of Russia.

Sixth, the issues of interaction between civil society and the state are very relevant and topical in jurisprudence. According to some scientists[5], Russian Freemasonry in the 18th – the first quarter of the 19th centuries was an institution of the nascent civil society. This institution had certain goals and objectives, ensured the reproduction of existing values, and carried out the functions of both the modernization (in the second half of the 19th century) and conservation (in the

---

[1] A. P. Semitko "The culture of law and the 'common good'" // Legal state: theory and practice. # 2 (52). 2018. Page 31.

[2] V. V. Lapaeva "The types of legal understanding: legal theory and practice." M.: RAP, 2012. Page 302.

[3] A. N. Lushin "The state-legal views of Russian Freemasons at the turn of the XVIII-XIX centuries": A thesis of a Candidate in Legal Sciences: 12.00.01. - Nizhny Novgorod, 2004. - 161 p.

[4] The Rosicrucianism is a type of Freemasonry that arose in Prussia in the 18th century. The main differences of it were the practice of metaphysics and alchemy, competition with the Knights Templar (chivalry), and the use of higher degrees.

[5] Such positions are held, in particular, by S. V. Arzhanukhin and M. Abassy. See S. V. Arzhanukhin "The philosophical views of Russian Freemasonry... Page 139; Malgorzata Abassy "A Russian Mason on the Paths of his Native Culture. The Case Study of Nicolas Novikov." Krakow. 2014. P. 63.

first quarter of the 19th century) of social, including state-legal, phenomena and processes.

There is no doubt that the state tried to put Freemasonry under police surveillance. The state thought that Freemasonry was a "state within a state" and a basis for various kinds of secret societies[1].

Seventh, it is impossible to present the subject of research in a qualified manner within the framework of the history of the teachings of the state and law without involving the tools of other sciences and disciplines due to the interdisciplinarity of the subject of research. A haphazard study of the state and legal ideas of Russian Freemasons will not benefit either Russian Freemasonry as a section of historical science, the history of the state and law, or the history of doctrines about the state and law. Unless you see the "picture" as a whole, you can find that the Freemasons had a variety of ideas and notions about the state and law. In other words, they had the whole spectrum of ideas of a free person, fitting into the historical context.

A certain integrative research program is required to highlight the main, essential, and mass ideas of the Russian Freemasons regarding the state-related legal orientation, their origins and forms, and the transmission of ideas in the socio-cultural space. This program should include the involvement of information blocks from Russian domestic history and the history of foreign countries (some knowledge of the history of the 18th and the first quarter of the 19th centuries), the history of the state and law of the Fatherland (some knowledge of jurisprudence, noble and government constitutionalism), philosophy (some knowledge of the metaphysics of law and moral philosophy), and history of the theory of law (some knowledge of the concepts of the natural law of the XVII and XVIII centuries and the first quarter of the XIX century). Bringing all the blocks together and creating meaning-uniting connections is difficult, but at the same time, necessary, being a very urgent task for the future history of the doctrine of the state and law, as a way of the "holistic consideration of the past of mankind."[2]

---

[1]Considering the history of Russian Freemasonry, the following striking events were demonstrating the attitude of the state monarchy towards the Masonic Lodges: the case of N. I. Novikov and the Moscow Martinists in 1792, an attempt by M. M. Speransky on the reform of Freemasonry in 1810-1811, the prohibition of the activities of Masonic Lodges and secret societies on August 1, 1822.

[2]The author of the statement is Donald Kelly (A journal on the history of ideas. A citation was quoted from L. P. Repina's "Historical science at the turn of the XX-XXI centuries: social theories and historiographical practice." – M.: Krug, 2011. Page 340.

Picture 2. A masonic sign is in the form of an owl, acacia, and wild stone. The late 18th - an early quarter of the 19th century. Metal, engraving. Published in the catalog of the exhibition of the State Hermitage Museum in 2013[1].

Freemasons were not homogeneous in their philosophical, moral, and state-related legal views. They belonged to different classes: noble (hereditary and personal nobility) and free[2] (merchants, scientists, writers, musicians, etc.). Russian Freemasons consisted of Russified foreigners (I. A. Fessler, G. A. Rosenkampf, I. G. Schwartz (Shvarts in the Russian sources)) and native citizens of Russia (N. I. Novikov, M. M. Speransky, I. A. Pozdeev). The native language for some Freemasons was a foreign one; for others - Russian. Freemasons consisted of public leaders (I. A. Pozdeev, N. I. Novikov, and I. V. Beber) and Freemasons that had senior governmental positions (A. B. Kurakin, M. M. Speransky, and A.D. Balashov). In addition, Freemasons were grouped by interests: the circle of I. P. Elagin, the circle of N. I. Novikov, the circle of I. A. Fessler, and others. Some Freemasons left political and public life (the Freemasons of the 18th century), while others came to replace them (the Freemasons of the 19th century).

---

[1]G. A. Mirolyubova, I. N. Ukhanova "Everybody was a Freemason at that time" // The Wisdom of Astrea: The Freemasonry monuments of the 18th – first third of the 19th century in the Hermitage collection: exhibition catalog / The State Hermitage Museum - St. Petersburg: The Publishing House of the State Hermitage, 2013. - 480 p.: ill. Pages 9-26. Page 20.
[2]The concept of a free estate is a conditional term used in this work to define the totality of personally free people (not nobles) that are members of Masonic Lodges.

The same individuals had a completely different Masonic worldview. When being students and comrades, they had certain ideas about the state and law (for example, N. M. Karamzin and A. S. Shishkov had a Comrade Degree[1]). However, they obtained completely different notions about the state and law already during the transition to a Master's Degree. And finally, their opinions about the state and law changed dramatically upon initiation into the higher degrees. Brothers received some new intellectual experience by using the initiation systems of other Masonic Systems. After leaving Freemasonry, a person underwent a change or serious restructuring of his worldview. The worldview of Russian Freemasons largely depended on the sphere of the activity of a Freemason (for example, I. N. Boltin and A. I. Musin-Pushkin were engaged in historic research, I. G. Schwartz and A. M. Bryantsev devoted themselves to Pedagogy and Philosophy, G.A. Rosenkampf and M. M. Speransky occupied themselves with some legislative and state activities) and his involvement in court parties (N. I. Panin, V. P. Kochubei, M. M. Speransky, etc.).

When Russian Freemasons "took off their apron," they ceased, with rare exceptions, to be guided by Masonic rules and concepts. They had to hide their membership in Masonic Lodges, Masonic Symbols, and secrets. Therefore, it would not be entirely correct to discuss the state-related legal ideas of Russian Freemasonry only by actions and decisions and the writings of statesmen and public figures[2].

It should be noted that there was a separate existence of the mystical-idealistic and practical political and legal worldviews among the members of Masonic Lodges.

There was an attempt made in this book to consider the certain State and legal views of some state, scientific, and public figures of the Russian Empire. Those people were members of the Masonic Lodges. This historical excursion demonstrates the semantic connection of the Masonic worldview with the political and legal constructions of a particular author, as well as with the political and legal worldview of the Russian Monarchs (Catherine II, Paul I, and Alexander I),

[1]There is some information about the Comradely Degree of Nikolai Mikhailovich Karamzin in the Lodge of the Golden Crown in Simbirsk in the summer of 1784. See A. I. Serkov "Russian Freemasonry. 1731-2000": An Encyclopedic Dictionary. / A. I. Serkov. - M., 2001. Pages 376, 989. There is some information about the Honorary Fellowship Degree of Alexander Semenovich Shishkov in the Lodge of Neptune to Nadezhda in Kronshtadt in 1780-1781. A. I. Serkov "Russian Freemasonry. 1731-2000." Page 950.

[2] The influence of Masonic ideology and symbolism on the legislation, diplomatic correspondence, literature, architecture, state awards in the Russian Empire cannot be denied. However, this influence was carried out through the gradual convergence of the worldview of one or another historical figure with Masonic views and ideals.

expressed in the sources of the personal origin and legislative acts of the Russian Empire. This connection is comprehensively considered and limited by the framework of the theory of the "common good." Therefore, the book does not exhaust the range of possible questions and problems regarding the history of the political and legal teachings of the Russian Freemasons of the 18th and 19th centuries.

Picture 3. A white husky puff with blue silk piping. Russia. The end of the 18th century. Published by Yu. V. Plotnikova in the catalog of the exhibition of the State Hermitage Museum in 2013[1].

When preparing the book, the following historiographic base was used: research by different scientists on national history, the history of philosophy, state and law, and political and legal doctrines. Legal Science has begun considering the problems of the state and legal ideas of Russian Freemasons only in the XXI century. There were no special studies carried out for some objective reasons until the XXI century. A significant number of documents and materials on Russian Freemasonry were destroyed or taken abroad[2]. Only one serious monographic study containing a detailed picture of the formation and development of the state-related legal views of Russian Freemasons at the turn of the 18th - 19th centuries was fulfilled by A. N. Lushin.

---

[1]The Wisdom of Astrea: The monuments of the Freemasonry of the 18th - the first third of the 19th centuries in the Hermitage Collection: an exhibition catalog / The State Hermitage Museum - St. Petersburg: The Publishing House of the State Hermitage, 2013. - 480 p.: ill. Page 184.

[2] For example, the conspiratorial part of the Freemasons-Rosicrucians "had a firm rule to burn all the current documents at the end of the year at the last quarterly conference." See Yu. E. Kondakov "The secret instructions of the Russian Rosicrucians of the XVIII-XIX centuries." - Moscow: Ganga, 2018. Page 34.

The main trend of the pre-revolutionary period was the development of an empirical base: various publications on the history of Freemasonry. The first studies of Freemasonry began at the beginning of the 19th century. After prohibiting Masonic Lodges in 1822, many researchers of the 19th century introduced the categories and concepts of "Russian Freemasonry" and "Masonic Literature" into scientific circulation. The concept of "Russian Freemasonry" was also included in the subject of social and humanitarian sciences at that time.

The factual base on the Freemasonry of the 18th century was formed by the research of M. N. Longinov (1823-1875), C. B. Eshevsky (1829-1865), P. P. Pekarsky (1827-1872), and A. I. Nezelenov (1845-1896). Those authors compiled the biographies of N. I. Novikov, I. G. Schwartz (Shvarts in the Russian sources), I. V. Lopukhin, S. I. Gamaleya, and M. M. Kheraskov. In addition, they noted the influence of Masonic ideas on the life of the Russian society of the 18th century and described the works of Freemasons. Some acts and regulations of the lodges were published by the above-mentioned scholars. The materials of the investigation file against the Martinists were also detailed (that investigation was initiated by Catherine II in 1792).

The scientists A. N. Pypin, T. O. Sokolovskaya, V. I. Semevsky, and G.V. Vernadsky investigated the socio-political views of Freemasons and the connection of the Masonic worldview and literature with social and political practice. They were the first ones to try to give a historical analysis of the normative documents of Freemasons. Also, some aspects of the topic are touched upon in the biographical literature dedicated to N. I. Novikov, I. A. Fessler, M. M. Speransky, Catherine II, Paul I, Alexander I, etc.

The study of the worldview of the Russian Freemasons of the 18th - 19th centuries contradicted the officially promoted line of the ruling Communistic Party in Soviet times. Therefore, the issues of the contribution of Russian Freemasons to the development of state and legal doctrines have practically not been studied at all. The topic of Russian Freemasonry is touched upon within the framework of literary criticism and linguistics (P. N. Sakulin, B. S. Meylakh, G. A. Gukovsky, N. L. Rubinstein (Rubinshtein in the Russian sources), and V. V. Vinogradov).

The research interest in the history of Russian Freemasonry started returning only in the 1970s, including the contribution of Russian Freemasonry to the history of Russian constitutionalism and Russian philosophical thought. The theses of S. N. Nekrasov and N. V. Minaeva were defended on the topic of Freemasonry. The questions related to Masonic themes have been touched upon in the studies of historians T. A. Bakunina, V. O. Klyuchevsky, and M. M. Safonov, philologists V. I. Novikov and K. V. Pigarev, philosophers V. V. Zenkovsky, G. V. Florovsky, and others[1].

Some scientific works by various specialists also appear in the post-Soviet period (historians T. V. Andreeva, V. M. Bokova, V. Yu. Zakharov, T. N. Zhukovskaya, Yu. E. Kondakov, and A. I. Serkov, philosophers S. V. Arzhanukhin, E. L. Kuzmishin, Yu. L. Khalturin, and A. A. Fedorov, jurists S. V. Kodan, O. A. Kudinov, A. G. Moskvina, and A. N. Lushin). The closest attention in these scientific works has been paid to the problem of the genesis and influence of the state-related legal views of Russian Freemasons at the turn of the 18th - 19th centuries. The works made on the history of Russian Freemasonry by A. I. Serkov should be specially mentioned[2].

A monograph, "Philosophical Views of Russian Freemasonry" (based on the materials of the magazine "Freemasonry Shop")[3] by S.V. Arzhanukhin (published in Yekaterinburg in 1995) played an important role in the theoretical understanding of Masonic doctrine and Masonic organization. The scientist analyzed the work "The theoretical degree of Solomon Sciences" (Professor of the Moscow University I. G. Schwartz (Shvarts in the Russian sources) received that work from the Berlin Rosicrucians (Rozencraitsers in the Russian sources)). S. V. Arzhanukhin noted that the Russian Enlightenment would be "unthinkable without the fruitful and inspiring activity of Moscow Freemasons."

[1]The more detailed historiography is given in Paragraph 1.1 of Chapter I.
[2]A. I. Serkov "Russian Freemasonry. 1731-2000"; A. I. Serkov "The History of Russian Freemasonry of the 19th century" / Russian Freemasonry: Materials and Research. / Edited by M. V. Reizin and A. I. Serkov. – The 2nd edition (revised and extended). Volume 4. - SPb.: The publishing house named after N. I. Novikov, 2000, etc.
[3]S. V. Arzhanukhin "The philosophical views of Russian Freemasonry." 1995. - 223 p.

The leader of Moscow Freemasons at that time was I. G. Schwartz (Shvarts in the Russian sources)[1]. S. V. Arzhanukhin scientifically proved that the provisions of the Masonic statutes completely coincided with the opinion of the Masonic leaders. According to S. V. Arzhanukhin, the Masonic Order was a concrete historical form of the civil society of Russia in the 18th - 19th centuries as it had conscious goals and objectives, organizational structure, self-regulation, and continuity[2].

The state-related legal views of I. A. Pozdeev (he was another leader of the Russian Rosicrucian Freemasons) were described in the works of A. N. Pypin, G. V. Vernadsky, Yu. Kondakov, A. N. Lushin, and A. Yu. Minakov. I. A. Pozdeev was an honorary member of many Masonic Lodges and a leader of the Rosicrucians (Rozencraitsers in Russian sources). Other Freemasons constantly took into consideration the opinion of I. A. Pozdeev. The letters and notes of I. A. Pozdeev were published by P. I. Bartenev, A. A. Vasilchikov, and M. I. Sukhomlinov.

I. A. Fessler was one of the most prolific Freemason scholars. He published several dozen volumes of works. At the same time, comparatively little attention has been paid to I. A. Fessler in Russian historiography. According to I. G. Findel, I. A. Fessler, "by using his works, dispelled the fog that surrounded both the history and scientific side of the union, in general, for so long," gave the definitions of "inalienable Masonic freedom" and developed the "principles of social law[3]." The largest contemporary work that was devoted to the political and public views of I. A. Fessler was conducted by D. V. Gorbachev. D. V. Gorbachev believed that I. A. Fessler had not accepted the mystical elements of Freemasonry and had set himself the task of "cleansing" Freemasonry from any mysticism[4]. N. K. Gavryushin gave the characteristics of the philosophical heritage of I. A. Fessler.

M. V. Dovnar-Zapolsky, M. A. Korf, A. Yu. Minakov, A. E. Presnyakov, A. N. Pypin, and I. A. Chistovich wrote about the religious and mystical views of M. M. Speransky. Those scientists noted the similarity of the views of M. M. Speransky and I. A. Fessler, M. M. Speransky, and Emperor Alexander I. A. F.

[1]S. V. Arzhanukhin "From the lectures of I. G. Schwartz." Pages 78, 79.

[2]S. V. Arzhanukhin "The philosophical views of Russian Freemasonry." Page 139.

[3]I. G. Findel "The history of Freemasonry from its origin to the present": Translated from the 2nd German edition. Volumes 1-2 / The works of I. G. Findel. The edition of the Masonic magazine "DieBauhütte." - St. Petersburg: The printing house of N. Skaryatin, 1872-1874. – in 2 volumes; Volume 2. - 1874. Pages 59, 138.

[4]D. V. Gorbachev "The socio-political views of I. A. Fessler": An abstract of the thesis of a Candidate in Historical Sciences: 07.00.03. - Saratov, 2012. Page 15.

Bychkov published the handwritten texts of M. M. Speransky. Those texts expressed M. M. Speransky's philosophical, religious, and legal views.

The history of the official recognition of Freemasonry in the Russian Empire is the next block of the historiography of the state-related and legal ideas of Russian Freemasons. The historiography of the issue was presented in the descriptions of contemporaries (I. V. Beber, F. M. Gauenschild, E. A. Kushelev, V. V. Musin-Pushkin Bruce, Ya. I. De Sanglen, etc.). G. V. Vernadsky, Yu. E. Kondakov, M. N. Longinov, A. N. Pypin, A. N. Serkov, and T. O. Sokolovskaya studied the problem of relations between Freemasonry and the State. M. N. Longinov and G. V. Vernadsky's scientific studies were mainly limited to the 18th century and its main milestones in the relationship of Freemasonry and the State: the history of Swedish Freemasonry, the case of N. I. Novikov and his surroundings (I. V. Lopukhin, A. B. Kurakin, N. N. Trubetskoy, etc.). A. N. Pypin dealt with the projects of reforming Freemasonry and partly explained the history of the legislative regulation of Freemasonry in the 19th century in his writings on the history of Freemasonry at the beginning of the 19th century. T. O. Sokolovskaya comprehensively researched the Swedish System of Freemasonry. She arranged the history of the creation of the "Grand (Directory) Lodge Vladimir to the Order." A. I. Serkov made a serious attempt to study the process of reforming Russian Freemasonry at the beginning of the 19th century.He singled out the group affiliation of the reformers of Freemasonry (liberal, conservative, and apolitical) and noted the belonging of this or that historical figure to the Masonic Systems: the Rosicrucians (Rozencraitsers in the Russian sources), the Swedish System, the French System, and I. A. Fessler's Lodge. Yu. E. Kondakov, V. Yu. Zakharov, E. A. Vishlenkova, and A. Yu. Minakov were the first to outline a problem with the legalization of Freemasonry. The issues of granting liberty to Russian nobles, as well as the legislation of Catherine II and Paul I, were investigated by V. A. Tomsinov[1]. O. A. Omelchenko[2] carried out the coverage of the theme of enlightened absolutism in Russia in the 18th century. The influence of European culture on the intellectual choice of Russia at the turn of the 17th - 18th centuries was considered by M. S. Kiseleva[3].

---

[1]See, for example, V. A. Tomsinov "A Diploma on the rights, liberties, and advantages of the noble Russian nobility." Published in the edition of the Legislation of Empress Catherine II. 1783-1796 / Compiled by V. A. Tomsinov. An introductory article by V. A. Tomsinov. M.: Zertsalo, 2011. Pages XI–XL.

[2]O. A. Omelchenko "The monarchy of enlightened absolutism in Russia: Political doctrine, legal policy, state reforms": A thesis of a Ph.D. in Legal Sciences: 12.00.01.-Moscow, 2001. - 389 p.

[3]M. S. Kiseleva "The intellectual choice of Russia in the second half of the 17th-early 18th centuries: from ancient Russian literacy to European scholarship." - M.: Progress-Tradition, 2011. - 471 p.

The history of the influence of European thought on the political and legal thought of Russia in the 18th-first quarter of the 19th century was investigated by K.D. Bugrov, M. A. Kiselev [1], and D. V. Timofeev[2]. T. V. Andreeva[3] showed the role of secret societies in developing government constitutionalism in the first quarter of the 19th century. The ideas of the correlation between the state, law, and morality in the history of political and legal thought were highlighted by Yu. V. Kostin[4]. The liberal-constitutional ideas in Russia at the beginning of the 19th century were revealed by V. M. Bokova[5]. The conservative legal ideology of Russia was formulated by A. A. Vasilyev[6]. t is worth noting the works of P. Buryshkin[7], T. Bakunina[8], L. Hass[9], A. Pyatigorsky[10], H. Reynalter[11], G.

---

[1] See, for example, K. D. Bugrov "The Natural Law and Virtue: The integration of European influence into the Russian Political Culture of the 18th Century" / K. D. Bugrov, M. A. Kiselev. - Yekaterinburg: The Publishing House of the Ural University, 2016. - 476, [3] p.

[2] See, for example, D. V. Timofeev "European ideas in the public consciousness and communicative practice of an educated Russian subject in the first quarter of the 19th Century: An experience in studying the basic socio-political concepts": An abstract of the thesis of a Ph.D. in Historical Sciences. - Chelyabinsk, 2011. - 34 p.

[3] See T. V. Andreeva "The secret societies in Russia in the first third of the 19th century ..." 2010. - 1101 p.

[4] Yu. V. Kostin "The ideas of the correlation of the state, law, and morality in the history of the political and legal thought of pre-revolutionary Russia in the second half of the 19th-early 20th centuries": An abstract of the thesis of a Ph.D. in Legal Sciences. - Moscow, 2008. - 46 p.

[5] V. M. Bokova "Liberal-constitutional ideas in Russia at the beginning of the 19th century (1801-1812): An abstract of the thesis of a Candidate in Historical Sciences. - Moscow, 1991. - 21 p.

[6] A. A. Vasilyev "The conservative legal ideology of Russia: the essence and forms of manifestation": An abstract of the thesis of a Ph.D. in Legal Sciences. - Yekaterinburg, 2015. - 55 p.

[7] Bourychkine Paul. Bibliographie sur la franc-maconerie en Russie, Completee et mise au point par Tatiana Bakounine. Preface de Roger Portal, 1967. 174 p.

[8] Bakounine T. La repertoire biographique des francs-masons russes (XVIII et XIX–e siecles). - Paris, 1967. - 655 p.

[9] Hass Ludwik. Wolnomularstwow Europie Srodkowo - WschodniejwXVIII – XIX wieku. – Wroclaw Zaklad N10 Wydawnictwo, 1982. - 572 s.

[10] Piatigorsky A. Who is afraid of Freemasons? The Phenomenon of Freemasonry. - London. The Harvill Press, 1997. - 398 p.

[11] Reinalter H. Die Freimaurer. München, 2006

Karlheinz[1], Fredericks[2], K. Grunwald[3], K. Lenning[4], B. Fey[5], D. Ward[6], and M. Abassy[7] among foreign researchers.

The works of I. A. Fessler (published in German)[8], B. Telepnev (published in English)[9], and Ch. F. Masson and L. F. Segur (translated from French into Russian)[10] can be considered foreign ones as well.

It is well-known that thousands of various sources have been published on the history of Russian Freemasonry. Therefore, it is easy to get confused with them. To prevent this from happening, three groups of information carriers were identified.

The first group includes the following regulatory sources:

---

1 Karlheinz Gerlach Die Freimaurer im Alten Preussen 1738-1806: die Loge in Berlin. Teil 1. Publisher, StudienVerlag, Innsbruck, Wien, Bozen 2014. – 1254 s.

2 Friedrichs. Geschichte der einstigen Maurerei in Russland. B., 1904.

3 Grunwald (Constantin de). Histoire de la Franc-Maconnerie en Russie // Traveau Villard de Honnecourt. T. 5. 1969. 424 p.

4 Lenning C. Allgemeines Handbuch der Freimaurerei, Leipzig. 1863. S. 551

5 La Franc-maconnerie et la Revolution intellectuelle Du XVIII siècle Par Bernard Fay Profeseur au Collere de France.EDITIONS DE CLUNY 35 et 37, RUE DE SEINE – PARIS VI, 1935; Revolution and Freemasonry 1680-1800 Bernard Faÿ. Boston. Little, Brown, and Company. 1935. - 349p.

6 Freemasonry: its aims and ideals by J.S.M. Ward B.A., F.S.S., F.R. Econ. Soc. Author of "Freemasonry and the ancient gods." ''The masonic handbook series, etc.," London. William Rider & Son, limited 8-II Paternoster Row, E.C.4 1923. – 232 p.

7 Malgorzata Abassy "A Russian Mason on the Paths of his Native Culture..." Krakow. 2014. – 195 p.

8 Fessler´s sämmtliche Schriften über Freymaurerey. Wirklich als Manuckript für Brüder. Berlin.1801.- 499 p.; Fessler´s sämmtliche Schriften über Freymaurerey. Wirklich als Manuckript für Brüder. Bd. 1. Zweite verbesserte und mit einem Anhange versehene Auflage. Freyberg, 1805; Fessler I. A. Resultate seines Denkens und Erfahrens als Anhang zu seinen Rückblicken auf seine 70-jaerige Pilgerschaft. Breslau, 1826.

9 The Rosicrucians (Rozencraitsers in the Russian sources) in Russia by Frater Boris Telepneff. Privately printed 1924. 17p.; Russian Masons by Bro. B. Telepneff, 1925. 32 p.; A Few Pages from the History of Swedish Freemasonry in Russia. ByBro. BorisTelepneff, 1928. 23 p.

10 Charles Francois Philibert Masson "The secret notes on Russia. And in the part about the end of the reign of Catherine II and the reign of Paul I." Volume I. Translated from the 2nd edition of N. Na-go. Moscow, 1918. Edited by I. I. Kazanov. The printing house "CULTURE" of A. K. Mieserova. - 94 p.; L. F. Segur "The notes of Count Segur on his stay in Russia during the reign of Catherine II (1785-1789)": Translated from French with the notes of the translator. - St. Petersburg: The printing house of V. N. Maykov, 1865. - 386 p.

1. The drafts and legislative acts that were drawn up in the middle of the 18th – the first quarter of the 19th centuries (the decrees and manifestos of Catherine II, Paul I, Alexander I, the Charter of the Deanery, the project of I. A. Fessler, G. A. Rosenkampf, and M. M. Speransky, the accompanying and analytical notes, the rules of tolerance for Masonic Lodges in 1811, etc.).

2. The acts of Masonic rule-making (instructions, codes, statutes, job descriptions, agreements, etc.).

The second group of sources consists of the political-related legal and moral-philosophical works containing ideas about the state and law (S. F. Pufendorf, V. N. Tatishchev, F. Prokopovich, Ch. L. De Montesquieu, J. F. Bielfeld (Ya. F. Bilfeld in the Russian sources), C. Beccaria, Catherine II, A. V. Khrapovitsky, A. I. Musin-Pushkin, N. I. Novikov, I. G. Schwartz (Shvarts in the Russian sources), A. M. Bryantsev, I. A. Fessler, M. M. Speransky, and others).

The third group included the following biographical sources:

1. Various sources of personal information: the memoirs, notes, letters, and reports of Russian Freemasons (I. V. Beber, F. M. Gauenschild, Ya. I. De Sanglen, V. V. Musin-Pushkin Bruce, E. A. Kushelev, M. M. Speransky, M. Ya. von Fock, A. B. Kurakin, A. R. Vorontsov, and others) and their contemporaries (Paul I, Alexander I, M. N. Karamzin, A. S. Shishkov, A. A. Arakcheev, A. N. Radishchev, V. N. Karazin, and others).

2. Different sources of objectified information: monthly words, biographical dictionaries, collections of historical materials, etc.

Picture 4. The Russian State Historical Archives in St. Petersburg. The main entrance. September 2018. A photo by A. V. Dmitriev.

The authors of the book used the following archival material:
1. The manuscripts of the funds of the Research Department of the Manuscripts of the Russian State Library - fund 013 (Arsenyev Vasily Sergeevich, Arsentyev Yuriy Vasilyevich), fund 014 (Arsenyev Vasily Sergeevich: a collection, XVIII-XIX centuries), fund 147 (Lanskoy Sergei Stepanovich (1787- 1862); Eshevsky Stepan Vasilyevich (1829-1865)).
2. The documents and materials of the State Archives of the Russian Federation - Fund 48 (The Investigative Commission (Committee) and The Supreme Criminal Court in the case of the Decembrists of 1825-1826), Fund 109 (The Third Section of His Imperial Majesty's Own Chancellery), list of contents 1a (The secret archive. The revolutionary and social movement in Russia in 1826-1880), fund 1137 (Georgy Vladimirovich Vernadsky, Historian, Professor of Russian History at Yale University (New Haven, the United States of America), fund 1463 (A collection of the individual documents of personal origin), fund 1165 (The Special Office of the Ministry of the Interior), list of contents 1 (An inventory about the anti-government actions, the situation of the peasants, about the Patriotic War of 1812 and other issues in 1810-1826), list of contents 2 (An inventory on the fight against espionage, surveillance of foreigners, and other issues in 1808-1826), list of contents 3 (An inventory list # 3 in 1811-1826).
3. The cases of the Russian State Archive of Ancient Acts - fund 7 (Rank VII. Preobrazhensky Order, Secret Chancellery, and Secret Expedition), fund 8 (Rank VIII. The Kalinkin House and Cases of Crimes Against Morality), list of contents 1 (The cases of the Main Police Chief Chancellery and "Kalinkin's Commission" on the fight against prostitution. The case of N. I. Novikov. The documents about the Freemasons in Russia and Masonic manuscripts), fund 146 (The investigative files - (a collection) from the funds of the Ambassador Order

and the Collegium of Foreign Affairs), case 23 (the correspondence of the Curator of Moscow University I. Melissino on the Freemasons (1783-1790)), fund 1261 (the Vorontsov family, Counts, the landowners of the central, southern, and south-eastern provinces).

4. The manuscripts of the funds of the research archive of the St. Petersburg Institute of History of the Russian Academy of Sciences - fund 36 ("The Vorontsov family - an ancient noble family: Vorontsov Mikhail Illarionovich (1714-1767), Count and Vorontsov Roman Illarionovich (1707-1783), Count").

5. The documents and materials of the funds of the Russian State Historical Archive - fund 90 (The Russian Technical Society), fund 733 (The Department of Public Education, list of contents 1. A secretarial desk. The personal files of the employee, list of contents 142. The rank of Scientific Institutions), fund 938 (the documents collected by the Head of the General Archive of the Ministry of Foreign Affairs G. V. Esipov (Collection)), fund 1101 (the documents of personal origin that do not constitute separate funds), fund 1163 (The Committee for the Protection of General Security under the State Council), fund 1260 (The Commission for Drafting Laws under the State Council), fund 1287 (Economic Department of the Ministry of Internal Affairs. Inventory 45. A secretarial desk; Chancellery).

The main sources are the works of Lawyers N. M. Azarkin, F. G. Bauze, Ya. F. Bilfeld, A. A. Vasilyev, G. V. Vernadsky, Z. A. Goryushkin, M. M. Kovalevsky, S. V. Kodan, S. A. Korf, Yu. V. Kostin, O. A. Kudinov, O. E. Leist, A. N. Lushin, I. V. Mikheeva, A. G. Moskvina, V. S. Nersesyants, B. E. Nolde, O. A. Omelchenko, A. A. Pavlov, S. Pufendorf, S. A. Pokrovsky, M. A. Reisner, A. P. Semitko, M. M. Speransky, B. I. Syromyatnikov, V. M. Syrykh, V. N. Tatishchev, V. A. Tomsinov, G. F. Shershenevich, V. G. Shcheglov, and J. G. Justy (I. G. Yusti in the Russian sources).

The works of the following authors were also used: M. Abassy, V. N. Alekseev, T. V. Andreeva, S.V. Arzhanukhin, T. V. Artemyeva, V. G. Bazanov, T. A. Bakunina, V. M. Bokova, K. D. Bugrov, O. P. Vedmin, E. A. Vishlenkova, I. P. Voronitsyn, K. Gerlach (Gerlakh in the Russian sources), D. V. Gorbachev, N. E. Dorokhova, V. E. Evgenyev-Maksimov, B. V. Emelyanov, A. V. Zavrazhin, V. Yu. Zakharov, Ivanov-Razumnik, S. P. Karpachev, M. S. Kiseleva, Yu. E. Kondakov, N. D. Kochetkova, E. L. Kuzmishin, V. V. Kuchurin, S. S. Landa, Yu. S. Limanskaya, M. N. Longinov, A. McKay, N. V. Minaeva, A. Yu. Minakov, M. Moramarco, A. I. Nezelenov, S. M. Nekrasov, V. S. Nersesyants, V. I. Novikov, P. P. Pekarsky, D. I. Pigarev, N. K. Piksanov, M. N. Pokrovsky, A. E. Presnyakov, A. N. Pypin, H. Reinalter, L. P. Repina, N. A. Rozhkov, A. V. Romanovich-Slavatinsky, N. L. Rubinstein (Rubinshtein in the Russian sources), P. N. Sakulin, F. Sevastyanov, V. I. Semevsky, A. V. Semeka, V. P. Semennikov, A. I. Serkov, T. O. Sokolovskaya, V. Startsev, P. V. Stegniy, M. I. Sukhomlinov, B. Telepnev, D.

V. Timofeev, V. N. Tukalevsky, L. L. Fedotova, B. Fey, I. G. Findel, G. V. Florovsky, Yu. L. Khalturin, L. Khass, I. A. Stark (Shtark in the Russian sources), and N. K. Shilder.

The purpose of the book is to identify the main state and legal ideas of Russian Freemasons. These notions fit into the theory of the "common good" (this statement will be proved later). Also, the book aims to explain the role of Russian Freemasons in the life of the Russian Empire at the end of the 18th – the first quarter of the 19th centuries. Therefore, the author of this scientific study was assigned the following tasks:

1. Analyzing historiography, sources, and theory on the research topic.
2. Determining the conceptual, main ideas, concepts, and approaches to the state and law on the part of Russian Freemasons in the studied period.
3. Determining the main provisions and approaches to the theory of the "common good" (the welfare of all and everyone).
4. Identifying and showing the origin and development of the theory of the welfare of all and everyone in the documents and worldview of Russian Freemasons.
5. Assessing the role of Russian Freemasonry in the development and implementation of the theory of the welfare of all and everyone and the development of the state and law of the Russian Empire.

The book focuses on the study of those ideas of Russian Freemasons that are set out in acts, lectures, notes, projects, manuscripts, books, and letters and are of a state-related legal nature. In other words, these notions meet such areas as the state and law. Particular attention is paid to the process of the formation and development of ideas about the "common good" among the Russian Freemasons of the late 18th – the first quarter of the 19th centuries. The time covered by the book's description shows the middle of the 18th century – the first quarter of the 19th century. The influence of the theory of the "common good" on the worldview of the nobles in Russia began in the first half of the 18th century. The noticeable spread of Masonic Lodges in Russia started in the second half of the 18th century. The history of Russian Freemasonry in the 18th century has been described in detail by Historians.

The process of the formation of the legal worldview of Russian Freemasons ends in the 1780s. This process largely coincides with Russian Freemasonry's acquisition of independence from the foreign Chapters and the formation of its governing bodies. The Masonic assemblies come under legislative regulation, and the formation of Freemasonry as a social institution begins at that time. At the same time, the ideas of the "common good" were formed in the political and legal worldview of the Russian Monarchs (Paul I and Alexander I).

That was the time of the transition of the Masonic subculture to the intercultural influence[1]. The philosophical, moral, and legal ideas of the Professors of the Moscow University I. G. Schwartz (Shvarts in the Russian sources) and A. M. Bryantsev and the ideas of some statesmen (Count, the Actual Privy Councilor N. I. Panin, Count, General-in-Chief P. I. Panin, Chief Hofmeister I. P. Elagin, Actual Privy Councilor (1793) A. I. Musin-Pushkin, Actual Privy Councilor (1801) A. V. Khrapovitsky, and the Actual Privy Councilor (1807) I. V. Lopukhin) were formed at that time. The liberal state-related legal concepts of Professor I. A. Fessler and Officials G. A. Rosenkampf (Rozenkampf in the Russian sources) and M. M. Speransky and the conservative concepts of E. A. Kushelev and I. A. Pozdeev became prevalent at the beginning of the 19th century. Freemasons strove to disseminate the moral and legal ideas and notions of serving the Tsar, Fatherland, and Society in Russian Society at that time. Freemasonry ceased to exist as a social institution after the prohibition of Masonic Lodges and other Secret Societies on August 1, 1822.

The book shows for the first time that the doctrine of the state and law of Russian Freemasons lies in the mainstream of the theory of the "common good," developed by both Western and Russian thinkers. An attempt has been made in the book to prove to the respected reader that Russian Freemasons were the adherents of the theory of the "common good" in its religious natural-legal interpretations. The book demonstrates the interpretations of the theory of the "common good" by Russian Freemasons for the first time. Ultimately, the reader will conclude that the state-related legal ideology in Russia and the ideas of Russian Freemasons about the state and law were largely the same.

Research methodology and methods

Various general scientific methods were used in the book. The inductive method, analysis, and synthesis allowed us to describe Russian Freemasonry as a community and highlight the state-related and legal ideas of the individual representatives of Freemasonry. The sources of the state-related and legal ideas of Russian Freemasons and their organic connection with the theory of the "common good" were discovered by the deductive method. The concept history method allows building a text-related sequence of the formation, change, and interpretation of ideas and their storage and transmission[2]. The methods of intellectual history allowed us to analyze the texts and ways of conceptualizing the surrounding world of nature and society by Russian Freemasons and establish the forms, means, and institutions of the

---

[1] See Malgorzata Abassy "A Russian Mason on the Paths of his Native Culture..." Pages 176-177.
[2] See D. V. Timofeev "European Ideas in the Public Consciousness..." 2011. – 35 p.

intellectual communication of Russian Freemasons in a socio-cultural context[1]. An attempt was made to comprehensively analyze the topic under consideration in this scientific work. The author considered the subject from the standpoint of historical and legal science, the history of political and legal doctrines by using the empirical data of Russian history and theoretical generalizations from the field of the philosophy of law by historical and legal reconstruction and source analysis.

For disclosing the topic in detail, the historical-genetic method was used as a procedure for studying the genesis (the origin and stages of development) of the concrete historical phenomena and the analysis of the causality of changes[2] and the historical-biographical way[2]. The mode of historical and legal reconstruction was also used to clarify the logic of the main stages in the development of the research subject. Means of internal and external criticism were used to characterize some historical and legal documents and establish the authorship and the year of their origin. Along with this, the techniques of the statistics of the non-included observation of Russian Freemasons were applied to characterize the subject of research. According to the methodological approach of Yu. L. Khalturin, the text must be written by a Freemason and intended only for Freemasons. The text should contain various philosophical ideas and refer to the canonical Masonic texts, connecting the philosophical ideas and Masonic symbols[3]. Therefore, the texts of the Masonic statutes, acts, and instructions addressed to different members of Masonic Lodges are extremely important.

It should be said separately about the definition of Freemasonry. T. O. Sokolovskaya and A. N. Pypin considered Freemasonry by 3 different aspects: social movement, mystical teaching, and organization.

S. V. Arzhanukhin proved that Masonic Lodges are “a form of civil society”:

1. Masonic Lodges “play the role of a kind of the spiritual schools of civil society in Russia[4].”

2. “The Masters of the Lodges are the leaders of the religious and moral movement of civil society[5].”

---

[1] L. P. Repina “Historical science at the turn of the XX-XXI centuries.: social theories and historiographical practice” / L. P. Repina; - Moscow: Krug, 2011. Pages 343, 371.
[2] L. P. Repina “Historical science at the turn of the XX-XXI centuries.: social theories and historiographical practice” / L. P. Repina; - Moscow: Krug, 2011. Pages 343, 371.
[3] Yu. L. Khalturin “The philosophy of the Russian Masons of the late 18th - early 19th centuries: a critical reconstruction”: A thesis of a Candidate in Philosophical Sciences: 09.00.03 - Yekaterinburg, 2010. Page 32.
[4] S. V. Arzhanukhin “The philosophical views of Russian Freemasonry ...” Page 134.
[5] Ibid. Page 165.

3. "Being the leaders of civil society that developed and preached the spiritual, moral, and religious norms of thinking and human behavior in everyday life, they considered themselves responsible for the spiritual health and prosperity of the nation and consciously entrusted themselves with determining the ways to revive and improve the human race[6]."

4. "Russian Freemasonry was the first manifestation of civil initiative."

5. "The Masonic Order <...> acted as an organizational and religious-ideological formation of the civil society of Russia in the 18th-19th centuries." And "the civil society should have (and, at that time, it had) the conscious goals and objectives and be concerned about its welfare and watch over its preservation. And the Masonic Order was such a social form of self-organization[1]."

6. "The active fulfillment of moral duties outside the Lodges leads to the formation of the ethics of civil society[2]." Yu. E. Kondakov also notes the influence of Freemasons on the formation of civil society in Russia[3]. The Polish researcher M. Abassy considered Masonic Lodges as an institution of civil society[4].

Thus, the Freemasonry in the book is considered as an organization having a regulatory component that is very important: a set of documents (constitutions (statutes), patents, acts containing some rituals, as well as some instructions and protocols). Freemasons create the organizational and legal support of the activities of the particular Masonic System (English, French, Zinnendorf (Tsinnendorfskaya in the Russian sources), Swedish, Rosicrucian (Rozenkreytserskaya in the Russian sources), etc.), the Mother's Lodge (for example, the Sphinx in Moscow in the 18th century, Peter to the Truth in St. Petersburg in the 19th century[5]), the governing body of several lodges (for example, the Chapter of Beneficial (Charitable) Knights at the beginning of the 19th century[6]), the Union of Lodges (the Grand Lodge of Astrea, the Great Provincial Lodge, etc.), as well as their Officials (the Grand Provincial Master, the Grand Master, Great Local Master, 1st Overseer, 2nd Overseer, Chair Master, etc.).

The main ideas that were demonstrated in this scientific work

1. The theory of the "common good" was widespread in Europe at the end of the 18th – the first quarter of the 19th century. This theory had its conceptual

[1]S. V. Arzhanukhin "The philosophical views of Russian Freemasonry..." Page 139.
[2]Ibid. Page 162.
[3]Yu. E. Kondakov "The Order of the Golden and Rose Cross in Russia..." Page 5.
[4]Malgorzata Abassy "A Russian Mason on the Paths of his Native Culture." Page 63.
[5]A. I. Serkov "Russian Freemasonry. 1731-2000." Page 954.
[6]Ibid. Page 1025.

apparatus (the “common good,” the “common harm,” the benefit of “all and everyone”) and a natural-legal basis. This theory was called the theory of the welfare of all and everyone in the Russian Empire.

2. The “common good” in the political and legal discourse began being considered as a goal of the possession of things, a punishment of a criminal, the restriction of rights, rule, conclusion, and execution of a contract, in terms of interest (“open sea,” “virtues,” “life,” “the preservation of faith,” “the fulfillment of promises,” “the fulfillment of contracts,” “prosperity,” “the greatest benefit,” “justice,” “silence,” “peace,” “faith and fear of God,” “the construction of bridges, roads,” “general and individual happiness,” etc.), and as a method (when making decisions). The opposite of the “common good” is the “common harm” that is extremely negative. A person guided by the theory of the “common good” should direct his or her actions towards his or her good for the benefit of “all citizenship” and other citizens. He or she must coordinate his or her will with the will of others and, if necessary, limit it to achieve this.

3. The “common good” is possible only if the good of everyone is realized (Ch. L. Montesquieu) and the “common good” is equal in value to the good of everyone, and they do not contradict each other (J. G. Justi and C. Beccaria). The legislation that takes into consideration the good of all and everyone is good. And on the contrary, the legislation that does not take it into account is bad, being “torture” (C. Beccaria, J. G. Justi). Some attempts have been made to implement these provisions of the theory in the state and legal policy of Russia.

4. The principles of the theory of the welfare of all and everyone:

4.1 The “common good” is inextricably linked with the rights (privileges) and liberties of a Monarch and all estates.

4.2. The “common good” serves as a balance of the interests between the state and citizens.

4.3. The well-being of all and everyone requires a good knowledge of the “condition, titles, and exercises” of citizens and the world around them for organizing life for the “common good,” as well as for knowing their rights and responsibilities.

5. The Russian theory of the welfare of all and everyone was developed by I. G. Reichel (Reikhel in the Russian sources), Catherine II, Z. A. Goryushkin, and other scientists and thinkers. The “common good” was understood as general and individual happiness (the greater good), a criterion for making decisions, and a method for aligning interests. The good of all was rooted in the Common Law (State Law), and the good of everyone - in the Special Law (the Civil Law). The benefits that flow from autocratic rule are equal to the benefits that liberty gives. Laws had to be arranged in such a way that everybody, when achieving his or her benefit, benefited the general one, and vice versa.

6. Some Russian Monarchs (Catherine II, Paul I, and Alexander I) adopted the terms and principles of the theory of the welfare of all and everyone, proclaiming the welfare of all and everyone and the prevention of the "common harm" as the goal of their rule. The "common good" was considered by them as the interest, balance (of the interests between the state and citizens), and method (a way to make decisions). The phrase "We have recognized for good" became a stable expression for denoting the legislative will of a Monarch.

7. The theory of the welfare of all and everyone was disseminated both in the legislative, official, business, and diplomatic practice of the Officials of the Russian Empire and in the documents of Masonic Lodges, the writings, and correspondence of Russian Freemasons. The vocabulary of the theory of the "common good" was present in the Masonic acts, documents, and speeches, which have become widespread among Brothers-Freemasons: both "Knightly Systems" and the Rosicrucians (Rozencraitsers in the Russian sources). The welfare of all and everyone was the goal of the Masonic Order.

8. The term "common good" appeared in the vocabulary of Russian Freemasons in the 1750s and survived until the prohibition of Russian Freemasonry in 1822. Russian Freemasonry inspired and encouraged the Brothers to use the vocabulary of the "common good" in their works. This influence was manifested even when the author of the work stopped attending Masonic meetings.

9. Russian Freemasons shared and supported the theory of the welfare of all and everyone. That theory was the root of their political and legal ideas. Russian Freemasons rejected any violent methods of overthrowing the government as incompatible with the principles of the "common good," excluding any political radicalism, and condemned any actions leading to the "common harm," prolonged wars, and civil disasters. Russian Freemasons strengthened the statehood of the Russian Empire: they supported and disseminated the dominant political and legal ideology, spread "peace and quiet" in the state, and fought any radical political and legal ideas (atheistic, materialistic, and revolutionary).

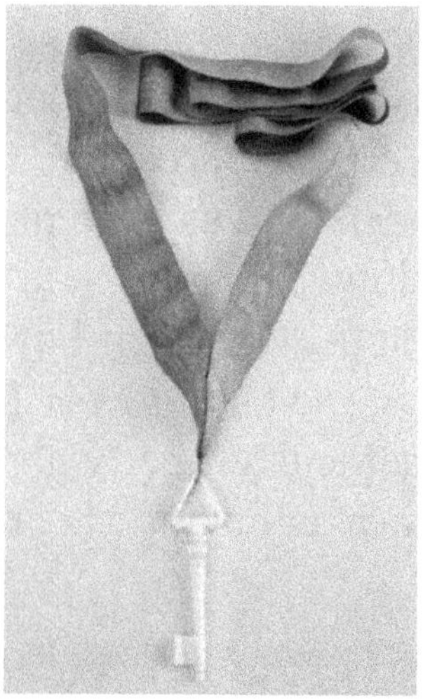

Picture 5. A sign is in the form of a bone Master Key on a blue moire neck ribbon. Russia. The late 18th - early 19th centuries. Published by I. N. Ukhanova in the catalog of the

exhibition of the State Hermitage Museum in 2013[1].

The role of the book is that the main provisions and conclusions formulated in it complement and develop the sections of the history of the state and law and legal teachings of Russia. The natural-legal concept of the "common good" in the interpretation of Russian Freemasons allows us to take a fresh look at the history of the teachings of the state and law. A theoretical analysis of the new sources on the history of the state and law significantly expands the research area of science.

The study of the legal ideas of Russian Freemasons gives the options for solving the problems of modern legal science: a balance of the institutions of the state and civil society, an actualization of the theory of the "common good," and a consideration of the problems of the ratio of private and public, issues of protecting the human rights, and weighing various interests in a new way. The book will be interesting for Lawyers, Historians, Philosophers, and Political Scientists interested in the topic. The developed historical and legal problems provide a more objective assessment of the past historical experience of Russia. The scientific and legal assessment of the culture of the past is the only basis for the development of the culture of future generations. The content of the book can be used in research on the history of the state and law, legal doctrines, and teaching courses in the national history of the state and law, the history of Russia, political science, philosophy, and comparative jurisprudence in various higher educational institutions.

The structure of the book

The book consists of an introduction, three chapters (two paragraphs in the first chapter and four paragraphs in the second and third chapters), a conclusion, a bibliography, and five appendices.

The first chapter reveals the basics of the historiography and source study of the state and legal ideas of the Russian Freemasons of the late 18th – the first quarter of the 19th century. The second chapter considers the content of the theory of the "common good" (the welfare of all and everyone) and its implementation in

[1]The Wisdom of Astrea: the monuments of the Freemasonry of the 18th - the first third of the 19th century in the Hermitage collection: an exhibition catalog / The State Hermitage Museum - St. Petersburg: The Publishing House of the State Hermitage, 2013. - 480 p.: ill. Page 141.

the legislation and vocabulary of Masonic Lodges in the Russian Empire of the 18th century - the first quarter of the 19th century. The third chapter shows the use and interpretation of the theory of the welfare of all and everyone in the vocabulary of Russian Freemasons from 1750 to 1822.

The introduction substantiates the relevance of the chosen topic. The author tried to determine the conceptual content of the state and legal ideas of Russian Freemasons, their genesis, and their inseparable connection with the theory of the "common good." The object and the subject have been determined (the theory of the welfare of all and everyone, outlined in the acts, lectures, notes, projects, manuscripts, and books of prominent Russian Freemasons). The chronological framework of the study from 1780 to 1822 was grounded. The introduction describes the degree of the scientific elaboration of the topic and the source base. Also, the introduction shows some works on Russian Freemasonry by some domestic and foreign authors of the past and present (A. N. Pypin, T. O. Sokolovskaya, V. I. Semevsky, A. I. Serkov, S. V. Arzhanukhin, G. Karlheinz (Karlheints in the Russian sources), A. N. Lushin, Yu. E. Kondakov, and others). The study identified the following three groups of sources: normative sources, political-legal philosophical writings, moral-philosophical writings, and some sources of a biographical nature (personal and objectified information). Some archival sources were mentioned separately. A theoretical basis of the study was the work of Historians, Lawyers, and Philosophers (G. V. Vernadsky, S. V. Kodan, A. N. Lushin, S. V. Arzhanukhin, E. A. Vishlenkova, G. V. Florovsky, T. V. Andreeva, V. Yu. Zakharov, Yu. E. Kondakov, and others). The research methodology was presented by general and special modes, including induction and deduction, means of historical reconstruction, comparatively legal, intellectual history, etc. The certain nine main ideas of the book were formulated. The theoretical and practical significance of the book was emphasized.

The first chapter comprehensively analyzes the historiography and sources on the research topic. The citations show the questions of the worldview of Russian Freemasons developed in the Tsarist, Soviet, and Post-Soviet times. The importance of archival sources and foreign literature is pointed out.

Paragraph 1.1, "The historiography of the state-legal ideas of Russian Freemasons," describes and analyzes the literature, main stages in the study of the state-legal ideas of Russian Freemasons, and approaches to the study of the topic.

Paragraph 1.2, "The source study of the state and legal ideas of Russian Freemasons," provides the analysis of sources on Russian Freemasonry, the problems of the source study of Russian Freemasonry, the stages of the author's processing of existing sources, and the introduction of some new sources into the scientific circulation.

The second and third chapters of this scientific work consider the sources, content, approaches, and dissemination of the theory of the "common good" (the welfare of all and everyone) from the points of view of Russian scientists, Russian Monarchs, and Russian Freemasons in the studied period.

Paragraph 2.1, "The theory of the 'common good' in the Russian Empire," reveals the genesis and content of the theory and its interpretation in the understanding of Russian jurists. This paragraph also analyzes the terms "common good," "common harm," "welfare of all and everyone," etc.

Paragraph 2.2, "The domestic theory of the welfare of all and everyone," shows and analyzes the spread of the theory of the "common good" in science, politics, and education in Russia in the 18th – the first quarter of the 19th century, providing the examples of the development of the theory by Russian scientists and interpreting the theory by Catherine II.

Paragraph 2.3, "The welfare of all and everyone in the imagination of Paul I and Alexander I," proves that Paul I and Alexander I had the "common good" goal of reigning, interpret this category, and summarizes the development of the theory of the welfare of all and everyone in the first quarter of the 19th century.

Paragraph 2.4, "The welfare of all and everyone and Russian Freemasonry," demonstrates the influence of Western European Masonic Lodges and associations on the Russian Lodges and analyzes the spread of the vocabulary of the "common good" in the statutes, acts, and instructions of Masonic Lodges.

Paragraph 3.1, "The 'common good' in the first generation of Russian Freemasons (1750-1769)," shows the spread of the vocabulary of the theory of the "common good" among the nobility that attended Masonic Lodges in 1750-1769 and analyzes the "common good" in the works of I. N. Boltin, A. R. Vorontsov, G. P. Gagarin, A. P. Sumarokov, M. M. Kheraskov, and others.

Paragraph 3.2, "The welfare of all and everyone in the second generation of Russian Freemasons. Part 1 (1770-1779)," reveals the views of some Russian Masons (that visited the lodges in 1770-1779) on the "common good" and the good of everyone, demonstrating the excerpts from the works of F. G. Bauze, A. I.

Vasilyev, A. B. Kurakin, and others, and showing the similarities and differences in the approach to the "common good" by A. R. Radishchev.

Paragraph 3.3, "The welfare of all and everyone in the second generation of Russian Freemasons. Part 2 (1780-1789)," provides the views of some Russian Freemasons (I. I. Betsky, I. A. Pozdeev, Kh. A. Chebotarev, and others) on the bliss of all and everyone.

Paragraph 3.4, "The welfare of all and everyone in the third and fourth generation of Russian Freemasons (1790-1822)," proves the spread of the vocabulary of the "common good" in the letters and works of I. P. Turgenev, A. A. Chartoryisky, M. Yu. Vielgorsky, and P. D. Lodiy. Also, it shows the positive role of Russian Freemasons in the development of domestic legal thought and in fighting against any radicalism in the public and political consciousness.

A conclusion substantiates the achievement of the declared goal and objectives of the author and shows the scientific novelty. The conclusion also states the legitimacy of the main ideas of the book and their theoretical, logical, and empirical validity. This research filled some gaps in the modern scientific knowledge of the history of the state and law and introduced some new sources into scientific circulation. No doubt, this scientific work helps overcome some common misconceptions about the role and nature of Russian Freemasonry, assessing the contribution of Russian Freemasonry in the formation of legal culture and civil society in Russia. The author proved the spread of the theory of the "common good" in the Russian Empire in the 18th and the first quarter of the 19th centuries, highlighted the vocabulary and principles of the theory, the correspondence of the state-related legal ideas of Russian Freemasons to the theory of the welfare of all and everyone, shared by some Russian Monarchs. The work concludes the positive role of Russian Freemasonry in the formation and development of Russian Statehood.

The bibliography cited consists of 339 titles and 53 of which are archival (51 of them have never been published). The book contains 40 illustrations.

Chapter I

The issues of the historiography and source study of the state and legal ideas of the Russian Freemasons of the late 18th – the first quarter of the 19th century

§1.1. The historiography of the state and legal ideas of Russian Freemasons

The historiographic basis of the study included the works of scientists on Russian national history, the history of philosophy, state and law, and political and legal doctrines. Legal Science only in the XXI century began considering the problems of the state and legal ideas of Russian Freemasons. No special research has been fulfilled for any objective reasons yet. A significant number of various papers and materials on Russian Freemasonry were destroyed or taken abroad[1]. A. N. Lushin accomplished a serious monographic study containing a detailed picture of the formation and development of the state-related legal views of Russian Freemasons at the turn of the 18th century -19th century.

The historiography of the matter can be divided into the Pre-Revolutionary, Soviet, and Post-Soviet writings of history.

The main tendency of the Pre-Revolutionary Period was the development of the empirical base: different publications on the history of Freemasonry. The first studies of Freemasonry started at the beginning of the 19th century. After prohibiting the Masonic Lodges in 1822, the researchers of the 19th century introduced the following categories and concepts into the scientific circulation: "Russian Freemasonry" and "Masonic Literature." Moreover, the term "Russian Freemasonry" was included in the subject of Social Sciences and Humanities.

The research of M. N. Longinov (1823-1875), S. B. Eshevsky (1829-1865), P. P. Pekarsky (1827-1872), and A. I. Nezelenov (1845-1896) formed the factual base on Freemasonry in the 18th century. Those scientists compiled the biographies of N. I. Novikov, I. G. Schwartz (Shvarts in the Russian sources), I. V. Lopukhin, S. I. Gamaleya, and M. M. Kheraskov, noted the influence of Masonic ideas on the life of Russian society in the 18th century and gave a detailed description of the works of Freemasons. The above-mentioned scientists published

---

[1]For example, the conspiratorial part of the Freemasons-Rosicrucians "had a firm rule to burn all the current documents at the end of the year at the last quarterly conference." See Yu. E. Kondakov "The secret instructions of the Russian Rosicrucians of the XVIII-XIX centuries." - Moscow: Ganga, 2018. Page 34.

the acts and regulations of the lodges and detailed the materials of the investigation file against the Martinists (initiated by Catherine II in 1792).

A. N. Pypin, T. O. Sokolovskaya, V. I. Semevsky, and G. V. Vernadsky studied the socio-political views of Freemasons and the connection between the Masonic worldview and literature with social and political practice. Those scientists tried to give a historical analysis of the normative documents of Freemasons for the first time.

Picture 6. Alexander Nikolaevich Pypin. A photo of the young scientist (from open sources).

The writer and historian A. N. Pypin (1833-1904) was a prominent researcher of Freemasonry. His article was published in the Europe Bulletin # 6, "Russian Freemasonry before Novikov," in 1868[1]. "The materials for the history of Masonic Lodges" were published in the Europe Bulletin # 1, 2, and 7 in 1872[2]. "The Chronological index of Russian Lodges from the first introduction of Freemasonry till its prohibition, 1731-1822" was issued by the Printing House of M. Stasyulevich in St. Petersburg in 1873[3]. The book "The Russian Freemasonry of the 18th and the first quarter of the 19th centuries: Research and materials on the age of Catherine II and Alexander I"[4] was published in 1916 and then reprinted in 1918 and 1997. A. N. Pypin considered the systems (English, Swedish, Zinnendorf, etc.) and the unions of Masonic Lodges in Russia (Elaginsky, Novikovsky, the Rosicrucians (Rozencraitsers in the Russian sources), etc.), showed the chronology and place in the general history of Freemasonry, indicated the personal membership, and

---

[1]Europe Bulletin. 1868. N# 6. Pages 546-589.
[2]Europe Bulletin. 1872. # 1. Pages 174-214. # 2. Pages 561-603, # 7. Pages 244-288.
[3]A. N. Pypin "The chronological index of Russian Lodges from the first introduction of Freemasonry to its prohibition, 1731-1822." SPb.: The printing house of M. Stasyulevich, 1873. - 43 p.
[4]A. N. Pypin "The Russian Freemasonry of the 18th and the first quarter of the 19th century: research and materials on the era of Catherine II and Alexander I." Edited by G. V. Vernadsky. The notes by G. V. Vernadsky. Petrograd, 1916. -571 p.

published the documents of the lodges.

Picture 7. Vladimir Vasilyevich Semevsky. A photo of the young scientist (from open sources).

V. I. Semevsky (1848-1916) published a significant number of works on Freemasonry and Russian history at the end of the 18th – the first quarter of the 19th centuries. V. I. Semevsky published his book “From the history of social trends in Russia in the 18th and the first half of the 19th century”[1] in 1885. Then, in 1906, his work “The question of the transformation of the state system in the 18th and the first quarter of the 19th centuries: essays from the history of political and social ideas”[2] was issued. After that, in 1907, his article “Speransky's first political treatise”[3] was published by the magazine “Russian Wealth.” Afterward, in 1908, the articles by the magazine “The Past Years” under the title “Decembrists-Masons”[4] were issued. Later, in 1911, the article “Liberal plans in government spheres in the first half of the reign of Alexander I”[5] (reprinted in 1912) and the article “The Fall of Speransky”[6] (reprinted in 1912) was published in the 2nd volume of the collection “The Patriotic War and Russian Society 1812-1912” year). V. I. Semevsky was one of the first to create the review and political and legal analysis of the views of the educators and philosophers, statesmen, and public figures of the 18th-19th centuries. He researched the ideas and projects of the state reforms of S. E. Desnitsky, D. Diderot, N. I. Panin, M. A. Fonvizin, D. I. Fonvizin, M. M. Shcherbatov, A. N. Radishchev, the constitutional and constituent projects of A. Chartoryiskiy, N. S. Mordvinov, M. M. Speransky, and N. N. Novosiltsev, and liberal social ideas considered in the works of A. S. Pushkin and K. F. Ryleev. V. I. Semevsky gave a commentary on various Masonic documents and examined the “The Charter of Freemasons” (1782) and “The Code of the Great Masonic Lodge of Astrea” (1815). When researching, he referred to the protocols of

[1]V. I. Semevsky “From the history of social movements in Russia in the 18th and the first half of the 19th century,” St. Petersburg: The literature of Apostolov, 1885. - 203 p.

[2]The past. 1906. # 1-3.

[3]Russian wealth. -1907. # 1. - Pages 41-88.

[4]The past years. 1908. # 2 Pages 1-50; # 3. Pages 127-170; # 5-6. Pages 379-433.

[5]The Patriotic War and Russian society 1812-1912. M.: Publisher: The publishing house of the partnership of I. D. Sytin. 1912. - Volume 2. - Pages 174 - 178.

[6]The Patriotic War and Russian society. 1812-1912. M., 1911. Volume II. Pages 221-246.

the lodges. V. I. Semevsky paid the closest attention to M. M. Speransky's state activities. Ya. L. Barskov (a historian of the Russian literature of the 18th century and a teacher, 1863-1937) published several works on the history of Russian Freemasonry: "Materials for the history of the Novikov Friendship Society of 1782 with notes by N. P. Poludensky"[1] (1863), "Lopukhin Ivan Vladimirovich: The biographical feature article. A separate reprint from the 'Russian Biographical Dictionary'"[2] (1914), "The Correspondence of the Moscow Freemasons of the XVIII century. 1780-1792"[3] (1915), and "The letters of A . M. Kutuzov"[4] (1917). Ya. L. Barskov showed some information about the scientific and educational activities of Freemasons-Professors of the Moscow University and published a significant number of the diaries and letters of many Freemasons (N. I. Novikov, I. P. Turgenev, A. M. Kutuzov, G. Ya. Shreder, and many others).

Many publications on the history of Freemasonry started flourishing in the first quarter of the 20th century. Many new works were added to the works of the above-mentioned authors of the early XX century. Tira Ottovna Sokolovskaya (a member of the Council and a Secretary of the Imperial Society of the Zealots of history, 1884-1942) presented more than 50 articles and several small books: "The Chapter of the Phoenix: The Highest Secret Masonic Rule in Russia (1788-1822),"[5] a book "Materials on the history of Russian Freemasonry in the 18th-19th centuries,"[6] "Russian Freemasonry and its significance in the history of the social movement (XVIII and the first quarter of the XIX century),"[7] "A list of Officers of the Russian Army that admitted their belonging to Freemasonry (1826): from the materials for the history of Russian Freemasonry[8]." By using the extensive historical and literary material, T. O. Sokolovskaya highlighted the following

---

[1]The Russian archive. 1863. # 3. Pages 204-212.

[2]Ya. L. Barskov "Lopukhin Ivan Vladimirovich: a biographical feature article." A separate print from the "Russian Biographical Dictionary". St. Petersburg, 1914. – 33 pages.

[3]Ya. L. Barskov "The correspondence of the Moscow Freemasons of the 18th century. 1780- 1792." - Petrograd: The Printing House of the Department of Russian Language and Philology of the Imperial Academy of Sciences, 1915. - 335 p.

[4]The Russian Historical Journal. 1917. Books 1-2. Pages 131-140.

[5]T. O. Sokolovskaya "The Chapter of the Phoenix: The highest secret Masonic rule in Russia (1788-1822)." Petrograd: The printing house of P. P. Soykin, 1916. - 100 p.

[6]T. O. Sokolovskaya "The materials on the history of Russian Freemasonry in the 18th-19th centuries." M.: The Publishing House of the State Public Historical Library of Russia, 2000. - 165 p.

[7]T. O. Sokolovskaya "Russian Freemasonry and its significance in the history of the social movement (XVIII and the first quarter of the XIX century)." SPb.: The printing house of N. Glagolyev, 1910. - 184 p.

[8]T. O. Sokolovskaya "A list of the Officers of the Russian army that recognized their belonging to Freemasonry (1826): from the materials for the history of Russian Freemasonry," St. Petersburg, 1907. - 69 p.

features of Russian Freemasonry about the state: the equality before the law, Russian "truth" and Russian "originality," moral self-improvement, love for the Fatherland, and the humanization of the criminal punishment and the customs of war. T. O. Sokolovskaya took into consideration the fact that Freemasons had had their own rules of conduct - laws (she published the Laws for the Scottish Master, the Laws of the Order of Freemasons, the Laws of the Russian Grand National Lodge, and others) and the presence of the internal legal proceedings. She cited some provisions of the Code of the Grand Masonic Lodge of Astrea, gave the corresponding analysis of the Code, admission to Freemasons, Masonic rituals and symbolism, and Masonic teaching saying that the Divine Law (love for one's neighbor, Brother, and humanity) is superior to the Human Law.

V. N. Tukalevsky (a historian and a bibliographer, 1881-1936) published an article, "From the history of philosophical trends in Russian society in the 18th century (An experience of characterizing the ideological trends in the Russian Freemasonry)"[1] in the magazine of the Ministry of Public Education (# 2) in 1911. Also, he published a small book, "The Search of Russian Freemasons (From the History of Philosophical Trends in the Russian Society of the 18th Century)"[2] and an article "N. I. Novikov and I. G. Schwartz (Shvarts in the Russian sources)"[3] in the collection "Freemasonry in its Past and Present" in 1911. V. N. Tukalevsky was the first scientist to theoretically comprehend the influence of the cultural and ideological trends of the 18th century (French rationalism and Russian "Voltaireism") on Russian society in the context of the age-old struggle of "reason" and "faith," "spirit" and "body" in the minds of people. He also explained the emergence of Russian Freemasonry as a natural response to the spiritual and moral quest of the Russian nobility. V. N. Tukalevsky showed the influence of the books of Saint-Martin (Sen-Marten in the Russian sources), I. Arndt, J. Boehme (Beme in the Russian sources), F. Kempiysky on the ideological searches of Russian Freemasons (N. I. Novikov, I. G. Schwartz (Shvarts in the Russian sources), and I. V. Lopukhin) and their handwritten and printed periodicals and monographs. V. N. Tukalevsky supposed that the Freemasonry of Russia at the end of the 18th century had formed as the mystical (Christian idealism) and materialistic (Alchemy and Magic) currents.

---

[1]A Journal of the Ministry of Public Education. 1911. # 5. Pages 1-69.
[2]V. N. Tukalevsky "Russian Freemasons' quest (from the history of philosophical trends in Russian society in the 18th century)" // St. Petersburg: The Senate Printing House. 1911. - 73 p.
[3]Freemasonry in its past and present / Edited by S. P. Melgunov, N. P. Sidorov. In 2 volumes. M., 1914-1915 (Reprinted in 1991). Volume I. -M.: SP IKPA, 1991. - Pages 175-226.
[4]G. V. Vernadsky "Russian Freemasonry in the reign of Catherine II." Pg.: The Printing House of the Imperial Academy of Sciences. 1917. XXIV, -286 p.

Historian G. V. Vernadsky (1887-1973) defended a Master's thesis on the topic "Russian Freemasonry in the reign of Catherine II"[4] and published the book "Nikolai Ivanovich Novikov"[1] in 1917. G. V. Vernadsky was the first scientist to group and give a detailed analysis of sources on the history of Russian Freemasonry in his thesis: the official government documents concerning Freemasons, official Masonic documents, printed and handwritten Masonic literature, the correspondence, diaries, and memoirs of Freemasons. G. V. Vernadsky comprehensively showed the similarities and differences between Voltaire and Freemasonry. He was the first scientist to highlight the rationalist trend in Freemasonry in detail, represented in the "first Elagin Union" (I. P. Elagin, M. M. Kheraskov, A.V. Vorontsov, and others), and to enumerate the translated books of the Voltaireans and Encyclopedists (published by "Rationalist Freemasons" earlier). The author was the first scientist to note the enthusiasm of Freemasons for the works of sentimentalists (J. J. Rousseau (Russo in the Russian sources), H. F. Gellert, H. M. Wieland (Viland in the Russian sources), and others). The author also gave a thorough analysis of the translated ancient and new mystical literature, the literature of Ancient Greece, Ancient Rome, and the Middle Ages, showing their influence on the work of Russian Freemasons. G. V. Vernadsky was the first to try to bring the ethics and philosophy of Freemasons into a system and highlighted the main points of this philosophy. The author also covered in detail the political and legal views of Freemasons on the state and law (these views were also the result of familiarization with the translated literature of Bielfeld, Justi, and Saint-Martin (Sen-Marten in the Russian sources): a description of the natural legal views of Vladimir Zolotnitsky, M. M. Shcherbatov, I. P. Elagin, S. I. Gamaleya, I. G. Schwartz (Shvarts in the Russian sources), and O. A. Pozdeev and other socio-political utopias of M. M. Shcherbatov and I. V. Lopukhin). G. V. Vernadsky demonstrated the political and social positions of the Freemasons, expressing the concepts of modernization (R. L. Vorontsov, A. A. Rzhevsky, A. S. Stroganov, etc.) and conservatism (G. P. Gagarin, N. V. Repnin, A. B. Kurakin, and others). G. V. Vernadsky showed some new circumstances in the case of N. I. Novikov in connection with the interference of Masonic Leaders in the foreign policy issues of the Russian Empire (with Prussia) and the issue of succession to the throne (the Freemasons trained and instructed Tsarevich Pavel Petrovich, preparing the highest place in the Masonic hierarchy for him). The historian made a startling conclusion: the "Pavel's state" with its three-day corvee, military settlements, ideas of the Holy Tsar, and notions of the Holy Union was the

[1] G. V. Vernadsky "Nikolai Ivanovich Novikov". Pg.: The Ninth State Printing House, 1918. - 165 p.

result of Masonic ideas and notions that influenced the worldview of Pavel Petrovich.

Some aspects of the topic are touched upon in the biographical literature dedicated to N. I. Novikov, I. A. Fessler, M. M. Speransky, Catherine II, Paul I, Alexander I, etc.

Russian Freemasonry was studied within the framework of literary studies and linguistics in the USSR (P. N. Sakulin, B. S. Meylakh, G. A. Gukovsky, N. L. Rubinstein (Rubinshtein in the Russian sources), and V. V. Vinogradov). The research interest in the history of Russian Freemasonry returned in the 1970s. The contribution of Russian Freemasonry to the history of Russian constitutionalism and Russian philosophical thought started being studied. S. N. Nekrasov and N. V. Minaeva defended their theses on the topic of Freemasonry. The studies of some historians (T. A. Bakunina, V. O. Klyuchevsky, and M. M. Safonov), philologists (V. I. Novikov and K.V. Pigarev), and philosophers (V. V. Zenkovsky, G. V. Florovsky, and others) considered the matters related to the Masonic themes.

Picture 8. Ivanov-Razumnik Razumnik Vasilievich (from open sources).

The literary critic Ivanov-Razumnik (1878-1946) published the 5th edition of Part 1 of "The History of the Russian Social Thought" in 1918. He touched on the issue of the correlation between Freemasonry and Decembrism[1].

According to the author's opinion, Decembrism and Freemasonry were meaningfully incompatible. Also, he thought that the Masonic form (structure and rituals) had been incapable of creating or supporting the Decembrist Movement[2]. For example, the "Union of Welfare" replaced the questions of ethics with the questions of politics (incompatible with the Masonic Rules[3]) in its activities.

N. K. Piksanov (1878 - 1969) read his paper "The reappraisal of Russian Freemasonry"[4] in the Sociological Department of the State Academy of Arts on

[1]Ivanov-Razumnik "The history of Russian social thought" [Text] / Ivanov Razumnik. - The 5th edition (revised). - Ptg. : Revolutionary Thought, 1918. - 21 cm. Part 1: From Radishchev to the Decembrists [Text]. - 1918. - 192 p.

[2]Ibid. Page 144.

[3]Ibid. Pages 146-149.

[4]The State Academy of Artistic Sciences. A report ... [Text] / The State Academy of Artistic Sciences. - Moscow, 1926-. - 25 cm. 1921-1925. - 1926. Pages 14, 86.

March 2 and March 9, 1922. N. K. Piksanov was a student of A. N. Pypin, like P. N. Sakulin and preserved the tradition of the imperial cultural-historical school. N. K. Piksanov made an important discovery saying that the Russian Freemasonry of the 18th century had been heterogeneous and constantly evolved. In other words, some Freemasons did not bring anything specifically Masonic to the literature they wrote, but some Freemasons experienced an evolution of views (from Voltaireism to Mysticism).

A. E. Presnyakov (a Corresponding Member of the Russian Academy of Sciences, a Ph.D. in Russian History 1870-1929) published his rare and surprising content book (because it contrasted with the official political line) "Alexander I"[1] in 1924. That scientist, in his book, described in detail the connection of Masonic philosophy with the mystical aspirations of Alexander I, reflected in the text of the Act of the Holy Union (1815). The author noted that both Alexander I and M. M. Speransky had been attracted by "the religious and moral basis of Masonic books." Moreover, after reading the act of the Holy Union in the reference, M. M. Speransky recognized the fulfillment of his long-standing "dream of the possibility of improving governments and an application of the teachings of the God-man to the affairs of society"[2] in it.

Volume 1 of "The Cases of the Supreme Criminal Court and the Commission of Inquiry Concerning State Criminals" was published in the collection "The Decembrist Uprising"[3] in 1925. The volume mainly contained the protocols of the interrogations of the Decembrists: Prince S. P. Trubetskoy, K. F. Ryleev, Nikita Muravyov, Alexander Bestuzhev, Mikhail Bestuzhev, and others. The protocols of the interrogation of Prince Trubetskoy showed that the rituals of the secret societies of Decembrists had not been Masonic either in form or in content, and the agitation in favor of Decembrism within the Masonic Lodges (by P. Pestel and N. Muravyov) had not been successful. An anniversary collection, "The Decembrist revolt" (1825-1925), was published in Leningrad in 1926. N. F. Lavrova, in her article "The Dictator of December 14," in this collection provided some important information separating Freemasonry and Decembrism[4]. Thus,

---

[1]A. E. Presnyakov "Alexander I" / Professor A. E. Presnyakov. - Petersburg, 1924. - 188 p.
[2]Ibid. Page 157.
[3]The uprising of the Decembrists [Text]: documents / The Central archive; Edited by M. N. Pokrovsky. A preface by M. N. Pokrovsky. – Moscow. Leningrad, 1925-. - 26 cm. - (The materials on the history of the Decembrist uprising). Volume 1: The cases of the Supreme Criminal Court and the Commission of Inquiry, regarding the state criminals. - 1925. Pages 24-25.
[4]N. F. Lavrova "Dictator of December 14: The revolt of the Decembrists." An anniversary collection. 1825-1925 / Edited by Yu. G. Oksman and P. E. Shchegolev. - Leningrad: The publishing house "Byloye," 1926. - 400 p.

many Decembrists were in the lodge of the "Three Virtues": Prince Trubetskoy, Pavel Pestel, Alexander Muravyov, Prince Shakhovskoy, Prince Dolgoruky, Pavel Lopukhin, Pavel Pestel, and others. They did not achieve their political goals in the lodge. For this reason, they created their organization, "The Union of Salvation." The "Masonic forms and rituals" in the Charter of the Union of Salvation promoted "a firm discipline of this secret society that would guarantee its safety." According to the Charter of the Union of Salvation, the members of the Union were divided into three degrees: "Brothers," "Men," and "Bolyars." "The successive Elders, Chairman, two Overseers or Keepers, and Secretary were elected from the Bolyars monthly. The first Elders were as follows: Trubetskoy (Chairman), Lopukhin and Alexander Muravyov (Overseers), and Nikita Muravyov (Secretary)." "According to the indisputable testimony of the number of the members of the Salvation Union, the ultimate goals of the Salvation Union were the introductions of the monarchical constitutional rule and the liberation of peasants.[1]"

The third edition of "The History of Atheism" by I. P. Voronitsyn (1885-1938) was published in Ryazan in 1930. The author pointed out the apolitical nature of Freemasonry in the book[2]. According to the author, all the information about the conspiracies of Freemasons was caused by their ideological competitors - "clerics" and the mystery of the Masonic Organization. I. P. Voronitsyn, like other contemporaries, shared Voltaireism and Freemasonry. He supposed that Catherine II, D. I. Fonvizin, I. P. Elagin, and I. V. Lopukhin had been Voltaireans in the early period. I. P. Voronitsyn, in his study, referred to A. N. Pypin, A. I. Nezelenov, V. I. Semevsky, V. N. Tukalevsky, A. I. Semeka, A. N. Veselovsky, P. N. Milyukov, G. V. Plekhanov, V. V. Sipovsky, P. K. Pisksanov, Ya. L. Barskov, V. P. Semennikov, N. P. Silvansky, and P. E. Shchegolev (it was substantially rich and extensive for research). The book critically evaluated the views and showed different opinions: Freemasons, Voltaireans, and Constitutionalists (F. V. Krechetov and E. M. Kravkov), state scholars (I. B. Shad and A. P. Kunitsyn), participants in "The Case of Professors" (K. I. Arsenyev, A. I. Galich, K. F. German, and E. V. S. Raupakh). A Professor of the University of Paris, T. A. Bakunina (1904-1995), published her book "Famous Russian Freemasons"[1] in Paris in 1935. According to T. A. Bakunina, Russian Freemasonry turned the teaching of the Order into popular moral philosophy[3]. T. A. Bakunina gave a brief description of the history of Freemasonry, highlighting the main, in her opinion, features of this cultural phenomenon of public life. According to her, when Catherine's reigning, the basis of the activity of Russian

---

[1] N. F. Lavrova "Dictator of December 14: The revolt of the Decembrists." Pages 141, 142.

[2] I. P. Voronitsyn "The history of atheism" [Text] / I. P. Voronitsyn. - The 3rd edition (revised and supplemented). - Ryazan, 1930. Pages 175-286.

[3] T. A. Bakunina "Famous Russian Freemasons" [Text]; Freemasons / T. A. Bakunina. - Moscow: Joint Venture "Interbuk," 1991. - 141 p.

Freemasonry was education, and when Alexander I was ruling, the socio-political issues were main. The author discussed the propaganda of the ideas of Decembrism among Freemasons and the cases of using the lodges to cover up anti-government activities. Considering the apolitical nature of the lodges that were not suitable for the Decembrist anti-government movement, T. A. Bakunina notes that, according to the "General Laws" adopted in the lodges, it was forbidden even to "talk about the religion-related, legal, state affairs, and strife under a fine of 5 rubles for the poor[1]." She concluded that Freemasonry "goes exclusively into political thought, changing its real ideology[2]." The author provided some quantitative and social characteristics of membership in lodges. The total number of Freemasons fluctuated between 1,300 members in 1816-1818 and 1,600 members in 1820-1822. The St. Petersburg lodges had a significant number of members (700-800 and more). The Moscow lodges had (700-800 and more) as well. The provinces had the rest[3].

The book "Russian historiography" by N. L. Rubinstein (Rubinshtein in the Russian sources) (1897-1963) was published in Moscow in 1941. The book comprehensively described the activities of M. M. Shcherbatov as a historian, his political and philosophical works[4] were indicated, and historiography was given. The author noted some connection between M. M. Shcherbatov's political ideas and doctrine of the state with Ch. L. Montesquieu and Ch. Beccaria[5]. According to the author, M. M. Shcherbatov read and quoted David Hume, using his methodology in his works[6]. Following the author, Freemasonry in the 18th century, "although contradictory," reflected the humanistic tendencies of the era. Freemasonry included "the moral idea of man and its assertion of the moral principle presupposed the general rights of the human person. Therefore, the educational activities of Novikov and other progressive trends of that period were also associated with Freemasonry in Russia."[7] N. L. Rubinstein (Rubinshtein in the Russian sources) defined Russian Freemasonry as "the right-wing of Western educational, social thought." "Freemasonry went towards the conservative tendencies of the nobility with its mysticism and apoliticism[8]."

---

[1] T. A. Bakunina "Famous Russian Freemasons" [Text]; Freemasons / T. A. Bakunina. - Moscow: Joint Venture "Interbuk," 1991. - 141 p., page 98.
[2] Ibid. Page 103.
[3] T. A. Bakunina "Famous Russian Freemasons." Pages 105, 106, 107, 114.
[4] N. L. Rubinshtein "Russian historiography" [Text] / N. L. Rubinshtein. - [Moscow], 1941. Pages 116-137.
[5] Ibid. Page 120.
[6] Ibid. Page 121.
[7] Ibid.
[8] Ibid. Page 168.

N. K. Piksanov (a researcher of the Russian literature of the 18th and 19th centuries, 1878-1969) published a serious essay called "Masonic Literature"[1] in 1947. He explained the policy of Catherine II towards Russian Freemasonry through some foreign policy factors. N. K. Piksanov noted that the Freemasons of the second half of the 18th century had a passion for the works of F.-M. Voltaire and J. J. Rousseau liking some of the beliefs of these authors (the criticism of religious superstitions, charlatanism, intolerance, the presence of the ideals of an enlightened monarch, secular education, love of nature, etc.). The author showed some Masonic and non-Masonic motives in the works of N. I. Novikov, A. P. Sumarokov, M. M. Kheraskov, and M. M. Shcherbatov.

V. G. Bazanov (1911-1981) published his book "Scientific Republic"[2] simultaneously in Moscow and Leningrad in 1964. By using the example of the "Chosen Michael" Lodge, he analyzed the provisions of the Code of the Grand Lodge of Astrea to find out the meaning of the word "Freemason," the duties of a "Freemason" towards other "Brothers," people outside the lodge, the state, and the institutions of the state[3]. The book provides an overview of the political and legal views of the members of the "Chosen Michael" Lodge: F. N. Glinka, A. D. Borovikov, Prince Dolgorukov, and others, described in their writings and conversations inside the lodge. The author considered the failure of the members of the lodge to comply with the Masonic Charter and an attempt to transform the Masonic rules under the Decembrist influence of "The Union of Salvation."

The second book of M. N. Pokrovsky, "The Russian history from the ancient times," in the publication "Selected Works" (1965-1967), was issued in 1965[4]. The author supposed that the socio-political events (the uprising of the Semyonov regiment, etc.) were the reasons for the prohibition of Freemasonry in Russia[5].

In 1973, in Moscow, K. A. Maiykova (an employee of the Lenin Library) compiled a list of contents of the collection of Masonic manuscripts by S. S. Lanskoy (1787-1862) and S. V. Eshevsky (1829-1865), fund # 147 (the manuscripts of the 18th - 19th centuries), 348 pieces, 644 storage units (as of

---

[1] N. K. Piksanov "Masonic Literature" // The history of Russian literature: in 10 volumes. Volume 4. Part 2. - M.; L. The Publishing House of the Academy of Sciences of the USSR. - 1947. Pages 51 - 85.

[2] V. G. Bazanov "Scientific Republic": [The Free Society of Russian Literature Lovers] / The Academy of Sciences of the USSR. The Institute of Russian Literature (The Pushkin House). – M.; L.: Nauka, 1964. - 463 p.

[3] V. G. Bazanov "Scientific Republic." Pages 57-85.

[4] M. N. Pokrovsky "Selected works": in 4 books. / Edited by an Academician M. N. Tikhomirov. – M.: Thought, 1965-1967. – in 4 volumes; Book 2: Russian history from ancient times. (Volumes 3-4). - 1965. – 664 pages.

[5] Ibid. Pages 201-220, 277-279.

12/15/2008 - 811 items of inventory)[1]. The inventory consists of the official documents (acts, laws, agreements, letters, minutes of meetings, lists of members, and instructions) of Masonic Lodges belonging to the Great Provincial Lodge in the east of St. Petersburg. The list of contents contains the important documents of the correspondence of Moscow Freemasons with abroad, the minutes of the Grand Directory Lodge of Vladimir to the Order of 1815-1816, an agreement between the Grand Provincial Lodge and the Lodge of Astrea in three languages, the affairs of the Grand Provincial Lodge of 1816-1817, and the official correspondence of Freemasons with the authorities, including the closure of the lodges in 1822 and 1826 in 3 languages. These documents testify to the internal organization and activities of Russian Freemasonry and its relationship to the state. K. A. Maiykova compiled another inventory in 1974 - the collection of Masonic manuscripts by V. S. Arsenyev (1829-1915), fund # 014 (the manuscripts of the 18th - 19th centuries), 1917 pieces, 1965 storage units[2]. This inventory contains some materials concentrated in one place and suitable for any historical and legal research on Russian Freemasonry. The list of contents consists of the statutes, laws, acts, materials of the Rosicrucians (Rozencraitsers in the Russian sources) and the carriers of the Theoretical Degree, minutes-books of lodges, minutes, lists of members, books, and manuscripts from the famous "Hermetic Library."

N. V. Minaeva defended her thesis for obtaining a Ph.D. in Historical Sciences, "Constitutional tendencies in the political projects of Russia at the beginning of the XIX century[3]," in Moscow in 1983. Her thesis outlined a range of the issues of reforms in the state and legal structure of Russia ("constitutionalism") at the beginning of the 19th century. The author comprehensively sets out the views and projects of A. R. Vorontsov, N. M. Karamzin, M. M. Speransky, A. P. Kunitsyn, and Decembrists N. M. Muravyov, and P. I. Pestel. N. V. Minaeva considered some historical and legal assessments of the works of the above-mentioned scientists and systematized them.

V. I. Rabinovich (1922-1995) published his book "Following Radishchev ...: F. V. Karzhavin and his surroundings"[4] in 1986. He mainly described F. V. Karzhavin's life and creative work. The author of the book supposed that a source

---

[1] Fund 147. Lanskoy Sergey Stepanovich and Eshevsky Stepan Vasilyevich: a collection, XVIII-XIX centuries. - 811 units of issue.

[2] Fund 014. Arsenyev Vasily Sergeevich: a collection, XVIII-XIX centuries. - 1967 units of issue.

[3] N. V. Minaeva "The constitutional tendencies in the political projects of Russia at the beginning of the 19th century": A thesis of a Ph.D. in Historical Sciences: 07.00.02. - Moscow, 1983. - 410 p.

[4] V. I. Rabinovich "Following Radishchev...: F. V. Karzhavin and his entourage." - M.: Thought, 1986.–221 p.

of the radical ideas of A. N. Radishchev and V. I. Bazhenov had been his friend, F. Karzhavin. Following the author, F. V. Karzhavin was an encyclopedist, rebel, and revolutionary and had a very negative attitude towards the Masonic views of his friends[1].

Picture 9. Vasily Osipovich Klyuchevsky (a photo of the young scientist, taken from open sources).

Volume 9 of "The Course of Russian History" in the 9-volume collection of the "Works" of V. O. Klyuchevsky (1841-1911)[2] was issued in 1990.

The author in his book comprehensively described "Russian Voltaireism" and "Novikov Circle" standing in the way of "Russian Voltaireism" and depicted the ideological searches of N. I. Novikov and I. V. Lopukhin from Voltaireism to Freemasonry. V. O. Klyuchevsky was convinced: "... when we read about such paroxysms of conscientious thought, perhaps, for the first time, we find an educated Russian person deep in thought. And he or she had this thoughtful condition earlier and will have it afterward ...."[3] I. N. Klyuchevsky explained the goals of Russian Freemasons: they "joined the 'small chosen people' of Freemasons only to process themselves into the suitable stones for the mental temple of Solomon for the future ideal Russian society."[4]

A collection, "On Russia and Russian Philosophical Culture: The Philosophers of the Russian-After-October Abroad," compiled by V. Zenkovsky (1881-1962), was published in Moscow in 1990[5]. The book showed the history of

---

[1] Ibid. Page 78.
[2] V. O. Klyuchevsky "The course of Russian history." Volume IX. - M., 1990. - 526 p.
[3] V. O. Klyuchevsky "The course of Russian history." Volume IX. - M., 1990. Page 47.
[4] Ibid. Page 49.
[5] On Russia and Russian Philosophical Culture: The philosophers of the Russian-after-October Abroad: Compiled by M. A. Maslin. An introductory article by M. A. Maslin, A. L. Andreev, pages 5-42. - M.: Nauka, 1990. - 528 p.

Russian philosophy and social thought of the 18th – the first quarter of the 19th centuries. The author identified the three main currents of the Russian philosophical thought of that period: "Russian Voltaireism" (nihilism and radicalism), secularized nationalism, and Russian Freemasonry ("meeting religious and philosophical requests outside the Church")[1]. V. Zenkovsky called Russian Freemasonry a school of humanism, awakening the intellectual interests in the principles of combining science and religion. According to the author, M. V. Lomonosov theoretically created it, for the first time, even before the emergence of Russian Freemasonry. "All the main characteristics of the future 'advanced' intelligentsia were formed in Russian Freemasonry. The primacy of morality, a sense of duty to serve society, and practical idealism, in general, were the basic things to follow. That was the way of ideological life and effective service to the ideal.[2]" V. Zenkovsky examined the biographies of I. G. Schwartz (Shvarts in the Russian sources), A. F. Labzin, and M. M. Speransky. The author demonstrated some religious and mystical perception of the law by M. M. Speransky, stated in his letters to Zeier (Tseyer in the Russian sources): "Speransky wrote to him: people are mistaken, stating that the spirit of the Kingdom of God is incompatible with the principles of political societies..." And he added further: "I know no single state issue that could be reduced to the Gospel.[3]" V. Zenkovsky showed "the ideological traditions of Freemasonry" of Professor Prokopovich Antonsky, "the traces of Freemasonry" in the works of A. P. Chaadaev, the searches of A. I. Hertsen, and the teachings of N. F. Fyodorov.

The historians T. V. Andreeva, V. M. Bokova, V. Yu. Zakharov, T. N. Zhukovskaya, Yu. E. Kondakov, A. I. Serkov, philosophers S. V. Arzhanukhin, E. L. Kuzmishin, Yu. L. Khalturin and A. A. Fedorov, lawyers S. V. Kodan, O. A. Kudinov, A. G. Moskvina, and A. N. Lushin issued some scientific works in *the post-Soviet period*, considering the problem of the genesis and influence of the state-legal views of Russian Freemasons at the turn of the 18th-19th centuries. A. I. Serkov published some good works on the history of Russian Freemasonry[4]. Thanks to A. I. Serkov, that gave the biography of A. R. Vorontsov, who served as Diplomatic Representative in Austria, England, and Holland (from 1761 to 1768), Senator (from 1779), a Member of the State Council (1803), Chancellor (1802-

---

[1] On Russia and Russian Philosophical Culture: The philosophers of the Russian-after-October Abroad: Compiled by M. A. Maslin. An introductory article by M. A. Maslin, A. L. Andreev, pages 5-42. - M.: Nauka, 1990. - 528 p., page 61.

[2] Ibid. Page 129.

[3] Ibid. Page 139.

[4] A. I. Serkov "Russian Freemasonry. 1731-2000"; A. I. Serkov "The history of the Russian Freemasonry of the 19th century" / Russian Freemasonry: Materials and Research. / Edited by M. V. Reizin and A. I. Serkov.

1804) and had the rank of Actual Privy Councilor and the rank of Actual Chamberlain from 1803, the relationship of Freemasonry and the state and law could be traced. A. R. Vorontsov attended the Lodge (the United Muses) of Urania (operating from 1773) several times in 1773-1775, and the "meetings were held there on Saturdays every other week." "A. R. Vorontsov was supposed to receive the Degree of the Scottish Master in September 1776 and become a Member of the Great English (from 1762), Provincial (from 1777) Lodge in St. Petersburg. All the Masters of the lodges visited that lodge."[1] A. N. Pypin studied the influence of A. R. Vorontsov on the worldview of Alexander I[2]. V. I. Semevsky noted the political views of A. R. Vorontsov on the state structure of Russia[3]. V. N. Alekseev issued the work describing the contribution of the Counts of the Vorontsov family to the public and political life of the Russian Empire[4]."

A. I. Serkov undertook significant efforts to publish some works on Russian Freemasonry over the past quarter of a century. He continued the work of T. A. Bakunina-Osorgina, created a dictionary of the biographies of Freemasons, and compiled a register of the lodges that worked in the 18th and 19th centuries. A. I. Serkov published four multivolume books on Russian Freemasonry before 2020.

Yu. E. Kondakov is a prominent scientist that highlighted the activities of the Rosicrucians (Rozencraitsers in the Russian sources) (they did not stop their work after banning all the secret societies) and the Knightly Systems of Freemasonry in Russia. He published a considerable number of the acts of the

---

[1] It is noteworthy that his father, Roman Illarionovich Vorontsov held the position of Grand Provincial-Local Master in the Great English (Provincial) Lodge in 1772-1775. A. I. Serkov "Russian Freemasonry. 1731-2000." Pages 200, 959, 971, 973.

[2] A. N. Pypin "Social movement in Russia under Alexander I." M., 2001.

[3] V. I. Semevsky "The questions about the transformation of the state system in Russia in the 18th and the first quarter of the 19th centuries. An essay on the history of political and social ideas" // Byloye, 1906. # 1.

[4] V. N. Alekseev "The Counts of the Vorontsov family in the political and public life of Russia in the 2nd half of the 18th – the 1st half of the 19th centuries.": an abstract of the thesis of a Candidate in Historical Sciences: 07.00.02. - Vladimir, 2010. - 23 p.

Masonic Systems and characterized them[1]. S. P. Karpachev[2], V. V. Kuchurin[3], E. A. Vishlenkova[4], A. Yu. Minakov[5], O. P. Kikin[6], D. E. Kharitonovich[7], V. Yu. Zakharov[8], P. D. Nikolaenko[9], S. V. Belykh[10], and A. Yu. Palyulin[11] issued their

---

[1] Yu. E. Kondakov "The Order of the Gold and Rose Cross in Russia. The theoretical degree of Solomon Sciences: a monograph" / Yu. E. Kondakov. - St. Petersburg, 2012. - 615 p.; Yu. E. Kondakov "Liberal and conservative trends in religious movements in Russia in the first quarter of the 19th century: a monograph." The Russian State Pedagogical University (named after A. I. Herzen). - St. Petersburg, 2005. - 343, [1] p.; Yu. E. Kondakov "The Rosicrucians, Martinists, and 'Internal Christians' in Russia in the late 18th – the first quarter of the 19th centuries". The Russian State Pedagogical University (named after A. I. Herzen). - St. Petersburg, 2011. - 499 p.; Yu. E. Kondakov "'Knightly' Freemasonry systems in Russia: 1772-1822" / Yuri Kondakov; a foreword by R. Collis; an afterword by A. I. Serkov; an article by R. A. Gorodnitsky. - Moscow, 2017. - 595 p. and other works.

[2] S. P. Karpachev "The art of Freemasons [Text]: a scientific reference monograph" / S. P. Karpachev. - Moscow: Forpost, 2015. - 475 p.; S. P. Karpachev "The Freemasonry and Freemasons of Russia of the XVIII-XXI centuries. [Text]: the features of the Russian 'royal art'" / Sergey Karpachev. - Saarbrücken : Palmarium acad. publ., 2013. - 323 p.; S. P. Karpachev "The Russian Freemasonry of the XVIII-XX centuries: A tutorial for a special course" / S. P. Karpachev; The Ministry of Education of the Russian Federation. The Moscow State Open Pedagogical University - M.: Alfa, 2000. - 70, [1] p. and other works.

[3] V. V. Kuchurin "From the history of the political struggle at the beginning of the 19th century: an unrealized project of the Masonic reform of M. M. Speransky" // The Petersburg Historical Journal. St. Petersburg Institute of History of the Russian Academy of Sciences. # 3 (11) 2016. - Pages 6-18, and other works.

[4] E. A. Vishlenkova "Religious policy in Russia, the first quarter of the 19th century,": A thesis of a Ph.D. in Historical Sciences: 07.00.02. - Kazan, 1998. - 466 p.

[5] A. Yu. Minakov "Russian conservatism in the first quarter of the 19th century.": A thesis of a Ph.D. in Historical Sciences: 07.00.02 / Minakov Arkadiy Yuryevich; [The place of protection: The Belgorod State University]. - Voronezh, 2011. - 611 p. and other works.

[6] O. P. Ved'min "Freemasons in Russia, 1730-1825" [Text] / O. P. Vedmin; The Ministry of the General and Professional Education of the Russian Federation. The Kemerovo State University - Kemerovo: Kuzbassvuzizdat, 1998. - 212 p.

[7] D. E. Kharitonovich "Freemasonry" / Dmitry Kharitonovich. - M.: All the world, 2001. - 223 p.

[8] V. Yu. Zakharov "The Russian constitutionalism of the 2nd half of the 18th – the 1st quarter of the 19th centuries in the context of the development of Western European legal thought." 1142 p.

[9] P. D. Nikolaenko "Prince V. P. Kochubey and the problem of reforming the public administration apparatus in Russia in the first third of the 19th century": An abstract of the thesis of a Ph.D. in Historical Sciences. - St. Petersburg, 2013. - 54 p.; P. D. Nikolaenko "V. P. Kochubey and the Freemasons of the Ministry of Internal Affairs in 1822" // A Bulletin of the Catherine Institute. A Science Magazine. - 2011. - # 4 (16). - Pages 130-135.

[10] V. S. Belykh "Freemasonry: history, the state, and law" // Law and the State, # 2 (67). 2015. - Pages 82-87; V. S. Belykh "Russia. Yesterday, today, tomorrow" [Text] / V. S. Belykh. - Moscow: Prospekt, 2017. - 248 p. and other works.

[11] A. Yu. Palyulin "The ideas of law and the state in the Gnostic teachings": A thesis of a Candidate in Legal Sciences: 12.00.01. 2014. - 171 p.

good works on Masonic themes as well. The following researchers: historian T. N. Zhukovskaya[1], philologist V. I. Novikov[2], philosopher A. A. Fyodorov[3], lawyers S. V. Kodan[4] and A. G. Moskvina[5], lawyer-historian O. A. Kudinov[6], and some others created good works on this theme, too. K. D. Bugrov[7], A. N. Dolgikh[8], S. V. Dubova[9], A. M. Dubrovsky[10], D. V. Bukharov[11], T. I. Zaeva[12], K. I. Kiychenko[13], and K. A. Rudenko[14] are also interested in this topic now.

---

[1] Noble liberalism under Alexander I: The disputes about the constitutions and "slavery" in Russian journals 1800-1810. – Petrozavodsk: The Petrozavodsk State University. 2002, - 42 p.
[2] V. I. Novikov "Freemasonry and Russian culture." - M.: Art, 1996. - 495 p.
[3] A. A. Fyodorov "The evolution of the idea of the perfect state and person in the philosophical anthropology of the Russian Freemasons of the XVIII century" // The state structure and people: The dialogue of worldviews. - Nizhniy Novgorod, 1997. – Pages 108-110.
[4] S. V. Kodan "M. M. Speransky about the ranks and rank-making in Russia" // The Ural Historical and Legal Yearbook. Yekaterinburg, 2004. Pages 27-34, and other works.
[5] A. G. Moskvina "The formation of Russian jurisprudence: XVIII century." SPb., 2000. - 142 p.
[6] The development of constitutional and legal theories by Russian state scientists in the XIX - early XX centuries." // O. A. Kudinov. A scientific editor: A. Ya. Malygin - M.: Sotsium, 2002. - 181 p.
[7] K. D. Bugrov "Natural Law and Virtue: The integration of European influence into the Russian political culture of the 18th Century. A monograph" / K. D. Bugrov, M. A. Kiselev. Yekaterinburg: The Publishing House of the Ural University, the University Publishing House, 2016. - 480 p.
[8] A. N. Dolgikh "Conservative Freemasons and the Peasant Question in Russia at the Beginning of the 19th Century (I. V. Lopukhin and O. A. Pozdeev)" // History: Facts and Symbols. A peer-reviewed scientific, theoretical, and applied journal. - Yelets, 2015. - Issue. 1 (# 2). - Pages 52 - 63.
[9] S. V. Dubova "The Charter, or the Rule of Freemasons by I. P. Elagin as a source of the formation of the Masonic Worldview System" / S. V. Dubova // Text, context, intertext: A collection of the scientific articles based on the materials of the International Scientific Conference "XIII Vinogr. reading" (Moscow, October 15–17, 2013); The Department of Education of Moscow, GBOU VPO MGPU), The Institute of Humanitarian Problems. - M., 2014. - Volume 3. - Pages 138 -142.
[10] A. M. Dubrovsky "The Freemasonry of the XVIII-XIX centuries and the Bryansk Territory (to the formulation of the question)" / / The problems and trends in the development of the socio-cultural space of Russia: history and modernity. The materials of the III International Scientific and Practical Conference. The Bryansk State Engineering and Technological University. Edited by T.I. Ryabova. 2016. - Pages 121-124.
[11] D. V. Bukharov "The state and charitable activities of a Freemason I. V. Lopukhin in the Kaluga Province in February-April 1807" / / A Bulletin of the Bryansk State University. # 3 (26) (2015). Bryansk: RIO BGU, 2015. - Pages 84-86.
[12] T. I. Zaeva "Senator I. V. Lopukhin on the problems of the civil liability of an individual" // A Bulletin of the Murmansk State Technical University. - 2014. - Volume 17, # 4. - Pages 681-686.
[13] K. I. Kiychenko "The proceedings of Louis Claude De Saint-Martin and their influence on the development of Russian Martinism" // The scientific-technical sheets of St. Petersburg. The State Polytechnic University, # 4 (232). Pages 109-117.

Gavrilov[1], S. V. Dubova[2], A. M. Dubrovsky[3], D. V. Bukharov[4], T. I. Zaeva[5], K. I. Kiychenko[6], and K. A. Rudenko[7] are also interested in this topic now.

The fundamental work of S. V. Arzhanukhin is still very important in the field of philosophy, acting both as a methodology and as a subject of research. The comprehensive work of S. V. Arzhanukhin is the monograph that was published in Yekaterinburg in 1995: "The philosophical views of Russian Freemasonry: Based on the materials of the magazine "Freemasonry Shop's[8]." This study introduced the sources that were relevant to the history of political and legal doctrines. In particular, "The Theoretical Degree of Solomon Sciences"[9] deserves to be noted. S. V. Arzhanukhin provides the author's analysis of the text in his study. The third paragraph of "The Theoretical Degree ..." - "About the proper obedience to the authorities" defines the duties of a Freemason about the state and his status in society: each member of this community must be a loyal subject to his Sovereign, willingly submitting to his authorities, peaceful citizen, or average man in his place

---

[1] S. V. Gavrilov "The problem of interaction between the Decembrist and Masonic organizations in the studies of V. I. Semevsky" / The problems of history, philology, culture. 2016. # 1 (51). Pages 296–308.

[2] S. V. Dubova "The Charter, or the Rule of Freemasons by I. P. Elagin as a source of the formation of the Masonic Worldview System" / S. V. Dubova // Text, context, intertext: A collection of the scientific articles based on the materials of the International Scientific Conference "XIII Vinogr. reading" (Moscow, October 15–17, 2013); The Department of Education of Moscow, GBOU VPO MGPU), The Institute of Humanitarian Problems. - M., 2014. - Volume 3. - Pages 138 -142.

[3] A. M. Dubrovsky "The Freemasonry of the XVIII-XIX centuries and the Bryansk Territory (to the formulation of the question)" / / The problems and trends in the development of the socio-cultural space of Russia: history and modernity. The materials of the III International Scientific and Practical Conference. The Bryansk State Engineering and Technological University. Edited by T.I. Ryabova. 2016. - Pages 121-124.

[4] D. V. Bukharov "The state and charitable activities of a Freemason I. V. Lopukhin in the Kaluga Province in February-April 1807" / / A Bulletin of the Bryansk State University. # 3 (26) (2015). Bryansk: RIO BGU, 2015. - Pages 84-86.

[5] T. I. Zaeva "Senator I. V. Lopukhin on the problems of the civil liability of an individual" // A Bulletin of the Murmansk State Technical University. - 2014. - Volume 17, # 4. - Pages 681-686.

[6] K. I. Kiychenko "The proceedings of Louis Claude De Saint-Martin and their influence on the development of Russian Martinism" // The scientific-technical sheets of St. Petersburg. The State Polytechnic University, # 4 (232). Pages 109-117.

[7] K. A. Rudenko "The secrets and ideas of Kazan Freemasonry in the late 18th – the early 19th centuries" // A Bulletin of the Kemerovo State University of Culture and Arts. 2012. # 19-1. – Pages 238-241.

[8] S. V. Arzhanukhin "The philosophical views of Russian Freemasonry." The Publishing House of the Ural State University, 1995. - 224 pages.

[9] Ibid. Page 39.

of residence, peacemaker in fear and originator (founder) of tranquility and unanimity. He must extremely watch the interests of the state, avoiding inflicting any harm on it. In general, this community always receives great protection from the kings, princes, and state due to the impeccable behavior observed[1]."

The manuscripts of Schwartz's (Shvarts' in some Russian sources) lectures formed the basis of the articles of V. V. Sipovsky ("Novikov, Schwartz (Shvarts in some Russian sources), and Moscow Freemasonry") and A. V. Semeka ("The Russian Rosicrucians (Rozencraitsers in the Russian sources) and the attitude of Empress Catherine II towards them")[2]. S. V. Arzhanukhin, M. I. Nevzorov, and A. D. Tyurikov published the lectures of I. G. Schwartz (Shvarts in some Russian sources).

M. N. Longinov, S. E. Eshevsky, and V. N. Tukalevsky fulfilled an assessment of the creative heritage of I. G. Schwartz (Shvarts in the Russian sources). The researchers assessed the correlation between the teachings of Freemasonry (Schwartz (Shvarts in the Russian sources) drew his ideas from them) with Christianity, as well as with the ideas of state power. S. V. Arzhanukhin noted that the Russian Enlightenment would be "unthinkable without the fruitful and inspiring activity of Moscow Freemasons." I. G. Schwartz (Shvarts in the Russian sources) was a leader of Moscow Freemasons at that time[3]. S. V. Arzhanukhin proved that the provisions of Masonic statutes completely coincided with the opinion of Masonic leaders. According to S. V. Arzhanukhin, the Masonic Order was a concrete historical form of civil society in Russia in the 18th century-19th century as it had conscious goals and objectives, organizational structure, self-regulation, and continuity[4].

A. N. Pypin, G. V. Vernadsky, Yu. Kondakov, A. N. Lushin, and A. Yu. Minakov described the state-related legal views of I. A. Pozdeev (he was another leader of the Russian Rosicrucians (Rozencraitsers in the Russian sources) Freemasons) in their works. I. A. Pozdeev was an honorary member of many Masonic Lodges and a leader of the Rosicrucians (Rozencraitsers in the Russian sources). Many Freemasons followed his opinion. Bartenev, A. A. Vasilchikov, and M. I. Sukhomlinov published the letters and notes of I. A. Pozdeev.

I. A. Fessler was one of the most prolific scholarly Freemasons. He published several dozen volumes of his works. At the same time, comparatively

---

[1] PB. OSRK. Q.III.139. Page 5.

[2] G. V. Vernadsky "Russian Freemasonry in the reign of Catherine II." SPb., 1999. Page V.

[3] S. V. Arzhanukhin "From the lectures of I. G. Schwartz 'On the three cognitions: curious, useful, and pleasant'" // Philosophical Sciences. The scientific and theoretical journal, 1992, # 1. Pages 78, 79.

[4] S. V. Arzhanukhin "The philosophical views of Russian Freemasonry": Based on the materials of the journal "Freemasonry Shop." Page 139.

little attention has been paid to him in Russian Historiography. According to I. G. Findel, I. A. Fessler, "by using his works, cleared the fog that had surrounded both the history and scientific side of the union for a long time," gave the definitions of the "inalienable Masonic freedom," and developed "the principles of social law."[1] D. V. Gorbachev produced the largest contemporary work devoted to the political and public views of I. A. Fessler. D. V. Gorbachev believes that I. A. Fessler did not accept the mystical elements of Freemasonry and decided "to clean" the Freemasonry from any mysticism[2]. N. K. Gavryushin gave some characteristics of the philosophical heritage of I. A. Fessler.

M. V. Dovnar-Zapolsky, M. A. Korf, A. Yu. Minakov, A. E. Presnyakov, A. N. Pypin, and I. A. Chistovich described the religious and mystical views of M. M. Speransky in their works. These scientists noted some similarities between the views of M. M. Speransky and I. A. Fessler, M. M. Speransky, and Emperor Alexander I. A. F. Bychkov published the handwritten texts of M. M. Speransky, expressing his philosophical, religious, and legal views.

Yu. L. Khalturin described the philosophy of Rosicrucianism (Rozencraitserstvo in the Russian sources)[3]. E. L. Kuzmishin established the continuity of Western and Russian Freemasonry and translated some normative documents on the history of Western Freemasonry[4]. He published one of his last monographs in 2019[5].

A. N. Lushin was the first in the Russian historical jurisprudence to study the process of the formation and influence of the state and legal views of Russian Freemasons (at the turn of the 18th - 19th centuries) on the formation and development of the law and legal doctrines in Russia. He researched it in 2004[6]. He

---

[1] I. G. Findel "The history of Freemasonry from its origin to the present": Translated from the 2nd German edition. Volumes 1-2 / The works of I. G. Findel. Published by a Freemasonry magazine "DieBauhütte." - St. Petersburg: The printing house of N. Skaryatin, 1872-1874. – in 2 volumes; Volume 2. - 1874. Pages 59, 138.

[2] D. V. Gorbachev "The socio-political views of I. A. Fessler": An abstract of the thesis of a Candidate in Historical Sciences: 07.00.03. - Saratov, 2012. Page 15.

[3] Yu. L. Khalturin "'Heavenly Science': European Alchemy and Russian Rosicrucianism in the 17th-19th Centuries: a monograph." - St. Petersburg: The Publishing House of the RKhGA, 2015. - 376, [2] p. and other works.

[4] The history of Freemasonry in documents / E. L. Kuzmishin. -M.: The printing house of the publishing house "Ars Tectonica," 2010. - 404 p. and other works.

[5] E. L. Kuzmishin "Freemasonry" / Evgeny Kuzmishin; a foreword by A. I. Serkov, Yu. E. Kondakov; an article by R. A. Gorodnitsky and E. L. Kuzmishin. – The 2nd edition corrected and supplemented - Moscow: Ganga, 2019. - 547, [3] p.

[6] A. N. Lushin "The state-legal views of Russian Freemasons at the turn of the XVIII-XIX centuries": A thesis of a Candidate in Legal Sciences: 12.00.01: Nizhny Novgorod, 2004. - 161 p.

showed the Masonic activities of two order directions in his dissertation: Brothers-Counts N. I. Panin and P. I. Panin and their St. Petersburg entourage and Moscow Freemasons (Martinists) headed by Senator I. V. Lopukhin. According to the author's research, the theoretical reasoning of Russian Freemasons touched upon the issues of equality and inequality, preferred state structure for Russia, necessary legal reforms, effective and humane legal proceedings, etc. Freemasons remained the consistent supporters of the preservation of the monarchical way of government for Russia with the preservation of the estate system and serfdom and the option of the harmonious relationship between the landowners and peasants proposed by them. A. N. Lushin was the first scientist (in the history of the Russian legal doctrines) that analyzed the works of I. P. Elagin's "Experience of Narration about Russia" and "Notes" by I. V. Lopukhin. This author demonstrated that the representatives of the Masonic community (I. P. Elagin, S. E. Desnitsky, brothers-Counts N. I. Panin and P. I. Panin, D. I. Fonvizin, I. V. Lopukhin, and Count M. M. Speransky) had stood at the origins of Russian Law in the late 18th – the early 19th centuries and had not "blindly" copied the Masonic ideas of the French or Swedish versions but had creatively developed them with the traditions of Russian Law.

Some historians of Freemasonry (T. O. Sokolovskaya, A. I. Serkov, and Yu. E. Kondakov) think that it is quite acceptable to use the following terms "Laws[1]," "Masonic Laws[2]," "Masonic Legislation[3]," and "Masonic Lawmaking[4]" for denoting the normative acts of Masonic Lodges. Yu. E. Kondakov dedicated Paragraph 5.1 of his book "The 'Knightly' systems of Freemasonry in Russia: 1772-1822"[5] to the Russian Masonic Legislation. However, these authors did not provide the rationale for the use of these terms, as well as their content.

---

[1] Russian Freemasonry: Materials and Research. / Edited by M. V. Reizin and A. I. Serkov. Russian Freemasonry in the reign of Catherine II / G. V. Vernadsky. - SPb., 1999. Pages 15, 85, 268.

[2] T. O. Sokolovskaya "The secret archives of Russian Freemasons." - Moscow, 2007. Pages 26, 159, 271, 289, 331.

[3] The "Knightly" Systems of Freemasonry in Russia: 1772-1822 / Yu. E. Kondakov. Moscow, 2017. Pages 11, 159, 168, 221,233, 326, 402; The history of Freemasonry in documents / E. L. Kuzmishin. - M., 2010. Page 4; I. G. Findel "The history of Freemasonry from its origin to the present": Translated from the 2nd German edition. Volumes 1-2 / The works of I. G. Findel. - St. Petersburg, 1872-1874. – in 2 volumes. Volume 1. - 1872. Page 58. I. G. Findel "The history of Freemasonry." Volume 2. - 1874. Page 310.

[4] Ibid. Page 159.

[5] Ibid. Pages 381-401.

The authors of this study analyzed the work “A discourse on the support of the monarchical power in Russia by Freemasons[1].” It was established that S. P. Fonvizin was writing it under the dictation of I. A. Pozdeev. This “reasoning” demonstrated the continuity of the state and legal ideas of the domestic political and legal thought of the 18th and 19th centuries. The text of the work was addressed to some Brothers-Freemasons involved in the political discussions about the emancipation of peasants and the establishment of the Basic Laws (Constitution) in the Russian Empire in 1814-1818. The reasoning was aimed at supporting the Estate Statehood of Russia and the Monarchical Form of Government in the first quarter of the 19th century among the Masonic Brothers.

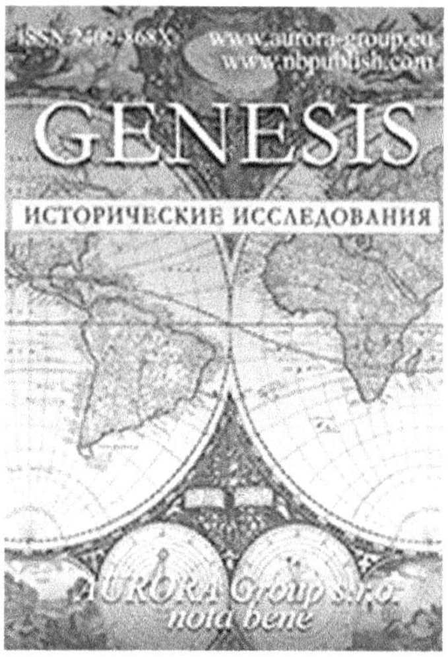

Picture 10. A cover of the magazine “GENESIS: The historical research” by the Publishing House “Nota Bene” at the website https://www.nbpublish.com/e_hr/ (accessed: March 29, 2021: open access).

The reasoning was fully consistent with the Masonic rules and regulations. The discourse demonstrated a commitment to social peace based on “good morals” and to the conscientious performance of class duties, being rich in the elements of the organic theory of the state and natural-legal argumentation.

Some contemporaries (I. V. Beber, F. M. Gauenschild, E. A. Kushelev, V. V. Musin-Pushkin Bruce, J. I. De Sanglen, etc.) described the historiography of the issue of the official recognition of Freemasonry in the Russian Empire. G. V. Vernadsky, Yu. E. Kondakov, M. N. Longinov, A. N. Pypin, A. N. Serkov, and T. O. Sokolovskaya dealt with the problem of the relationships between Freemasonry and the state. M. N. Longinov and G. V. Vernadsky mainly researched the 18th century and its main milestones in the relationship of the state and Freemasonry: the history of Swedish Freemasonry, the case of N. I. Novikov and his entourage (I. V. Lopukhin, A. B. Kurakin, N. N. Trubetskoy, etc.). A. N. Pypin touched upon the projects of reforming the Freemasonry and partly explained the history of the

[1]The publication is scheduled for 2021 in Genesis: Historical Studies.

legislative regulation of Freemasonry in the 19th century in his writings on the history of Freemasonry at the beginning of the 19th century. T. O. Sokolovskaya comprehensively studied the Swedish System of Freemasonry, putting the history of the creation of the Great (Directory) Lodge "Vladimir to Order." A. I. Serkov made a serious attempt to study the process of reforming Russian Freemasonry at the beginning of the 19th century. He singled out the group affiliation of the reformers of Freemasonry (liberal, conservative, and apolitical) and considered the belonging of this or that historical figure to the following Masonic Systems: the Rosicrucians (Rozencraitsers in the Russian sources), the Swedish System, the French System, and the Lodge of I. A. Fessler. Yu. E. Kondakov, V. Yu. Zakharov, E. A. Vishlenkova, and A. Yu. Minakov identified a problem with the legalization of Freemasonry for the first time. V. Yu. Zakharov considered the process of the legalization of Freemasonry in the context of the constitutional projects in the Russian Empire of the 18th and 19th centuries.[1] He supposed that Freemasonry had been legalized in Russia in 1803-1804[2]. E. L. Kuzmishin thought about the same[3]. E. A. Vishlenkova analyzed a concept of the legalization of Freemasonry in the 19th century regarding the reforms of Freemasonry under the leadership of I. A. Fessler and M. M. Speransky[4]. Yu. E. Kondakov used the term "legalization" to explain the recognition of a lodge by the government[5] and in the context of the opposition to I. A. Pozdeev's legalization of the Masonic Lodges, initiated by I. A. Fessler[6].

The authors of this study studied a matter of the official recognition of Freemasonry in the Russian Empire. After weighing all the arguments "for and against" the recognition of Freemasonry as tolerant (this term at that time meant official recognition, and not the admissibility of an unwanted and disapproved movement by the state), it was found that the introduction (in the secret regime – only for using in a special office of the Ministry of Police) of the rules of the tolerance of the Masonic Lodges of 1811 served as a model for the modernization of relations between the state and public organizations. S. V. Kodan noted the cycles of Russian modernization: adoption of the rules in 1811 had corresponded

[1]V. Yu. Zakharov "The Russian constitutionalism of the 2nd half of the 18th – the 1st quarter of the 19th centuries in the context of the development of Western European legal thought …." Page 146.
[2] Ibid. Page 148.
[3] According to E. L. Kuzmishin, under the conditions of monarchical rule, the decisive word for recognizing any social movement as lawful ("tolerant") always remains with the Sovereign-Emperor.
[4] E. A. Vishlenkova "Religious policy in Russia, the first quarter of the 19th century." 1998. Pages 122-133.
[5] Yu. E. Kondakov "The Order of the Gold and Rose Cross in Russia." Page 400.
[6] Ibid. Page 464.

to the cycle of reforms (1801-1811), while the prohibition of Masonic Lodges in 1822 had been quite consistent with the cycle of transition to the counterreforms (1811-1825). And the legislative regulation of that sphere of life fitted into those cycles very well. Thanks to the norms formulated in the rules, the Masonic Lodges were tolerated by the Russian Government from 1811: some individual lodges were opened with the governmental knowledge and consent, other lodges were closed, and the regular reports, information about the members and extracts from the minutes of the meetings of the lodges were sent to the Ministry of Police.

V. A. Tomsinov researched the matters of granting liberty to the Russian nobles, as well as the legislation of Catherine II and Paul I[1].

M. S. Kiseleva[2] considered the influence of European culture on the intellectual choice of Russia at the turn of the 17th - 18th centuries.

K. D. Bugrov, M. A. Kiselev[3], and D. V. Timofeev[4] studied the history of the influence of European thought on the political and legal thought of Russia in the 18th-the first quarter of the 19th century.

T. V. Andreeva[5] showed the role of secret societies in the development of governmental constitutionalism in the first quarter of the 19th century.

Yu. V. Kostin[6] highlighted some ideas of the correlation between the state, law, and morality in the history of political and legal thought.

---

[1]See, for example, V. A. Tomsinov's "A Diploma on the rights, liberties, and advantages of the noble Russian nobility. Published in the publication: The Legislation of Empress Catherine II. 1783-1796" / Compiled by V. A. Tomsinov. An introductory article by V. A. Tomsinov. M.: Zertsalo, 2011. Pages XI–XL.

[2] M. S. Kiseleva "The intellectual choice of Russia in the second half of the 17th-the early 18th centuries: from the ancient Russian literacy to the European scholarship." - M.: Progress-Tradition, 2011. - 471 p.

[3] See, for example, K. D. Bugrov's "Natural law and virtue = Naturallawandvirtue: The integration of European influence into the Russian political culture of the 18th century" / K. D. Bugrov, M. A. Kiselev. - Yekaterinburg: The Publishing House of the Ural University: The University Publishing House, 2016. - 476 p.

[4] See, for example, D. V. Timofeev's "European Ideas in the Public Consciousness and Communicative Practice of an Educated Russian Citizen in the First Quarter of the 19th Century: An Experience in Studying the Basic Socio-Political Concepts." - Chelyabinsk, 2011. - 34 p.

[5] See T. V. Andreeva "Secret societies in Russia in the first third of the 19th century," 2010. - 1101 p.

[6] Yu. V. Kostin "The ideas of the correlation of the state, law, and morality in the history of the political and legal thought of pre-revolutionary Russia in the second half of the 19th-the early 20th centuries": An abstract of the thesis of a Ph.D. in Legal Sciences. - Moscow, 2008. - 46 p.

V. M. Bokova[1] revealed the liberal-constitutional ideas in Russia at the beginning of the 19th century.

A. A. Vasilyev[2] formulated the conservative-legal ideology of Russia.

O. A. Omelchenko[3] proved a positive role of the ideology of enlightened absolutism in the history of the state and Law of Russia.

It is worth noting the works of P. Buryshkin[4], T. Bakunina[5], L. Hass[6], A. Pyatigorsky[7], H. Reynalter[8], G. Karlheinz (Karlheints in the Russian sources)[9], Frederiks[10], K. Grunwald[11], K. Lenning[12], B. Fey[13], D. Ward[14], and M. Abassy[15] among foreign researchers. The works of I. A. Fessler (published in German)[16], B.

---

[1] V. M. Bokova "Liberal-constitutional ideas in Russia at the beginning of the 19th century (1801-1812)": An abstract of the thesis of a Candidate in Historical Sciences. - Moscow, 1991. - 21 p.

[2] A. A. Vasilyev "The conservative legal ideology of Russia: the essence and forms of manifestation": An abstract of the thesis of a Ph.D. in Legal Sciences. - Yekaterinburg, 2015. - 55 p.

[3] O. A. Omelchenko "The monarchy of enlightened absolutism in Russia: Political doctrine, legal policy, state reforms": A thesis of a Ph.D. in Legal Sciences: 12.00.01.-Moscow, 2001. - 389 p.

[4] Bourychkine Paul. Bibliographie sur la franc-maconerie en Russie, Completee et mise au point par Tatiana Bakounine. Preface de Roger Portal, 1967. 174 p.

[5] Bakounine T. La repertoire biographique des francs-masons russes (XVIII et XIX-e siecles). - Paris, 1967. - 655 p.

[6] Hass Ludwik. Wolnomularstwow Europie Srodkowo – Wschodniejw XVIII – XIX wieku. – Wroclaw Zaklad N10 Wydawnictwo, 1982. - 572 s.

[7] Piatigorsky A. Whos afraid of Freemasons? The Phenomenon of Freemasonry. - London. The Harvill Press, 1997. - 398 p.

[8] Reinalter H. Die Freimaurer. München, 2006

[9] Karlheinz Gerlach Die Freimaurer im Alten Preussen 1738-1806: die Loge in Berlin. Teil 1. Publisher, StudienVerlag, Innsbruck, Wien, Bozen 2014. – 1254 s.

[10] Friedrichs. Geschichte der einstigen Maurerei in Russland. B., 1904.

[11] Grunwald (Constantin de). Histoire de la Franc-Maconnerie en Russie // Traveau Villard de Honnecourt. T. 5. 1969. 424 p.

[12] Lenning C. Allgemeines Handbuch der Freimaurerei, Leipzig. 1863. S. 551

[13] La Franc-maconnerie et la Revolution intellectuelle Du XVIII siècle Par Bernard Fay Profeseur au College de France. EDITIONS DE CLUNY 35 et 37, RUE DE SEINE – PARIS VI, 1935; Revolution and Freemasonry 1680-1800 Bernard Faÿ. Boston. Little, Brown, and Company. 1935. - 349p.

[14] Freemasonry: its aims and ideals by J.S.M. Ward B.A., F.S.S., F.R. Econ.Soc. Author of "Freemasonry and the ancient gods," "The masonic handbook series, etc." London. William Rider & Son, limited 8-II Paternoster Row, E.C.4 1923. – 232 p.

[15] Malgorzata Abassy "A Russian Mason on the Paths of his Native Culture. The Case Study of Nicolas Novikov." Krakow. 2014. – 195 p.

[16] Fessler´s sämmtliche Schriften über Freymaurerey. Wirklich als Manuckript für Brüder. Berlin.1801.- 499 p.; Fessler´s sämmtliche Schriften über Freymaurerey. Wirklich als Manuckript für Brüder. Bd. 1. Zweite verbesserte und mit einem Anhange versehene Auflage. Freyberg, 1805;

Telepnev (published in English)[1], and Ch. F. Masson and L. F. Segur (Segyur in the Russian sources) (translated into Russian)[2] can be considered as foreign works.

G. Grotius, S. F. Pufendorf, J. G. Justi, J. F. Bielfeld, F. Prokopovich, V. N. Tatishchev, Catherine II, Ch. L. Montesquieu, C. Beccaria, I. G. Reichel, Z. A. Goryushkin, M. A. Balugyansky, I. P. Turgenev, P. D. Lodiy, M. M. Speransky, V. S. Solovyev, M. A. Reisner, and V. S. Nersesyants considered the issues of the theory of the "common good." K. D. Bugrov, D. I. Dedov, V. V. Lapaeva, A. P. Semitko, G. A. Gadzhiev, and P. L. Likhter (modern scholars) touched upon the matters of the "common good." O. A. Omelchenko noted the influence of the theory of the "common good" on the political and legal doctrine and legislation of the Russian Empire in the 18th century. He proved that the category of the "common good" had been perceived by some Russian politicians and Police, and an ideology of state liberalism had become a base of the public law doctrine of a Russian Monarchy, being concretized in legislation[3]. Nevertheless, noting this undoubtedly remarkable work, the theory of the "common good" merged with the doctrine of enlightened absolutism, the content of the theory of the "common good" was not disclosed as there were no constituent parts of the theory and interpretations in the socio-political and legal discourse in the Russian Empire of the 18th-19th centuries.

Nowadays, the matters of borrowing and creative processing the Anderson Constitution and provisions of the Wilhelmsbad Convention in Russian Masonic Statutes (the Grand Lodge of Astrea and other lodges) have not been practically investigated in the legal literature, and the corresponding analysis has not been fulfilled. The state-related legal ideas of I. G. Schwartz (Shvarts in the Russian sources) (1751-1784), A. F. Labzin (1766-1825), R. A. Koshelev (1749-1827), and A. B. Kurakin (1759-1829) should be studied in terms of their influence on the formation of the Russian state and law and the history of Russian political and legal thought.

Fessler I. A. Resultate seines Denkens und Erfahrens als Anhang zu seinen Rückblicken auf seine 70-jaerige Pilgerschaft. Breslau, 1826.

[1] The Rosicrucians (Rozencraitsers in the Russian sources) in Russia by Frater Boris Telepneff. Privately printed 1924. 17p.; Russian Masons by Bro. B. Telepneff, 1925. 32 p.; A Few Pages from the History of Swedish Freemasonry in Russia. ByBro. BorisTelepneff, 1928. 23 p.

[2] Charles Francois Philibert Masson "The Secret Notes on Russia. And in the part about the end of the reign of Catherine II and the reign of Paul I. Volume I. Translated from the 2nd edition of N. Na-go. Moscow, 1918. Edited by I. I. Kazanov. The printing house "CULTURE" of A. K. Mieserova. - 94 p.; L. F. Segur "The Notes of Count Segur about his stay in Russia during the reign of Catherine II. (1785-1789)": Translated from French with the notes of the translator. - St. Petersburg: The printing house of V. N. Maykov, 1865. - 386 p.

[3] O. A. Omelchenko "The Monarchy of Enlightened Absolutism in Russia: Political doctrine, legal policy, state reforms." Pages 56, 118, 268, 281, 332, 335, 337.

There are other studies (not considered in this book) showing Russian Freemasons' understanding the freedom, equality, and law (in the subjective and objective sense) and considering the preferable and ideal forms of government and governing. However, it should be noted that the empirical material containing information about the corresponding ideas of Russian Freemasons (about freedom, law, the state, etc.) does not have any provisions that conflict with the content of this book.

The issues of the dynamics of the development of ideas about the state and law in the life of a particular author and his or her greater or lesser interest in the theory of the welfare of all and everyone were not considered in the book. There was no comparative analysis of various works (by the same author) for the presence of other state-legal ideas and their comparison in quantitative and qualitative terms with the theory of the welfare of all and everyone in this book. This work was limited to citing some sources that contain the vocabulary of the theory of the welfare of all and everyone or reasoning on this issue.

Considering all the material studied, several general theoretical generalizations can be made.

First, the pre-revolutionary authors created an empirical basis for researching the history of Freemasonry. M. N. Longinov, A. I. Nezelenov, V. I. Semevsky, E. S. Shumigorsky, Ya. L. Barskov, E. I. Tarasov, V. N. Tukalevsky, M. A. Korf, A. V. Romanovich-Slavatinsky, Yu. A. Veselovsky, and other scientists published some biographical literature. M. N. Longinov, S. V. Eshevsky, P. P. Pekarsky, V. I. Semevsky, Ya. L. Barskov, T. O. Sokolovskaya, and E. I. Tarasov issued some new sources on the history of Russian Freemasonry in the 18th century and put them into circulation. A. N. Pypin and V. N. Tukalevsky provided information on certain Masonic Systems (English, Swedish, Zinnendorf (Tsinnendorf in the Russian sources), etc.) and the unions of Masonic Lodges in Russia (Elaginsky's union, Novikovsky's union, the Rosicrucians (Rozencraitsers in the Russian sources), etc.). A. N. Pypin, T. O. Sokolovskaya, and G. V. Vernadsky presented the history of Freemasonry in its chronological order from the 18th century to the first quarter of the 19th century.

Second, some pre-revolutionary historians and literary scholars tried to theoretically comprehend the Masonic doctrine and heritage. M. N. Longinov, A. I. Nezelenov, V. N. Tukalevsky, A. V. Semeka, and G. V. Vernadsky researched the literary and ideological trends in Freemasonry in the 18th century, and this study considers their research. M. N. Longinov, A. N. Pypin, and T. O. Sokolovskaya studied Freemasonry in three aspects at the same time: as a social movement, teaching, and organization. G. V. Vernadsky was the first to fulfill a comprehensive source study analysis of the history of Russian Freemasonry.

Third, M. N. Longinov and G. V. Vernadsky started studying the socio-political activities of the Freemasons of the 18th century before 1917. M. N. Longinova, P. P. Pekarsky, and G. V. Vernadsky comprehensively studied the investigation of the "Martinist" N. I. Novikov. G. V. Vernadsky fulfilled a political and legal analysis of the views of the educators, philosophers, statesmen, and public figures of the 18th century. V. I. Semevsky carried out the same analysis but for the XVIII-XIX centuries. V. I. Semevsky and T. O. Sokolovskaya analyzed the "Charter of Freemasons" (1782) and "Code of the Great Masonic Lodge of Astrea" (1815). And G. V. Vernadsky assessed the influence of Freemasonry on the policy of the state and the development of social and political thought. The result of that influence was the "Pavel's State" (with its three-day corvee, military settlements, the ideas of the Holy Tsar and the Holy Union) and the notions of the Decembrist G. S. Batenkov, Slavophiles V. F. Odoevsky, and I. V. Kireevsky, and Pochvennik A. A. Grigoryev (Pochvenniki were pursuing the national local ideas of improving Russia by using only various local resources).

Fourth, G. V. Vernadsky, M. N. Pokrovsky, P. N. Sakulin, I. P. Voronitsyn, T. A. Bakunina, N. L. Rubinstein (Rubinshtein in the Russian sources), V. V. Vinogradov, V. G. Bazanov, V. I. Startsev, V. V. Zenkovsky, G. V. Florovsky, and A. E. Presnyakov considered the following important things: 1) the main characteristics of Russian Freemasonry are a combination of the mysticism and rationalism, Orthodox Christianity and moral improvement, ethical individualism, cosmopolitanism, and patriotism; 2) the differences between Russian and Western Freemasonry are in the presence of the moral philosophy, apoliticism, and lack of protectionism; 3) the centers of Russian Freemasonry are St. Petersburg and Moscow; 4) I. P. Elagin, I. V. Lopukhin, N. I. Novikov, and D. I. Fonvizin recorded some changes in the worldview from "Voltaire" to "Masonic," A. N. Radishchev noted some alterations in the worldview from "Masonic" to "rationalistic," and N. M. Karamzin observed that some changes in the worldview from "Masonic" to "sentimental" had taken place. Ivanov-Razumnik, M. N. Pokrovsky, and N. F. Lavrova noted the incompatibility of Freemasonry and Decembrism.

Fifth, the documents and literature in the archives were barely developed during the Soviet period. The research in the USSR was mainly based on the Masonic documents and books that had been published during the tsarist times. The main work on the publication of various archival documents will be already directed at the post-Soviet period.

Sixth, in Soviet times, the researchers V. G. Bazanov, G. V. Vernadsky, V. V. Zenkovsky, N. V. Minaeva, A. E. Presnyakov, and N. L. Rubinstein (Rubinshtein in the Russian sources) characterized the legal and political views and projects of A. R. Vorontsov, R. L. Vorontsov, G. P. Gagarin, S. I. Gamaleya, I. P. Elagin, V. l. Zolotnitsky, A. B. Kurakin, I. V. Lopukhin, O. A. Pozdeev, N. V. Repnin, A. A. Rzhevsky, M. M. Speransky, A. S. Stroganov, M. M. Shcherbatov, and I. G. Schwartz (Shvarts in the Russian sources). The above-mentioned researchers discovered the following signs and tendencies: 1) the conservative and modernist currents of the political and legal thought of Russian Freemasons were identified; 2) an interference of Russian Freemasons in the foreign policy issues of the Russian Empire (the relations with Prussia), as well as in the issue of the succession to the throne was established (Freemasons were preparing Pavel Petrovich for the occupation of the highest position in the Masonic hierarchy); 3) various Masonic ideas influenced the state policy (the reforms of Paul I and Alexander I), Decembrists, Slavophiles, and Pochvenniki; 4) Freemasonry was a progressive phenomenon in the public life of Russia, assuming the moral ideal and general rights of a person; 5) the origins of Russian Freemasonry were taken from the Western moral-mystical and political-legal ideas; 6) the rights and obligations of a Freemason were determined on the basis of the analysis of the Code of the Grand Lodge of Astrea and the violations of the Masonic statutes were shown on the example of the activities of the Lodge of “Chosen Michael” (departed from Freemasonry to Decembrism).

Seventh, the preservation of Freemasonry on the agenda in Soviet times (even though as the literary monuments and literary phenomenon, as well as among Russian emigrants) opened Russian Freemasonry to the history and philosophy of the post-Soviet period. So, history and philosophy started studying Masonic ethics, ritualism, and socio-political views from the beginning of the 90s of the XX century. A. I. Serkov and S. P. Karpachev published their reference books on Freemasons. A. I. Serkov, Yu. E. Kondakov, S. P. Karpachev, and E. L. Kuzmishin defended and issued their fundamental monographic works on the history of Freemasonry. S. V. Arzhanukhin published several fundamental works in the field of philosophy. Yu. L. Khalturin made a serious contribution to the development of the philosophy of Russian Freemasonry. All the above-mentioned made a breakthrough in the fields of history and philosophy in the post-Soviet period.

V. V. Kuchurin, E. A. Vishlenkova, A. Yu. Minakov, O. P. Vedmin, D. E. Kharitonovich, V. Yu. Zakharov, P. D. Nikolaenko, S. V. Belykh, and A. Yu. Palyulin contributed to the development of "Freemasonry." And some interest in the topic of Russian Freemasonry has recently increased in the scientific community.

Eighth, there are still many unexplored questions due to the specificity of the topic and because of the combination of objects from several scientific branches of knowledge: philosophy, history, philology, law, and others. The thesis of A. N. Lushin is still the only fundamental work in the field of the history of political and legal doctrines after 1990. He researched the Masonic activities of the currents of two Orders and introduced some new sources into scientific circulation. A. N. Lushin proved that Freemasons had remained the consistent supporters of a Monarchy with the preservation and harmonization of the estate system and serfdom and that the representatives of the Masonic Community had been one of the first to formulate Russian Law in the late 18th and the early 19th centuries. Considering the literature of the XXI century, Yu. E. Kondakov, E. L. Kuzmishin, A. I. Serkov, and some other authors disclosed the ideology, views, and issues of the history of Russian Freemasonry in the XVIII and the first quarter of the XIX century. V. A. Tomsinov[1] studied the political and legal worldview of the Russian Monarchs: Paul I and Alexander I. M. A. Reisner and O. A. Omelchenko researched the theory of the "common good" in the history of the state and Law of Russia. F. Y. Ford and A. V. Dmitriev (the authors of this work) made some modest contributions in the form of the introduction of the following two documents into scientific circulation: "The rules on the tolerance of Freemasonry in the Russian Empire" (1811) and "The discussions on the support of Freemasons for the monarchical power in Russia" (1817). In addition, he carried out the source analysis. The author of this scientific work also emphasized the role of the theory of the "common good" (the welfare of all and everyone) in the history of the state and Law of Russia and the doctrine of the state and law. By considering the state-

[1]See, for example, V. A. Tomsinov's "Emperor Paul the First (1754–1801): Statesman and Legislator // The Legislation of Emperor Paul I." - M.: Zertsalo, 2008. - Pages XV–LXIV; V. A. Tomsinov "The main directions of the legislative policy of Alexander I // The Legislation of Emperor Alexander I, 1801-1811." - M.: Zertsalo, 2011. - Pages XV-XXVIII.

legal ideas of Russian Freemasons in this book, the theory of the "common good" was considered for the first time.

§1.2. The source study of the state and legal ideas of Russian Freemasons

A source base of the study was made up of the following three groups of information carriers.

The first group consists of the normative sources that are divided into two large subgroups: a) the projects and legislative acts drawn up in the middle of the 18th – the first quarter of the 19th centuries (the decrees and manifestos of Catherine II, Paul I, and Alexander I, the highest approved projects, etc.); b) the acts of the Masonic rule-making (the instructions, regulations, statutes, job descriptions, agreements, etc.).

The first subgroup allows determining the place and forms of expressing the theory of the "common good" in the context of the public law doctrine and government constitutionalism.

The second subgroup of sources considers the significance of the theory of the "common good" in the system of the rules according to which Masonic Systems, Masonic Unions, Masonic Lodges and their Officials, and Freemasons, in general, operate.

The second group of research sources embraces the political-legal, ethical-philosophical, and even artistic compositions containing the vocabulary or doctrine of the welfare of all and everyone (S. F. Pufendorf, V. N. Tatishchev, F. Prokopovich, Ch. L. de Montesquieu, J. F. Bielfeld, C. Beccaria, Catherine II, A. V. Khrapovitsky, A. I. Musin-Pushkin, G. P. Gagarin, M. M. Speransky, and others).

The third group includes the following biographical sources: a) the sources of personal information – the memoirs, notes, letters, and reports of Russian Freemasons (A. R. Vorontsov, A. B. Kurakin, A. M. Kutuzov, etc.) and their contemporaries (Paul I, Alexander I, M. N. Karamzin, A. N. Radishchev, and others); b) the sources of objectified information – the monthly words, biographical dictionaries, collections of historical materials, etc.

The authors of this scientific work used the following archival material:

1. The manuscripts from the funds of the research department of the manuscripts of the Russian State Library - fund 013 (Arsenyev Vasily Sergeevich and Arsenyev Yuriy Vasilyevich), fund 014 (Arsenyev Vasiliy Sergeevich: a collection, the XVIII-XIX centuries), fund 147 (Lanskoy Sergey Stepanovich (1787-1862); Eshevsky Stepan Vasilyevich (1829-1865)).

2. The documents and materials of the State Archives of the Russian Federation - Fund 48 (The Investigative Commission (Committee) and the Supreme Criminal Court in the case of the Decembrists of 1825-1826), fund 109 (The Third Section of His Imperial Majesty's Own Chancellery), list of contents 1a (The secret archive. The revolutionary and social movement in Russia in 1826-1880), fund 1137 (Georgy V. Vernadsky, historian, Professor of Russian History at Yale University (New Haven, The United States of America), fund 1463 (A collection of the individual documents of personal origin), fund 1165 (The Special Chancellery of the Ministry of Internal Affairs), list of contents 1 (The inventory of anti-government actions, the situation of the peasants, the Patriotic War of 1812, and other issues. 1810-1826), list of contents 2 (The inventory of the fight against espionage, the observation of foreigners, and other issues. 1808-1826), list of contents 3 (The inventory list # 3. 1811-1826).

3. The files of the Russian State Archive of Ancient Acts - fund 7 (Rank VII. The Preobrazhensky Order, Secret Chancellery, and Secret Expedition), fund 8 (Rank VIII. The Kalinkin House and Cases of Crimes Against Morality), the Commission "for the fight against prostitution." The case of N. I. Novikov. The documents about Freemasons in Russia and Masonic manuscripts), fund 146 (The investigative files - (a collection) from the funds of the Ambassador Order and the Collegium of Foreign Affairs), case 23 (the correspondence of the curator of Moscow University I. Melissino about Freemasons (1783-1790)), fund 1261 (The Vorontsov family: the counts, landowners of the central, southern, and southeastern provinces).

4. The manuscripts of the funds of the research archive of the St. Petersburg Institute of History of the Russian Academy of Sciences - fund 36 ("The Vorontsov family are an ancient noble family: Vorontsov Mikhail Illarionovich (1714-1767), Count; Vorontsov Roman Illarionovich (1707-1783), Count").

5. The documents and materials from the funds of the Russian State Historical Archive - fund 90 (The Russian Technical Society), fund 733 (The

Department of Public Education, list of contents 1. A Secretary's desk. The personal files of an employee, list of contents 142. The rank of scientific institutions), fund 938 (The documents collected by G. V. Esipov, the Head of the General Archives of the Ministry of Foreign Affairs (a Collection)), fund 1101 (the documents of the personal origin that do not constitute separate funds), fund 1163 (The General Security Committee under the State Council), fund 1260 (The Commission for drawing up laws under the State Council), fund 1287 (The Economic Department of the Ministry of Internal Affairs. Inventory 45. A Secretary's desk; Chancellery).

The specifics of the sources formulate the following tasks: 1) an identification of the author's belonging to Freemasonry, a variety of Freemasonry with an indication of the lodge, the union of lodges, chapter, and position; 2) the historical significance of the researched personality (in public, political, and scientific life); 3) a study of the official and unofficial opinion of a Freemason about the law in its manifestations, a critical attitude towards existence (the existing state-political orders) and due (an idealistic attitude towards the state and law); 4) a study of the relationship of the Masonic Doctrine with the official and unofficial texts that showed the views of the Freemason of the period researched.

The authors of the book used the following main literature as the sources: the works of lawyers N. M. Azarkin, F. G. Bauze, Ya. F. Bielfeld, A. A. Vasilyev, G. V. Vernadsky, Z. A. Goryushkin, M. M. Kovalevsky, S. V. Kodan, S. A. Korf, Yu. V. Kostin, O. A. Kudinov, O. E. Leist, A. N. Lushin, I. V. Mikheeva, A. G. Moskvina, V. S. Nersesyants, B. E. Nolde, O. A. Omelchenko, A. A. Pavlov, S. Pufendorf, S. A. Pokrovsky, M. A. Reisner, A. P. Semitko, M. M. Speransky, B. I. Syromyatnikov, V. M. Syrykh, V. N. Tatishcheva, V. A. Tomsinov, G. F. Shershenevich, V. G. Shcheglov, and J. G. Justi.

F. Y. Ford and A. V. Dmitriev also utilized the works of some other authors: M. Abassy, V. N. Alekseev, T. V. Andreeva, S. V. Arzhanukhin, T. V. Artemyeva, V. G. Bazanov, T. A. Bakunina, V. M. Bokova, K. D. Bugrov, O. P. Vedmin, E. A. Vishlenkova, I. P. Voronitsyn, K. Gerlakh, D. V. Gorbachev, N. E. Dorokhova, V. E. Evgenyev-Maksimov, B. V. Emelyanov, A. V. Zavrazhina, V. Yu. Zakharov, Ivanov-Razumnik, S. P. Karpachev, M. S. Kiseleva, Yu. E. Kondakov, N. D. Kochetkova, E. L. Kuzmishin, V. V. Kuchurin, S. S. Landa, Yu. S. Limanskaya, M. N. Longinov, A. McKay, N. V. Minaeva, A. Yu. Minakov, M. Moramarco, A. I. Nezelenov, S. M. Nekrasov, V. I. Novikov, P. P. Pekarsky, D. I. Pigarev, N. K.

Piksanova, M. N. Pokrovsky, A. E. Presnyakova, A. N. Pypin, H. Reynalter, L. P. Repina, N. A. Rozhkov, A. V. Romanovich-Slavatinsky, N. L. Rubinstein (Rubinshtein in the Russian sources), P. N. Sakulin, F. Sevastyanov, V. I. Semevsky, A. V. Semeka, V. P. Semennikov, A. I. Serkov, T. O. Sokolovskaya, V. Startsev, P. V. Stegniy, M. I. Sukhomlinov, B. Telepnev, D. V. Timofeev, V. N. Tukalevsky, L. L. Fedotova, B. Fey, I. G. Findel, G. V. Florovsky, Yu. L. Khalturin, L. Khass, I. A. Stark (Shtark in the Russian sources), and N. K. Shilder.

Before proceeding to the description of the source study of the state and legal ideas of Russian Freemasons regarding the theory of the "common good," it is necessary to consider the problems discovered in this area.

First of all, there is a problem with the correct interpretation of words and expressions. The history of the 18th – the first quarter of the 19th century took place more than 200 years ago. Many generations of people have changed, the alphabet and culture have changed, and the whole world has become completely different during this period. It would be incorrect to consider the state and legal problems of the 18th and the first quarter of the 19th centuries from the standpoint of not only the 21st century we live in but also the 20th century. Therefore, when researching, it was very important to tell the readers about the subject, minimally distorting the original meaning. When citing the manuscripts and monographs of the 18th century, even removing the "yat'" and "hard signs" is some interference with the authentic vocabulary. However, what is more important, when maintaining the form, some words and phrases have dramatically changed their original meaning over time (for example, the words "revolution" and "tolerance"[1]).

[1]Tolerance today is understood as "A characteristic, the ability to tolerate something, to endure something." See an explanatory dictionary of the Russian language: [4 volumes / D. N. Ushakov and others]; Edited by D. N. Ushakov. - M.: Rus. dictionaries, 1994. - 21 cm. [Volume 4: C-Ya]. - M.: Russian Dictionaries. – Page 1500 by 2 columns. "Tolerance" is usually not used in modern Legislation (such definitions as "lawfulness," "legality," etc. are used instead of this term). But the certain normative acts, where tolerance is understood as "an active attitude based on recognizing the universal human rights and fundamental freedoms," are an exception to the rule. See "The Declaration of Principles on Tolerance." Adopted by resolution 5.61 of the UNESCO General Conference on November 16, 1995//https://www.un.org/ru/documents/decl_conv/declarations/toleranc.shtml (Accessed: August 08, 2021). Tolerance was understood as a synonym for official recognition, permission in the XVIII – the early XIX centuries. For example: according to §7 Art. 295 of the Code of the Laws of the Russian Empire, the provincial authorities, together with the provincial guards, solve the issues of maintaining "the order in the church rites of all confessions, tolerable by laws." See §7 Art. 295 of the Code of the Laws of the Russian Empire, compiled by the order of the

Picture 11. A photo of one of the globular nodules in the Torysh tract on the Mangistau Peninsula, Kazakhstan (from open sources). A wild stone in construction - different types of natural stones of various origins that have an uneven chipped surface and an irregular shape. The "wild stone" in Russian Freemasonry often denoted an uneducated and uninitiated person but ready to cognize God, nature, and himself.

It should be said about the problems of access to the sources and their correct interpretation. According to the Masonic tradition, a person that does not belong to Freemasonry (a layman) has no right to get acquainted with any documents of the lodge. In addition, many Masonic documents have corresponding differences because there are different systems in Freemasonry (English, Swedish, French, and other ones). According to the general rule, a Freemason of another system has no right to get acquainted with the acts of other lodges and attend any meetings of the lodges of another system. Also, it is usually banned to get acquainted with the documents of the Officials of the higher degree lodge unless the researcher is a carrier of the same degree. However, this rule is not followed in the academic environment. It is assumed that the scholars researching the activities of Masonic Lodges have the necessary level of education and culture to "preserve and increase" the knowledge about Freemasonry. Thus, they are "devoted" by another usage - research tradition.

At the same time, there is still a certain barrier of misunderstanding for the researchers that have never undergone any consecrations and initiations into any public organizations and have been familiar with the symbols and procedures for holding the meetings, rituals, and models of behavior in a few societies and communities. Those people that have had such an experience know that there are the following periods in the life of each fellow member ("Brother"): 1) some inspiration and enthusiasm for ideas; 2) some active participation and fulfillment of public duties; 3) "respectable but modest presence." The thoughts about the

---

Sovereign Emperor Nikolai Pavlovich: [15 volumes]: The 2nd edition - St. Petersburg: The Printing House of the Second Department of His Imperial Majesty's Own Chancellery, 1833. - 25 cm. [Volume 2]: The Code of state and provincial institutions. Part 2: Provincial Institutions. - 1833. - [6], 903, [4] c.

purpose of the lodge, his role in the lodge, and his function in the surrounding world (the family, state, law, etc.) during these periods will, of course, differ. It is important to understand that the personal ideas about the state and law of each Freemason will also differ, depending on his social origin, place of residence, the available rank of public service, and age. Therefore, the "Masonic" notions proper will be the certain general ideas arising, first of all, from the normative requirements of the Masonic acts and statutes. The above-mentioned ideas give a certain scope for self-expression. Strictly speaking, these patterns of behavior were inspired by the texts and speeches of the Brothers. The activities of a Freemason within the lodge play a huge role. The perception and assimilation of the rules of Freemasonry, the Masonic System, and a Masonic Lodge almost always occur inside a person. At first, an initiate does not usually believe in what he is told about. Or he draws the "castles in the air," imagining something unreal. But, after receiving the position in the lodge and when performing his duties within the lodge, Brother is more and more filled with the principles that led him to the lodge. This involvement in Freemasonry stamps his life as a whole: his family, service, hobbies, etc. And, vice versa, leaving Freemasonry, stopping attending the meetings of the lodges, and ceasing performing his positions (duties) in the lodge gradually erase "Brother's" memories of Freemasonry and its ideals.

A problem of the preservation of sources should be separately noted. After the official prohibition of Freemasonry in Russia on August 1, 1822, the Russian Freemasonry of the researched period sank into oblivion. Many documents were destroyed due to the former Freemasons' fears of persecution. After the Decembrist uprising on December 14, 1825, the process of destructing the documents only accelerated. However, the former Freemasons (A. F. Benkendorf, S. S. Lansky, M. M. Speransky, and others) continued occupying the highest positions in the Russian state. Nevertheless, some archives have survived. A. I. Serkov[1] reported on this in his research in detail. Also, it should not be forgotten about internal and external censorship. Many Authors could not write and publish everything they wanted to report because of this. Lots of works were published decades after the death of the authors or abroad (for example, the works by M. M. Shcherbatov, K. A. Geyking, and others). Some secret prohibition was imposed on the coverage of some events during the Russian Empire (the circumstances of the assassination of Paul I, Russian Officials' membership in the Masonic Lodges, and other incidents).

---

[1]A. I. Serkov "The fate of Masonic meetings in Russia. 500 years of gnosis in Europe. The Gnostic Tradition in Printed and Manuscript Books": Moscow - St. Petersburg / A catalog of the exhibition in the All-Russian State Library for Foreign Literature, Moscow and the All-Russian Museum of A. S. Pushkin, Petersburg. - Amsterdam, 1993. - Pages 27-34.

Of course, nobody should be a Freemason to write about Freemasons. At the same time, it is extremely important to decide who should be considered a Freemason. For example, A. I. Serkov and S. P. Karpachev suppose that the "New Israel" Leshchitsa-Grabyanka[1] society of people can be attributed to the Masonic organizations. It is also well known about the membership of N. M. Karamzin in the Masonic Lodge "Golden Crown" in Simbirsk. He was initiated to the 2nd degree in 1784 but closed the work in 1789[2]. And, after coming back from a trip to Europe, N. M. Karamzin never returned to the Masonic activities. The next example is demonstrated by the meetings of the "Dying Sphinx" Lodge in St. Petersburg. That lodge was attended by Anna Evdokimovna Labzina (the wife of A. F. Labzin - the Master of the Lodge)[3]. So, should any secret societies be classified as Masonic? Should the Brothers that left the Freemasonry and women be classified as Freemasons? This is a question... Therefore, the criteria according to which people can or should not be considered Freemasons are very important.

The authors of this scientific work used the following three main criteria for determining who can be considered a Freemason and who cannot be named a Freemason:

1. A sexual criterium (only a man could be a Freemason).

2. An age (a man had to be at least 21 years old).

3. A documented membership in a Masonic Lodge. The main proof of membership in Freemasonry can only be the information that was gleaned from the protocols, acts, and statutes of the lodges. This data is in the archives and the historians of Freemasonry. P. P. Pekarsky, S. E. Eshevsky, V. I. Semevsky, A. N. Pypin, T. O. Sokolovskaya, A. I. Serkov, Yu. E. Kondakov and others partially published it. The additional evidence is the autobiography, memoirs, and correspondence of some Freemasons themselves. Those Freemasons demonstrated their affiliation with Freemasonry in these documents. The additional evidence is also the information that can be obtained from the Dictionaries of Freemasons (some review materials and studies), compiled by T. A. Bakunina, A. I. Serkov, S. P. Karpachev, and others. Mentioning a particular person in the literature on the history of Freemasonry can also testify to belonging to Freemasonry. It would be

---

[1]S. P. Karpachev "The art of Freemasons" [Text]: a scientific reference monograph / S. P. Karpachev. - Moscow, 2015. Page 460; A. I. Serkov "Russian Freemasonry. 1731-2000." Page 1051.

[2] A. I. Serkov "Russian Freemasonry. 1731-2000." Pages 376-377, 989.

[3] Ibid. Pages 1096, 1097.

impossible to create and complete this scientific work without using the reference book of Freemasons and Masonic Lodges, compiled by A. I. Serkov[1]. The 7-volume dictionary by A. I. Serkov (published in 2019-2020) gives the most complete information about the Freemasons of the 18th and 19th centuries.

The next problem is the proper selection of sources. Researching Freemasonry started almost at once after prohibiting the Masonic Lodges in the Russian Empire by Alexander I in 1822. Nowadays, according to the calculations of the author of this research, the number of sources on Russian Freemasonry exceeds several thousand bibliographic units. And there are at least several hundred studies among them. Therefore, it is very important to select the most representative sources (allowing us to consider the research topic in full) from the entire set of them.

The depth and breadth of the study were comprehensively demonstrated in the description of the algorithm for working with sources.

In the first stage, the dissertation studies on Freemasonry were taken as a basis. The authors of this work selected the theses from a list of the specialties of the scientific nomenclature (from the abstracts and manuscripts of the dissertations directly or indirectly related to the Freemasonry of the studied period): in law (23 dissertations), in philosophy (13 dissertations), in history (49 dissertations), in philology (33 dissertations), in cultural studies (3 dissertations), in political science (1 dissertation), and in psychology (1 dissertation). In total, 123 dissertations were taken as a basis for the period considered from 1990 to 2015 (a quarter of a century)[1]. Considering the quantitative ratio, the legal research in the total mass of research does not exceed 1/5: 20% of the total mass of research (18.6%). The research proper on Freemasonry in different areas of humanitarian knowledge (there is the word "Freemasonry" and its derivatives in the name of them) consists of 21 dissertations. And there are only 5 theses in law among them: less than ¼ (23. 8%). The bibliography of these dissertations allowed us to determine the range of the sources that should be consulted on the research topic. When compiling, more than 20 thousand bibliographic items were found. In addition, the most popular reprinted works and the most prolific authors in terms of the number of works published were also revealed (T. O. Sokolovskaya, A. N. Pypin, etc.). A review of sources lets us conclude that ¾ of all the sources on Freemasonry (the nonlegal researchers rely on) are not available for legal science; these sources have not been studied and given a scientific assessment yet. Some sources that have not been considered in legal science yet are the "Charter of Freemasons, approved at

---

[1]A. I. Serkov "Russian Freemasonry. 1731-2000": An Encyclopedic Dictionary. - M., 2001. - 1222 p.

the General Council of the Convention that took place in Wilhelmsbad 5787 (XVIII-XIXb.b.). From the history of Russian Freemasonry,"[1] "The Code of the Great Masonic Lodge of Astrea on V. S.-Petersburg,"[2] "The questions answered by I.E.Sh."[3]

In the second stage, the authors of this book selected the sources (from the Soviet period from 1917 to 1990) that were placed in the electronic catalog of the Russian State Library as of September 22, 2017. In total, this catalog contained the 369 titles of publications under the keyword "Freemasonry." The above-mentioned works were published from 1917 to 1990 inclusive[4].

Finally, 65 substantial works were selected from these works:

1. 35 theoretical works.
2. 18 biographical works.
3. 9 works of a journalistic nature.
4. 3 bibliographic works.

The term "Russian Freemasonry" is defined in some theoretical works. These works help understand the essence of Russian Freemasonry and its place in the social, religious, and political life of the country, including the state and law. The biographical literature, accordingly, covers the biography of the Freemasons of the studied period, some information about the membership in the lodges, civil service positions, public vocations, and literary works. The journalistic literature consists of the apologetics of Freemasonry and conspiracy literature ascribing purely negative semantic characteristics to the Freemasons. This group of sources allows us to formulate concrete antitheses. When refuting these antitheses, we can come to some scientific conclusions. The bibliographic works contain some information for historiographers.

---

[1]As of May 2018, according to the calculations, 132 dissertations were defended, addressing the topic of Russian Freemasonry: in law (23 dissertations), in philosophy (15 dissertations), in history (55 dissertations), in philology (33 dissertations), in cultural studies (3 dissertations), in political science (2 dissertations), in psychology (1 dissertation). Of these, research on Russian Freemasonry - 23 works. The statute of Freemasons (approved at the General Council of the Convention that was held in Wilhelmsbad in 5787 (XVIII-XIXb.b.)). From the history of Russian Freemasonry. SPb.: Econ. typo-lit. 1907. - 16 p.

[2] The Code of the Grand Masonic Lodge of Astrea in the East of St. Petersburg; The Laws of the Grand Masonic Lodge of Astrea in the East of St. Petersburg or Under the constitution of the Grand Lodge of Astrea of the Masonic Union. Bipartite. 1815. Parts 1-2. SPb., 1816. - 345 p.

[3] The questions answered by I.E.Sh. NIOR RGB. Fund 14. Unit of issue # 681.

[4] As of May 12, 2018, this catalog contained 441 items for the keyword "Masonry." As of August 08, 2021, the same catalog contains 558 items for the keyword "Freemasonry." A significant block of the new receipts for 2018-2021 consists of the literature in German, English, and French (24 titles in total).

In the third stage, the authors of this scientific work managed to work at the funds of Moscow and St. Petersburg, studying the important primary sources, as well as the materials related to the secret, classified information of the Secret Chancellery, the Special Chancellery of the Ministry of Internal Affairs, the Special Chancellery of the Ministry of Police, etc.

Fund 146, located in the Russian State Archive of Ancient Acts, is very interesting (particularly, storage unit 23, "The cases of the secret expedition"). The dispatches from the curator of the Imperial Moscow University, Privy Councilor Ivan Ivanovich Melissino, to the Commander-in-Chief in Moscow, Prince Alexander Alexandrovich Prozorovsky, with the attachment of his 59-page correspondence with Ober Kamerger Shuvalov and other persons about the reputed Friendly Scholar Society, now colloquially known under the name "Martinists" on June 13, 1790. Studying this case, we can learn that one Freemason from one system wrote a denunciation against a Freemason from another system. Considering Fund 1261, an 84-page storage unit # 2951, "The Highly Philosophical Discourse on Freemasonry" by S. R. Vorontsov, we can conclude that S. R. Vorontsov was interested in education and Freemasonry, but after not finding interest in Freemasonry, he got disappointed with it and left it. This data shows that Freemasonry was not homogeneous, and membership in the Masonic Lodge was very limited to the interests of a particular person.

The Scientific and Historical Archives of the St. Petersburg Institute of History of the Russian Academy of Sciences (NIA SPb II RAN), fund 176, contains the cases testifying to many projects of the state and legal transformations addressed to Monarch Alexander I from 1803 to 1810. The following storage units of the fund are very interesting: 1) 235 "March 24, 1803. Yakov Markevich's letter to Alexander I with the attachment of projects on the improvement of the state"; 2) 236 "October 1, 1803. Demyan Polyansky's letter to Alexander I" with the attachment of 3 projects "for the improvement of the 'common good'"; 3) 269" August 21, 1804. Poet S. S. Bobrov's letter to N. N. Novosiltsev with the transmission of his essay "The Historical Review of Russian Legislation"; 4) 289 "April 3, 1804. The subject serving as a matter for proving information about jurisprudence." Fund 36 (list of contents 1, the sheets of the storage unit 753) contains one of the lists of I. V. Lopukhin's notes, later published in London, "The notes of I. V. Lopukhin, Book VII, 1802."

The funds of the Russian State Historical Archive contain many documents testifying to the spread of the category of the "common good": fund 938, list of contents 1, file 66 - "The regulations on the state structure" (related, as the author found, to the middle of the 18th century); fund 938, list of contents 1, file 440, Page 1 - "The Masonic notes written by Count M. Yu. Vielgorskiy"; fund 1101, list of contents 1, file 230, 169 pages - "The Statute of the Masonic Order

(The system of the highly respectable, strong, and wise Order of the Knights and Brothers of the Light, from the seven wise Fathers, heads of seven churches in Asia)"; fund 1260, list of contents 1, file 578, 45 pages - "The case of drawing up a draft of the Church Charter for Protestants. It started on July 23, 1806, and ended on January 02, 1808."

A Research Department of the Manuscripts of the Russian State Library (NIOR RGB) contains the interesting fund 014, case 4: "The general laws of Freemasons." They were at the disposal of the Three-Banner Lodge in Moscow under the direction of P. Tatishchev[1], consisting of the general institutions (12 members) and the general laws proper (52 paragraphs). The general laws were characterized by high legal techniques for the Masonic documents of that time. Unlike other documents, it provided for a mechanism of responsibility for violating the Masonic Rules: 1) the persuasion or monetary fines in favor of the poor; 2) doubling the fine or excluding from the lodge for a time or permanently. The unreliable persons were not accepted as Freemasons. The candidates for disciples were also subject to the Masonic Laws. The visitors' ignorance of the Masonic Laws and regulations exempted them from any responsibility. The laws provided for the rules for raising the degree and the legal and moral obligations of Brothers.

Fund 014 of the NIOR RGB also contains Case 6, which includes the Charter of the Freemasons of the early 19th century[2]. This Charter is one of the fundamental documents of Masonic Lodges as its provisions were developed at the general Masonic Convention in Wilgelsbadt in 1782 and recommended as models for the Masonic Lodges that had sent delegates to that Convention. It consists of a preamble, 9 chapters, and a conclusion. The Charter has a poetical and artistic form with some elements of reasoning and pathetic assertions, containing a system of religious, public, social, Masonic, family, and personal obligations. The document has a humanitarian (assistance to the weak, the poor, and children) and patriotic orientation (love and service to the Fatherland and Tsars), containing the ideas of cosmopolitanism and self-designation - "Civil Society." The paper traces the transition from strict obedience to Masonic Leaders to the religious and moral obligations, an all-estates character, cosmopolitanism, the transition from the unconditional support of the sovereign to the unconditional support of the state and replacing the use of the Masonic "Laws" with the Masonic ceremonies and signs.

---

[1]The general laws of Freemasons. See "The Research Department of the Manuscripts of the Russian State Library." Fund 014 (Arseniev Vasily Sergeevich: a collection, the XVII-XIX centuries). # 4 (The general laws of Freemasons). 10 p.

[2] In RGB. NIOR. Fund 14. # 6. 10 pages. The charter was published by T. O. Sokolovskaya at the beginning of the 20th century. See T. O. Sokolovskaya "The secret archives of Russian Freemasons" / T. Sokolovskaya, D. Lotareva. - Moscow: Veche, 2007. - 477, [1] p.

There are “The Laws of the All-Russian State Grand Lodge”[1] in Fund 014 of the NIOR RGB in Case # 34. These laws applied to a whole union of Masonic Lodges. Therefore, for the sake of studying, they are very interesting.

There are “The positions R.K. of the ancient system in the junior assemblies read by Chrysophiron with the appendix of other Brothers’ speeches in 1782”[2] in Fund 014 of the NIOR RGB in Case # 1657. This document characterizes the Order of the Russian Rosicrucians (Rozencraitsers in the Russian sources) that played a significant role both in the history of Russian Freemasonry and in the history of Russia at the end of the 18th century – the first quarter of the 19th century.

NIOR RGB mainly contains the manuscripts and documents relating to the archives of Masonic Lodges, allowing the reconstruction of some views of Freemasons on the state and law. On the contrary, there are chiefly cases and reports of the public and secret nature in the funds of the State Archive of the Russian Federation (G.A. R.F.) and the Russian State Archive of State Archives (RGADA). They allow us “to see” the objective picture already by state Officials, to understand the hidden mechanisms of the regulation of Freemasonry, as well as the practice of their application. Moreover, the information from the NIOR RGB and the State Archive of the Russian Federation (G.A. R.F.) and the Russian State Archive of State Archives (RGADA) are like two halves of the event: if they factually, chronologically, and substantively coincide, then that event took place, was not invented and exaggerated. For example, a report by I. A. Fessler and G. A. Rosenkampf[3] was found in the NIOR RGB fund. It only showed the preparation for the Masonic reform described in the studies of V. V. Kuchurin and A. Yu. Minakov. And the rules of the tolerance of Freemasonry that were based on that report are in the State Archives of the Russian Federation (G.A. R.F.)[4]. Besides, the name of the document was borrowed from G. V. Vernadsky, that researched at

---

[1] The Laws of the State All-Russian Grand Lodge. Held on January 05, 1780. The Laws of the State Grand Lodge//RGB. NIOR. Fund 14. Case # 34. 4 pages.
[2] RGB. NIOR. Fund 14. # 1657. “The Positions of R.K. of the ancient system read by Chrysofiron with the application of speeches and other Brothers in 1782 at the junior meetings.”
[3] NIOR RGB Fund 147 (Sergei Stepanovich Lanskoy (1787-1862); Stepan Vasilievich Eshevsky (1829-1865)). # 6 /m1883/ (The documents of the 18th and 19th centuries: A Note on Freemasons, compiled after the report of Rosenkampf and Fessler). Pages 108-129.
[4] The State Archive of the Russian Federation. Fund 109 (The Third Branch of His Imperial Majesty's Own Chancellery). List of contents 1a (A secret archive. The revolutionary and social movement in Russia in 1826-1880). Case # 2246 (The draft conditions for the existence of societies, partnerships, brotherhoods, and other organizations, including the Masonic Lodge “Vladimir to Truth” authorized by the government).

the beginning of the 20th century. His notes can be found in the fund of the same name of the State Archives of the Russian Federation (G.A. R.F.)[1]. Only when utilizing the information of the funds in the aggregate can we reconstruct the events quite reliably. It should be noted that the report of I. A. Fessler and G. A. Rosenkampf was, in fact, one of the first studies on the legislative regulation of Freemasonry, fulfilled by the Freemasons themselves.

In the fourth stage, the authors studied various research materials in the reading rooms of the Russian State Library (Moscow), the Russian National Library (St. Petersburg), the Sverdlovsk Regional Universal Scientific Library named after V. G. Belinsky (Yekaterinburg), the Central City Public Library named after V. V. Mayakovsky (St. Petersburg), the State Library of Berlin (Staatsbibliothek Zu Berlin), the National Library of the Republic of Kazakhstan (Almaty), and the National Library of Estonia in Tallinn (Eesti Rahvusraamatukogu). The following publications that have not received coverage or have been thoroughly forgotten in the Russian-language literature on Freemasonry should be considered.

The book "Über arbeiteteun der weiterte Neuauflageü"[2] in the article "Alexander I" shows that the official recognition of Freemasonry in Russia took place in 1810 due to the work of the commission consisting of the Minister of Education, Count A. K. Razumovsky, the Minister of Police A. D. Balashev, Count Mikhail Speransky, and I. A. Fessler that created a favorable opinion-report on Freemasonry (günstiges Gutachten[3]). An article on the history of Freemasonry during the reign of "Paul I. Alexander I." contains some information about the most numerous lodges - "Les Amis Reunis," "La Palestine," and "Alexander the Crowned Pelican." Grand Duke Constantine, Count Stanislav Pototsky, Count Ivan Vorontsov, General Osterman-Tolstoy, Alexander von Benckendorff, Prince Alexander Vurtemberga, Chamberlain Alexander Naryshkin, and many other Courtiers were in the Masonic Lodges. The source demonstrates the inner ideology of the Masonic Lodges. For example, "Les Amis Reunis" was a very liberal lodge

---

[1] GA RF. Fund 1137 (Georgy Vladimirovich Vernadsky, historian, Professor of Russian History at Yale University (New Haven, USA). List of contents 1 (Vernadsky Georgy Vladimirovich, a Professor of Russian History at Yale University. 1857-1931). Case # 126 (The Notes (without a signature). "On Masonic Lodges and other secret societies" from 1811-1826 (from the Secret Department of the Military Scientific Archive). Copies). 69 pages.

[2] Über arbeiteteun der weiterte Neuauflageü (StandFebruar 2000) der Ausgabe von 19322000 by F.A. Herbig Verlags buchhandlung GmbH, München 951p.

[3] Ibid. Page 63.

fighting against any prejudices of any kind (Vorurteilealler Art), fanaticism, religious hatred, and the enmity between nations. Also, that Lodge had a pacifist program. Prince Alexander Ypsilantis (Ipsilanti in the Russian sources), taking part in the "Palestine" Lodge, developed a wide-ranging activity aimed at gaining freedom for Greece. The article shows that Russian Freemasons were true patriots and statesmen. The elite of the Russian army consisted of Freemasonry during the Napoleonic Wars. The communication with the Prussian Freemasons strongly impressed the Russian Officers, especially when returning home through the territory of Prussia. A. I. Mikhailovsky-Danilevsky noted that some Russian Officers had seen the patriotism in its most majestic (erhebendsten) form in the German field Lodges and the Russian Lodges of "St. George" and "Alexander to loyalty." Certainly, the Russian Officers did not hear anything in the lodges about the "world conspiracy," but instead, they got an idea of the desire for the highest development of the Russian national culture (nationaler Kultur)[1]. This data shows us, firstly, the connection between Russian Freemasonry and Prussian Freemasonry and, secondly, the fact that Freemasons shared both liberal natural-legal ideas and conservative and monarchist ideas.

When studying the book "La Franc-maçonnerie et la Revolution intellectuelle Du XVIII siècle" by Bernard Fey[2], we can learn that French Freemasonry became anti-Christian in 1792-1815[3]. At first, in 1790, Freemasonry in France tried to modernize the Catholic religion and was tolerant of it[4], but, starting from 1800, it became anticlerical and demanded that Catholic Churches be closed and the clergy disbanded[5]. Russian Freemasonry, unlike French Freemasonry, did not imagine itself without the state and religion. For this reason, Russian Freemasonry rejected the French political and legal doctrine, along with French Freemasonry in Russia.

The book "Revolution and Freemasonry 1680-1800" by Bernard Fey revealed some important circumstances explaining the participation of Freemasonry in the revolution in France. French Freemasonry attempted to create a new religion based on the principles of ecumenism but failed. The Masonic Lodges

---

[1]Über arbeiteteun der weiterte Neuauflageü (StandFebruar 2000) der Ausgabe von 19322000 by F.A. Herbig Verlags buchhandlung GmbH, München 951p., pages 730-731.

[2]Bernard Faÿ "Revolution and Freemasonry 1680-1800." Boston. Little, Brown, and Company. 1935. – 349 pages.

[3] Ibid. Page 298.

[4] Ibid. Page 299.

[5] What the Russian Freemasons will later call the "common harm."

in France at the end of the 18th century were very popular, but, at the same time, they could not boast of unity: "This mixture of booze, songs, fraternity, lectures, philanthropic activities, religion, goodwill towards each other, nebulous mysticism, false chivalry, and serious ambition was the headiest drink of the eighteenth century." The frivolity and idealism of French Freemasonry provoked completely undesirable social consequences. The author of the book notes the false optimism of Freemasons in 1789: "Even when French people killed each other, they, at the same time, kissed, sang, and danced in the squares, praising the happiness of humanity and the joy of virtue to the skies"[1]. "The three main principles of 18th century Freemasonry - freedom, equality, and brotherhood" lost the character of spiritual principles because they started meaning the "political equality, civil liberty, brotherhood of the people, and charity."[2] French Freemasonry believed in progress, the power of the human mind, and the absolute value of science that became the foundation of all knowledge, the source of all confidence, even the religious faith[3]. French Freemasons believed in humanity and progress and were completely convinced that they had rights, wanting to defend them without any remorse. Freemasons were present in the National Assembly and all the Ministries, holding the key positions there, as well as in the clubs that governed the street masses, thus playing a leading role in the French Revolution. "Considering all the intellectual products of Freemasonry, it can be said that the most important and, perhaps, at the same time, the most dangerous product was optimism[4]."

Picture 12. A gang of French peasants in revolt in 1789. A reproduction of the painting of the early 20th century by P. A. Svedomsky[5]. The color processing by A. N. Makarov.

[1] Revolution and Freemasonry. Page 300.
[2] Ibid. Page 307.
[3] Ibid. Page 308.
[4] Ibid. Page 300.
[5] An Album of historical painting [Text]: in engravings from the paintings by Russian and foreign artists. - [St. Petersburg]: The edition of the journal "World Illustration," [1891]. - [53] p.: ill. Page VII.

"France became a victim of 'terror' between 1792 and 1794. The bloodshed was encountered everywhere: the war raged on all borders, the civil war was in the west and southeast, there were a lot of massacres and persecution in all cities and robberies and murders on the highways and in the villages[1]." Therefore, many lodges "fell asleep," the criticism arose within Freemasonry about the happening events, and the Duke of Orleans publicly renounced the Order and condemned it. After getting crushed by the elements of the revolution, Freemasonry left France. The intellectual and social foundations of Freemasonry were defeated, and the aristocrats (the members of Masonic Lodges) were beheaded or forced to flee. There was no organized Masonic activity in France from 1793 to 1797. Freemasonry in France got revived only under Napoleon Bonaparte, that headed Freemasonry. B. Fay notes that, in England, starting from 1790, Freemasonry began acquiring a "militant-patriotic," more religious and national character (instead of a cosmopolitan one), entirely different from the character of French Freemasonry[2]. Freemasonry was attacked, persecuted, and accused of preparing and carrying out the French and American revolutions at the beginning of the 19th century in England and the United States[3]. And B. Fay believes that this accusation was quite correct as Freemasonry had prepared the ground for the revolutions of 1688, 1776, and 1789 and even participated in them.

It can be read in the book "Freemasonry: its aims and ideals" by John Ward[4] that French Freemasonry at the turn of the XVIII-XIX centuries was political[5]. According to the author, the main reason for this was some struggle of the Catholic Church against Freemasonry[6]. At the same time, British and American Freemasons distanced themselves from politics by harboring social ideals. The political goals of Freemasonry destroy the state Freemasonry is located.

Also, any political aspirations destroy any Freemasonry itself (the author points out four consequences of the lodge's enthusiasm for politics):
1. Such goals will surely spoil the spirit of harmony in the lodge.
2. Power in the lodge can pass into the hands of extremists.
3. The secret nature of the meetings of Freemasonry can turn them into "the most formidable weapon against a constitutionally established government."

---

[1] Revolution and Freemasonry. P. 301.
[2] Revolution and Freemasonry. P. 302-305.
[3] Revolution and Freemasonry. P. 305.
[4] Freemasonry: its aims and ideals by J.S.M. Ward B.A>, F.S>S., F.R. Econ. Soc. London. William Rider & Son limited 8-II Paternoster Row, E.C.4 1923. – 232 pages.
[5] Ibid. Page16.
[6] Ibid. Page33.

4. All of the above-mentioned lead to “the dishonest and unconstitutional activities of the members of the Order,” acting according to the imperative political instructions[1].

S. P. Karpachev, in his article “M. M. Kovalevsky[2],” examines the biography of the famous lawyer M. M. Kovalevsky. M. M. Kovalevsky and his friend E. V. de Roberti joined the “Cosmos” Lodge of the Scottish Charter in Paris (under the leadership of the famous Russian inventor-electrical engineer P. N. Yablochkov)[3] in 1888.

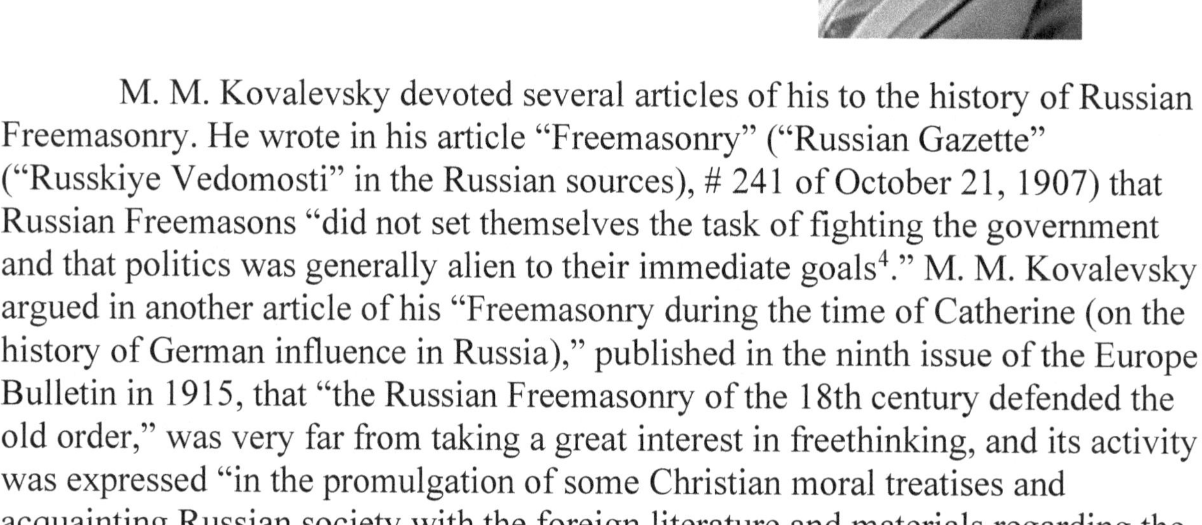

Picture 13. A photo of Maxim Maksimovich Kovalevsky (1851-1916, from open sources)

M. M. Kovalevsky devoted several articles of his to the history of Russian Freemasonry. He wrote in his article “Freemasonry” (“Russian Gazette” (“Russkiye Vedomosti” in the Russian sources), # 241 of October 21, 1907) that Russian Freemasons “did not set themselves the task of fighting the government and that politics was generally alien to their immediate goals[4].” M. M. Kovalevsky argued in another article of his “Freemasonry during the time of Catherine (on the history of German influence in Russia),” published in the ninth issue of the Europe Bulletin in 1915, that “the Russian Freemasonry of the 18th century defended the old order,” was very far from taking a great interest in freethinking, and its activity was expressed “in the promulgation of some Christian moral treatises and acquainting Russian society with the foreign literature and materials regarding the Russian history[5].”

[1] Freemasonry: its aims and ideals by J.S.M. Ward B.A>, F.S>S., F.R. Econ. Soc. London. William Rider & Son limited 8-II Paternoster Row, E.C.4 1923. – 232 pages. Page 32.
[2] S. P. Karpachev “M. M. Kovalevsky” // Freemasonry and Freemasons. A digest of articles. Issue I. “Era,” Moscow, 1994 – 123 pages. - Pages 76-90.
[3] Ibid. Page 86.
[4] S. P. Karpachev “M. M. Kovalevsky” // Freemasonry and Freemasons. A digest of articles. Issue I. “Era,” Moscow, 1994 – 123 p. – Page 88.
[5] Ibid. Page 89.

M. M. Kovalevsky, in his article "The struggle of a German influence with a French influence at the end of the 18th and the first half of the 19th century[1]" wrote that the first centers of "German influence (this influence rapidly increased in the second half of the reign of Alexander I and during the reign of Nikolai Pavlovich") had been "next to the Masonic Lodges continuing the tradition of Catherine era and its dependence on Germany[2]," as well as in the universities.

Some rare books of the early 20th century contain some important assessments of Russian Freemasonry: A. V. Mezieres's "In Search of Truth and the Meaning of Life (an Essay from the History of Russian Freemasonry)" (1906)[3] and S. M. Propper "Freemasonry and its Significance for Cultural Success" (1907)[4]. The English-language literature written by a Freemason for Freemasons is very interesting to study. Boris Telepnev wrote many small books on the history of Russian Freemasonry. They were originally presented in the form of reports at the meetings of Masonic Lodges in England in the first quarter of the XX century. The author in his book "Russian Freemasons" (1925)[5] reported on three periods of Russian Freemasonry: from the moment of opening and until the complete closure of the lodges in 1792-1794; from the restoration of the lodges in the early years of the 19th century and until their complete closure in 1822 and from 1822 to 1924. B. Telepnev pointed to the "royal road" of Masonic Lodges and various deviations from it by Russian Freemasons.[6] The author emphasizes some specific ideals shared by Freemasonry against the background of the ideas of the Enlightenment: "The dangerous network of the ideas of French origin (they confused many Russians in that era) forced many serious thinkers to appreciate the inner strength and beauty of Freemasonry and united them under the banner of fighting their common enemies - skepticism, materialism, atheism, and revolutionary aspirations. Those views that penetrated Russia on the eve of the revolution in France were received by the Empress at first quite benevolently. Those French ideas were consistent with her rationalistic and skeptical mind. Also, French morality corresponded to her character and the character of her courtiers[7]." However, soon, many Russian nobles became dissatisfied with the new *"brilliant, but shallow*

---

[1] M. M. Kovalevsky "The struggle of German influence with French at the end of the 18th and in the first half of the 19th century" // M. M. Kovalevsky "The selected works": bipartite - Part 2. - M.: Russian Political Encyclopedia (ROSSPEN), 2010. - 448 p. Pages 85-126. Page 91.

[2] Ibid. Page 91.

[3] A. V. Mezier "In Search of the Truth and Meaning of Life (An essay on the History of Russian Freemasonry)"//History and Public Issues # 112, O. N. Popova, 1906. St. Petersburg. – 142 p.

[4] S. M. Propper "Freemasonry and its importance for the success of culture.". SPb. 1907. - 60 p.

[5] Russian Masons by Bro. B. Telepneff. 32 p. By Pencil II 1925. 4707.

[6] Ibid. Page 1.

[7] Russian Masons by Bro. B. Telepneff. 32 p. By Pencil II 1925. 4707. Page 6.

ideas that undermined morality, national traditions, and the authority of religion"[1] (*emphasized by the authors of this scientific work*). The author continued: the nobility of the Russian Empire had found some "help and light" in Freemasonry, and it had rallied under the banner of Freemasonry. "Henceforth, there was the important and useful value of Russian Freemasonry during the time of Empress Catherine, consisting of *the ideas of morality, religion, Christian mysticism, and loyalty to national traditions* that were shared by some of the most serious Russian patriots and Orthodox Christians"[2] (*it was emphasized by the authors of this research*). Further, the author wrote that Russian Freemasonry "had become not only a temple of Christian secrets, but also a bulwark against revolutionaries, materialists, and atheists[3]." The book also described the differences between the Swedish and French systems of Freemasonry in Russia and the Russian Rosicrucians (Rozencraitsers in the Russian sources). B. Telepnev, in his book "The Rosicrucians (Rozencraitsers in the Russian sources) in Russia" (1924)[4] reported that, in terms of politics, the Rosicrucians (Rozencraitsers in the Russian sources) were loyal to the monarchical government, opposing the "revolutionary ideas." The Russian Rosicrucians (Rozencraitsers in the Russian sources) thought that the doctrines of the "Illuminati" were especially dangerous. The author concluded that the Russian Rosicrucians (Rozencraitsers in the Russian sources) in Russia had prevented a revolution similar to the French one and saved Russia from the revolutionaries. B. Telepnev showed in his book "A Few Pages from the History of Swedish Freemasonry in Russia" (1928)[5] that Swedish Freemasonry had set itself the goal of protecting moral principles, religion, law, and order from any atheistic and radical ideas existing at that time throughout Europe. Despite the harsh measures taken in Russia against the Order, the ideals that inspired its members survived into the nineteenth century and beyond[6].

The book by a Polish researcher M. Abassy "A Russian Mason on the Paths of his Native Culture. The Case Study of Nicolas Novikov" (2014)[7], contains

---

[1] Russian Masons by Bro. B. Telepneff. 32 p. By Pencil II 1925. 4707. Page 6.
[2] Ibid. Page 6.
[3] Ibid. Page 13.
[4] The Rosicrucians (Rozencraitsers in the Russian sources) in Russia by Frater Boris Telepneff. Privately printed by Dr. W. Wynn Westcoit. 1924. 17 p.
[5] A Few Pages from the History of Swedish Freemasonry in Russia. By Bro. Boris Telepneff. 1928. 23 pages.
[6] A Few Pages from the History of Swedish Freemasonry in Russia. By Bro. Boris Telepneff. 1928. Pages 20-21.
[7] Malgorzata Abassy "A Russian Mason on the Paths of his Native Culture. The Case Study of Nicolas Novikov." Krakow. 2014. – 195 p.

some interesting conclusions on the history of Russian Freemasonry. This Case Study is practically unknown to Russian readers.

The book by A. Makei "Principles of Masonic Law: A Treatise on the Constitutional Laws, Customs, and Landmarks of Freemasonry"[1] (the first edition was published in 1856) revealed the meaning and role of a Master's Degree - the main degree in Freemasonry.

In the fifth stage, it seemed to the author of this work that the work had reached a dead end:

1. A. N. Lushin proved the belonging of Russian Freemasons to the conservatives and liberals.
2. A. I. Serkov wrote that Russian Freemasonry had been extremely different in its political and legal views and had not represented a single community with any common goals and objectives.
3. S. V. Arzhanukhin argued that Russian Freemasonry had formulated the ethical and moral imperatives becoming the legal norms over time and acquiring a formal legal form. The author of this book realized that the development of the ideas of any of the researchers had not made a significant contribution to science, and the work on the ideas of each Masonic Lodge and the ideas of each Freemason had turned the work into a Sisyphean work[2]. A lot of primary sources did not have a date or an author. Therefore, they could not (and cannot) be introduced into scientific circulation without a preliminary source analysis.

In addition, during the analysis and verification of various sources, it turned out that Russian Freemasons had not been able to have normatively and practically any different (from the officially recognized political and legal ideology) ideas about the state and law.

First, it was prohibited by Masonic landmarks (Anderson's constitution) and Masonic statutes. Secondly, the members of the Masonic Lodges consisted of the noble elite (the members of the Royal families, Senators, the Rectors of universities, the deans of universities, Governors-General, etc.). That elite was very

---

[1] The principles of Masonic law: a treatise on the constitutional laws, usages, and landmarks of Freemasonry/by Albert Mackey [Luton; England]: Andrews U.K. Ltd., 2010. – 235 p.

[2] In this case, it would be necessary to describe the state-legal views of every person that left a mark on history and visited the Masonic Lodge. A qualified presentation of the state-legal views of every Freemason is, in fact, independent thesis research.

conservative and loyal to the government as part of Russian society[1]. Thirdly, to be promoted, all Russian Officials and nobles were obliged to share the ideas and principles officially declared by a Monarch's will. The search for such ideas and principles among Russian Monarchs is, at the same time, an answer to the question about the state-legal ideas of Russian Freemasons.

In the sixth stage, during the analysis and systematization of sources, the author of this work discovered a theoretical construction of the "common good" in the documents, speeches, and writings of Russian Freemasons. The statements of the theorists and historians of law (V. V. Lapaeva, M. A. Reisner, A. P. Semitko, A. V. Tomsinov, V. S. Nersesyants, and O. A. Omelchenko) helped a lot for a theoretical understanding of the concept of the "common good" in the historical and legal context. The presentation of the material would not be possible without the use of some developments in the field of the intellectual history of the following authors: M. S. Kiseleva, M. A. Kiselev, K. D. Bugrov, and D. V. Timofeev. The central sources of the theory of the "common good" were the works of G. Grotius (Grotsy in the Russian sources), S. F. Pufendorf, J. G. Justi, J. F. Bielfeld, F. Prokopovich, V. N. Tatishchev, Ch. L. de Montesquieu, C. Beccaria, I. G. Reichel, Z. A. Goryushkin, Catherine II, and Pavel I. Based on the fact that the terms of the "common good" were consolidated in the legislation, political, and legal documents, we can conclude about the legal nature of the theory that was well-known in the Russian Empire as the theory of the welfare of all and everyone. The author found out that the sources of the state and legal ideas of Russian Freemasons contain the terminology of the theory of the welfare of all and everyone.

They can be divided into the following sources:

1. The sources proving the normatively binding nature of the theory of the welfare of all and everyone for Russian Freemasons (the materials of the Wilhelmsbad convention of 1782 that influenced the history of Freemasonry in Russia; the acts and statutes of Masonic Lodges, partially published by Yu. E. Kondakov and T. O. Sokolovskaya and partially located in the archival funds).
2. The sources of the personal origin that use the vocabulary of the theory of the welfare of all and everyone or provide the arguments about the welfare of all and everyone (books, memoirs, notes, testimonies, etc., belonging to one person or a group of persons). The personal convictions of a Freemason at a certain stage of

---

[1] A decrease in the number of conservative-minded nobles and an increase in young officers in the Masonic Lodges gave rise to liberal and even radical views that caused a threat to the existence of Freemasonry in Russia, as I. A. Pozdeev and E. A. Kushelev declared many times.

his life in the latter case coincide with the requirements of Masonic normative documents and the content of the official political and legal ideology.

The translated literature should be mentioned separately: the books of I. A. Stark (Shtark in the Russian sources) "The Apology, or Defense of the Order of Freemasons" and K. G. L. Von Plumenek "The Open Influence of the True Freemasonry, etc." The circulation of these books in the Masonic world, both in Russia and abroad, was very noticeable. Reading these books that enjoyed authority among Russian Brothers-Freemasons also contributed to the spread of the theory of the welfare of all and everyone.

Many sources (over 95 percent) are primary sources published in the 18th, 19th, and early 20th centuries. Only a small number of works were cited through cross-citation (for example, citing A. F. Labzin based on P. Bessonov's essay and A. A. Czartorysky's memoirs based on A. N. Arkhangelsky's book "Alexander I").

The research on the legal source studies has not been fulfilled in this work. In other words, the research into the issues of the legislative regulation of Russian Freemasonry and its legalization at the beginning of the 19th century only partially concerns the state-legal ideas of Russian Freemasons. These questions were reflected in the publication of A. V. Dmitriev's "The Rules on the Tolerance of Freemasonry in the Russian Empire in 1811: Source Analysis." The author concluded that this document had been preserved in the secret archive of the III Department of His Imperial Majesty's Chancellery, as well as in the military-scientific archive of the General Headquarters. T. O. Sokolovskaya, V. I. Semevsky, G. V. Vernadsky, and A. I. Serkov read the document and made up their own opinion about it. This document does not have any name and belongs to the category of resolutions. It was called "the rules" in the official secret correspondence of 1826. T. O. Sokolovskaya, V. I. Semevsky, and G. V. Vernadsky also called the document "the rules" (however, there were other names: the draft of conditions, a note on societies, etc.). The rules were finally drawn up in 1811 (after the official recognition of the acts of the Swedish System), and they began to be guided by the Minister of Police and the Heads of the Masonic Lodges.

The issues of reflecting the ideas about the state and law of Russian Freemasons in the "secret" documents and records of Russian Freemasons were analyzed by using the example of the article by A. V. Dmitriev, "A discourse on the support of Freemasons for the monarchical power in Russia in 1817: a source analysis" (hereinafter - "Reasoning"). It was established during the research that "The Reasoning" had been written down by S. P. Fonvizin from the words of its author - Iosif Alekseevich Pozdeev, in 1817. “The Reasoning” refers to the documents and materials that were passed on by Russian Freemasons from generation to generation until this document came to a researcher N. P. Kiselev and, finally, ended up in the Research Department of the Manuscripts of the Russian State Library. The publication of this article on the pages of the magazine “Genesis” in the “Historical Research” section was scheduled for 2021. These studies introduce the relevant documents (with the establishment of the year of compilation, authorship, authenticity, and value) into the science of the history of the state and law, the doctrine of the state, and law.

The collection, analysis, and synthesis of the sources of the official (the legislation and political-legal projects) and unofficial (the acts of Masonic Lodges, correspondence, and essays) origin allow us to conclude about their reliability, consistency, and semantic unity. The theory of the welfare of all and everyone was widespread both in the legislative, official business, and diplomatic practice of the officials of the Russian Empire and in the documents of Masonic Lodges, writings, and correspondence of Russian Freemasons. This theory did not become the subject of any censorship during the tsarist era, it was bypassed in Soviet times, and an interest in it began to wake up again in the post-Soviet times.

The sources used by the authors confirm the main conclusions of the study:
1. The existence of the theory of the “common good” in Europe awakened the theory of the welfare of all and everyone in the Russian Empire.
2. The theory of the welfare of all and everyone became part of the culture of the nobility, officials, and the reigning house of the Romanov family (Catherine II, Paul I, and Alexander I) in the Russian Empire.
3. The theory of the “common good” was reflected in the acts of Masonic Lodges in Russia and abroad.
4. The theory of the welfare of all and everyone was reflected in the writings and correspondence of the members of Masonic Lodges in Russia.

To sum up, it can be concluded that all the sources of the research can be conditionally divided into the normative acts (the acts of Masonic Lodges, legislation, and legislative projects), the essays of a different nature, and biographical data (the notes, memoirs, dictionaries, and collections of materials). They, taken together, allow us to give an objective picture of the spread of the theory of the “common good” as the main idea of Russian Freemasons about the state and law: to determine the biography of the author, the author's affiliation with

Freemasons, the connection between the ideas of a Freemason and the attitudes of Masonic acts and legislation.

A significant block of sources was presented in the form of the archival material from the funds of the NIA SPB II RAN (1 fund), RGB (3 funds), RGADA (4 funds), G.A. R.F. (5 funds), and RGIA (7 funds).

The scientific literature underlying the research was divided into a block of primary sources: the works of the 18th – the first quarter of the 19th centuries (F. G. Bauze, J. F. Bielfeld, Z. A. Goryushkin, S. Pufendorf, M. M. Speransky, V. N. Tatishchev, I. A. Stark (Shtark in the Russian sources), and J. G. Justi); a block of the literature of the second half of the 19th century - the first half of the 20th century (G. V. Vernadsky, M. M. Kovalevsky, S. A. Korf, B. E. Nolde, M. N. Pokrovsky, M. A. Reisner, A. I. Semevsky, T. O. Sokolovskaya, B. I. Syromyatnikov, B. Fey, etc.), and a block of the Soviet and post-Soviet literature (M. Abassy, T. V. Andreeva, S. V. Arzhanukhin, T. V. Artemyeva, K. D. Bugrov, E. A. Vishlenkova, K. Gerlakh, V. Yu. Zakharov, S. V. Kodan, Yu. E. Kondakov, A. N. Lushin, A. Yu. Minakov, V. S. Nersesyants, O. A. Omelchenko, A. P. Semitko, A. I. Serkov, V. A. Tomsinov, etc.). The number of primary sources and representatives of the other generations of authors was evenly distributed.

The problems of the source study are as follows:

1. An author's membership in Masonic Lodges. According to the authors of this scientific work, the determining factor of membership in a Masonic Lodge is the presence of the protocol of the lodge. Piece of additional evidence is the autobiography, memoirs, correspondence of some Freemasons themselves, reference, and historical literature.

2. A problem of the secrecy and safety of Masonic documents, especially in the light of the requirements of the Masonic statutes on the secrecy of documents for the members of another Masonic system and in the light of censorship prohibitions on any publications after 1822.

3. A problem with the proper selection of sources (the number of these sources on the research topic exceeds several thousand bibliographic items).

The abundance of sources on Russian Freemasonry let the authors of this research study them in several consecutive stages:

1. An analysis of dissertation research on Freemasonry was carried out. After considering 132 dissertations for the period from 1990 to May 2018, it can be concluded that ¾ of the existing sources (the dissertations in other sciences (philosophy, history, cultural studies, etc.) are based on) were not used in any legal research related to Freemasonry.

2. A selection of sources was made for the period from 1917 to 1990 (the Soviet period). The Soviet period contains important sources of a theoretical, biographical, and bibliographic nature.

3. The authors of this work managed to work in the archives on the history of Freemasonry in Moscow and St. Petersburg (NIOR RGB, RGADA, GA R.F., RGIA, and NIA SPB II RAN). It can be possible to reconstruct the events and intellectual history with a sufficient degree of reliability only by using the information of the funds in their aggregate as the funds contain the primary sources of information, as well as the materials related to the information of limited access.

4. Some literature in foreign languages was studied. Nowadays, this literature is practically unknown to specialists in the history of Russian Freemasonry. Also, these literary materials are completely unknown to specialists in the history and theory of the state and law, the doctrine of the state, and the tenet of law. The main provisions of this literature confirm the theses about rejecting the French political and legal doctrine and French Freemasonry in Russia as Russian Freemasonry was apolitical, did not imagine itself outside the institutions of the state and church, had a conservative character, and showed loyalty to the government. On the contrary, French Freemasonry had a political nature and paved the way for and participated in the French Revolution of 1789. Russian Freemasons cleared Russia of any representatives of the revolutionary movement, preventing any revolution in Russia.

5. The authors of this research started studying some sources of the official political and legal doctrine of the Russian Empire in the second half of the 18th and the first quarter of the 19th centuries, as it turned out that Russian Freemasons had not been able to have an idea of the state and law, different from the officially recognized political and legal ideology.

6. A theoretical construction of the “common good” was discovered in the documents, speeches, and writings of Russian Freemasons, and a corresponding selection was made. The same construction was found in the legislation of the

corresponding period of Russian history and the political and legal documents. The etymology of the terms led to the doctrinal sources: the works of the foreign and domestic jurists that are united by a common theory of the "common good," known in Russia as the theory of the welfare of all and everyone.

7. An analysis of various sources allowed the author to conclude their reliability, consistency, and semantic unity. The theory of the welfare of all and everyone was widespread both in the legislative, official business, and diplomatic practice of the Officials of the Russian Empire and in the documents of Masonic Lodges, the writings, and correspondence of Russian Freemasons.

Chapter II

The "common good" in the theory, legislation, and worldview of Russian Freemasons in the Russian Empire of the 18th century – the first quarter of the 19th century.

§2.1. The theory of the "common good" in the Russian Empire

The theory of the "common good" is a forgotten topic in jurisprudence, but scientists have recently started taking an interest in it. Today, the phrase "common good" can often be found in the bylaws of the Russian Federation and legal literature. The "common good" as a category was consolidated in the constitutions of Europe, America, and Asia. The references to the "common good" are contained in the judgments of the Constitutional Court of Russia and the European Court of Human Rights. The theoretical legal thought tries to give the concept of the "common good" and find the content of the "common good," its origins, and regularities. The idea of the "common good" as the goal of state power was not considered scientific in Soviet times[1]. For this reason, no scientific attention was paid to it at all. The theory of the "common good" is absent among the theories of the Age of Enlightenment, named in the famous textbook on the history of political and legal doctrines, edited by O. E. Leist and V. A. Tomsinov[2]. O. A. Omelchenko's study dedicated to the doctrine of enlightened absolutism in Russia is an exception. The theory of the "common good" in this research was considered the basis of a public law doctrine[3]. There is an opinion (widespread in the modern literature) saying that the category of the "common good" considered without any reference to geography, historical period, and other factors "turns into an empty abstraction and a good wish that "everything is good[4]." On the other hand, there is another opinion (widespread among the legal theorists) saying that "the interpretation of the 'common good' in Russia was dominated by the Cathedral-Collectivist (Byzantine) framework (not by the Universalist (Western) approach).

---

[1]N. S. Prozorova "The political and legal views of John Lilburn." M.: The State Publishing House of Legal Literature. 1960, page 31.

[2] The history of political and legal doctrines. A textbook for high schools. The 3rd edition supplemented / Edited by a Ph.D. in Legal Sciences, Professor O. E. Leist and a Ph.D. in Legal Sciences, Professor V. A. Tomsinov. M.: Zertsalo Publishing House, 2009. - 584 p.

[3] O. A. Omelchenko "The monarchy of enlightened absolutism in Russia: Political doctrine, legal policy, state reforms": A thesis of a Ph.D. in Legal Sciences: 12.00.01.-Moscow, 2001. - 389 p.

[4] A. P. Semitko "The culture of law and the 'common good'"//Legal state: theory and practice. # 2 (52). 2018. Page 31.

According to this handling, the 'common good' was considered as a kind of higher principle dominating over the individual" and referring to the transcendental divine sphere[1]. Anyway, these statements are debatable.

To reveal the theory of the "common good," the author of this work used the "history of concepts" method that involves identifying the "broad political, socio-economic, and cultural contexts," as well as "studying any changes in the content of a concept in a historical retrospective" and "comparing different meanings and contexts" of using the concept for one or two generations[2]. V. S. Nersesyants and K. D. Bugrov noted that the concept of the "common good" went back to ancient socio-political and legal thought. Socrates argued that virtue could give the knowledge "that ensures the choice of good and the rejection of evil[3]." Also, he said that like-mindedness in obedience to the laws is "the greatest good for the state[4]." According to Socrates, the management of the affairs of the polis based on knowledge is "the only reliable path to the 'common good'[5]." Archon Solon supposed that the greatest good for society was in order and law. Also, he thought that the greatest evil was "in the lawlessness and civil strife[6]." Plato (Platon in the Russian sources) counted that the correct laws were the laws "that were established for the 'common good' of the entire state, not for some narrow ruling group only[7]." The concept of the "common good" became widespread in the modern era as it had been successfully embedded both in the political and theological reasonings based on the idea of God as a source of good and in the natural legal concepts showing that the source of good was "an agreement on the unification between people in the name of their earthly well-being[8]." The works of Aristotle, "Politics,"[9] and Foma Akvinsky, "Sum of Theology,"[10] were the most famous works on the "common good" of ancient times

---

[1] V. V. Lapaeva "The types of understanding Law: legal theory and practice." - M., 2012. Page 302.

[2] D. V. Timofeev "European Ideas in the Public Consciousness and Communicative Practice of an Educated Russian Citizen in the First Quarter of the 19th Century: An Experience in Studying Basic Socio-Political Concepts": An Abstract of the Thesis of a Ph.D. in Historical Sciences. 2011. Page 14.

[3] V. S. Nersesyants Socrates [Text] / V.S. Nersesyants; The Academy of Sciences of the USSR. - Moscow: Nauka, 1977. Page 33.

[4] Ibid. Page 49.

[5] Ibid. Page 57.

[6] Ibid. Page 40.

[7] V. S. Nersesyants "Plato" / V. S. Nersesyants. - Moscow: Legal Literature, 1984. Page 64.

[8] K. D. Bugrov "Natural Law and Virtue: The Integration of European Influence into the Russian Political Culture of the 18th Century". 2016. Page 116.

[9] Aristotle "Politics." The works: 4 volumes - M.: Thought, 1983. - Volume 4. Page 380.

[10] Thomas Aquinas "The sum of theology" / Translated by S. I. Eremeeva and A. A. Yudin. Part I—II. Questions 90-114. Kiev: Nika-Center, 2010. - 432 p. Part 2. Book one. Question 96. Chapter 1 and 4.

and the Middle Ages. Eberhard Isenmann revealed the "common good" in detail. The "common good," in his opinion, is a normative and regulatory idea that is similar to the notion of the social contract and popular sovereignty. It has an undoubted axiomatic value[1], in addition, to his mind. The concept of the "common good" Bonum Commune, Utilitas Publica has been a universal formalized theoretical concept of political thought since the days of Greco-Roman antiquity[2]. According to Dante Alighieri (Aligyery in the Russian sources), the meaning of the concept is the creation and preservation of the "common good": "cuiuslibet societatis finis est commune sociorum bonum[3]." This maxim means that the "common good" is a mandatory principle and the final goal of both "the legitimate political action of any ruler" and any subject that "must contribute to the 'common good,'" following his or her capabilities[4]. A concept of the "common good" in the Latinized Christian world manifests itself in political theory, diplomatic correspondence, legal texts and laws, attorneys' opinions, and reform projects[5].

Academician V. S. Nersesyants devoted an entire chapter of his book "The Philosophy of Law" to the legal concept of the "common good," fully comprehending the problem of the "common good" and making the greatest conceptualization of the "common good." V. S. Nersesyants wrote that "the 'common good' is the recognition and result of the natural-legal equality of individual goods. Thus, the concept of the 'common good' presents a legal model for identifying, agreeing, recognizing, and protecting various interests (conflicting in many respects), claims, and wills of the members of this community[6]." According to him, the "common good" was "not a denial of the differences in interests, claims, wills, goals, etc. of individual subjects, but some general

---

[1] Eberhard Isenmann "The notion of the 'Common Good', the concept of politics, and practical policies in Late Medieval and Early Modern German cities" // De Bono Communi. Discourse and Practice of the "Common Good" in the European City (13th-16th c.)/ Edited by ElodieLecuppre-Desjardin & Anne-Laure Van Bruaene. 2010, Brepols Publishers n.v., Turnhout, Belgium. P. 110.
[2]Eberhard Isenmann "The notion of the 'Common Good', the concept of politics, and practical policies in Late Medieval and Early Modern German cities" // De Bono Communi. Discourse and Practice of the "Common Good" in the European City (13th-16th c.)/ Edited by ElodieLecuppre-Desjardin & Anne-Laure Van Bruaene. 2010, Brepols Publishers n.v., Turnhout, Belgium. P. 110.
[3] Alighieri Dante, *Monarchia,* R. IMBACH&C. FLÜELER (ed. Andtr.), L.II, v,2, Stuttgart, 1989. Translated by V. P. Zubov: "the goal of any society is the 'common good' of its members." Dante Alighieri "A Monarchy". – M.: "Kanon-press-C" – "Kuchkovo field," 1999. Page 66.
[4] Eberhard Isenmann "The notion of the 'Common Good'..." P. 107.
[5] Ibid.
[6] V. S. Nersesyants "The Philosophy of Law." A textbook for high schools. - M.: INFRA Publishing Group • M - NORMA, 1997. Page 69.

condition of their possibility. Law does not subordinate life to itself, unify different interests, destroy the free will of individual subjects, etc., but only represents and expresses the necessary order (norms, forms, scales, institutions, and procedures) for an equal (identically free for everybody) external manifestation of these differences[1]."

A theorist of law, M.A. Reisner (1868-1928), noted at the beginning of the 20th century that the theory of the "common good" had been a basis of the works of a Prussian philosopher H. Wolf, a philosopher of the Prussian Police Science Justi, the provisions of an Austrian lawyer Sonnenfels (Zonnenfels in the Russian sources), and the Great Prussian King Frederick II (Fridrikh II in the Russian sources). The concept of the "common good" as an integral part of the theory of the absolute state became a universal dogma in Western Europe in modern times[2]. The category of the "common good" was enshrined in the Bavarian Civil Code of 1756, the French Declarations of the Rights of the Man and Citizen of 1791 and 1793, and the Prussian Zemstvo Code of 1794. The "common good" as a category in the Russian Empire was reflected in the translated works of D. Nettelbladt, J. Bielfeld, and C. Beccaria. According to M. A. Reisner, many Russian compositions were "heavily influenced by the same theory[3]." The "common good" was one of the central themes in the works of Z. A. Goryushkin, N. M. Karamzin, and P. N. Gulyaev. Following M. A. Reisner, the doctrine of the "common good" was the theory that had become the legal basis of the political system[4]. Nevertheless, noting the existence of the abuse of the term "common good" in political practice, M. A. Reisner defined the "common good" as "that which is determined by natural law, this good is normal, reasonable, and moral." According to him, the good includes safety, health, free using the results of one's labor, the good of the family heart and marital happiness, and the good of religious, moral, and mental education[5].

---

[1] V. S. Nersesyants "The Philosophy of Law." A textbook for high schools. - M.: INFRA Publishing Group • M - NORMA, 1997. Page 70.
[2] M. A. Reisner "The 'common good' and the absolute state"//The Bulletin of Law: The Magazine of the Legal Society at the Imperial St. Petersburg University. - SPb., 1871-1906. Volume XXXII. 1902, # 9/10 (Nov.-Dec.). Pages 3-6.
[3] M. A. Reisner "The 'common good' and the absolute state..." Page 7.
[4] Ibid. Pages 15-16.
[5] Ibid. Pages 67-68.

Picture 14. A photo of Mikhail Andreevich Reisner (1868-1928). From open sources

John Lilburn (a lieutenant colonel, a participant in the English Revolution, and a leader of Levellers, 1614-1657) used the terms of the "common good" long before their appearance in Russia. John Lilburn argued that people had to use power "by mutual agreement or consent ... for the kind use and good of everyone, and not for the evil, detriment, or harm of anyone[1]." The aim of the law was the "common good" of citizens in this case.

It can be read in the manifesto of the lieutenant colonel of April 14, 1649[2]: "No man is born exclusively for himself or herself, but he or she is bound by the laws of nature (and these laws apply to everyone), the laws of Christianity (we must obey these laws as Christians), and the laws of the state and government to guide our efforts to increase the overall happiness concerning us and others as well[3]." D. Lilbern and his party moved in one main direction: the equalization of people. He declared the need to obtain "a general agreement of all and everyone among all the people in terms of equalization[4]." The manifesto of D. Lilbern, Walvin, Pins, and Overton suggested that the laws adopted by society and the state as a whole "should direct the efforts of people to increase overall happiness" and comply with "God's word," "the law of nature," and "brain[5]." Later, that approach resulted in the teaching of Jeremiah Bentham (Ieremiya Bentam in the Russian sources) (1748-1832) about law as an art of happiness. The main principle of that art was to achieve "the greatest happiness of the greatest number of individuals."

---

[1]The citation was quoted from N. S. Prozorova's "The political and legal views of John Lilburn." Moscow: The State Publishing House of Legal Literature. 1960. - 53 p.

[2] A Manifesto of Lieutenant Colonel John Lilburn / / D. Lilburn "Pamphlets." M.: The state socio-economic publishing house. 1937. Pages 94-107.

[3] Lieutenant Colonel John Lilburn "Manifesto..." Page 94.

[4] Ibid. Page 98.

[5] N. S. Prozorova "The political and legal views of John Lilburn." Moscow: The State Publishing House of Legal Literature. 1960. Page 48.

According to J. Bentham (I. Bentam in the Russian sources), the rights useful for society had to be included in the legislation, and the harmful and useless for people's rights had to be excluded[1].

The philosophers of the Age of Enlightenment (T. Hobbes, D. Locke, P. Holbach, J. Lametrie, and J. J. Rousseau (Zh. Zh. Russo in the Russian sources)) also appealed to the "common good." T. Hobbes placed the social contract based on the state. In his opinion, this social contract was concluded for the "common good[2]." But it should be considered that, according to that philosopher, this agreement was devoid of morality and ethics. The state power of the ruler and parliament was absolutized and unlimited, being limited only by the strength of the state itself[3]. T. Hobbes believed that "sharing the power of the state means destroying it as the divided powers can mutually destroy each other[4]."

D. Locke substantiated the right of people to revolt when the authorities encroach upon freedom, property, and other inalienable natural benefits[5].

Following P. Holbach, the supreme power in society was exercised by "the members that had been chosen by society to express its will, act on its behalf, and direct the activities of all other citizens for the 'common good.'[6]"

J. Lametrie and J. J. Rousseau thought that the "common good" was the goal of public relations: "the wisdom of government, the effectiveness of laws, the incorruptibility of rulers, the trust of people, harmony between all classes and, most importantly, the universal striving for the "common good[7]." According to J. J. Rousseau, the task of any state is the welfare of its citizens. If "the people diminished in number and depleted,"[8] then this is the worst form of government. J. Lametrie and J. J. Rousseau supposed that people had to have a sovereign and indivisible will[9].

---

[1] Something about the legal doctrine of Jeremy Bentham (I. Bentam in the Russian sources): A. N. Ostroukh "Bentham's doctrine of law": A thesis of a Candidate in Legal Sciences: 12.00.01. - Moscow, 2002. - 240 pages.

[2] K. Yu. Milovanov "The legal state in the Philosophical and Historical Discourse of the Age of Enlightenment" // Professional Education and Society, 2019, N# 1. Page 26.

[3] Ibid. Pages 28, 30, 32.

[4] K. Yu. Milovanov "The legal state in the Philosophical and Historical Discourse of the Age of Enlightenment" // Professional Education and Society, 2019, N# 1. Page 31.

[5] Ibid. Page 38.

[6] Quoted from K. Yu. Milovanov's "The legal state in the Philosophical and Historical Discourse of the Age of Enlightenment." Part 2 // Professional Education and Society, 2019, N# 2. Pages 61-62.

[7] Ibid. Page 67.

[8] Ibid. Page 74.

[9] Ibid. Page 68.

According to M. V. Alpatov, G. Mably also considered it important to curb passions and strive for the "common good": "...a historian helps foster a citizen that can serve the public good, educating a patriot, a person of high morality, capable of fighting passions[1]." However, G. Mably excluded religion from this process, allowing universal equality and the overthrow of a government[2].

M.V. Alpatov noted that J. J. Rousseau had presented the historical process in the form of a "relentless regression[3]." Therefore, it is not surprising that his ideas were adopted by Jacobins in France. It is well-known that Jacobins allowed any revolutionary terror.

Russian Freemasons also used the category of the "common good," like the enlighteners that considered the "common good" as the main goal of the state and society. However, as we can see below, they rejected any violent methods of overthrowing power as incompatible with the principles of the "common good." It should be noted that Russian Freemasons allowed peaceful resistance to despotic power. During the armed coup in France in 1789, the ideas of the enlighteners (those ideas were not limited to the theory of the "common good," religion, and the rule of law) resulted in radicalism and pogroms, leading to the "common harm," prolonged wars, and civil disasters. European society paid a high price for those speculative ideas at that time.

Because the "common good" as a category is widespread in science and legislation, being used in various contexts and filled with different meanings by some authors, the authors of this scientific work consider it appropriate to classify varied cases of the wording of this concept in the 17th-19th centuries. That could, in turn, allow us to identify the general patterns of using the "common good."

The authors of this research identified three main types of the "common good" as a category:
1. The "common good" as a goal of society, government, and legislation).
2. The "common good" as an interest of the majority, all and everyone, etc.
3. The "common good" as a method of conflict resolution, decision-making, etc.).

---

[1] M. V. Alpatov "Russian historical thought and Western Europe (the XVIII - the first half of the XIX centuries)." [Text] / M. A. Alpatov. - Moscow: Nauka, 1985. Pages 91-92.
[2] It should be noted that such an approach was incompatible with the ideals of English, Prussian, and Russian Freemasonry.
[3] M. V. Alpatov "Russian historical thought and Western Europe (the XVIII - the first half of the XIX centuries)" [Text] / M. A. Alpatov. - Moscow: Nauka, 1985. Pages 95-96.

Depending on the context in which the category “common good” is used, we can get an opportunity to define the content of the category in the historical context more accurately.

The origins of the theory of the "common good" in Russia

Hugo Grotius (a Dutch lawyer, an advocate, and a Doctor of Law, 1583-1645) was one of the first authors known in Russia to use the principle of the "common good." The following works were translated into Russian in the 18th century: "Hugo Grotius interpreted, or Hugona Grotsia on the right of war and peace, three books abridged before, and now they were issued in full, with the privilege of His Imperial Majesty, in Gray, by Johann Adam Pleneur, the type of Daniel Shtarkia, 1693" (translated from Latin into Russian by Ivan Sagarov in 1748)[1]; "Reasoning against atheists and neutralists" (translated from Latin by Amvrosy (A. S. Zertis-Kamensky) and published in 1765)[2]; "True Christian piety: Proved against the godless, pagans, Jews, and Mahometans" (translated by Peter Alexiev, an ecclesiarch of the Moscow Big Uspensky Cathedral in 1768)[3].

Hugo Grotius (Gugo Grotsy in the Russian sources) considered the "common good" as the goal of owning things, the goal of punishing the criminal[4], the goal of limiting rights ("for the 'common good'")[5], the goal of government ("the good of government is the happiness of its subjects"; "the ruler has a duty to care more for the good of the whole, rather than about the good of the parts")[6], the purpose of concluding and fulfilling an agreement[7] and a motive of the citizens' behavior ("love often inspires and, sometimes, commands to prefer the good of many people to the personal good")[8], as interest (the author refers "the open sea," "greater good," "benefit," "virtue," "life" to the "common good")[9], as a method of decision-making: it is necessary to avoid the actions having the consequences that

---

[1] G. Hugo Grotius "Grotius Interpreted, or Hugon Grotius on the Law of War and Peace, three books abridged before, and now they were issued in full, with the privilege of His Imperial Majesty, in Gray, by Johann Adam Plener." Printed in the printing house of Daniil Shtarkia, 1693 [manuscript]: original / translated from Latin into Russian by Ivan Sagarov. - 1748. - 112 pages.

[2] G. Grotius "Reasoning against atheists and neutralists" / Translated from Latin [by Ambrose (A. S. Zertis-Kamensky)]. - Moscow: Printed in the Senate Printing House, 1765. - [2], 66 p., the 2nd edition was released at the Novikov Printing House in 1881.

[3] G. Grotius "True Christian piety: Proven against atheists, pagans, Jews, and Mohammedans" / Translated by Peter Aleksiev, an ecclesiarch of the Moscow Big Uspensky Cathedral. - [Moscow]: Printed at The Imperial Moscow University, 1768. - [20], 220 p.

[4] Hugo Grotius "On the Law of War and Peace": A reprint from the edition of 1956 - M.: Ladomir, 1994. Pages 69, 102.

[5] Ibid. Page 368.

[6] Ibid. Pages 161, 559.

[7] Ibid. Pages 561, 765.

[8] Ibid. Page 191.

[9] Ibid. Pages 216, 363, 474, 551-552.

can be foreseen, "if the good (our action is directed towards) insignificantly exceeds the evil that should be feared, or if the hope of achieving the good with the equality of the good and evil exceed the fear of evil a little bit." The choice must be made prudently so that, "in case of doubt, this choice will always lean in the direction that is more beneficial to another person than to himself or herself[1]." A. A. Pavlov (a modern researcher of the creative heritage of H. Grotius) noted that Grotius' concept of law "is based on the idea of the good (benefit) of an individual, the state, and the world community[2]."

In addition to the works of G. Grotius, the common European scientific paradigm of the first half of the 18th century included the creative legacy of an encyclopedist, philosopher, and lawyer Christian Freiherr von Wolff (1679-1754). O. A. Omelchenko noted that "the initial and key concept of Wolff's political philosophy (that philosophy became main for the new state idea as well)[3] was the idea of the 'common good'"[4] (italics supplied by O. A. Omelchenko). According to C. Wolff, the "common good" is the achievement of "the greatest happiness that every person could enjoy on the Earth under his or her condition"[5] (italics supplied by O. A. Omelchenko). For this reason, the best ruler on the throne will be a philosopher that will search for the "common good" and ensure the happiness of his or her subjects.

Another well-known in Russia popular author of the theory of the "common good" was a German legal theorist, historian, and philosopher Samuel Freiherr von Pufendorf (1632-1694). He wrote many works, and some of them should be mentioned: "The Elements of Universal Jurisprudence" (1661), "Natural and Popular Law" (1672), and "On the duties of man and a citizen according to the Natural Law" (1673) (that book was translated into Russian by order of Peter I and published in 1726)[6].

---

[1] Hugo Grotius "On the Law of War and Peace." Page 579.

[2] A. A. Pavlov "The legal concept of Hugo Grotius": An abstract of the thesis of a Candidate in Legal Sciences: 12.00.01 / The North-West Academy of the State Services. - St. Petersburg, 2002. Page 8.

[3] By talking about the new state idea, O. A. Omelchenko, first of all, means enlightened absolutism. His thesis having the same name was devoted to it.

[4] O. A. Omelchenko "The Monarchy of Enlightened Absolutism in Russia: Political Doctrine, Legal Policy, State Reforms": A thesis of a Ph.D. in Legal Sciences. - Moscow, 2001. Page 61.

[5] A citation was quoted from: O. A. Omelchenko "The Monarchy of Enlightened Absolutism in Russia: Political Doctrine, Legal Policy, State Reforms": A thesis of a Ph.D. in Legal Sciences. - Moscow, 2001. Page 62.

[6] S. Pufendorf "On the duties of man and a citizen according to the natural law": Translated into Russian by V. M. Kruglov in 1726: in 2 volumes. Volume I. - St. Petersburg: Nestor-History, 2011. - 214 p.

The structure of the book "On the duties of man and a citizen according to the Natural Law" is remarkable: after the chapters about the duties, general and natural law, there are the chapters "On the duties of man to God ...," "On the duties of man to himself or herself...," and "On the duties of man to other people, society, and the state[1]." The order of presentation means that the theory of S. Pufendorf is based on the concept of human "duties" that should be understood as "human actions under the force of obligation to the laws of good[2]." In S. Pufendorf's opinion, the law is "a decree or a directive, and, by using this instruction, the supervisor obliges his or her subordinate to coordinate his or her actions according to this charter[3]." The duty is "a union of law that should be followed to fulfill the commandment if need be[4]." The "common good" is derived from the general natural law and is the goal of human duty. And this aim is usefulness to society ("fellowship")[5]. According to the natural law, "nobody should harm another person, but, on the contrary, everyone should take care of another person's use and benefit[6]." Even though man as an animal loves his or her benefit most of all, "a person foresaw some benefit from the civil friendship[7]." A striking example of the "common good" as an interest is to help the "natural human condition" of a child that "would die without the help of others" but that is raised and trained by society for the "common good[8]." The content of the general benefit as interest also includes the preservation of faith, the fulfillment of promises, and the execution of contracts. And "the major portion of the benefit will perish without all of the above-mentioned because the benefit occurs from the mutually created actions in the human race[9]." An example of the "common harm" is the perjury of people in court based on friendship, hatred, revenge, and dependence[10].

The opposite of man as an animal striving for his or her benefit is man as a citizen ("Civil or Political animal," "good citizen"). A good citizen is one that "strives for the common benefit and good with all his or her might" and prefers the general benefit to his or her use; when performing any actions for his or her benefit, he or she foresees to provide "the benefit of all citizenship" and other

---

[1] It is worth noting a significant similarity between the main provisions of the subsequent political and legal literature and the charters of Masonic Lodges in Russia in the 18th century with the structure of presentation proposed by S. Pufendorf in the 17th century.
[2] S. Pufendorf "On the duties of man and a citizen according to the Natural Law." Page 19.
[3] Ibid. Page 31.
[4] Ibid. Page 32.
[5] Ibid. Page 41.
[6] Ibid. Page 141.
[7] Ibid. Page 156.
[8] Ibid. Page 137.
[9] Ibid. Page 83.
[10] Ibid. Page 141.

citizens' benefit by these acts.[1] To achieve the "common good" as an interest, everybody must coordinate his or her "will" with the "will of all and everyone."[2] S. Pufendorf used the "common good" as a method to determine the usefulness of any teaching: "...any human teaching that is futile and vain <...> and gives no human or civil benefit" should not be applied[3].

Feofan Prokopovich (1681-1736) and Vasily Nikitich Tatishchev (1686-1750) took up the theory of the "common good" at the beginning of the 18th century in Russia. F. Prokopovich was known as a Russian writer on theology, philosophy, law, and pedagogy, philosopher, the first Vice-President of the Holy Governing Synod (from 1721), and Archbishop of Novgorod (from 1725). He reflected his views on the state and law in his work "The Truth of the Monarch Will" (1722). V. N. Tatishchev (a Russian historian, geographer, philosopher, lawyer, and statesman) created works that traced his state and legal views: "The Spiritual of Vasily Nikitich Tatishchev" (1733-1734), "A conversation about the benefits of sciences and schools" (1733-1736), and "A discourse on state government" (1746-1750). F. Prokopovich and V. N. Tatishchev were united by European education and the use of secular rhetoric. Both studied and lived abroad among different cultures and religions for a long time: F. Prokopovich lived in Poland, German Duchies, Prussia, and the Papal region, and V. N. Tatishchev resided in the Czech Republic, German Duchies, Prussia, Sweden, and Denmark.

As for F. Prokopovich, he tried to combine a principle of the absolute and unlimited power of a Monarch and the theory of the "common good." Therefore, the Monarch in his works was limited only by divine law, had to have some positive moral qualities, and strive for the "common good."[4] A special case of this rule is the possibility and obligation of the Monarch to change the heir in certain cases[5]. After the Monarchs took the throne, his subjects (F. Prokopovich used the term "subjects") were obliged to endure his abuses to avoid the "common harm[6]."

Considering the works of V. N. Tatishchev, it can be noted that they mainly contain a simplified and abbreviated presentation of the concept of the "common good" of S. Pufendorf. This reduction does not contain any definitions of the concepts. But the author assimilated the main idea: the importance of combining wills, limited by love and a contract. All citizens must fulfill their estate duties for the "common good" according to that agreement[7]. A ruler, on the other

---

[1] S. Pufendorf "On the duties of man and a citizen according to the Natural Law." Page 157.

[2] Ibid. Pages 161-162.

[3] Ibid. Page 212.

[4] F. Prokopovich "The truth of a Monarch's will". M., August 07, 1722. Pages 1, 15, 18, 22, 29, 30.

[5] Ibid. Pages 27-30, 37, 41, 59.

[6] Ibid. Pages 31, 32.

[7] V. N. Tatishchev "The Spiritual of Vasily Nikitich Tatishchev". - Leipzig: Wolfgang Gerhard, 1862. Pages 25, 27;

hand, must take care of the benefits and peace of citizens, pass the laws, and rule according to the divine rules[1]. V. N. Tatishchev noted that there was also some reasoning about the need to have an absolute rule and autocracy for a large territory[2].

The new authors that worked in line with the concept of the "common good" gained fame in Russia in the middle of the 18th century: J. F. Bielfeld (Ya. F. Bilfeld in the Russian sources) and J. G. Justi. Jakob Friedrich von Bielfeld (1716-1770) was a German economist, lawyer, statesman, and adviser to the Prussian King Frederick the Great. He was made (ordained) a Freemason in Hamburg in 1737. J. F. Bielfeld published "The Political Directions" ("Institutions politiques," 1760) in French. The book "The Political Directions" was translated into Russian by the decree of Catherine II by Prince Fyodor Shakhovsky and Professor Anton Barsov[3]. Johann Heinrich Gottlieb von Justi (1717-1771) was a German economist, lawyer, professor, and Prussian minister. The following works of his should be mentioned: "The Plan for Good Government" (1759), "The Foundations of the Power and Bliss of States" (1760-1761), and "The Principles of Police Science" (1782). Avraham Volkov translated his work "An Essential Image of the Nature of People's Societies and All Kinds of Laws[4]." Then that book became widespread in Russia. When creating the Order on drawing up a draft of a new code in 1767, Catherine II was guided by his works.

Some analysis of the works of scientists shows that the commonplace is the concept of the "common good" and the good of everyone. This idea says that the "common good" can be achieved only if the good of everyone can be realized. The "common good" is understood as the unification of wills by limiting the private wills within reasonable limits. Scientists demonstrate to us a principle of the unity of power, society, and even the concepts understood by them as homogeneous entities. This principle is opposed to the principle of power-sharing.

V. N. Tatishchev "A conversation between two friends about the benefits of science and schools" / / Tatishchev V. Collected Works: in 8 volumes (in 5 books): Book. 5/Volume 7. Russian history. Volume 8. The selected works: M.: Ladomir, 1996. Pages 83-85, 86, 111, 117, 121, 122, 128.

[1] V. N. Tatishchev "A conversation between two friends about the benefits of science and schools" / / V. N. Tatishchev "The collected Works": in 8 volumes (in 5 books): Book. 5/ V.7. Russian history. Volume 8. The selected works: A reprint from the edition of 1968, 1979 - M.: Ladomir, 1996. Pages 51-132. Pages 85, 86, 117, 119, 124, 125.

[2] V. N. Tatishchev "The arbitrary and consensual reasoning and opinion of the assembled Russian gentry about state government"// V. Tatishchev "The collected works": in 8 volumes. Volume 8. - M.: Ladomir, 1996. Page 147.

[3] Ya. F. Bielfeld "The Instructions of a Political Baron Bielfeld." M.: Printed at the Imperial Moscow University, 1768-1775. Part 1. 1768. - 462 p.; Part 2. 1775. - 498 p.

[4] J. G. Justi "An essential depiction of the nature of folk societies and all kinds of laws" / Composed by Mr. Justi; translated from German into Russian by Avraam Volkov. - M.: Published at the Imperial Moscow University, 1770. - 384 pages.

An important part of the general concept is the principle of fulfilling the obligations of both the subjects (citizens) and the ruler himself or herself. This, in turn, is the basis of the state and leads to the general benefit. Of course, if mutual obligations are not fulfilled, morals will be destroyed, and an inevitable fall of the state will occur. The morals and mutual obligations are strengthened by observing the following three types of laws: divine law, natural human law, and positive human law. The "common good" can be achieved by the implementation of these laws.

J. F. Bielfeld modernized the concept of the "common good." The "common good" as interest includes a "natural inclination" to prolong life and to "make your condition as good as possible[1]." This is the basis of politics. J. F. Bielfeld explained the connection between the whole and the private will. He singled out 25 reasons for the fall of the state, and a decline in morals was only one of many reasons[2]. To substantiate the integrity of state power, the author used the concept of "the unity of the circle.[3]" A sovereign there was a member of civil society that was obliged to love citizens and make them prosperous. The strength and reason for this were rooted in awareness and self-love. According to the concept of J. F. Bielfeld, a Sovereign must obey the requirements of natural and popular law, especially in the matter of the order of succession to the throne, as well as fulfill the agreements concluded by him or her[4]. An innovation of the concept was the substantiation of the possibility of regicide[5]: a tyrant on the throne can be killed for the good of the Fatherland (in fact, this provision of the concept theoretically explains the future assassination of Paul I that, according to his contemporaries, was a tyrant and interfered with the personal life of his subjects).

---

[1] J. F. Bielfeld "The instructions of a political Baron Bielfeld" / Translated from French into Russian by Collegiate Adviser and Eloquence Professor Anton Barsov. Part 2. - M.: Printed at the Imperial Moscow University, 1775. Page 124.

[2] Ibid. Page 467.

[3] J. F. Bielfeld "The instructions of a political Baron Bielfeld" / Translated from French into Russian by Collegiate Adviser and Eloquence Professor Anton Barsov. Part 2. - M.: Printed at the Imperial Moscow University, 1775. Page 460.

[4] Ibid. Pages 34, 46.

[5] Ibid. Page 485.

Picture 15. A frontispiece of the book by J. F. Bielfeld, "The Political Instructions of Baron Bielfeld" Part 1. M.: 1768.

Picture 16. A vignette of the table of contents of the book by J. F. Bielfeld, "The political Instructions of Baron Bilfeld" Part 2. M.: 1775.

Johann Heinrich Gottlob von Justi (J. G. von Justi) (I. G. von Yusti in the Russian sources) considered the concept of the "moral connection of wills" - a more developed abstraction[1]. The union of wills serves for "the 'common good,' the well-being of everyone and every kin[2]." According to J. G. von Justi, the "common good" included the only sources of natural law: "the urge to self-preservation, self-love, the multiplication of one's kin, love for children, the desire for pleasant pleasures, the aversion of disgusting and painful sensations, love for the delightful feelings that are given us by some people (we can see it in the children's love for the caregivers)[3]." The author deciphered the "common good" in even more detail, comprehending the "common good" as the desire of everyone for the well-being of everyone. J. G. Justi developed an additional provision saying that the good of all is equal to the good of everyone (these concepts in his interpretation were interrelated and interdependent)[4]. The scientist noted that "... the assurance of one's good is the only basis for obedience for a rational being" as "… the well-being of his or her being touches him or her more than the well-being

[1]J. G. Justi "An essential depiction of the nature of popular societies and all kinds of laws." - M.: Published at the Imperial Moscow University, 1770. Pages 29-30.
[2] Ibid. Pages 37.
[3] Ibid. Pages 243-244.
[4] Ibid. Pages 39, 47.

of another being[1]." The laws that "do not have this intention are not true." And they are "torture orders" aimed at the ruler's welfare[2]. The author categorically denies despotism (when a ruler allows the most severe injustices for the sake of his or her good). J. G. Justi noted that after everyone achieves his or her good, the "common good" is achieved, too. Therefore, every citizen was obliged to take care of both his or her own and the "common good" as well. To avoid abuse and to achieve the prosperity of his or her subjects and the monarch himself or herself, the monarch had to impose some restrictions on himself or herself[3]. This provision contradicts the concepts of an absolute and police state. The predecessors of J. G. Justi did not have this provision at all.

François Quesnay (Fransua Kyone in the Russian sources) (1694-1774) was a French economist and a member of the Paris Academy and the Royal Society of London. His ideas were practically unknown in Russia. Also, his books were not translated into Russian. However, the thoughts of François Quesnay in the presentation of Luzac's commentary on the Amsterdam editions of Montesquieu[4] were read by Empress Catherine II before her drawing up the "The instruction given to the commission on composing a draft of a new code[5]." The philosopher's ideas could be reflected in her political and legal worldview.

François Quesnay explained how to achieve the benefit of all and everyone. Confirming the possibility of the "stronger" becoming the head of the family, F. Quesnay denied the possibility of appropriating the "stronger" any natural rights of other people. The natural rights, in this case, are not destroyed but are subject to the order of "distributive justice" associated with the natural obligations and cooperation, "in which everyone contributes to the best of his ability to the 'common good." F. Quesnay noted that even though "everyone contributes in his or her way, but the occupations of one person serve to facilitate the occupation of another person," and "due to this mutual support, everyone contributes to the benefit of society almost to the same extent." Based on such cooperation, "everyone must use the entire totality of his or her natural rights under the prosperity that follows from the combination of social labor[6]."

---

[1] J. G. Justi "An essential depiction of the nature of popular societies and all kinds of laws." - M.: Published at the Imperial Moscow University, 1770. Pages 40, 251.
[2] Ibid. Pages 41, 233.
[3] Ibid. Pages 42, 75, 76, 78, 198, 199.
[4] O. A. Omelchenko "The Monarchy of Enlightened Absolutism in Russia: Political Doctrine, Legal Policy, State Reforms": A thesis of a Ph.D. in Legal Sciences. - Moscow, 2001. P. 111.
[5] V. A. Tomsinov "The Russian jurists of the 18th-20th centuries": The essays on life and work. In 2 volumes. M.: Zertsalo, 2007. Volume 1. P. 70.
[6] F. Quesnay "Natural Law" // F. Quesnay, A. R. J. Turgot, P. S. du Pont de Nemours "Physiocrats." The selected economic works / F. Quesnay, A. R. J. Turgot, P. S. du Pont de

Catherine II used the ideas of an Italian scientist, jurist, and philosopher Cesare Beccaria Bonezana (1738-1794), utilizing his notions as the basis for her famous Order. The "common good" in the book "On Crimes and Punishments" (that book was first translated into Russian under the Imperial Command in 1803)[1] was shown as the result of a social contract between the people and a sovereign that "became its legal guardian and manager[2]." The author supposed that the opposition of the "public good" and "the single good of each of the individuals separately" is a false concept[3]. Bad legislation forces some people to harm others, while good legislation aims for the "common good" and benefits "every citizen in particular[4]."

Charles Louis de Montesquieu (Sharl' Lui de Montesqyo in the Russian sources) (1689-1755) wrote many works. The "common good" in his works was also one of the main themes. Catherine II took up to 80% of the thoughts for her Order from his writings. Several of Charles Louis de Montesquieu's works were published in Russian in Russia in the 18th century: "The reflections on the causes of the majesty of the Roman people and their decline" (1769)[5], "Lysimachus" (1769), "The Temple of Cnidia" (1770), "On the Reason of Laws" (1775)[6], and "Persian Letters" (editions of 1789 and 1792). The author in his book "On the Reason of Laws" saw his calling in the prosperity of all people: "If I could do so that all people have some new reasons to love their duty, Sovereign, Fatherland,

---

Nemours; a foreword by P. N. Klyukin. Translated from French, English, and German into Russian by P. N. Klyukin. - M.: Eksmo, 2008. Pages 334-335.

[1] C. Beccaria "A discourse on Crimes and Punishments" / Translated from Italian into French by Andrei Morellet and from French into Russian by Dmitry Yazykov. With the addition of Diderot's notes and the writer's correspondence with Morellet. Published by His Highest Imperial Majesty's order. - In St. Petersburg: Under the Provincial Government, 1803. - XLIV, 268 p.

[2] On crimes and punishments. Translated from Italian into Russian / C. Beccaria. Compiled by M. Yu. Yumashev. Translated by Yu. M. Marinin and G. V. Cherdantsev. – The 5th edition (revised and enlarged). - M.: Stealth, 1995. Page 67.

[3] Ibid. Page 227.

[4] S. I. Zarudny "Beccaria on crimes and punishments in comparison with Chapter X of the Order of Catherine II and with modern Russian Laws": The materials for developing, comparing, and studying the theory and practice of Criminal Legislation / A collection of the works of S. Zarudny. - St. Petersburg: Printed in the Printing House of the Second Division of His Imperial Majesty's Own Chancellery, 1879. Pages 152, 153.

[5] Ch. L. Montesquieu "The reflections on the causes of the majesty of the Roman people and its decline" / Translated from French into Russian by Alexey Polenov. - St. Petersburg: Under the Imperial Academy of Sciences, 1769. - [8], 315, [2] p.

[6] On the Reason of Laws / The composition of Mr. Montesquia. Translated from French into Russian by Vasily Kramarenkov. - St. Petersburg: Under the Imperial Academy of Sciences, 1775.- Volume 1. - 1775. - [2], XXXIV, 424 p.

laws and can better feel their bliss in every land, every government, every place anyone is located now, then I would consider myself the happiest of mortals[1]."

Picture 17. Charles Louis de Montesquieu (1689-1755). A frontispiece of the book by Ch. L. Montesquieu, "On the essence of laws." Published by Vasily Sopikov. - Moscow, 1809 - 1814. Part 1. - XLVI, 310 pages.

Ch. L. Montesquieu pointed out in another place of his book that honor as the mainspring of government under monarchical rule leads to the "common good": "while thinking to keep in mind his or her good only, everyone strives for the public good[2]."

Thus, it can be concluded that the theory of the "common good" has its own ancient and medieval history. It was realized in political theory, some diplomatic correspondence, legal texts, laws, the opinions of lawyers, and the projects of reforms. The theory of the "common good" became a universal dogma in Western Europe in modern times. The theory of the "common good" contains a legal model for identifying, agreeing, recognizing, and protecting various interests, claims, and wills of the members of society. The theory of the "common good" spread in Russia by the end of the 18th century thanks to the translations of the works of G. Grotius, S. F. Pufendorf, J. G. Justi, and J. F. Bielfeld into Russian. This theory took root in Russian legal thought due to the efforts of F. Prokopovich and V. N. Tatishchev. According to this theory, the "common good" as a category started being considered as a goal of the possession of things, the punishment of a criminal, the restriction of rights, rule, the conclusion of a contract, and the execution of a contract, as interest ("open sea," "virtues," "life," "the preservation of faith," "keeping promises," "fulfilling contracts," "well-being," etc.), and as a method when making decisions. The "common harm" as an extremely negative

[1] Ch. L. Montesquieu "On the essence of laws" / The creation of Mr. Montesquieu. On the essence of laws. Part 1: The creation of Montesquieu. M.: Sopikov, 1809. Pages V-VI.

[2] Ch. L. Montesquieu "The Spirit of Laws": The creation of the famous French writer de Montescu: in 3 parts / Translated by E. Karneev. A foreword by E. Karneev. Parts 1-3. - St. Petersburg: The printing house of N. Grech, 1839. – in 3 volumes. Page 46.

phenomenon was opposite to the "common good." Following S. F. Pufendorf, V. N. Tatishchev, J. F. Bielfeld, and J. G. Justi, a person guided by the theory of the "common good" had to direct his or her actions towards his or her good for the benefit of "all citizenship" and other citizens, coordinating his or her will with the will of others and, if necessary, limiting it. The same principle acted on a ruler (Sovereign). In other words, a regent had to either behave absolutely (F. Prokopovich) or impose restrictions on himself or herself (J. G. Justi). The "common good" could be achievable only if the good of everyone could be realized (Ch. L. Montesquieu). According to J. G. Justi and C. Beccaria, the value of the "common good" was equal to the good of everyone, and they did not contradict each other.

F. Quesnay supposed that the "common good" could be achieved by "distributive justice" associated with natural obligations and cooperation to the best of one's abilities. The legislation that considers the good of all and everyone is good, and, on the contrary, the legislation that does not take it into account is bad and "torture" (C. Beccaria and J. G. Justi).

§2.2. The domestic theory of the welfare of all and everyone

The concept and basic provisions of the well-known theory of the "common good" in Russia (created by the leaders of Western Europe) were considered in the previous paragraph. F. Prokopovich and V. N. Tatishchev were also mentioned as the domestic followers of the theory of the "common good." The theory of the "common good" became well-known in the Russian Empire as the theory of the welfare of all and everyone. It can be concluded by the name of the theory that the basic provisions of the "common good" (known to Western Europe) were preserved by the domestic theory. This paragraph will discuss the interpretation of these provisions in domestic legal thought.

V. N. Tatishchev was one of the first to take into consideration the category of the "common good" (the common use). He entrusted in his work "Dukhovnaya" (compiled in 1733): "when servicing an Emperor and the State, you must be faithful and diligent; when fulfilling any affairs assigned to you, you should take care of the 'common good' like dealing with your good[1]." V. N. Tatishchev, in his work "The conversation about the benefits of sciences and schools" (1733), shows "the necessity of teaching and the benefits of science for the state, in general," and "for every class, in particular[2]." He considers the interests of the state as the "common good" and the interests of every class as the good of everyone. Some attention should also be paid to the certain language construction "for ..., in general" and "for ..., in particular." It will be repeated in many works of Russian thinkers, prose, poetry, and legislation.

M. V. Lomonosov (1711-1765), in his "Letter to I. I. Shuvalov on the Use of Glass," placed the following lines: "As the 'common good' to the Fatherland is the insight, this teaching should be expanded into the seas[3]." M. V. Lomonosov, in his letter to I. I. Shuvalov, refers to the "common good" as the goal of creativity: "Analyzing my writings, I found some old notes of my thoughts extending to the increment of the 'common good'"[4]. It can be read in the next sentence of the letter: "Upon considering, I judged myself for good...." This phrase logically results from

---

[1]V. N. Tatishchev "The Spiritual of Vasily Nikitich Tatishchev." - Leipzig, 1862. Page 25.

[2] The materials for studying the works of Tatishchev. I. The talk about the benefits of sciences and schools. (A statement of the content according to the article by K. N. Bestuzhev-Ryumin). // Vasily Nikitich Tatishchev. 1685-1750. - St. Petersburg: I. Glazunov, 1896. Page 54.

[3] M. V. Lomonosov "A letter about the benefits of glass to I. I. Shuvalov" // The works of M. V. Lomonosov. - Petrograd: Kopeyka, [1916]. Pages 33-43. Page 43.

[4] M. V. Lomonosov (1711-1765) "A letter from the late Mikhail Vasilyevich Lomonosov to Ivan Ivanovich Shuvalov": From the Magazine of Ancient and Modern Literature published by Mr. Olin. - St. Petersburg: The printing house of the Department of Public Education, 1819. Page 2.

the author's desire for the "common good." It is necessary to memorize this speech turnover "judged for the good" as it will be repeated in many official business letters and legislative acts in Russia in the 18th – the first quarter of the 19th centuries. M. V. Lomonosov, in his letter "On the reproduction and preservation of Russian people" (1761), to me I. Shuvalov also referred to the adherence to the "common good," noting the need for "some correction of morals[1]." It can also be read in Lomonosov's work "From the praiseworthy words to Peter the Great" (1755): "... the great benefit comes to a person and the whole state from a curious journey to the foreign lands[2]." P. I. Shuvalov (a Field Marshal General, Conference Minister, and Senator, 1711-1762) clarified the idea of the "common good." In his opinion, the welfare of the state follows from the nationwide benefit: if the people are oppressed, then the state bears losses: "the death of the people and harm to the state" is inseparable[3]. K. D. Bugrov[4] pointed out that the category of the "common good" (common use) was also used in the works of other domestic scientists: F. G. Strube (Shtrube in the Russian sources) de Pyrmont (1704-1776), V. K. Tredyakovsky (1703-1769), and P. I. Rychkov (1712-1777).

The Russian theory of the welfare of all and everyone was developed by the following scientists of the 18th – the first quarter of the 19th centuries. Professor of General History of Moscow University Johann Gottfried Reichel (1727-1778) defined the goal of the well-being of all and everyone ("the well-being of all, in general, and everyone, in particular") as universal and individual happiness: "to make all and everyone happy[5]." He considered the following benefits: internal and external security, "the preservation and multiplication of

---

[1]M. V. Lomonosov "On the reproduction and preservation of the Russian people" // The selected philosophical works / M. V. Lomonosov. Edited by G. S. Vasetsky. A preface by G. S. Vasetsky. - [Moscow]: Gospolitizdat, 1950. Page 598.

[2] M. V. Lomonosov "From a word of praise to Peter the Great" / / The selected Philosophical Works. Page 494.

[3] O. A. Omelchenko "The Monarchy of Enlightened Absolutism in Russia: Political Doctrine, Legal Policy, State Reforms": A thesis of a Ph.D. in Legal Sciences. - Moscow, 2001. Page 71.

[4] K. D. Bugrov "The Natural Law and Virtue: the integration of European influence into the Russian political culture of the 18th Century". 2016. Pages 216, 227, 266.

[5] A convolute. The flourishing state and glory of Russia following the heroic virtues of Her Autocrat: On the celebrated-on June 30, 1772, ten-year triumph of the prosperous reign of the August Monarch of the Great Sovereign Catherine II, Empress and Autocrat of All Russia, and so on at the public meeting held in the Imperial Moscow University / With the deepest zeal, an orator John Gottfried Reichel, Professor of History, Public Ordinary Librarian, Secretary of the University conference, a member of Leipzig Scientist Society. Translated from Latin by Teacher of History Khariton Chebotarev. - [Moscow]: Printed at the Imperial Moscow University, [1772]. Page 8.

common use and benefits," the approval of laws, the poll tax, the development of sciences and arts, the upbringing of children, etc[1]. Achieving these benefits does not happen "by chance" and not "by itself yourself," but it is "the result of great works and zeal for the 'common good[2].'" According to J. G. Reichel, the "common good" was the Fatherland (a city, a region, a country, and the place of residence)[3]. At the same time, J. G. Reichel argued that thought about the "common good" should be a criterion for all actions of citizens: "Do their private and own benefits agree with the common welfare or are they pernicious and harmful to it?[4]." Citizens themselves considered the "great ranks," "wealth," "lust for power," "luxurious life and its delights," "idleness," "laziness," etc., as personal good. The desires of citizens were immoderate and fickle. These wishes could not fulfill their whims in the pursuit of imaginary happiness.

Therefore, they needed a boss - the Sovereign that "will know and understand better than everyone else" what is the "common good" and the good of everyone. This Monarch could apply "the most appropriate and effective means" to preserve and increase wealth and, finally, make all and everyone happy[5]. J. G. Reichel proved that the "common good" needed the work and zeal for the well-

---

[1] A convolute. The flourishing state and glory of Russia following the heroic virtues of Her Autocrat: On the celebrated-on June 30, 1772, ten-year triumph of the prosperous reign of the August Monarch of the Great Sovereign Catherine II, Empress and Autocrat of All Russia, and so on at the public meeting held in the Imperial Moscow University / With the deepest zeal, an orator John Gottfried Reichel, Professor of History, Public Ordinary Librarian, Secretary of the University conference, a member of Leipzig Scientist Society. Translated from Latin by Teacher of History Khariton Chebotarev. - [Moscow]: Printed at the Imperial Moscow University, [1772]. Pages 6, 11, 12.

[2] A convolute. The flourishing state and glory of Russia following the heroic virtues of Her Autocrat: On the celebrated-on June 30, 1772, ten-year triumph of the prosperous reign of the August Monarch of the Great Sovereign Catherine II, Empress and Autocrat of All Russia, and so on at the public meeting held in the Imperial Moscow University / With the deepest zeal, an orator John Gottfried Reichel, Professor of History, Public Ordinary Librarian, Secretary of the University conference, a member of Leipzig Scientist Society. Translated from Latin by Teacher of History Khariton Chebotarev. - [Moscow]: Printed at the Imperial Moscow University, [1772]. Page 12.

[3] A Convolute. A word about how the ancients aroused in the citizens love for the Fatherland: On the highly solemn birthday of the August Monarch of the Great Sovereign Catherine II, Empress and Autocrat of All Russia, and so on, celebrated with the deepest reverence at the Imperial Moscow University on April 22, 1775 / Spoken by Johann Gottfried Reichel, a Public Ordinary Professor of History. Translated from Latin by a University Sublibrarian Khariton Chebotarev. - M.: Published at the University Printing House, [1775]. Pages 5, 6.

[4] A Convolute. The blooming state and glory of Russia... Page 7.

[5] Ibid. Pages 7-8.

being of the people, in general, and that citizens often had the opposite interests. Therefore, every citizen had to coordinate his or her interests with the interests of other citizens, and everybody also needed a ruler that could take care of the "common good."

Zakhary Anikeevich Goryushkin (1748-1821), a lawyer and Professor of law at Moscow University, wrote in his "Guide to the Study of Russian Law Art...": "the pretext of autocratic rule is not taking away people's natural freedom but directing their actions towards receiving the greatest good from all people." Z. A. Goryushkin, in his book, reproduced and developed the provisions of the Commission's Order on drawing up a new code of Catherine II. So, he thought that the state law contained "the regulations prescribing the certain means that could be used for achieving the well-being of all and everyone, especially for the people living under these Laws" (paragraph 2152). The state law consisted of general and specific (civil) law. General law constituted "the common benefit of peoples" - "the body of the State" "for the preservation of the integrity, good order, and silence of the State[1]."

Z. A. Goryushkin supposed that well-being from liberty and well-being from any autocratic rule could be equalized ("many great deeds promote the well-being of a Monarch's subjects"). The aim of any autocratic rule was the well-being and "happiness of a Sovereign's subjects." Such a government limits the natural liberties "less than others" and "corresponds to the end that is gazed relentlessly in the establishment of civil societies" (The Order of the Commission of the Code. Article 14). "The intention and end of any autocratic rule is the glory of the citizens, the State, and a Sovereign" (Article 15 of the Order)[2]. The author also mentioned the quality of the employees of the "middle government" (Officials). The qualities of an employee of the "middle government" were his or her "work, loyalty, and impartiality" ("the art, hard work, loyalty to the fulfillment of the assigned, good and impartial behavior" that is indicated in the oath)[3].

Z. A. Goryushkin explained that the goal of law and canon was the well-being of all and everyone: "the civil rights and laws can be honored in such ways that everyone living in society and marching steadily for the sake of his or her good could reach that great intention that constitutes the well-being of all and everyone[4]."

---

[1] Z. A. Goryushkin "The guide to the knowledge of Russian Law Art, containing the State Law, the Law of the People, and, finally, the Laws on Animals." Binding 4. M.: Printed at the University Printing House. 1816. Page 1427.

[2] Z. A. Goryushkin "The guide to the knowledge of Russian Law Art." Pages 1430-1431.

[3] Ibid. Page 1438.

[4] Z. A. Goryushkin "The description of judicial actions, or the easiest way to fast obtain the proper knowledge for the administration of the positions in the Judicial Places, especially those

Mikhail Andreevich Balugyansky (1769-1847) came from the noble class of Hungary, studied at the Faculty of Law at the University of Vienna, taught various courses in political science, police, financial, and commercial law at the Faculty of Law of the Civil Academy in Gross-Vardane (Nad'varad, The University of Pest), taught courses in history, law, finance, and statistics was a Ph.D. in Law and Professor at the University of Pest, headed the Department of History, Statistics, Public, and Popular Law, was Dean of the Faculty of Law in Nad'varad. He and P. D. Lodius were invited to Russia to teach in 1803. After coming to the Russian Empire, he received the position of an Ordinary Professor of Political Science, taught courses in political economy, finance, and diplomacy, received a Ph.D. in Law, and was a member of many scientific societies. Mikhail Andreevich Balugyansky worked at the Commission for Drafting Laws for more than 15 years, was a teacher of jurisprudence with the Grand Dukes Nikolai and Mikhail Pavlovich, Dean of the Faculty of Philosophy and Law of the Main Pedagogical Institute, the first Rector of St. Petersburg University), starting from 1819, rose to the rank of Privy Councilor, the Head of the II Department of the Chancellery of His Imperial Majesty, and the position of a Senator. He was also the author of theoretical developments in the system of Russian Law[1].

M. A. Balugyansky, in the article of his book "The National Wealth," defined the "common good" as the sum of all private goods: "Every person knows better what is more useful for him or her from the point of view of economists. However, the benefit of everybody should not contradict the benefit of the state as the 'common good' is nothing more than the sum of all private goods <...> Only the benefit and harm of one's neighbor can be put within the limits of productive activity. The government cannot determine the former, and the latter can be determined by the civil and criminal laws ...[2]."

The theory of the welfare of all and everyone deeply penetrated Russian education in the 18th – the first quarter of the 19th centuries. One of the most prevailing books studied by students of seminaries, universities, and academies was the book "On the position of man and a citizen, a book for reading determined in the public city schools of the Russian Empire, published by the highest

---

that will be used in the Civil Service without having a chance to practice the Domestic Laws." - Moscow: Printed at the University Printing House of Lyubiya, Gariya, and Popov. M., 1807. Page 34.

[1] Russian Freemasons. 1721-2019. A Biographical Dictionary. Century XIX. Volume I // A. I. Serkov, M.: Ganga, 2020. Pages 141-145.

[2] M. A. Balugyansky "The national wealth. An image of various economic systems" // Statistical magazine. SPb., 1806. Volume one. Part 2. Page 62.

command of the reigning Empress Catherine II," by I. I. Felbiger), published for the first time in 1783 at the behest of Catherine II and reprinted many times[1].

The structure of the book consists of the following 4 chapters: Chapter 1, "On the human virtues," Chapter 2, "On the duties to God," Chapter 3, "On the duties to one's neighbor," and Chapter 4 - "On the duties to oneself."

"After acquiring some thorough knowledge of our duties, we must move away from delusions and false opinions as a person possessed by false opinions cannot know the true good and what is useful for him or her. And for this, starting from our very young years, we must learn about ourselves and others, imitate varied kind and honest people, willingly accept various wise instructions, run away from any evil and vicious directions carefully, and intelligently arrange our actions in advance for every day."[2] It should be noted that Russian Freemasons taught the same in the student lodges. J. G. Reichel wrote about the same as well. I. I. Felbiger mentioned in his book that "the best way to counteract pride is to learn oneself[3]." The "common good" was primitivized and mixed with the good of the state in the book. The civil union based on the love of the citizens of different classes for the Fatherland was presented in the most general form. The book popularly reported how this love had to be expressed.

P. M. Zakharyin wrote and published his book "The path to good morality or the Abbreviated Instruction to learning youth, containing the useful and moral rules for every rank and condition of people" in 1793 and 1796[4]. The reader can read there that by using paternal authority and the unification of families, the citizens elected a Sovereign that was entrusted with the care of the "common good." The book consistently reveals the responsibilities of citizens to God, parents, the Supreme Authority, and the bosses determined by it, relatives, teachers, etc.

---

[1] I. I. Felbiger "On the positions of man and a citizen, a book determined for reading in the public city schools of the Russian Empire, published by the highest command of the reigning Empress Catherine II." St. Petersburg, 1783 - 180 pages.

[2] Ibid. Page 16.

[3] Ibid. Page 34.

[4] P. M. Zakharyin "The path to good manners, or an Abbreviated Instruction to learning youth, containing the useful and moralistic rules for every rank and condition of people" / A composition by Peter Zakharyin; Dependent of the Moscow Merchant Semyon Nikiforov. - Moscow: The printing house of A. Reshetnikov, 1796. - [2], VI, 1-64, 69-104 [=100] p.

Picture 18. An Engraving ["Prayer"]. P. M. Zakharyin "The path to good behavior or an Abbreviated Instruction to learning youth," Moscow: A. Reshetnikov's Printing House, 1796. VI, 1-64, 69-104 pages.

As a result, the books of I. I. Felbiger and P. M. Zakharyin became very popular and prevailed in the 18th century. These books presented the interpretation of the theory of the "common good" in a simplified and censored form. According to K. D. Bugrov, these books became the official textbooks of the Russian Empire, and Thomism (obedience to the social role received by a person) was demonstrated there[1]. Following the correct notion of K. D. Bugrov, society, in this case, was represented by "a combination of different groups (warriors, judges, 'teachers' (priests), artisans, and farmers). Every group was associated with the performance of a certain kind of duties <...> Such a view on society was aimed at ensuring that every individual was satisfied with the performance of the 'duties' that had been assigned to him and did not strive for mobility[2]." Russian Freemasonry spread the same ideas. This can be verified further. The theory of the "common good" was not an empty phrase in political thought as well. The terminology of this theory became part of the official business turnover. The "common good" became the "flesh and blood" of bills on the state structure. So, the Statute on the state structure, relating to the period of the reign of Peter III[3], mentioned the "common

[1] K. D. Bugrov "A formation of the ideas of republicanism in the Russian socio-political thought of the XVIII century": An abstract of the thesis of a Ph.D. in Historical Sciences. - Yekaterinburg, 2018. Page 30.

[2] K. D. Bugrov "A formation of the ideas of republicanism in the Russian socio-political thought of the XVIII century": An abstract of the thesis of a Ph.D. in Historical Sciences. - Yekaterinburg, 2018. Page 29.

[3] This is evidenced by the phrase: "La Couronne, qui est le plus haut héritage des Empire, peut descender au demi-sang du dernier Souverain, commes'il a la il le Sang du premier Monarque, car elle est descender de Pierre II a l' Imperatrie Anne et de cette-ci a L'Imperatrie Elisabette, qui etait respectivement demi-sang l'un a l'auble." The crown, being the highest heritage of empires, can descend to the bearer of the same blood of the last Ruler as the blood of the first Monarch,

good" as the goal of the legislation. This Statute in the form of a manuscript consists of XIII sections on more than 69 pages, written partly in Russian and partly in French (I. The General Provisions. II. On the Supreme Power. III. On the succession. IV. On the Imperial Family Name. V. The state orders (central) VI. The state orders (local) VII. On the subjects, in general, the rights and obligations. VIII. On the estates. IX. On the clergy. X. On the foreigners. XI. The flying marks of different content. XII. The historical remarks. XIII. The critical remarks)[1]. Page 12 says: "Every subject must recognize, honor, and defend the above-mentioned and any other legalization useful to the 'common good[2].'" Section V "The state orders.

The higher" refers to the "common good" as a doctrine that should be guided by the highest Officials: "The Duty of Our Important Personage is:

1. To give us the best pieces of advice according to the ability and thought of each of us.

2. We should be guided by the 'common good,' the honor of His Imperial Majesty and the Empire, impartiality, doubt, or fear[3]."

---

because it is transferred from Peter II to Empress Anna, and from her to Empress Elizabeth that, accordingly, was of the same blood from the first to the last carrier (translated by the author). It mentions the Monarchs from Peter II to Elizabeth Petrovna. The latter was mentioned in the past tense ("etait"). See "The regulations on the state structure" // RGIA. Fund 938. List of contents 1. Case # 661. Page 10.

[1] RGIA. Fund 938. List of contents 1. Case # 661.

[2] Ibid. Page 8.

[3] Ibid. Pages 12-13.

Picture 19. An illumination of the St. Petersburg Academy of Sciences (dated September 6, 1750) presented: The prosperity pours the flowers and fruits on the free sciences and shows those practicing in these sciences a new way towards zealous diligence about them, and, in addition, the prosperity protects them with the citation of the name of Her Imperial Majesty: [print] / Grid. Ivanovich Sokolov from the Academy of Sciences and Arts - [St. Petersburg, 1750]. - 1 l. An illumination theater in the form of a wooden platform, erected on the Neva in front of the buildings of the Kunstkamera and the Academy of Sciences, is shown. The allegorical scene presented at the illumination theater depicted a picture of the prosperity of the arts and sciences in Russia under the benevolent patronage of Empress Elizabeth Petrovna.

The central place in the domestic theory of the welfare of all and everyone is occupied by the legal views of the Russian Monarchs that not only led the Russian Empire but were also the representatives of the Imperial House.

Before taking the throne, they were Grand Dukes and Princesses, receiving the best education and upbringing at that time. The nobility had to reckon with their opinion (and for the other estates, they were "demigods").

The imitation of their views was a rule of good manners and a condition for any promotion.

The first in the line of Monarchs was the Grand Duchess (her legal views will be given below). Later, she became Empress Catherine II (1729-1796). The legal views of Ekaterina Alekseevna, the Autocrat of Russia, can be understood from the legislative acts, correspondence, and writings.

Empress Catherine II motivated the termination of the Prussian campaign of the Russian corps with the "silence and prosperity" of the throne in her encrypted Decree to Count Zakhar Grigoryevich Chernyshev on June 28, 1762[1].

Empress Catherine II[2] placed a noteworthy line in her circular rescript, dated July 9, 1762: "Defining ourselves to advance *the welfare of our faithful subjects and all mankind* as a whole, we also want to take upon ourselves the burden of presenting to all the belligerent powers that it is necessary to stop shedding innocent blood and restore general silence" (*emphasized by the authors of this scientific work*).

Catherine the Great indicated in her handwritten note to the Siberian Governor and Commander of the Chinese border (dated December 4, 1762) that "justice," "silence," and "peace" had been included in the concept of bliss[3]. Some instructions were given to the extraordinary envoy on the issue of Sweden's choice of the form of government in the encrypted Rescript # 28 to Count Osterman to Stockholm, drawn up by Prince A. Golitsyn on October 22, 1763, according to the project of N. I. Panin, following a nominal decree of Her Imperial Majesty with the handwritten resolution of Her Imperial Majesty "To be this way." It was stated in it, in particular: "Those that directly love their Fatherland and are attached to its lasting bliss can reliably take the Aglinsky *Sharter* (*Catherine the Great's italics*) or their unshakable fundamental charter. Then, after purifying their form of government, they can leave the royal reassuring and acts of the Seim's conclusions from all the zemstvo laws, rituals, and institutions that are at different times subject to them. After that, they should firmly enact in this decree the following points their general rights and freedoms are based on: the rights and advantages that belong to the Royal Majesty as the head of all the people subject to him, the government power to maintain a balance between the King and the nation, the steadfast rights and liberties of the people and legislator's right given to the officials of the state for keeping the national loyalty, a declaration of war, the conclusion of peace, the adoption of new obligations with other world powers, the determination and arrangement of duties and taxes, the urgent convocation of the Seimas, and the dependent power of the Seim Deputies from these fundamental statutes that are firm and not subject to the Seim Deputies' large number of votes....[4]" It should be noted that the bliss of the Fatherland includes the general rights and freedoms of the King and subject people, the immovable rights and

---

[1]Catherine II "The political correspondence of Empress Catherine II." - [St. Petersburg: without publishers], 1885-1914. / Russian Historical Society). Volume 48: 1762 and 1763. 1885. Page 1.

[2] Ibid. Pages 14-15.

[3] Ibid. Page 202.

[4] Catherine II "The political correspondence of Empress Catherine II." - [St. Petersburg: without publishers], 1885-1914 / Russian Historical Society. Volume 51: 1763 and 1764 - 1886. Page 47.

freedoms of the people, the legislative powers, and the balance of interests "between the King and nation." Even though this provision served as an argument for some diplomatic influence and was not subject to wide publicity, this legal thought was introduced into the political and legal vocabulary of the Russian "High Society" (the highest statesmen of the Russian Empire): a senior member of the foreign collegium, an actual Privy Councilor N. I. Panin, Vice-Chancellor A. M. Golitsyn, and Empress Catherine II.

So, Rescript # 21 to the Baron of Corfu in Copenhagen on August 30, 1762 (and a copy of Rescript # 19 to the envoy Musin-Pushkin in Hamburg), signed in pursuance of the Highest Will by Count M. Vorontsov and Prince A. Golitsyn, informed about the welfare of the cities, Hamburg and Lubeck. That well-being was associated with the liberties, rights, and freedom from the entry of Danish troops[1]. The "benefit" and "welfare" of Poland were noted in Rescript # 31 to Rzhichevsky to Warsaw of September 19, 1762[2], signed in pursuance of the Highest Will by Count M. Vorontsov and Prince A. Golitsyn. "The welfare of the Polish Republic" and "the welfare of the fatherland" were mentioned in Rescript # 2 to Count Keyserling to Warsaw, signed on January 2, 1763, in fulfillment of the Highest Will by Count M. Vorontsov and Prince A. Golitsyn[3]. "The silence and well-being of the German Empire," "concern for the welfare of the Empire and each co-member of it, and the protection of imperial legalizations" were mentioned in Rescript # 23 to Prince Golitsyn to Vienna (encrypted), signed on April 29, 1763, in pursuance of the Highest Will by Count M. Vorontsov and Prince A. Golitsyn[4]. It can be read about the assurance of "indispensable concern for the welfare of the empire and each co-member of it" in Rescript # 12 to Minister Simolin in Gegensburg, signed on April 29, 1763, in fulfillment of the Highest Will by Count M. Vorontsov and Prince A. Golitsyn[5].

The terms liberty ("liberte") and the welfare of your Fatherland ("bien-etre de sa patrie") were used together in a copy of the Empress' letter to the Primate of the Kingdom of Poland on February 24, 1764[6], being the goal for the "zeal and devotion" of the Primate of the Kingdom of Poland. The adherence of Catherine II to the "tranquility of the Rzeczpospolita," its "inner peace," and "the preservation of its rights" was emphasized in the letter of the Empress to the Polish King

---

[1]The political correspondence of Empress Catherine II. Volume 48: 1762 and 1763. 1885. Page 113.
[2] Ibid. Pages 132-133.
[3] Ibid. Pages 245-246.
[4] Ibid. Page 465-466.
[5] Ibid. Page 466-467.
[6] The political correspondence of Empress Catherine II. Volume 51: 1763 and 1764 - 1886. Page 222.

Stanislav August (the draft was handwritten by N. I. Panin) on September 19, 1764, while Stanislav August was the guarantor of the country's welfare (bien-etre)[1].

The "official benefit" and "public welfare" in Order # 27 of the Empress "On the idea of the doubtful matter," printed on July 6, 1765, were associated with "the privileges given and confirmed to this nation[2]." All management issues were "under the good care and order" of the Governor's office, and if it was impossible to resolve the issues, the Governor presented them to the Governing Senate.

Regarding the Cherkasy people and the inhabitants of the Sloboda province, it was fixed in Order # 28 of the Empress that the intention of Her Imperial Majesty was "making the state and people's benefit with the better order and success by using the new Orders." It should be noted that the people's benefit in the document was inseparable from the "granted and not canceled privileges[3]."

Prosperity in the Police Regulations of 1766 was understood as "the faith and fear of God" among the lands and cities[4].

An introductory part of the Declaration (the Declaration was approved by Catherine the Great (the phrase "To be in this way" informs about this) and given by the highest name of Her Majesty the All-Russian Empress to the noble knighthood and zemstvo, especially for Courland and Semigalia (1766)) indicated: "Her Majesty the Empress in such a generous reasoning for the 'common good' for good, thinking that it is profitable and necessary, told her Minister ....[5]" The

---

[1] The political correspondence of Empress Catherine II. Volume 51: 1763 and 1764 - 1886. Page 490.

[2] Catherine II "The Decrees of the Most Eminent and Greatest Sovereign Empress Ekaterina Alekseevna, Autocrat of All Russia: Held from July 01, 1765 up to January 01, 1766." / Printed by the Highest Command of Her Imperial Majesty. - St. Petersburg: Under the Senate, 1779. Page 19.

[3] Catherine II "The Decrees of the Most Eminent and Greatest Sovereign, Empress Ekaterina Alekseevna, Autocrat of All Russia: Held from July 01, 1765 up to January 01, 1766." / Printed by the Highest Command of Her Imperial Majesty. - St. Petersburg: Under the Senate, 1779. Page 19-20.

[4] A Convolute. The Decrees of the Most Eminent and Greatest Sovereign, Empress Ekaterina Alekseevna, Autocrat of All-Russia: Held on July 01, 1765, up to January 01, 1766. / Printed by the Highest Command of Her Imperial Majesty. - In St. Petersburg: Under the Senate, 1779. Page 347.

[5] A Declaration made by the Highest Name of Her Imperial Majesty, All-Russian Empress to the Noble Chivalry and Zemstvo, and, especially, located in Courland and Semigallia // Catherine II "The political correspondence of Empress Catherine II". St. Petersburg: A Collection of the Imperial Russian Historical Society. Volume 67: 1766-1767, 1889. Pages 37-41.

translated "Declaration on behalf of Her Majesty the All-Russian Empress (the Declaration was made by the Extraordinary and Plenipotentiary Ambassador of Catherine II, Prince Repnin to the assembled at the Sejm of 1766 Polish Republic[1]," outlined in French, and approved by Catherine the Great) informed: "Recommending this matter and asking the King and his people to treat it with all the attention and respect that it deserves in its importance for the 'common good,' Her Majesty the Empress considers it from two points of view: spiritual and secular." The "common good" in the French text of the declaration was denoted by the phrase "le bien général."

A modernized theory of the welfare of all and everyone was reflected in the Order (drawn up by Catherine II on July 30, 1767) for the Commission on the drafting of a new Code. The Order has been studied in the literature in detail.

The state and legal views of Empress Catherine II (set out in the Order) can be summarized in the following eight provisions:

1. The establishment of an indispensable law[2].
2. The guarantees of the freedom of citizens (nobles, townspeople, and peasants)[3].
3. The equality of everybody before the law[4].

---

[1] The Declarations on behalf of Her Imperial All-Russian Majesty, made by Her Ambassador, Extraordinary and Plenipotentiary Prince Repnin to the Polish Republic assembled at the Seim of 1766 // Catherine II "The political correspondence of Empress Catherine II." St. Petersburg: A Collection of the Imperial Russian Historical Society. Volume 67: 1766-1767, 1889. Page 88.

[2] Catherine II "An Order of the commission on drafting a New Code" // Catherine II "The works of Empress Catherine II": Volumes 1-3. - St. Petersburg: A. Smirdin, 1849-1850. – in 3 volumes; 17. - (The complete works of Russian authors). Volume 1. - 1849. Page 10. Catherine II - Article 44. Beccaria - Paragraphs 25 and 41. See S. Belikov "The significance of Beccaria in the science and history of Russian Criminal Law". Pages 158-232 / / Beccaria, Cesare "On the crimes and punishments" / Translated from Italian with an etude "The Significance of Beccaria in the Science and History of Russian Criminal Legislation" [S. Belikov]. - [Kharkov]: S. Ya. Belikov, 1889. - XIV, 232 p.

[3] Catherine II "An Order of the commission on drafting a New Code" // Catherine II "The works of Empress Catherine II": Volumes 1-3. - St. Petersburg: A. Smirdin, 1849-1850. – in 3 volumes; 17. - (The complete works of Russian authors). Volume 1. - 1849. Pages 8-9, 17-18, 21-24, 82-84. Catherine II - Articles 33-39. Beccaria - Paragraphs 25 and 27, Montesquieu - Book XI, Chapters 3 and 6. Catherine II - Articles 83, 87, 88. Montesquieu - Book VI, Chapters 9 and 12. Catherine II - articles 98, 104, 106, 112, 114. Beccaria and Montesquieu - no analogues. Catherine II - Articles 341-345. Beccaria and Montesquieu - no analogues.

[4] Catherine II "An Order of the commission on drafting a New Code" // Catherine II "The works of Empress Catherine II": Volumes 1-3. - St. Petersburg: A. Smirdin, 1849-1850. – in 3 volumes; 17. - (The complete works of Russian authors). Volume 1. - 1849. Pages 8-9, 32, 61. Catherine II - Articles 33-39, Beccaria - Paragraphs 25 and 27, Montesquieu - Book XI, Chapters 3 and 6. Catherine II - Article 149. Beccaria - Paragraph 3. Catherine II - Article 244. Beccaria - Paragraph 41.

4. The education of citizens on the rules of morality and respect for the law[1].
5. The limitation of a monarchy by law and morality[2].
6. The development of legislation in the form of the establishment of laws and orders, the adoption of statutes, and the issuance of decrees[3].
7. The inequality of superiors and subordinates to preserve the morals and monarchical form of government[4].
8. The selective application of Western ideas based on experimental experience[5]. The last four provisions have no analogs in the teachings of Ch. L. de Montesquieu and C. Beccaria (that served as the ideological source of the Mandate). Paragraph 13 of the text of the Order for the Commission on drafting a New Code (dated July 30, 1767) points out the fact that Catherine II understood the greatest benefit of the "common good." This point says that the aim of the autocratic ruling is "not taking away the natural freedom of people. On the contrary, the real goal of it is directing the actions of people towards receiving the greatest good from everybody[6]." The interests of the "common good" are protected by law. The grave violation of these interests will destroy society. The "easiest" breach of the interests will bring "irritation" to a particular person[7]. The Order introduced the term "well-being-established state" (the state organizing the provision of work to workers "according to their strengths" and

---

[1] Catherine II "An Order of the commission on drafting a New Code" // Catherine II "The works of Empress Catherine II": Volumes 1-3. - St. Petersburg: A. Smirdin, 1849-1850. – in 3 volumes; 17. - (The complete works of Russian authors). Volume 1. - 1849. Pages 8-9, 12, 61, 82-87. Catherine II - articles 33-39. Beccaria - Paragraphs 25 and 27, Montesquieu - Book XI, Chapters 3 and 6. Catherine II - Articles 58-60. Montesquieu - Book XIX, Chapters 2 and 14. Catherine II - Articles 244-249. Beccaria - Paragraph 41. Catherine II - Articles 341-356. Beccaria and Montesquieu - no analogues.
[2] Catherine II "An Order of the commission on drafting a New Code" // Catherine II "The works of Empress Catherine II": Volumes 1-3. - St. Petersburg: A. Smirdin, 1849-1850. – in 3 volumes; 17. - (The complete works of Russian authors). Volume 1. - 1849. Pages 114-115. Catherine II - Articles 511-513. Beccaria and Montesquieu - no analogues.
[3] Ibid. Page 100. Catherine II - Articles 444-446. Beccaria and Montesquieu - no analogues.
[4] Ibid. Pages 112, 114. Catherine II - Articles 503 and 509. Beccaria and Montesquieu - no analogues.
[5] Catherine II "An Order of the commission on drafting a New Code" // Catherine II "The works of Empress Catherine II": Volumes 1-3. - St. Petersburg: A. Smirdin, 1849-1850. – in 3 volumes; 17. - (The complete works of Russian authors). Volume 1. - 1849. Page 116. Catherine II - Articles 520-522. Beccaria and Montesquieu - no analogues.
[6] Catherine II "An Order of the commission on drafting a New Code" / / The works of Empress Catherine II: Volumes 1-3. - St. Petersburg: A. Smirdin, 1849-1850. – in 3 volumes. Volume 1. - 1849. Page 5.
[7] Ibid. Pages 56-57.

being obliged "to give all citizens the reliable maintenance, food, decent clothing, and a kind of life that does not harm human health)[1]."

Two groups of duties (the implementation of them benefits the common use) among the duties of the state were identified in the Supplement to the Grand Order of April 8, 1768 (Paragraphs 576-578). Number 2 on the list of duties indicated: "the maintenance of internal order, peace, and safety of everyone, in particular, and all people, in general"; the maintenance of "people for the administration of justice, decency, and supervision over various orders serving the common use." Some duties (number 3 on the list of duties) were envisaged for common use: "building cities and roads, making canals by digging, cleaning rivers, establishing schools and hospitals," etc.[2] It is worth mentioning the terms "the wholeness of the people" and "the wholeness of things" used in Paragraphs 647 and 648 of the Addendum to the Great Order of April 8, 1768. It was typical for the 18th century to recognize the unity of things and phenomena in nature. Therefore, the appearance of this term in the Grand Order Supplement was not surprising. "The wholeness of the people" presupposed some knowledge of the condition of people, their rank, and their exercise. "The wholeness of things requires a good knowledge of each of them in detail and in general so that you can judge their mutual relationship and make them useful to society, considering them all together[3]."

Both terms were subordinate to the term the "common good," deriving from it. This connection was especially emphasized in paragraph 655: "... all parts are included in one another in this chapter, according to their decent relationship with each other, as there is not one of them that would not depend on others ...[4]," and, taken all together, they had to serve the security of the state, the welfare of the people, and the glory of an Autocrat.

---

[1] Catherine II "An Order of the commission on drafting a New Code" / / The works of Empress Catherine II: Volumes 1-3. - St. Petersburg: A. Smirdin, 1849-1850. – in 3 volumes. Volume 1. - 1849. Page 84.

[2] Ibid. Page 127.

[3] Ibid. Page 157.

[4] Catherine II "An Order of the commission on drafting a New Code / / The works of Empress Catherine II: Volumes 1-3. - St. Petersburg: A. Smirdin, 1849-1850. Volume 1. - 1849. Page 158.

Picture 20. Action 1 of the wicked fire of the entertainment lights, presented at the end of the wedding celebration of their imperial highnesses, in St. Petersburg, in October 1773: Russia before the altar in the temple of bliss erected by the great Catherine begs heaven for the continuation of its prosperity. As a result of the prayer heard, the good geniuses fly down, wearing the signs of a marriage union, two flaming hearts, and the fiery marriage candles / Gravé par S. M. Roth; I. de Stehlin inv [eni] t; performance by M. Nemov. – SPb. 1773. - 1 page.

It was written in the Outline on the completion of the commission of the draft of the New Code of April 8, 1768, in the introductory part of the provision: "We are obliged to do good to each other as much as possible" and further, summing up: "... every honest person in society has a desire or will to see his or her whole Fatherland at the highest degree of prosperity, glory, bliss, and tranquility," "and every citizen, in particular," "must be protected by laws" that would not suppress his or her welfare, protecting him or her from all opposing this rule enterprises[1]." It can be seen from these provisions that the well-being of all and everyone in the text of the Outline was associated with the well-being of the state (Fatherland) and the well-being of a citizen. "The order and nature of things"

[1]Catherine II "The Decrees of the Most Eminent and Greatest Sovereign, Empress Ekaterina Alekseevna, Autocrat of All Russia: held from January 1768 up to 1769" / Printed by the Highest Command of Her Imperial Majesty. - St. Petersburg: Under the Senate, 1786. Page 18.

divided legislation into "The Mandate to the State" and "The Mandate to a Citizen." "The Common Right that is established for the common use of the peoples[1]" (capital letters - from the source) was formulated in "The Mandate to the State." "The Special Right that is made for every person especially" (capital letters - from the source) was formulated in "The Mandate to a Citizen." Common Law included certain general rituals necessary "to preserve the integrity, good order, and silence of the state" that constituted "the existence of the supreme power," legislative, protective, and perfecting power, a form of state structure, legal proceedings[2], etc., in other words, everything that is called public law today. Special Law included "all those legalizations and regulations that bring benefit and security to every citizen living with others in society, both in the reasoning of himself or herself and in the discussion of his or her property and obligations[3]." That Special Law was divided into persons, things, and obligations[4]. It can be assumed that the theory of the welfare of all and everyone became a project used for creating a New Code of Law in the Russian Empire.

Catherine II used the phrase "we exhort all of them, in general, and each of them, especially[5]" in her manifesto to the Slavic peoples of the Balkan Peninsula on January 19, 1769. The Empress wrote to the Governor of the Province Pomerelsky, Count Fleming, on September 7, 1769, making the following line in her letter: "No private difficulties of my Empire, no plans of the enemies of Poland's tranquility and envious persons of the participation that I take in its welfare, no worries, no means for its pacification." Welfare is spelled "bien-être" in the French original. "A Draft of the Noble Rights composed by the Commission on the State Clans and signed by its members[6]" (1771) is a notable but little-known document. Fyodor Kozlovsky was the author of the text. An introductory part of the project says: "When undertaking to compose and publish a new statute, Her

---

[1]Catherine II "The Decrees of the Most Eminent and Greatest Sovereign, Empress Ekaterina Alekseevna, Autocrat of All Russia: held from January 1768 up to 1769" / Printed by the Highest Command of Her Imperial Majesty. - St. Petersburg: Under the Senate, 1786. Page 18-19.

[2] Catherine II "An Order of the commission on drafting a New Code" / / The works of Empress Catherine II: Volumes 1-3. -St. Petersburg: A. Smirdin, 1849-1850. Volume 1. - 1849. Pages 141-153.

[3] Ibid. Page 154.

[4] Ibid. Pages 154-165.

[5] A Manifesto to the Slavic peoples of the Balkan Peninsula // The political correspondence of Empress Catherine II. - St. Petersburg, 1885-1914. A Collection of the Imperial Russian Historical Society. Volume 87: 1768-1769 - 1893. Page 324.

[6] A Collection of the Imperial Russian Historical Society. - St. Petersburg, 1867-1916. - 148 volumes. Volume 32: Some historical information about the Catherine Legislative Commission for drafting a New Code. Part 4. - St. Petersburg.: The printing house of N. A. Lebedev, 1881. Pages 573-585.

Imperial Majesty added the bliss of all and everyone to the glory of Her statehood and the nobility of Russia ....” The project revealed the content of the bliss of all and everyone: “… although the distinguished virtue and its righteous retribution are the first pillars of universal good deeds, this is not enough for the above-mentioned subject - the bliss of all and everyone. At first, it is necessary that all and everyone, according to their state, would exactly know about their rights and obligations and how to use their privileges and fulfill the duties[1].” It is already clear from this line that the bliss of all and everyone did not consist only in striving for everything good but also had a legal character: it provided for the knowledge of rights and obligations. It is explained below: “The bliss does not lie in having everything that pleases a whimsical desire as that could be only the bliss of the strong people. In effect, happiness exists in *having all those rights and benefits of everybody that he or she may justly and judiciously want* (*an emphasis was added by the authors of this work*). These rights and benefits should be real, not dreamy, and even more reliable, better shielded, and attached. The necessary conjugation and alliance among all citizens say that all citizens should not enjoy all the same rights and advantages as that would be universal confusion. But the order should reign. According to this order, all the separate belonging rights should be divided. For example, *the nobility should see their benefit in the use and benefit of the petty bourgeoisie* (*it was emphasized by the authors of this research*), and, in turn, the petty bourgeoisie should see their benefit in the use and benefit of the lower to them classes, etc[2].” The theory of the bliss of all and everyone was dominant and determined the content of this document: “Perhaps, not all rights that can be dreamt of and written about were mentioned here but it can be said that only those privileges that correspond to the condition of the state and the bliss of all and everyone were observed[3].” The line of the project indicated the fundamental nature of the theory: “The equal rule will probably be observed in the following projects as well.” According to V. A. Tomsinov, this project was identical to the Granted Diploma to the Nobility in 1785 in the ideological content, spirit, style, and terminology[4].

The terminology of the theory of the “common good” can also be seen in the Imperial Decree from the College of Foreign Affairs to the Chargé d'Affaires in

---

[1] A Collection of the Imperial Russian Historical Society. - St. Petersburg, 1867-1916. - 148 volumes. Volume 32: Some historical information about the Catherine Legislative Commission for drafting a New Code. Part 4. - St. Petersburg.: The printing house of N. A. Lebedev, 1881. Page 575.

[2] Ibid. Page 576.

[3] Ibid. Page 576.

[4] The Legislation of Empress Catherine II, 1783-1796 / Compiled by V. A. Tomsinov. An introductory article by V. A. Tomsinov - Moscow: Zertsalo, 2011. Page XXIX.

Paris N. K. Khotinsky, signed by Count N. Panin and Prince A. Golitsyn on August 12, 1772[1]. According to the author of the Decree, the content of the well-being of the Polish State included: “the restoration of its members of the Greek and other Christian denominations (in the rights of citizenship and equality) that were gradually driven out of them by an excellent number of Catholics by violence alone, despite the exact clear laws and the very foundations of the republic, where the private freedom and equality of every citizen constitutes the chain of the common freedom and equality,”[2] “general peace and quiet.” The “common good” was a way of making decisions: the Seim “found a way to reconcile the interests of dissidents with the constitution and the direct good of the republic and to also approve these interests by enacting the new and permanent laws in favor of its liberty.”[3] The “common harm” as opposed to the “common good” and included: “the flame of fanaticism, indignation, and robbery could creep in and spread. Nevertheless, the evil itself would not reach the edge it was in afterward if the government of the republic remained under its previous resolution to regard the troublemakers as troublemakers and did not begin to bring itself into complete oblivion because of the intrigues of some power-hungry and vain people that considered the multiplication of anxiety in their Fatherland as the safest and best way to raise their ranks and achieve their dangerous views opened at the coronation Seim”[4]; “everyone can easily imagine the consequences of civil disorder and war: the merchant class and trades were suppressed and ruined everywhere, lots of disrupters tortured, tormented, and killed the dissidents everywhere, the villagers, quietly staying in their houses, were deprived of their estates and food, many cities and villages were burned and devastated… In other words, the traces of murder and the most brutal barbarism are visible everywhere …[5].” As the subjects of Poland “… have a lot of harm through the suppression of any communication and lots of evil disasters can further easily grow everywhere …,” the Emperor of the Holy Roman Empire, Empress-Queen, King of Prussia, and Empress Catherine II decided to take Polish territory under their guardianship.

Empress Catherine II wrote to Count P. A. Rumyantsev in 1773, referring to love for “the true good of the Empire.”[6] When writing a letter to Field Marshal

---

[1] The political correspondence of Empress Catherine II. SPb. 1885-1914. A Collection of the Imperial Russian Historical Society. Volume 48: 1762 and 1763. 1885. Pages 196-202.

[2] Ibid. Page 197.

[3] Ibid. Page 198.

[4] Ibid. Page 199.

[5] Ibid. Page 200.

[6] The letters of Empress Catherine II to Count Rumyantsov 1773 / / The works of Empress Catherine II: Volumes 1-3. - St. Petersburg: A. Smirdin, 1849-1850. – in 3 volumes. Volume 3. - 1850. Page 255.

General Prince Golitsyn in 1780, Catherine II emphasized: "The subject of My reign is the delivery of blessings and tranquility to the Fatherland and the ascension of glory and greatness of it without acquiring any empty names[1]." When compiling a letter to Actual Privy Counselor Mr. Panin on August 16, 1773, the Empress referred to "the benefit of the Empire" and "the good arrangement of everything given by the power of the Almighty" as the basis of the state rule[2].

One of the famous favorites of Catherine II, General-In-Chief, Governor-General of several provinces of the Russian Empire, writer, and poet Pavel Sergeevich Potemkin (1743-1796) assured Catherine II (in his report dated July 26, 1774) that he had "for the first subject in life <...> the good of society and loyalty to the sacred person ...[3]": The Empress.

Catherine II wrote (in her Decree "On the necessary corrections in the teaching of Sciences in the Artillery and Engineer Cadet Corps," dated February 21, 1784)[4] to Lieutenant-General Melissino: "The country where the government accepts the execution of such an important task is blessed. However, Russia is a hundred times more blessed as not only the wise and humane Monarch cares about this part of the general well-being ...[5]."

An introductory part of the landmark document of the 18th century (the Letters Patent to the Russian Nobility of 1785) indicated that the "common good" was a goal of the activities of the subjects of the Russian Empire: "... when the united labor and love for the Fatherland strive mainly for the 'common good' ...." When talking about the aim of her reign, Catherine II mentioned the delivery of "the firm and strong resolutions to all the loyal subjects in all the necessary parts of the internal State administration to increase the prosperity and order for the future."[6] Clause 20 of the Letters Patent emphasized that "... the service of the

---

[1] A letter to Field Marshal Prince Golitsyn // The works of Empress Catherine II: Volumes 1-3. - St. Petersburg: A. Smirdin, 1849-1850. – in 3 volumes. Volume 3. - 1850. Page 374.

[2] From the Empress to Mr. Real Privy Counselor Panin // The correspondence of Empress Catherine II with various persons. SPb., 1807. Pages 15-17.

[3] Ya. K. Grot "P. S. Potemkin during the Pugachev events. The materials for the history of Pugachev's rebellion in 1774" // Russian antiquity. - 1870. - Volume 2. - The 3rd edition. SPb., 1875. Page 404.

[4] The Nominal Order "On the necessary corrections in the teaching of Sciences in the Artillery and Engineering Cadet Corps" given to Lieutenant-General Melissino on February 21, 1784 / / The Legislation of Empress Catherine II, 1783-1796 / Compiled and edited by V. A. Tomsinov. An introductory article by V. A. Tomsinov – M.: Zertsalo, 2011. Pages 15-30.

[5] Ibid. Page 16.

[6] Catherine II "On the nobility": [Letters Patent. Approved on April 21, 1785]. - [St. Petersburg]: Printed in the Senate on April 24, 1785. Pages 2, 4.

nobility to the "common good" is necessary and needed...[1]." The provisions of the Letters Patent were proclaimed for the benefit of the Russian nobility. The Russian nobility was the first estate in the Russian Empire and deserved "firm and solid decisions." The theory of the welfare of all and everyone was not exclusively a noble asset. It touched upon the life of the other classes of the Russian Empire as well. In particular, the Charter on the Rights and Benefits of the Cities of the Russian Empire (dated April 21, 1785)[2] depicted a mechanism. According to that mechanism, the city society presented "its public needs and benefits" to the Governor. Moreover, any public inquiries and responses to the Governor's inquiries had to be similar "to both legalization and general good ..." (paragraphs 36-38)[3]. Paragraph 81 of the Charter indicated that "the cities from Our ancestors and ourselves were founded not only for the people living there but also for the public good. Those cities multiply the state revenues, providing the citizens with the ways for acquiring the property through the trade, crafts, handicrafts, and crafts ...[4]." Being part of the theory of the welfare of all and everyone, the wording "to all and everyone" entered the legal text as a verbal cliche, a stamp of legal speech: "The petty bourgeoisie is free to start the manufacturing of all kinds and produce all kinds of handicrafts by it without any other permission or order: this article allows it to all and everyone ..." (paragraph 90)[5].

Empress Catherine II revealed the essence of the policy following the theory of the welfare of all and everyone in her Manifesto "On the Establishment of the State Loan Bank" of June 28, 1786[6]: "We disdained the rules of a hellish policy instilling that the people should be in shortage or poverty for being hardworking and obedient. The prosperity of humanity and, especially, Our subjects is the law of Our thoughts and the feelings of Our hearts. Being guided by this, We recognize that the enrichment of people is the wealth of a Sovereign and the industriousness and handicraft can achieve perfection and mostly flourish in the places where these people live in complete contentment because people are attracted by an abundance of money everywhere, and the money is taken for the price of all things[7]." Catherine II also extended the provisions of this policy to the

---

[1] Ibid. Page 3.

[2] The Diploma of rights and benefits to the cities of the Russian Empire April 21, 1785 / / The Legislation of Empress Catherine II, 1783-1796 / Compiled and edited by V. A. Tomsinov. An introductory article by V. A. Tomsinov - Moscow: Zertsalo, 2011. Pages 52-89.

[3] Ibid. Page 57.

[4] Ibid. Page 65.

[5] Ibid. Page 65.

[6] A Manifesto "On the establishment of the State Loan Bank" (dated June 28, 1786) / / The Legislation of Empress Catherine II, 1783-1796 / Compiled and edited by V. A. Tomsinov. An introduction article by V. A. Tomsinov - Moscow: Zertsalo, 2011. Pages 98-113.

[7] Ibid. Page 99.

newly created banks: "... so that our Banks, resting on a fundamental and immutable law, thus, should pass any harmful conclusions and empty talk, acquire the respect and faith of other European peoples, and *spread the good that comes from there not only for the government benefit but also, even more, for the benefit of different states of people"*[1] (*it was emphasized by the authors of this work*). There is the wording "we certify and encourage all and everyone"[2] in Paragraph 1. This also testifies to the manifestation of the above-mentioned theory in the text of the normative legal act of the Russian Empire of the 18th century.

There was the wording "it is commanded to all and everyone to bring their complaints after getting offended and insulted ...[3]" in Paragraph 49 of the Manifesto "On the Duels" (dated April 21, 1787)[4]. It can be seen in the Manifesto "On the non-recovery of salary income to the treasury from the regions newly acquired from Poland until 795" (dated April 13, 1793): "Our main intention and will in this acquisition lies and will consist in protecting the inhabitants by their peace and giving them our ruling based on our firm and unshakable foundations and justice flowing to everyone. Spreading many good deeds and making everyone happy are our most pleasant responsibilities and duties, given from above ...[5]." The following were the benefits that had been included in the concept of happiness: protecting personal and property security, compensating for any losses incurred from any confusion and strife, and not collecting and exacting "the government salary income ...." It is worth paying attention to the following phrases mentioned in the Nominative Decree given to the Livonian, Estland, and Lithuanian Governor-General, Prince Repnin "On the division of the Grand Duchy of Lithuania into three parts and on the way of ruling over them" (dated October 30, 1794)[6]: "... I let you know that all and everyone, starting from the noblest

---

[1] Ibid. Page 102.

[2] Ibid. Page 102.

[3] A Manifesto "On the Duels" (dated April 21, 1787) / / The Legislation of Empress Catherine II, 1783-1796 / The Moscow State University named after M. V. Lomonosov, The Faculty of Law. Compiled and edited by V. A. Tomsinov. An introductory article by V. A. Tomsinov. - Moscow: Zertsalo, 2011. Pages 144.

[4] Ibid. Pages 136-144.

[5] A Manifesto "On the non-collection of salary income to the treasury from the newly acquired from Poland Regions, until 795" (dated April 13, 1793) / / The Legislation of Empress Catherine II, 1783-1796 / Compiled and edited by V. A. Tomsinov. An introductory article by V. A. Tomsinov. - Moscow: Zertsalo, 2011. Pages 190-191.

[6] A Nominal Order given to the Lifland, Estland, and Lithuanian Governor-General, Prince Repnin "On the division of the Grand Duchy of Lithuania into three parts and on the manner of governing them" (dated October 30, 1794) / / The Legislation of Empress Catherine II, 1783-1796 / Compiled and edited by V. A. Tomsinov. An introductory article by V. A. Tomsinov. – M.: Zertsalo, 2011. Pages 204-221.

nobility to the last one that is due, should make a solemn oath of fidelity and obedience …[1]"; "… everyone is encouraged and invoked to leave the vain attachment to debauchery ...."[2] Empress Ekaterina Alekseevna was also well-known as a writer. She created such works as "The Secret of the Anti-Absurd Society" (1759), "The Invisible Bride" (1786), and many others. The theory of the welfare of all and everyone was reflected in the literature of Catherine II. So, the following lines are of interest, in particular, in the "Grandmother's Alphabet to the Grand Duke Alexander Pavlovich" (1783): "Man has a nature endowed with good …[3]," "The world produces good consent and, in turn, good consent makes a multitude of benefits and pleasures; on the contrary, any quarrels and disagreements diminish and depress all good …[4]," "Power is entrusted to the one for the sake of servicing the multitude …[5]," "When citizens show jealousy to each other as if giving or fulfilling the best advice for the benefit of the Fatherland, then nobody prefers his or her benefit to the common benefit …[6]," "Alexander asked Diogenes if he was afraid of him? Diogenes answered by using the question: 'Are you good or evil, Alexander?' Alexander said: 'I am blessed.' And Diogenes, lifting his voice, said: 'Who ever saw the fear of the good?'[7]," "If you want to be good, reject all the condemnatory characteristics you can find in others from yourself …[8]," "When suddenly shining, the sun will be joyfully received from everyone; the same can be said about the person that voluntarily creates good …[9]." The theory of the welfare of all and everyone received a touch of light irony from the servant Praskovya in her dialogue with Nekopeikov in the comedy "The Name Day of Mistress Vorchalkina[10]." When asked by Praskovya why Nekopeikov is here, he replies: "… I am here for the 'common good'"; the welfare of the Fatherland binds me here …." When continuing the dialogue, Praskovya criticizes Nekopeikov and notes that the "common good" depends not only on the "brainless head" of Nekopeikov[11].

---

[1] Ibid. Page 218.
[2] Ibid. Page 218.
[3] Catherine II "Grandmother's alphabet to Grand Duke Alexander Pavlovich" / Catherine II. - M.: MGI named after E. R. Dashkova, 2004. Page 2.
[4] Ibid. Page 28.
[5] Catherine II "Grandmother's alphabet to Grand Duke Alexander Pavlovich" / Catherine II. - M.: MGI named after E. R. Dashkova, 2004. Page 26.
[6] Ibid. Page 37.
[7] Ibid. Page 42.
[8] Ibid. Page 43.
[9] Ibid. Page 44.
[10] A name day of Mrs. Vorchalkina // The works of Empress Catherine II: Volumes 1-3. - St. Petersburg: A. Smirdin, 1849-1850. Volume 2. - 1849. - 612 pages.
[11] Ibid. Pages 242-243.

Catherine II left the following lines in one of her notes: "When meeting an intelligent person in my youth, an ardent desire was immediately born in me to see him or her used for the good of the country[1]." According to V. A. Tomsinov, the periods of the reign of Peter I and Catherine II were a time when the talents and abilities of gifted people brought many benefits to state government[2].

Following O. A. Omelchenko, the "common good" included the idea of a legitimate monarchy[3]. Mastering the terminology of the "common good" meant some innovations in legislation: the emergence of the new beginnings of the administration of justice resulted in the necessity of observing and ensuring in court not only the interest of a Monarch and the state law, in general but also the rights of every citizen[4]; a ban on the disposal of family estates and their transfer to heirs in case of inheritance by law[5]; the decriminalization of some crimes and the liberalization of punishments in the spiritual sphere[6]; the emergence of some additional duties for police officers ("zeal for the 'common good'")[7].

According to the research of O. A. Omelchenko, "the judicial-legal, criminal-legal, and organizational-law enforcement policy of the government was a systemic unity with the general legal policy of *enlightened absolutism*"[8] (*italics by O. A. Omelchenko*) that included the theory of the "common good."

Analyzing the drafts of the legal acts, letters, and essays of Catherine II, it can be logically and soundly argued that Catherine II perceived the terms of the theory of the welfare of all and everyone ("common good," "common use," "benefit to everyone separately," "to all and everyone," "welfare," "bliss," and "prosperity") and its principles: the "common good" is inextricably linked with the rights (privileges) and freedom of a Monarch and all estates; the "common good"

---

[1] A citation was quoted from V. A. Tomsinov's "Speransky." - M.: Young Guard, 2006. Page 63.
[2] Ibid. Page 63.
[3] O. A. Omelchenko "The Monarchy of Enlightened Absolutism in Russia: The Political Doctrine, Legal Policy, State Reforms": A thesis of a Ph.D. in Historical Sciences. - Moscow, 2001. Pages 104, 105.
[4] Ibid. Pages 121, 122.
[5] Ibid. Page 268.
[6] O. A. Omelchenko "The Monarchy of Enlightened Absolutism in Russia: The Political Doctrine, Legal Policy, State Reforms": A thesis of a Ph.D. in Historical Sciences. - Moscow, 2001. Page 287.
[7] Ibid. Page 335.
[8] Ibid. Page 337.

serves as a balance of interests between the state and citizens; the concept of welfare as an interest includes “the greatest benefit,” “justice,” “silence,” “peace,” “faith and fear of God,” “building bridges, roads,” etc.; the well-being of all and everyone requires a good knowledge of the “condition, titles, and exercises” of citizens and the world around them to organize life for the “common good,” as well as good learning people’s rights and responsibilities[1]. Catherine II made the bliss of all and everyone the goal of her reign, adapting the theory of the welfare of all and everyone for the legislation of the Russian Empire and building it under the provisions of the theory that was expressed in strengthening the protection of citizens' rights in the administration of justice, changing the legal status of family estates, decriminalizing the crimes, liberalizing the punishments in the spiritual sphere, and additional regulating many police activities.

[1] O. A. Omelchenko “The Monarchy of Enlightened Absolutism in Russia: The Political Doctrine, Legal Policy, State Reforms”: A thesis of a Ph.D. in Historical Sciences. - Moscow, 2001. Page 337.

§2.3. The welfare of all and everyone, as presented by Paul I and Alexander I

The next Monarch to fall into the sphere of the influence of the theory of the welfare of all and everyone was Grand Duke Pavel Petrovich, known as *Paul I,* during his reign of the Russian Empire (*1754-1801*). Despite his rejection of many of his mother's (Catherine II) undertakings, he was a supporter of the theory of the welfare of all and everyone. Paul I's contemporaries and historians characterized Paul I as "a capricious and despotic person changeable in his likes and dislikes." In addition, they indicated that his "government policy had been unpredictable and often devoid of elementary logic …[1]." At the same time, he had "unshakable moral foundations," including his beliefs about the bliss of all and everyone.

Paul I already expressed his attitude to the theory of the "common good" at the age of 24. It can be read in his letter to P. P. Panin of September 14, 1778: my intention and my thoughts are to nothing else, "but my ardent desire to tilt all things and make them flow in the proper and most precise order to a good end that is the 'common good' …[2]." Further, it can be seen: "The current state of affairs offends only the heart that is jealous of the good, and this insult is compelled to start by reasoning only for being on time to get ready by all means and as hard as possible to help the crept harm get in ...[3]."

The 1788 Order of the Grand Duke Pavel Petrovich[4] informs of the subject in more detail: "The subject of every society is the bliss of all and everyone. Society cannot exist if the will of everyone is not directed towards a common goal …[5]." It can be concluded from this thesis that "… there is no better image as an autocratic power because it combines the power of the Laws and the speed of the power of one …[6]."

By using this basis, Grand Duke Pavel Petrovich equates "the foundation of silence" and "the achievement of the goal of the law of God" to the bliss of all and everyone. The way to achieve and preserve the bliss of all and everyone is "the regulation of the rules of general security being born from the confluence of all

---

[1]A. V. Zavrazhin "Historical experience in the development of the political worldview of Russian society: 1721-1917": An abstract of the thesis of a Ph.D. in Historical Sciences - M., 2010. Page 34.
[2]Pavel I, P. I. Panin "The correspondence of Grand Duke Pavel Petrovich with Count Peter Panin" // Russian antiquity, 1882. - Volume 33. # 2. Page 411.
[3]Ibid. Page 416.
[4]Pavel I "The Order"// M. N. Semevsky "The materials for the Russian History of the XVIII century" // Europe Bulletin. Volume 1. March 1867. Pages 316-322.
[5]Ibid. Page 316.
[6]Ibid. Page 316.

things to one object[1]." These rules will be executed by the zemstvo and city police. Laws depend on the bliss of all and everyone, forming people's morals. Morals are "the pledge and foundation of everything," leading to the bliss of all and everyone[2].

After occupying the Russian throne, Paul I continued following the ideals inculcated in him. A phrase serving the improvement of the Church became an integral part of the preamble in the "Decree to Our Synod" (dated December 18, 1797): "... We have recognized for the good to make the following orders for the benefit of it ...[3]."

It can also be read in the Decree of February 13, 1798, regarding the rights, liberties, and freedom of trade in the Crimea: "... We recognized OUR encouragement for the good of trade and the strongest population and the establishment of cities and lands on this peninsula ...[4]."

It can be read in Paragraph 67 of the Charter of the State Auxiliary Bank for the Nobility, dated February 16, 1798[3] (approved by the Supreme Will), that all the ranks of the Bank, guided by the "intention based on the general benefit," must correctly and inviolably perform the positions prescribed for "everyone, especially, and all, in general, ...[5]."

The Decree (dated April 17, 1798) contained an indication that "... when wanting to expand their factories for the benefit of their own and the State ...," many of the merchants, factory owners, and manufacturers were breaking the law. Paul I acknowledged correcting this situation as "for the good," introducing a procedure of seizing the factories and mills of those factory owners that were "negligent about the public and private benefits[6]" by arresting and attaching that property to the state treasury.

The wording "... and, therefore, we recognized for the good to command ...[7]" was used in the May 1798 Decree prohibiting the transfer of an estate from one owner to another until making the final decision.

Starting from May 1798, the command formula in most cases changed to "We recognized for the necessity ...[8]."

---

[1] Pavel I "The Order"// M. N. Semevsky "The materials for the Russian History of the XVIII century" // Europe Bulletin. Volume 1. March 1867. Page 320.
[2] Ibid. Page 321.
[3] The Decrees of the Sovereign, Emperor Paul I, Autocrat of All Russia: [from January 1 to December 16, 1798]. - Moscow: The Senate Printing House, 1798. Page 11.
[4] Ibid. Page 77.
[5] Ibid. Pages 83-103.
[6] Ibid. Pages 102-103.
[7] Ibid. Pages 115-116.
[8] Ibid. Page 51.

It can be read in the Decree on the new establishment of the Order of St. John of Jerusalem (dated November 29, 1798): the order "... promoted both the common benefit of all Christianity and the private benefit of every State ...[1]."

When explaining the reason for the Decree on the acceptance of the title of a Master of the Order of Malta (that was an interstate act), printed in a printing house in St. Petersburg on December 16, 1798, Paul I said: "... while being in its respectful state for future times, this Order should be preserved with its previous regulations and advantages and should promote the good goal for achieving the common benefit as it was based on ...[2]."

A Decree of His Imperial Majesty from the Governing Senate (that Decree was passed in June 1799) mentioned the destruction of state forests and measures to preserve them: "... the malusage crept in has not yet been suppressed, and, for getting their private profits despite the general benefit, some ill-intentioned people do not stop destroying our state forests in various ways ...[3]."

Regarding the rank and title of Juncker, it can be read in the Decree of His Imperial Majesty from the Governing Senate (that Decree was passed in June 1799): "... to provide the Noble youth of our Empire with the methods and way for achieving the goal of every loyal subject by this means and using himself or herself for the benefit of us and the Fatherland. But <...> the renewal of this title <...> having preferences and satisfying the whims of the commanders do not serve the 'common good,' introducing the same malusage that was destroyed and will always be uprooted by us as our first goal ...[4]."

It was written in the Decree of His Imperial Majesty from the Governing Senate (that was passed in August 1799) regarding some reduction of the cases of the application of punishment for crimes in the form of the death penalty: "... We have recognized for the good that, starting from now, convict execution should be solely imposed for the murder, theft, and robbery[5]."

It can be read in the Decree of His Imperial Majesty from the Governing Senate on the settlement of Siberia along the border with China, printed in a printing house in St. Petersburg on November 4, 1799: "... looking for any ways for achieving everything that can serve its glory and benefit, we can see that the

---

[1] The Decree of His Imperial Majesty. Printed in the printing house of St. Petersburg on August 3, 1798, in Moscow - on August 19, 1798 // The Senate Printing House, 1798. Page 231.

[2] The Decrees of the Sovereign, Emperor Paul I, Autocrat of All Russia: [from January 1 to December 16, 1798]. - Moscow: The Senate Printing House, 1798. Page 229.

[3] A Convolute. The Decrees of the Sovereign, Emperor Paul I, Autocrat of All Russia: [From January 17 to December 30, 1799]. - Moscow: Printed in the Senate Printing House, 1799. Page 135.

[4] Ibid. Page 139.

[5] Ibid. Page 193.

Midday edge of Siberia, adjacent to the Chinese borders <...> does not bring the benefits that the State should receive from it …"; "In respect of it, we judged for the good to put …[1]."

The allied defensive treatise between Their Majesties, the Emperor of All Russia and the King of Sweden, concluded on October 18-29, 1799, was ratified by Paul I with his following words: "... after contentedly considering this allied defensive treaty, taking it for the good ...[2]."

It was said about the "common harm" and the "common benefit" in the Decree of His Imperial Majesty from the Governing Senate on customs tariffs on goods, printed in a printing house in St. Petersburg on December 17, 1799: "... generating an extortionate profit for a certain part of the profit-seekers, many different forgeries and tricks harm both *our* treasury and the greater number of honest merchants <...> our unshakable rule is to adjust the benefits of *our* treasury to the benefits of all and every *our* loyal subject, so We judged it for the good to call ...[3]."

It can be read in the Decree of His Imperial Majesty from the Governing Senate regarding the distribution and protection of forests, passed in December 1799: "... in respect of both the private interest of our loyal subjects and the common interest in that, we have recognized for the good ...[4]."

Thus, we can summarize that Paul I believed from his youth that all people should strive for a common goal - for the "common good" and prevent the "common harm." The concept of the "common good" as an interest included "silence" in the state, "achieving the goal of the law of God," and "common security." It was possible to achieve these benefits through the establishment of morals among citizens that, in turn, was formed through laws. Due to this, the role of the Monarch was extremely high as it combined the "power of the Laws" and the speed of the "power of one." The phrase "We have recognized for the good" became a stable expression to denote the legislative will of an Emperor. The "common good" included both the common (state) and private interests. Harm to both the state and individuals was the opposite of the "common good." The peculiarities of the legal worldview of Paul I, his literal and fanatical desire for the "common good," and his desire to make everyone serve the good of the Empire

---

[1] A Convolute. The Decrees of the Sovereign, Emperor Paul I, Autocrat of All Russia: [From January 17 to December 30, 1799]. - Moscow: Printed in the Senate Printing House, 1799. Page 231.

[2] Ibid. Page 247.

[3] A Convolute. The Decrees of the Sovereign, Emperor Paul I, Autocrat of All Russia: [From January 17 to December 30, 1799]. - Moscow: Printed in the Senate Printing House, 1799. Page 309.

[4] Ibid. Page 333.

turned into a sad end for him. M. M. Kovalevsky noted the desire of Paul I, like his predecessor Peter I at the beginning of the 18th century, for the "common good" that manifested itself in his petty tutelage over the people and taking care of all the interests of people[1]. This led to interference in the personal life of subjects. This meddling, in turn, resulted in the hatred of a significant part of the nobles and prompted them to a revolution (coup d'etat).

Picture 21. Emperor Alexander I. An engraving from a portrait painted by Veil in 1802, published in the book "The regicide on March 11, 1801: The notes of the participants and contemporaries (Sablukov, Count Bennigsen, Count Langeron, Fonvizin, Princess Lieven, Prince Chartoryiski, Baron Geyking, Kotzebue)": with 17 portraits, views, and plans. - St. Petersburg: the edition of A. S. Suvorin, 1907. - XLVIII, 375, [4] pages, [17] sheets of paper. Color processing by A. Makarov.

After the accession to the throne of the Grand Duke and then Emperor Alexander I (1777-1825), the theory of the "common good" continued to be the guideline of public policy.

The following line was included in the Manifesto on the annexation of the Georgian Kingdom of September 12, 1801[2]: "In the reciprocity of these generous *concerns of ours for the welfare of all and each of you* (*an emphasis was added by the authors of this work*), We demand that you take an oath of fidelity according to the form attached ...[3]." The oath, called "Oath Promise," in turn, contained the line: "I will not only announce about the harm to His Majesty's interests or the common benefit as soon as I know at once, but I will also prevent and forestall by all means ...[4]."

It was said in the preamble of the Nominative Decree "On the Organization of Specialized Schools" of January 24, 1803: "... And all our loyal

[1] M. M. Kovalevsky "From the history of the state power in Russia" // M. M. Kovalevsky "The selected works": 2 parts - Part 1. – M.: ROSSPEN, 2010. Page 122.
[2] A Manifesto of September 12, 1801 / / The Legislation of Emperor Alexander I, 1801-1811 / Compiled and edited by V. A. Tomsinov. An introductory article by V. A. Tomsinov. - Moscow: Zertsalo, 2011. Pages 51-53.
[3] Ibid. Page 53.
[4] Ibid. Page 53.

subjects will take an active part in these institutions established for the common benefit and the benefit of everyone ...[1]."

The Emperor thanked Empress Maria Fyodorovna in his Imperially approved project "On the establishment of widows' houses, treasuries, and hospitals" (dated February 1, 1803) and noted that "Projects <...> are a new experience of Your Imperial Majesty's unremitting efforts towards the "common good" that is the only goal of the everlasting desires of yours ...."[2]

It can be read about the connection between the good of the Fatherland and other goods in the given to the Senate Nominative Decree "On the inviolability of the rights granted to the Nobility" (dated March 21, 1803): "Connecting this with the spirit of laws existing on this subject in the Empire, the rights given to the Governing Senate, the benefit of the State service, the duty of every sensible and loyal subject, and the good of the Fatherland (the only subject of our deeds and the focus of all Our duties), We judged for the necessary ...[3]."

The Act of Approval for the Imperial University in Vilna (dated April 04, 1803) gives an important characteristic of the practical use of the theory of the welfare of all and everyone. That Act pointed to the "popular enlightenment" as the "natural foundation" of "the prosperity of all the areas of the Empire." The goal of the university was "the education of useful citizens for all states and all kinds of public service." The formula "and so they judged for the good[4]" was used in that Act.

There was also a place for the "common good" in the Charter of the Academy of Sciences[5] that was approved by the Highest on July 25, 1803. "The affirmation of the well-being of people" was associated with "the spread of

---

[1] A Nominal Decree given to the Senate "On the organization of schools" (dated January 24, 1803) / / The Legislation of Emperor Alexander I, 1801-1811 / Compiled and edited by V. A. Tomsinov. An introductory article by V. A. Tomsinov – M.: Zertsalo, 2011. Page 109.

[2] The highest approved project "On the establishment of widow houses, treasuries, and hospitals" (dated February 01, 1803) //// The Legislation of Emperor Alexander I, 1801-1811 / Compiled and edited by V. A. Tomsinov. An introductory article by V. A. Tomsinov – M.: Zertsalo, 2011. Page 115.

[3] A Nominal Decree given to the Senate, "On the inviolability of the rights granted to the Nobility" (dated March 21, 1803) //// The Legislation of Emperor Alexander I, 1801-1811 / Compiled and edited by V. A. Tomsinov. An introductory article by V. A. Tomsinov – M.: Zertsalo, 2011. Page 126.

[4] An approval act for the Imperial University in Vilna (dated April 04, 1803) // The Legislation of Emperor Alexander I, 1801-1811 / Compiled and edited by V. A. Tomsinov. An introductory article by V. A. Tomsinov - Moscow: Zertsalo, 2011. Page 128.

[5] The highest approved Charter of the Academy of Sciences on July 25, 1803 // The Legislation of Emperor Alexander I, 1801-1811 / Compiled and edited by V. A. Tomsinov. An introductory article by V. A. Tomsinov - Moscow: Zertsalo, 2011. Pages 150-170.

sciences and the improvement of useful knowledge[1]." The Emperor used the well-known formula "We judged for the good" to approve the new regulations and staff. It can be read in Paragraph 1 of the Charter: "The main duties of the Academy that are common to all Academies and scientific societies follow from the very purpose of its appointment: expanding the limits of human knowledge, improving science by enriching them with new discoveries, spreading enlightenment, and directing knowledge for the "common good" as much as possible ...[2]."

It can be read in the preamble of the Authorized Decree given to the Senate on February 28, 1804 "On the transformation of the Commission for Drafting Laws"[3]: "the formation of the Commission itself, the staff and all other <...> orders are such measures that <...> are completely consistent with Our intentions and cares about the establishment of the tranquility, benefit, and prosperity of *our* loyal subjects on the firm and unshakable foundations of the law ...[4]."

This Decree referred to the Order of Catherine II and quoted it: "It would be necessary to have the laws so good and so filled in all ways for the inviolable preservation of them to achieve the greatest good for the leading people so that everyone would be undoubtedly sure that he or she should keep these laws indissoluble for the sake of his or her own benefit ...." The following was given for interpreting these lines: "Of course, for achieving this necessary and only perfection of laws, there is the first and most important means for presenting the above-mentioned principles: their own righteousness will be the guarantee of sacred justice reigning in laws and over laws; their usefulness will assure everyone that *obedience to the laws has its own, obvious benefits"*[5] (*it was emphasized by the authors of this scientific work*).

An explanation was given below, mentioning the kind of laws that would have to satisfy this criterion: the certain laws "already approved by the seal of the people's welfare, befitting the welfare in the Empire, all the benefits of the local

---

[1] The highest approved Charter of the Academy of Sciences on July 25, 1803 // The Legislation of Emperor Alexander I, 1801-1811 / Compiled and edited by V. A. Tomsinov. An introductory article by V. A. Tomsinov - Moscow: Zertsalo, 2011. Page 151.
[2] Ibid. Page 151.
[3] A Nominal Decree "On the transformation of the Commission for Drafting Laws," given to the Senate on February 28, 1804 / / The Legislation of Emperor Alexander I, 1801-1811 / Compiled and edited by V. A. Tomsinov. An introductory article by V. A. Tomsinov - Moscow: Zertsalo, 2011. Pages 171-189.
[4] Ibid. Page 181.
[5] Ibid. Page 182.

situation, the spirit of the nation, and the main character of the peoples making up our nation ...[1]."

The general legal provisions included the arrangement of "different judicial places, the security of all and everyone," and the strict implementation of the laws "affirming the tranquility and prosperity of the State ...." "In reality," they are fair and useful "both for the State, in general, and, especially, for the subjects themselves ...[2]." Private statutes are needed only for some special cases when "the local circumstances require some exclusivity for their well-being in some respects ...."

The "common good" was the general criterion for making decisions in the Imperially approved Instruction to Senators appointed to inspect the Provinces (dated August 1, 1805)[3]. Paragraph 18 of the Instruction evidenced it: "Considering all of that, if something in these clauses was not specifically indicated and the Senators see and judge something worthy of respect, both in the interests and benefits of the State and in the general good; they should not leave it unattended in such circumstances, being guided in all by the importance of their oath, the dignity of their rank, and the rules of honor ...[4]."

Article 6 of the Manifesto, "On the new benefits granted to the merchants, differences, advantages, and new ways to spread and strengthen commercial enterprises"[5] (dated January 1, 1807) substantiated the Nobles' right to "external wholesale bargaining" as the "common good": "... so that the Nobles that are not in Our military and civil service could contribute to the 'common good' in the field of commercial industriousness ...[6]."

---

[1]A Nominal Decree "On the transformation of the Commission for Drafting Laws," given to the Senate on February 28, 1804 / / The Legislation of Emperor Alexander I, 1801-1811 / Compiled and edited by V. A. Tomsinov. An introductory article by V. A. Tomsinov - Moscow: Zertsalo, 2011. Page 183.
[2]Ibid. Page 184.
[3]The Highest Approved Instruction to the Senators appointed to inspect the Provinces (dated August 01, 1805) // The Legislation of Emperor Alexander I, 1801-1811/ Compiled and edited by V. A. Tomsinov. An introductory article by V. A. Tomsinov. - Moscow: Zertsalo, 2011. Pages 320-322.
[4]Ibid. Page 322.
[5]A Manifesto "On the new benefits granted to the merchants, differences, advantages, and new ways to spread and strengthen commercial enterprises" (dated January 1, 1807) // The Legislation of Emperor Alexander I, 1801-1811/ Compiled and edited by V. A. Tomsinov. An introductory article by V. A. Tomsinov. - Moscow: Zertsalo, 2011. Pages 327-338.
[6]Ibid. Page 322.

It can be read in one line of the preamble of the Manifesto of August 9, 1807, "On the conclusion of peace with the French Empire[1]": "The spirit of domestic jealousy, excited by the circumstances, instantly embraced all states and made the great experiments of courage, donations, and zeal for the 'common good' ...[2]." It can be additionally read in the section "Ratification": "After contentedly considering this treatise, *we* have accepted it for the good, confirmed, and ratified as if this is acceptable for the good, confirming and ratifying all its contents ...[3]."

A formula "We recognized for the good"[4] was similarly used in the Named Decree given to the Senate "On the establishment of a special Council under the Commission for Drafting Laws" (dated March 7, 1809)[5].

It was emphasized in the given to the Senate Named Decree "On the non-assignment of the ranks of Chamberlains and Chambers Junkers to any rank, either military or civil, and on the obligation of persons in these ranks to enter an active service and continue it under the established procedure, starting from the initial ranks" (dated 03 April 1809)[6] that "an encouragement in service and the excitement of all forces and abilities to work and be active for the common benefit constitute one of the most important charges of the Government" and that "... ancestors <...> bequeathed <...> to seek honor in business, and not in titles, and in the feat of domestic benefits to precede all other conditions ...[7]."

Article III in the Manifesto "On the conclusion of peace between Russia and Sweden" (dated October 1, 1809)[8] demonstrated an approval formula

---

[1] A Manifesto of August 9, 1807 "On the conclusion of peace with the French Empire" / / The Legislation of Emperor Alexander I, 1801-1811 / Compiled and edited by V. A. Tomsinov. An introductory article by V. A. Tomsinov. - Moscow: Zertsalo, 2011. Pages 338-346.

[2] Ibid. Page 339.

[3] A Manifesto of August 9, 1807 "On the conclusion of peace with the French Empire" / / The Legislation of Emperor Alexander I, 1801-1811 / Compiled and edited by V. A. Tomsinov. An introductory article by V. A. Tomsinov. - Moscow: Zertsalo, 2011. Page 346.

[4] A Nominal Decree "On the establishment of a special Council under the Commission for Drafting Laws," given to the Senate (dated March 07, 1809) / / The Legislation of Emperor Alexander I, 1801-1811 / Compiled and edited by V. A. Tomsinov. An introductory article by V. A. Tomsinov. - Moscow: Zertsalo, 2011. Pages 365-366.

[5] Ibid. Page 366.

[6] A Nominal Decree "On the non-assignment of the ranks of Chamberlains and Chambers Junkers to any rank, either military or civil, and on the obligation of persons in these ranks to enter an active service and continue it under the established procedure, starting from the initial ranks," given to the Senate (dated April 03, 1809) // The Legislation of Emperor Alexander I, 1801-1811 / Compiled and edited by V. A. Tomsinov. An introductory article by V. A. Tomsinov. - Moscow: Zertsalo, 2011. Pages 375-377.

[7] Ibid. Page 375.

[8] A Manifesto "On the conclusion of peace between Russia and Sweden" (dated October 01, 1809) // The Legislation of Emperor Alexander I, 1801-1811 / Compiled and edited by V. A.

"promises to continue accepting it for the good[1]." The section "Ratification" of the same Manifesto showed a formula "we took it for the good[2]."

The formula "We recognized for the good" was used in the preamble of the Manifesto "On privileges for various inventions and discoveries in arts and crafts" (dated June 17, 1812)[3].

One of the goals of the assembly (proclaimed in the Manifesto "On the collection of the zemstvo militia within the State," dated July 6, 1812[4]) was "the protection of the homes, wives, and children of all and everyone."

It can be read in the All-Merciful Manifesto "On the establishment of the crosses for the clergy and medals for the army, nobility, and merchants, and various privileges and favors" (dated August 30, 1814)[5]: "We have never felt so much great bliss, as when entering the boundaries of our blessed region, where *we* carried our filled with love for our worthy people heart and where we were greeted with universal zeal and joy. Now, although the regulation and arrangement of affairs in Europe for the common peace of all peoples requires our departure from Russia, we hope in the mercy of God that this departure will be already short-lived and, after completing our external affairs, we will return to the unhindered care of the internal good of our State ...[6]." The Manifesto instituted crosses and medals having the same image that was already on the medal of 1812 ("the all-seeing Eye") in honor of "the providence and mercy of God performed over *us*[7]" so that the noble Nobility (Paragraph 4 of the Manifesto) would increase "its care and concern for the welfare of its family members that are entrusted to it by God and laws; abstinence from luxury (the mother of vices) and household

---

Tomsinov. An introductory article by V. A. Tomsinov. - Moscow: Zertsalo, 2011. Pages 384-395.

[1] Ibid. Page 388.

[2] Ibid. Page 394.

[3] A Manifesto "On privileges for various inventions and discoveries in arts and crafts" (dated June 17, 1812) / / The Legislation of Emperor Alexander I, 1801-1811 / Compiled and edited by V. A. Tomsinov. An introductory article by V. A. Tomsinov. - Moscow: Zertsalo, 2011. Pages 3-6.

[4] A Manifesto "On the collection within the state of the zemstvo militia" (dated July 06, 1812) / / The Legislation of Emperor Alexander I, 1801-1811 / Compiled and edited by V. A. Tomsinov. An introductory article by V. A. Tomsinov. - Moscow: Zertsalo, 2011. Pages 6-7.

[5] The most merciful Manifesto "On the establishment of crosses for the Clergy and medals for the army, nobility, and merchants, and on various benefits and favors" (dated August 30, 1814) / / The Legislation of Emperor Alexander I, 1812-1825 / Compiled and edited by V. A. Tomsinov. An introductory article by V. A. Tomsinov. - Moscow: Zertsalo, 2011. Pages 61-66.

[6] Ibid. Page 61.

[7] Ibid. Pages 62-63.

housebuilding (a source of abundance, tranquility, and the purity of morals) will reward all the suffered disorders and losses to a large degree ...[1]."

The peasantry in the Manifesto was presented as an object of care and solicitude: "When considering the state peasants, the government will make every effort to provide them with all kinds of benefits; as for the landlord peasants, *we* are confident that our concern for their welfare will be fulfilled by their landowners' care for them. The connection was attributable to the Russian morals and virtues. That connection has existed between them for a long time, being marked by many experiences of their mutual zeal and a common love for the Fatherland, has not left the slightest doubt in us that, on the one hand, the landowners care for their peasants by using their paternal concern like looking after their children; and, on the other hand, the peasants fulfilling their filial responsibilities and duty like zealous household members will make themselves happy, flourishing like all the good-natured and prosperous families ...[2]." The benefit of all and everyone as an interest was realized in the form of benefits and favors in the Manifesto: the quitrent and poll taxes, fines and arrears from peasants up to May 1, 1813 were forgiven and not collected; the arrears and fines from trading peasants for 1812 and 1813 were forgiven and not collected; the arrears and fines from landlord income for 1812, 1813, and 1814 were forgiven and not collected; the penalties in criminal and government cases lasting more than 10 years were stopped; the penalties for state arrears, passing by inheritance, were consigned to oblivion; the people on state debts that were held in prison for more than 5 years and could not pay were released (while a recommendation was given to private people to do the same with their debtors); some extensive measures were introduced to amnesty criminals, "All-merciful forgiveness was extended to all people that committed crimes up to this day and they did not have to get executed for committing these crimes according to the laws, at least, due to the lack of publicity and the judicial investigation has not yet been started"; "general forgiveness" to those people that fought on the side of Napoleon was granted, an investigation against them was terminated, and their estate and property were returned to them[3].

---

[1] Ibid. Page 63.

[2] Ibid. Pages 63-64.

[3] The most merciful Manifesto "On the establishment of crosses for the Clergy and medals for the army, nobility, and merchants, and on various benefits and favors" (dated August 30, 1814) / / The Legislation of Emperor Alexander I, 1812-1825 / Compiled and edited by V. A. Tomsinov. An introductory article by V. A. Tomsinov. - Moscow: Zertsalo, 2011. Page 64-66.

The formula "We recognized for the good"[1] was used in the Manifesto "On the Treaties concluded for the Benefit of the State, on the accession the vast part of the Duchy of Warsaw (under the name of the Kingdom of Poland) to the Russian Empire, on raising the weapons again against Napoleon Bonaparte that left the Elba Island" (dated May 09, 1815)[2]. The following phrase is noteworthy: "His all-blessed providence for Us, turning any unmitigated evil into the good ...[3]." This phrase testified to the legal ideas of the author of the Manifesto, showing the coherent coexisting of the religion and the secular theory of the welfare of all and everyone.

A Manifesto "On the dissolution of the marriage of the Tsarevich and the Grand Duke Konstantin Pavlovich with the Grand Duchess, Anna Fedorovna, and the additional Decree on the Imperial Family" (dated March 20, 1820)[4] contained the wording "We recognize for the good" and "oblige everyone to whom this may concern …[5]."

Most of the landowners did not always agree with the interpretation of the "common good" offered by the most progressive part of the nobility and Alexander I. For example, when discussing the draft of the Commission for Drafting Laws prohibiting the sale of peasants individually and without land as the most consistent with the criterion of the "common good," the members of the Department of Laws remarked: "Of course, the public good is the primary subject of a charitable government, but this good consists in the observation of justice, the equality of everyone in the face of the law, the prohibition of the strong to oppress the powerless, and not in removing them from their due obedience and restraint; otherwise, when feeling their strength, they will put the yoke on the strong and will harm and destroy themselves in their fury …[6]."

---

[1] A Manifesto "On the Treaties concluded for the Benefit of the State, on the accession the vast part of the Duchy of Warsaw (under the name of the Kingdom of Poland) to the Russian Empire, on raising the weapons again against Napoleon Bonaparte that left the Elba Island" (dated May 09, 1815) // The Legislation of Emperor Alexander I, 1812-1825 / Compiled and edited by V. A. Tomsinov. An introductory article by V. A. Tomsinov. - Moscow: Zertsalo, 2011. Page 71.

[2] Ibid. Pages 70-73.

[3] Ibid. Page 72.

[4] A Manifesto "On the annulment of the marriage of the Tsesarevich and Grand Duke Konstantin Pavlovich with the Grand Duchess Anna Feodorovna and on an additional Decree on the Imperial Family" (dated March 20, 1820) / / The Legislation of Emperor Alexander I, 1812-1825 / Compiled and edited by V. A. Tomsinov. An introductory article by V. A. Tomsinov. - Moscow: Zertsalo, 2011. Pages 153-154.

[5] Ibid. Page 154.

[6] On the prohibition of the sale of emancipated people and peasants separately and without land // The Archives of the State Council. - St. Petersburg: Printed in the Printing House of the Second Department of His Imperial Majesty's Own Chancellery, 1869 - Volume 4: The reign of

Picture 22. Nikolai Semyonovich Mordvinov (1754-1845). A portrait of an unknown artist of the 1920s of the XIX century. From open sources.

The position of the department on this issue was revealed by the opinion of Admiral N. S. Mordvinov (1754-1845), dated December 2, 1820. Nikolai Semyonovich Mordvinov came from the noble Mordovian family of an admiral. He was a Senator, and a member of the Permanent Council and the State Council in civilian life. He is considered a follower of A. Smith and I. Bentham. He was the author of the projects for the emancipation of the peasants and a member of various Academies and Societies. Also, N. S. Mordvinov composed some works. In addition, he was a Master (a carrier of the 3rd Degree) of the Lodge of Silence in Moscow (1786-1787). He visited some lodges in England in the 1770s-1780s. The famous M. M. Speransky was his protégé[1].

N. S. Mordvinov supposed that the right of property was natural ("the Law of the Creator") and serfdom was Civil Law ("Human Law"). Serfdom could not contradict Natural Law. "The Creator of everything gave man the right to possess various things, but God put some mutual dependence between people: children depend on their parents, the wife depends on her husband, the weak depend on the

---

Emperor Alexander I (from 1810 to November 19, 1825). The Journals of the Department of Laws. Part 2: Drafting, considering, and approving the charters, regulations, and articles on various parts of the Legislation. - 1874 (a foretitle in 1875). Page 338.

[1] Russian Freemasons. 1721-2019. A Biographical Dictionary. Century XVIII. Volume II / A. I. Serkov, M.: Ganga, 2019. Pages 134-138; Russian Freemasons. 1721-2019. A Biographical Dictionary. Century XVIII. Volume III / A. I. Serkov, M.: Ganga, 2019. Pages 130, 288.

strong, and the stupid depend on the rational. As the right of ownership extends only to things, then a person cannot be the property of another person but can be dependent and subject to another. So, the Civil Law is consistent with the natural one …[1]." He explained that their differences from each other are in the presence of the limits of power: "The right of ownership gives unlimited possession over the thing. The right of the authorities has its limits and the mutual moral relationship between a Sovereign and an obedient person, the Master and servant …[2]." Mordvinov believed that "The dependence of a person on a person" "or the degree of this dependence is associated with the political, physical, moral, and statistical state of every particular land. The degree of this dependence must be consistent with it for the 'common good' and the particular good as well …[3]." Mordvinov thought that there had been the following reasons for the preservation of serfdom in Russia: "sparsely populated Russia," "great space," "the difference in the lean and fertile soils of the land," "the difference between cold and warm climates," "the degree of enlightenment," "lack of capital to patch crops before harvesting from fields," and "common welfare." According to the law, the attitude of landowners to peasants had to be like "household members." "Injuries" and "moral insults" were unacceptable. Serfs could file a complaint against the landowner in court. "The landowner could be deprived of the right of power over the peasants subordinate to him for any actions contrary to good behavior and for neglecting their welfare. After the deprivation of this power, he or she could even get deprived of the right to own his or her land (where his or her peasants lived and were offended by him or her …)[4]."

It was noted in the Named Decree "On the destruction of Masonic Lodges and all secret societies," given to the Governor of the Ministry of Internal Affairs, Count Kochubey, on August 01, 1822[5], that the "Masonic Lodges" initially had

---

[1]On the prohibition of the sale of emancipated people and peasants separately and without land // The Archives of the State Council. - St. Petersburg: Printed at the Printing House of the Second Department of His Imperial Majesty's Own Chancellery, 1869 - Volume 4: The reign of Emperor Alexander I (from 1810 to November 19, 1825). The Journals of the Department of Laws. Part 2: Drafting, considering, and approving the charters, regulations, and articles on various parts of the Legislation. - 1874 (a foretitle in 1875). Pages 342-343.
[2]Ibid. Page 343.
[3]Ibid. Page 343.
[4]Ibid. Page 344.
[5]A Nominal Decree "On the destruction of Masonic Lodges and all sorts of secret societies," given to the Governor of the Ministry of Internal Affairs, Count Kochubey on August 01, 1822 // The Legislation of Emperor Alexander I, 1812-1825: a collection of the legislative acts] / Compiled and edited by V. A. Tomsinov. An introductory article by V. A. Tomsinov. – M.: Zertsalo, 2011. Pages 265-266.

"the purpose of goodness," but "subsequently turned to the harm of the States' peace." Being guided by the notion of "what can harm the State," the Emperor "recognized for the good" to prohibit any Masonic and secret societies[1].

The wording "taking it for the good" in the Convention concluded in St. Petersburg between the Emperor of All Russia and the Government of the American United States "On the unshakable preservation of the friendly relationship between them" (dated April 17, 1824)[2] was preserved but the following addition appeared "In the name of the Most Holy and Inseparable Trinity." This addition testifies to the attention of the Emperor to various religious principles and symbols when drafting any international documents.

Reviewing the legal views of Alexander I, it can be seen that he believed that the goal of his ruling was to take care of the welfare of all and everyone in terms of his subjects and prevent the "common harm." The "common good" as interest included a wide list of benefits and ideas: "the spirit of laws," the rights of the Senate, "the benefit of the State service," "the duty of everyone and a sensible and loyal subject," the good of the Fatherland and the prosperity of the regions of the Empire, "useful citizens," "calmness, benefit, and the prosperity of subjects," "privileges and favors," "justice," "the equality of everyone in the face of the law," and "the prohibition of the strong to oppress the powerless." A formula "recognized for good" remained as a testament to the approval of the Supreme in many statutes. When obeying the laws, everyone had to see his or her own and obvious benefits (use). So, a special role was assigned to the laws: the laws that proved their usefulness, the laws that corresponded to "the benefits of the local situation," "the spirit of the nation," and "the character of the peoples" of Russia. Following the legal ideas of Catherine II, Legislation had to be divided into the general legal provisions related to the benefit of all (a judicial system, general security, "the tranquility and prosperity of the State") and the private legal provisions related to the benefit of individuals under the "local circumstances." The "common good" became a criterion for the adoption of orders by local Senators and the establishment of the legal status of peasants (depending on "the

---

[1]A Nominal Decree "On the destruction of Masonic Lodges and all sorts of secret societies," given to the Governor of the Ministry of Internal Affairs, Count Kochubey on August 01, 1822 // The Legislation of Emperor Alexander I, 1812-1825: a collection of the legislative acts] / Compiled and edited by V. A. Tomsinov. An introductory article by V. A. Tomsinov. – M.: Zertsalo, 2011. Page 265.

[2]The convention concluded in St. Petersburg between the Emperor of All Russia and the Government of the United States of America "On the unshakable preservation of the friendly relationship between them" (dated April 17, 1824) // The Legislation of Emperor Alexander I, 1812-1825: a collection of the legislative acts / Compiled and edited by V. A. Tomsinov. An introductory article by V. A. Tomsinov. – M.: Zertsalo, 2011. Pages 274-276.

political, physical, moral, and statistical state of the land"). Often, many legislative acts included the phrase "all and everyone" as part of the lexicon of the theory of the welfare of all and everyone.

A modern researcher of the political institutions of the 18th century K. D. Bugrov touched upon the issues of the "common good" in the life of the Russian society of that period. K. D. Bugrov supposes that the "common good" was used as the background for building the discussion about the role of a Monarch. According to K. D. Bugrov, the discussion about the role of a Monarch in the life of society in the court political context was a form of secular and provincial monarchism united by virtue and the "common good."[1] K. D. Bugrov believes that "there was a consensus among the Russian elites by the middle of the 18th century that the monarchical form of government itself for such a vast country as Russia was an integral part of the "common good" and that no other form of political organization could effectively achieve the "common good[2]." "The governance of the state with the help of the wise laws and power apparatus had the goal of creating the 'common good[3].'" This statement is true. This can be proved by the legal views of many Russian Monarchs, expressed in a variety of legislative acts, letters, and essays. Russian Freemasons demonstrated the same approach. I. A. Pozdeev showed the same. It can be seen further.

However, the following expression of K. D. Bugrov is quite disputable. K. D. Bugrov notes that the political environment of the Russian Empire of the 18th century "recognized the 'common good'" that coincided with the "*moral* good in general and the good of an individual, in particular. In this case, politics was a series of choices between good and harm, and the task of a well-informed ruler was to make the right choice"[4] (*italics by the authors of this scientific work*). At the same time, the Emperor acted as the "umpire." In contrast to the statement of K. D. Bugrov that the discussion in the 18th century was about "moral" good, we can note that the word "moral" in its modern reading and derivative phrases with the term the "common good" was not used in the political and legal texts of the 18th century. Moreover, the term the "common good" in legal documents of the 18th century was of a legal nature (just as this term has a legal nature today). According

---

[1]K. D. Bugrov "A formation of the ideas of republicanism in the Russian socio-political thought of the XVIII century": An abstract of the thesis of a Ph.D. in Historical Sciences. - Yekaterinburg, 2018. Pages 8, 22, 24.
[2]Ibid. Page 23.
[3]Ibid. Page 24.
[4]Ibid. Page 25.

to K. D. Bugrov, the "common good" of the 18th century referred only to the moral sphere of goods, excluding physical goods (food, clothing, housing, money, etc.). This fact is also questionable. As can be seen, the authors and followers of the theory of the "common good" included such goods as food, money, tax benefits, etc. as interest in the "common good." In other words, they placed quite material goods in the category of the "common good." If K. D. Bugrov, speaking of the "moral" nature of the "common good," considered *the moral and legal nature* of the good, then he was right as the jurists of the 18th and the first quarter of the 19th centuries did not divide law and morality. According to K. D. Bugrov, the law was largely ethical and moral in nature. This fact characterizes monarchical providentialism.

It must be said that the theory of the "common good" received a serious blow from critical philosophy in the first quarter of the 19th century. This theory fell out of favor, together with the names of H. Wolf and D. Nettelbladt at that time. It was replaced by the ideas of the new philosophy of I. Kant. These notions (along with the already prevalent theories of the enlighteners) spread in the Russian Empire at the beginning of the 19th century.

Some Freemasons (I. M. Shaden, F. G. Bauze, and H. A. Chebotarev) taught Lev Alekseevich Tsvetaev (1777-1835) at Moscow University. Then Tsvetaev went to study abroad at the University of Göttingen in 1801, listening to the lectures by August Schlözer (Avgust Shlyotser in the Russian sources) (historian, the author of Norman Theory) and Gustav Hugo (the founder of the Historical School of Law), and received his Ph.D. After that, he went to Paris to listen to lectures on the eighteenth-century encyclopedists from the legal historian Joseph Bernardi and became a member of the Paris Academy of Law. In 1805, Lev Alekseevich Tsvetaev entered the post of Extraordinary Professor at Moscow University to teach the History of Legislation and the Theory of Civil and Criminal Laws. Afterward, he became Dean of the Faculty of Morality and Politics and then the Vice-Rector of the university, teaching Political Economy, Natural, Civil, Criminal, Public, and Roman Law there. Delivering his lectures, he influenced the future Decembrists (N. I. Turgenev, I.D. Yakushkin, and others).

L. A. Tsvetaev became one of the jurists that gradually led the scientific community away from the problem of the "common good" and the "common harm." So, when looking through the book "The first principles of Natural Law, published for the guidance of students by Professor Lev Tsvetaev"[1] in 1816, it can be read about critical philosophy with its moral imperative that changes the concept of good and evil: "Our actions will be morally good if they follow the law

[1] The first beginnings of Natural Law, published for the guidance of students by Professor Lev Tsvetaev [Text]. - Moscow: Printed in the University Printing House, 1816. - [4], 86 pages.

of will and the rule that determines them can be represented in the general system of the laws of intelligent beings. Otherwise, they will be morally bad. That rule will prescribe evil. According to this evil, a free creature conforms to an external urge. This impulse itself can have no aim but can be comprehensively used by another person to achieve his or her own evil goal. And this is very bad. There is a common moral law saying: *do not consider humanity (either in yourself or others) as a method for achieving your or anybody's purpose only, but always examine it as an intention*"[1] (*italics by L. A. Tsvetaev*). As it can be seen, considering it within the framework of the problem of Natural Law, the theory of morality, being very speculative, subjective, and difficult to implement, appeared to replace the logical, clear, universal, and practical provisions of the theory of the "common good." This approach resulted in a new interpretation of historical facts: the revolution in France received a positive assessment - "Critical Philosophy transformed Philosophy and provided Natural Law with some great benefits; meanwhile, the French Revolution aroused a desire in many people to investigate and study the principles thereof, and, thereby, contributed to its improvement and dissemination …[2]."

Critical Philosophy and the Historical School of Law, being the most progressive teachings of that time, reduced the spread of the theory of the "common good" in Western Europe. Then, a wave of these new ideas swept over Russia. D. P. Runich and M. L. Magnitsky tried to fight those notions in Russia but unsuccessfully. The thoughts of the welfare of everyone, society, and the state were replaced by the suggestions of speculative morality, secularized Natural Law, political freedom (liberty), the growth of citizens' consciousness, and radical social modernization. Being extremely fanatical in their social narrowness in the Russian Empire, these views were deeply rooted in Russian society and resulted in the Decembrist uprising of 1825 at the time of the crisis of succession to the throne. The uprising was unsuccessful. When Decembrists were considering the process of the planned reorganization of the state, they had some ideas that could provide for the good of society and the state and implant through a violent change not constrained by means of government, misleading the ordinary performers and the people and leading to regicide. Most of the nobles that opposed the Decembrists could not agree with these principles and means. The concept of the "common good" in the program documents of the Decembrists (the Charter of the Union of Welfare, the draft constitution of N. M. Muravyov, and "Russkaya Pravda" of P. I.

[1]The first beginnings of Natural Law, published for the guidance of students by Professor Lev Tsvetaev [Text]. - Moscow: Printed in the University Printing House, 1816. - [4], 86 pages. Pages 5, 6.
[2] Ibid. Page 86.

Pestel) underwent some changes over the years of planning the coup. However, this is a topic for a specific study deserving a separate publication.

Summarizing the development of the domestic theory of the "common good" in the 18th – the first quarter of the 19th centuries, the conclusions mentioned below can be made up. The Russian theory of the welfare of all and everyone was developed thanks to I. G. Reichel (Reihel in the Russian sources), Catherine II, Z. A. Goryushkin, and other scientists and thinkers. The "common good" was understood as common and individual happiness (the greater good), a criterion for making decisions, and a method for aligning interests. The good of all was rooted in Common Law (State Law). The good of everyone was insinuated into Special Law (Civil Law). The benefits that flowed from autocratic rule were equal to the benefits given by liberty. The laws had to be arranged in such a way that everybody would benefit from the common use and vice versa while achieving his or her benefit.

The theory of the welfare of all and everyone extended its influence on education and politics. The "common good" was presented in a lightweight and censored form in the textbooks, being mixed with the good of the state, and manifested itself in the duties of citizens regarding God, parents, relatives, teachers, the Supreme Power, the Heads determined by this Power, etc.

The theory of the "common good" was not an empty phrase in political thought. The terminology of the theory became part of the official business turnover. The "common good" became the "flesh and blood" of bills on the state structure.

Analyzing the drafts of different legal acts, letters, and essays of Catherine II, Paul I, and Alexander I, it can be seen that those Monarchs adopted the terms and principles of the theory of the welfare of all and everyone, proclaimed the welfare of all and everyone and the prevention of the "common harm" as the goal of their rule. The "common good" was seen by them as an interest, a balance of interests between the state and citizens, and a method (a way to make decisions). A phrase, "We have recognized for the good," became a stable expression to denote the legislative will of a Monarch.

Catherine II adapted the theory of the welfare of all and everyone for the legislation of the Russian Empire, building it according to the provisions of the theory. For organizing the "common good," it was necessary to systematize Legislation so that everyone knew his or her rights and obligations. Paul I believed that the “common good” could be achieved through the establishment of morals among citizens, and those morals, in turn, could be formed through laws. Alexander I believed that everyone in obedience to the laws had to see his or her own and obvious benefits (use).

The “common good” became the subject of discussion about secular and provincial monarchism in Russia in the 18th century. At the same time, this category was mainly legal and jural but not very moral.

§2.4. The welfare of all and everyone and Russian Freemasonry

Russian Freemasonry was the result of the Russian Brothers' assimilating the Western directions of thought and the Western forms of Freemasonry. Therefore, to correctly understand the ideas of Russian Freemasons about the "common good," it is necessary to touch upon a broader context: the Masonic world's ideas about the "common good" and its relationship to the state and law.

Freemasonry in the German Kingdoms and Principalities is extremely important for understanding Russian Freemasonry. German Freemasonry's statutes precisely defined the relationship of Freemasonry to government institutions, politics, and religion. Firstly, it is the apolitical nature of Freemasonry: banning any discussions about changing the state system or political institutions in any Masonic Lodges. Every Freemason had to facilitate the politics of not shocking "the foundations of the state's well-being"[1]. The same was true for religion as well: "no dogmas, rituals, or church institutions had to be discussed in the Masonic Lodges[2]." Secondly, all Masonic Lodges had to be supra-national, supra-religious, and supra-political. Masonic Lodges tried to establish a new morality being tolerant of existing political and religious dogmas. Any Masonic Lodge, "according to the founders, should not serve as a place for uniting mankind by using a particular state system or political aspirations[3]." Any Masonic Lodge looked like a school of morality. Freemasonry was like a community "spreading true humanity by utilizing morality." At the same time, Freemasons emphasized that love for the Fatherland and commitment to the independence of their Motherland are inalienable qualities of a true Freemason[4]. A researcher of Freemasonry, writer, and publisher S. M. Propper (1855-1931) characterized Freemasonry as follows: it had to bring the "material sacrifices *for the 'common good'* (*an emphasis was added by the authors of this book*); in this respect, they should go hand in hand with all other good citizens without trying to attract any exclusive attention to themselves ...[5]." Thus, some nationalism, religious fanaticism, and political intolerance in the Masonic Lodges changed to the new

---

[1]S. M. Propper "Freemasonry and its importance for the success of culture." SPb. 1907. Page 17.
[2]Ibid. Page 18.
[3]Ibid. Page 18. These requirements stemmed from Anderson's Constitution, printed in London in 1723 and extending its effect to all Freemasons that recognized English Freemasonry (its rituals, system of degrees, governing bodies). Prussian and Russian Freemasons generally accepted English Freemasonry.
[4]Ibid. Page 19.
[5]Ibid. Page 46-47.

ideology and morality. As it can be seen further, the above-mentioned ideology and morality fitted into the theory of the "common good."

A classic example of "a philosopher on the throne" and the Head of a Masonic Order is the biography of Frederick II (the Great) (1712-1786), King of Prussia, that joined the Braunschweig branch of the Hamburg Masonic Lodge in 1738. Frederick II viewed Freemasonry as a valuable means of "raising people, making them the members of society, creating them kinder and more virtuous[1]." After he acceded to the throne, he openly declared his affiliation to Freemasonry and founded and headed the first Prussian Lodge of "Freemasons" in Charlottenburg on June 20, 1740. He considered himself "the first servant of the state, and *everyone could be happy in his or her way* in this state[2]" (*it was emphasized by the authors of this scientific work*). One of the features of the Age of Enlightenment can be seen in the activities of Frederick II: interweaving Masonic ideology and the theory of the "common good" in the context of the views of H. Wolf. Frederick II left a will before his death: "Our life is nothing more than a fleeting transition from the moment when we are born in the world to the moment when we die. During this short interval, the destiny of a person is *to work for the benefit of the society he or she is a member of*"[3] (*it was emphasized by the authors of this research*).

One of the most important Masonic documents of the 18th century is an extract from the acts of the general convention in Wilhelmsbad (dated September 01, 1782), signed by the President and all the Delegates to the convention[4]. At the convention, the delegates from different Masonic Lodges proclaimed rejecting the form that had no longer corresponded to "the customs and needs of the century." The Templar System was considered "dangerous in its consequences" and "capable of causing concern to governments." By considering "the first law of a Freemason instructing him to respect the Sovereign power" of the states, any attempts to recreate the Order of the Templars following the results of the convention were disavowed.

Part II indicated the goal of the Masonic Brotherhood – common welfare in the broadest sense: "... the sole purpose of our association is to make each of its

---

[1]S. M. Propper "Freemasonry and its importance for the success of culture." SPb. 1907. Page 27.
[2]Ibid. Page 27.
[3]Ibid. Pages 25-26.
[4]Please see the full text of the extract at https://www.le-ritdefrance.com/wp-content/uploads/1782-Wilhelmsbad.pdf (accessed on 10/17/2020) and http://triple-point.xooit.com/t1249-RER-%3A-Recès-du-Convent-de-Wilhelmsbad-%281782%29.htm (accessed on 10/11/2019)

members better and more useful for humanity through love and the study of truth, the deepest adherence to the dogmas, duties, and customs of our holy Christian religion, by active, enlightened, and universal charity in the broadest sense and through our obedience to the laws of our countries …[1].” Part IV of the excerpt stated: “We hope that, as the first law, we will establish the principles of tolerance towards other systems and the principles of active, enlightened, and universal charity as our characteristics. We will achieve the desired reunification with all good Freemasons. The first goal of ours is that we self-proclaim and declare that we recognize as false and contrary to true Freemasonry only those ranks whose principles would be opposed to religion, good morals, and social virtues …[2].”

The extract became famous in Russia. It was translated into Russian and kept in the archives of Masonic Lodges. The part XII of the book said, “... we [,] wanting more by advice [,] than by forcing [,] to lead to our opinion, and, hoping for the purity of our intentions, we had no other goal than to correct our statutes and combine all brotherhoods [,] burning with love for the good ...[3].” It is clear from the extract that “love for the good” and “charity” were the basis of the Masonic Brotherhood in the very broadest sense.

---

[1] In the original: “...l'unique but de notre association est de rendre chacun de ses membres meilleur et plus utile à l'humanité par l'amour et l'étude de la vérité, l'attachement le plus sincère aux dogmes, devoirs et pratiques de notre sainte religion chrétienne, par une bienfaisance active, éclairée et universelle dans le sens le plus étendu et par notre soumission aux lois de nos patries respectives.”

[2] In the original: “Nous avons lieu d'espérer qu'établissant pour première loi des principes de tolérance pour les autres régimes, et ceux d'une bienfaisance active, éclairée et universelle pour caractéristiques du nôtre ; nous obtiendrons la réunion désirée avec tous les bons Maçons : but que nous nous proposons principalement, et déclarons que nous ne reconnaîtrons pour fausses et contraires à la vraie Maçonnerie, que ces grades dont les principes seraient opposés à la religion, aux bonnes mœurs et aux vertussociales.”

[3] An extract from the acts of the general convention that was held in Wilhelmsbad in July and August 1782. Member XII / / NIOR. RGB. Fund 147. # 6. Page 74.

Picture 23. Johann August von Stark (Shtark in the Russian sources) (1741-1816). Painting by a German artist. From open sources.

The conductor of German influence in Russia was I. A. Stark. Johann August Stark (1741-1816) grew up in the family of a Lutheran Pastor, received a Ph.D. in Theology, and served as a Professor of Philosophy. He was initiated into Freemasonry in 1761 in the French Military Lodge in Göttingen. He was a President of the Chapter of the Templar System in St. Petersburg in 1765 and received the Order Name "Archimedes ab Aquilafulva." J. A. Stark founded the ZudendreiLowen (Three Lions) Lodge in Wismar in February 1767 and created a Chapter of Clerics (Weak Observation) in Wismar in 1770 (1768). He founded the Phoenix Chapter in St. Petersburg in 1768, attended the Three Crowns Lodge in Königsberg on September 3, 1769, and became a member of it in 1770. Then, he led the Chapter of Clerics, including the Chapter located in Königsberg, and received the order's name "Archimedes." Later he was a member of the Three Crowned Swords Lodge in Mitava, which operated from 1775 up to 1794[1].

It is worth paying attention to the iconic work of J. A. Stark, "An Apology, or Defense of the Order of Freemasons[2]." That book became exemplary not only for Western but also for the domestic Brothers of Freemasonry. The work of J. A.

[1]Russian Freemasons. 1721-2019. A Biographical Dictionary. Century XVIII. Volume II / A. I. Serkov, M.: Ganga, 2019. Pages 687-688; Russian Freemasons. 1721-2019. A Biographical Dictionary. Century XVIII. Volume III / A. I. Serkov, M.: Ganga, 2019. Pages 40, 115, 203, 204, 306.

[2]J. A. Stark "An Apology, or Defense of the Order of Freemasons" / Written by Brother ****, a member of the Scottish ** Lodge, in P **. Translated from German by I. P. Turgenev. - M.: The printing house of I. Lopukhin, 1784. - 224 pages.

Stark was translated into Russian by a Freemason I. P. Turgenev, and printed in the printing house of I. V. Lopukhin (another Freemason) in 1784. The book notes that the state has a law on general security and the right to measure all societies for compliance with the "common good," prohibiting the societies that do not correspond to it[1].

Freemasonry cannot become suspicious for the state, as it admits to its meetings "the first-class statesmen and even the Sovereigns themselves" so that a check on the criterion of general benefit could be carried out by them[2]. J. A. Stark, in his book, made the "common good" a criterion for assessing the usefulness and legitimacy of the existence of any society, using the terms the "common good" and "benefit of humanity[3]." Sovereigns and "other dignitaries" were obliged to lead the state to prosperity and, therefore, had to prohibit the activities of societies "leaning towards the harm of the State" or engaged in "any useless and vain things[4]." J. A. Stark considered the Order of Freemasons useful for the states due to its love of fellow men and invited all Sovereigns to join the Order[5].

The opinion of J. A. Stark on state and legal issues can be considered representative of the entire Russian Freemasonry of the 18th century as he took part in various Masonic Lodges for about 30 years, created several Chapters (Templars, Phoenix, Clerics) in St. Petersburg and Wismar, was a leader and a member of Masonic Lodges and Chapters, possessed high degrees, and expressed his thoughts in numerous works on History, Theology, Philosophy, Religious Societies, and Masonic Lodges[6].

---

[1]J. A. Stark "An Apology, or Defense of the Order of Freemasons" / Written by Brother ****, a member of the Scottish ** Lodge, in P **. Translated from German by I. P. Turgenev. - M.: The printing house of I. Lopukhin, 1784. - 224 pages. Page 46.

[2] Ibid. Page 54

[3] Ibid. Page 61, 92

[4] Ibid. Page 93.

[5] Ibid. Page 96

[6] See, for example, J. A. Stark's "The letters to a friend and testament to my son about the Order of St. K.": Translated from German into Russian. - St. Petersburg: The Marine Printing House, 1816. - [2], VIII, 224, [2] p.; J. A. Stark "An Apology, or Defense of the Order of Freemasons." - M.: The printing house of I. Lopukhin, 1784.- 224p.

Picture 24. A vignette from the book of J. A. Stark, "Apology, or the Defense of the Order of Freemasons" (1784). A compass, a plumb line, a ruler, and a shovel (the tools of a bricklayer) were depicted there. Those elements acquired a symbolic meaning in Freemasonry.

The diplomatic service was a channel for spreading Freemasonry in Russia. Counts of the Vorontsov family, Counts of the Panin Family, Princes of the Kurakin Family, and V. N. Repnin served abroad for some time, got acquainted with the Masonic Lodges there, and received initiation. After getting the Masonic aprons and gloves, the enlightened persons got deeply imbued with the desire for the "common good" (universal charity).

Another channel for distributing Freemasonry in the Russian Empire was the Courland, Semigalsk, Livonian, and Estonian nobility (the territory of the modern Baltic and Kaliningrad regions). As a rule, people from the families of the Baltic Barons obtained an excellent education at the German, Polish, and Baltic universities (Revel, Dorpat (Derpt in the Russian sources), and Vilna). Then, they usually entered the service in the Kingdom of Prussia, the Commonwealth, or the Russian Empire.

One of the representatives of the Courland nobility was Karl Aleksandrovich Geyking (1751-1809), an Actual Privy Councilor, a Senator, and a member of the Commission for Drafting Laws. As he noted in his first published French and German works, he loved the works of J. J. Russo[1]. K. A. Geyking also left notes about Courland, Poland, the reign of Paul I, and regicide (he was the biographer of Paul I). That is very valuable. K. A. Geyking published one work on

[1] K. A. Geiking "The days of Emperor Paul: The notes of a Courland Nobleman." St. Petersburg: F. I. Bulgakov, 1907. Page 46.

Monarchy as the best form of government in Latin: Regimen monarchicum ab ipsa natura et in corrupta ratione emanatum etc. a K. A. Ruttieniae Nobili[1].

In addition to achieving outstanding success when fulfilling the civil service in the Russian Empire, K. A. Geyking served in the Duchy of Saxony, the Rzeczpospolita, and the Kingdom of Sweden. But Freemasonry became an important field of his activity. According to A. I. Serkov, K. A. Geyking was initiated either in Germany or at the lodge of Catherine to the North Star in Warsaw. His first step was founding a new Masonic System of 3 Degrees in Dresden and the Lodge of the Friends of Experience (Amis l'éprouvé). He was a member of that lodge from 1770 up to 1780. Then K. A. Geyking founded the Warsaw Lodge of Catherine to the North Star. He established the Society of the Knights of St. Karl and two commandingdoms in Vilna and Warsaw in 1775-1776. K. A. Geyking became the Great Provincial Master of the Provincial Lodge to the North Star in Warsaw on November 24, 1779. He became the Plenipotentiary Representative of the Catherine to the North Star Lodge in Warsaw at the Royal York Lodge for Friendship in Berlin in 1780. K. A. Geyking founded the Lodge of Perfect Unification (Agreement) in Vilna in 1780, being a member of it in 1781. K. A. Geyking was a member of the Mitava Adoptive Lodge in 1782. Then, he founded the Liberty Lodge in St. Petersburg and subsequently created a similar lodge in Warsaw. K. A. Geyking became the Great Local Master of the Great East of Poland in 1781. He represented the Polish Lodge of the United Friends as a Deputy at the Masonic Congress in Paris in 1785. He was a member of the Goddess Eleusis Lodge in Warsaw, starting in 1787. K. A. Geyking was a participant at the Masonic Convention in Berlin in 1787. During the reign of Paul I, he was ordained a Knight of the Malta Order[2].

Therefore, reading about the views of K. A. Geyking on the state and law, it must be remembered that his views were, first, reflecting the general European ideas and, secondly, mirroring the Polish and Eastern nobility.

K. A. Geyking shared the terminology of the "common good" and the "common harm." So, for example, he wrote in "The Notes of a Courland nobleman" that the monopoly of eight Courland lawyers on conducting the cases is contrary to the law and brings "harm to the public[3]." Further, we read his commentary on the patronage of Paul I over the Malta Order: "To cheat the

---

[1] The data on the publication of the book in the library stocks of Russia, Estonia, and Germany were not found.

[2]Russian Freemasons. 1721-2019. A Biographical Dictionary. Century XVIII. Volume I / A. I. Serkov, M.: Ganga, 2019. Pages 354-356; Russian Freemasons. 1721-2019. A Biographical Dictionary. Century XVIII. Volume III / A. I. Serkov, M.: Ganga, 2019. Pages 12, 13, 40, 270-271.

[3]K. G. Geiking "The days of Emperor Paul." - SPb., 1907. Page 11.

members of the Order belonging to other nationalities and force them to approve such a lawless act, they obtained a special announcement from the Sovereign. According to that declaration, the Monarch promised to protect the Order, in general, and each Knight, in particular[1]." Because of the existing censorship in Russia, these lines were printed in Russia almost a century later.

The Courland and Semigal Knighthood (K. A. Geyking belonged to it) asked the Empress of the Russian Empire Catherine II, in 1762-1763, whether their rights, freedoms, and privileges would be changed or reduced. In response to this, a Declaration approved by Her Imperial Majesty on May 2, 1763[2] was adopted for the Courland Delegate, Mr. Geyking. That Declaration said that "Her Imperial Majesty will never be inclined to break this law that is wise and just. The rights, freedoms, and privileges of the Duchies of Courland and Semigalsk will be left on the same basis as they were during the Polish Kings' ruling as they were confirmed by an oath and will never be allowed to be changed in this respect[2]." Catherine II guaranteed the preservation of such rights, liberties, and privileges for future times.

However, although K. A. Geyking had 14 years of experience as a member of Masonic Lodges, held senior positions in some Masonic Lodges, founded some Masonic Lodges in Vilna and Warsaw, and a new Masonic System, his opinion cannot be considered representative of the entire Russian Freemasonry of the 18th century on the state and legal issues as his participation was mainly limited to the following foreign lodges: located in Poland and on the territory of the former Grand Duchy of Lithuania.

It can be noted that spreading the theory of the "common good" among Russian Freemasons was seriously influenced by the development of Freemasonry among Russian Germans. This circumstance was confirmed by G. V. Vernadsky[3]. The sessions of the Masonic Lodges were held "in French, English, and even Italian[4]," but the most common language was German. "Almost one-third of Freemasons in Russia consisted of Germans as a whole[5]." According to the confessional affiliation, German Freemasons were mainly Lutherans or Reformed, but there were also Catholics there. The influence of Germans was not limited to the German language. After the death of Frederick II in Prussia in 1786, Frederick

---

[1] K. G. Geiking "The days of Emperor Paul." - SPb., 1907. Page 38.

[1]The political correspondence of Empress Catherine II. SPb. 1885-1914. - 26 cm. – A collection of the Imperial Russian Historical Society. Volume 48: 1762 and 1763 - 1885. Pages 471-472.

[2]Ibid. Page 472.

[3]Russian Freemasonry in the reign of Catherine II / G. V. Vernadsky. - St. Petersburg.: The publishing house named after N. I. Novikov, 1999. - 567, [2] p.

[4]Ibid. Page 43.

[5]Ibid. Page 43.

[6]Ibid. Page 113-114.

Wilhelm II belonging to the Rosicrucian Order took the royal throne[6]. The influential Rosicrucians (Rozencraitsers in the Russian sources) together with him became the Head of the Kingdom of Prussia: Johann Christoph von Wöllner (1732-1800) received the post of Minister of Justice and Education, and Hans Rudolf von Bischofswerder (1741-1803) became Adjutant General and Minister of Foreign Affairs. They extended the influence of the Rosicrucians far beyond the borders of their state as senior officials. According to Yu. E. Kondakov, at the beginning of the 19th century, the Russian Rosicrucians (they did not lose contact with the Prussian Rosicrucianism and were under its organizational influence) were already "making some attempts to penetrate the higher spheres of the state power[1]." Prince A. N. Golitsyn was surrounded by R. A. Koshelev (Chief Chamberlain, Member of the State Council), N. F. Pleshcheeva (a wife of Vice Admiral S. I. Pleshcheev), P. D. Markelov, A. I. Kovalkov and his wife, Lefort, stepbrother of Prince D. M. Kologrivov, A. I. Turgenev and D. P. Runich. All of them were the persons that had either membership in the Order of the Rosicrucians or were their relatives and friends[2]. They distributed some religious literature of certain orientations and participated in the preparation of various government projects[3]. Their strongest influence in the first quarter of the 19th century could be observed in the Ministry of Spiritual Affairs and Public Education, the Bible Society, the Ministry of the Interior, and the Post Office.

The representation of German Freemasons in Russian Lodges, in comparison with the French and the British, was overwhelming. Their beliefs, university education (philosophical and legal), and views on Freemasonry formed the organization and ideology of Masonic Lodges in Russia, including their attitude to the government, state, and public institutions[4].

---

[1]Yu. E. Kondakov "Esoteric movement in Russia at the end of the 18th - the first half of the 19th century." – M.: Club Castalia. 2018. Page 637.
[2]Ibid. Page 637-638.
[3]Ibid. Page 639-643.
[4]See Appendix # 1.

Picture 25. A sign of the Lodge "Towards Three Globes." Prussia. Mid-18th century. The sign depicts an all-seeing eye shining in a triangle, superimposed on a silver snake holding its tail. Three gilded globes are placed on the snake's body[1].

Considering the 63 Great Masters identified by the author of this work based on the publications of A. I. Serkov[2], it can be said that 18 Great Masters out of the 63 Great Masters were of German origin, and their native language was German (about 1/3). They entered the highest governing bodies of Russian Lodges and founded new lodges and new Masonic Systems. For comparison, 5 Great Masters out of the 63 Great Masters were the conductors of French influence, and 2 *Great* Masters out of the 63 Great Masters were of English influence.

19 Great Masters out of the 63 Great Masters received legal education, scientific degrees in jurisprudence, and/or held the position of a lawyer, judge, or legal adviser. 12 Great Masters out of the 63 Great Masters received legal education at European Universities, mainly in Prussia and in the German Principalities (Leiden University, Leipzig University, University of Gaul, University of Jena, University of Turin, University of Königsberg, Collegium Nobilium in Warsaw, and the University of Vienna).

---

[1] Published in the Hermitage Collection. 2013, p. 238.

[2] The word "great" in this context does not mean the name of the position of a Freemason in a Lodge, meaning belonging to Freemasons that were visiting the lodges for a long time and/or holding the leadership positions in the lodges, Lodge Unions. See Appendix # 2. "The Great Master" usually means the position of the Head of the Lodge or the Head of the Union of Lodges in the Masonic lexicon.

7 Great Masters out of the 18 Great Masters of German descent have gained law degrees, degrees in jurisprudence, and/or held the position of a lawyer, judge, or legal adviser. Only 2 Great Masters out of the 5 Great Masters (the guides of French influence) obtained a law degree or held the position of a lawyer, judge, or legal adviser.

These circumstances indicate the decisive influence of German jurisprudence and German political and legal doctrine on Russian jurisprudence and Russian political and legal doctrine (as it was shown in the previous paragraphs), as well as the decisive influence of the ideology of German Freemasonry on the ideology and organization of Russian Freemasonry. These processes took place in parallel, with close interconnection and mutual influence.

The main Masonic acts, speeches, and notes testifying to the spread of the theory of the "common good" among Russian Freemasons will be considered further. The Russian "Knightly Systems" of Freemasonry in the 18th century, according to the classification of Yu. E. Kondakov will be shown first[1].

It can be read in the Plan or the general establishment of the Order of Freemasons in Member I of the Rules of the Charity Knights: "The Knights of the Holy City will be united by the union of close friendship, perfect equality and ardent love for truth and virtue; living under the shadow of the civil government, they are obliged to use the omnipotence of brain to facilitate the human race and especially comfort the weak, to preach the Holy Law of Jesus Christ and the moral integrity of *the civil benefits of each state* (*emphasized by the authors of this scientific work*) and to fulfill these things by word, deed, and example. By only one firm fulfilling the intention explicitly and helping the suffering people, they can renew the hope of being taken under the protection of civil authorities and enjoy the rights and advantages of cathedrals and communities tolerated by law.

So, they will observe exactly all civil duties and instill this duty in all of them. They *should expel and sweep aside all bad and obscene citizens from their ranks* (*an emphasis was added by the authors of the work*)."[2] Member 8 of the Rules directly speaks of the "common good" as a goal: "All knights of the Holy

[1] The "Knightly" Systems of Freemasonry in Russia: 1772-1822 / Yuri Kondakov. – M.: Ganga, 2017. Pages 249-253. See also: "A plan or general establishment of the Order of Freemasons" // RNB.OR.OSRK.D. OIII 14. Pages 2-103.
[2] The "Knightly" systems of Freemasonry in Russia: 1772-1822 / Yuri Kondakov. – M.: Ganga, 2017. Pages 249-250.

City that have already been admitted into the society must be revered as completely equal; may frank and fraternal friendliness reign among all Knights; may they give each other honor and courtesy, indispensable when communicating; let them feel how sweet it is to live together and unite mutual forces for the 'common good'; may they be kept by a sacred refuge of friendship, harmony, and hospitability to strangers[1]."

There are also some references to the "common good" in the Statute of the Masonic Order according to the System of the Highly Esteemed, Strong, and Wise Order of the Cavaliers and Brothers of Light in 1781, from the Seven Wise Fathers, Heads of Seven Churches in Asia. A copy of that Statute is kept in the Russian Historical State Archives[2]. The system consisted of five degrees[3]. To substantiate the establishment of the statute, it provides the assertion that "the preservation, permanent continuation, external and internal well-being of any society depends equally on their external and internal order, and, therefore, require some certain legalizations that produce this action and contain it in an everlasting activity[4]." The Statute also contains another vocabulary of the "common good": "all and everyone," "nothing against the people's rights, in general, and the rights of everyone, in particular"; "all of them together and each of them, in particular[5]." It can be noted that the vocabulary of the theory of the "common good" is associated with the "legalizations" and "people's rights." In other words, the vocabulary of the theory of the "common good" is legal.

It can be read in Paragraph 2 of the Laws of the State All-Russian Grand Lodge (dated January 5, 1780): "A Great Master or his Local Masters have the power and the right not only to be present in every working lodge but also to rule it, if they judge for the good, having a Master on the left[6]." The phrase "they will judge for the good" repeats the formula for expressing the Supreme Will in the

---

[1] The "Knightly" systems of Freemasonry in Russia: 1772-1822 / Yuri Kondakov. – M.: Ganga, 2017. Pages 249-250. Page 253.

[2] The Statute of the Masonic Order (the System of the Highly Esteemed, Strong and Wise Order of the Cavaliers and Brothers of the Light, from the Seven Wise Fathers, Heads of Seven Churches in Asia) / / RGIA. Fund 1101. List of contents 1. Case # 230. Pages 1-169.

[3] The system consisted of 5 types of degrees (from the lowest to the highest): "Chevalier Belets (Novice) of the 3rd year," "Chevalier Belets of the 5th year," "Chevalier Belets of the 7th year," "Leviticus," "Priest" // RGIA. Fund 1101. List of contents 1. Case # 230. Page 2.

[4] Ibid. Pages 1, 2.

[5] Ibid. Pages 96, 97, 99.

[6] The Laws of the State All-Russian Grand Lodge. Held on January 05, 1780. The Laws of the State Grand Lodge // RGB. NIOR. Fund 14. Case # 34. Page 2.

Imperial Decrees. This, in turn, testifies to the common (similar) legal vocabulary in the legislation of the Russian Empire and Masonic acts.

At the opening of the Provincial Lodge of the Swedish System in Moscow by Prince G. P. Gagarin in 1780, the Rhetorician of the lodge spoke by using the terms of the theory of the "common good" in the presence of Brothers. The Great Local Master, I. A. Pozdeev, was present at that opening. The speech was printed in the university printing house by N. I. Novikov in 1780 and published in Leipzig[1]. "We now see the just Radiance in the East, contemplating the Temple of Wisdom that is opening for us and feeling the general and private prosperity of every Freemason in our souls. The Great Architect pours out that prosperity to us."[2] The desire for the "common good" in the speech was combined with the construction of the Temple of Prosperity: "... who does not want to fill all the minutes of his life to restore the "common good" of Freemasons and build a Temple of Prosperity for himself in eternity …[3]." The Rhetorician finished his speech with the following words: "But if (from what may the Highest Right save us) <...> there is such a monster of cruelty among us that, after taking the work of masonry together with us, outrages our Society, brings dishonor to our name by dishonest deeds and violates the sanctity of our laws may such a brute be delivered to the Judgment of God and cut off from the number of our Brotherhood, *like a branch that makes the "common harm,"* to its eternal shame"[4] (*an emphasis was added by the authors of this research*).

There is the following line in the "Discourse on the true human welfare"[6] by Lavrenty Davydovsky, that was a student of the famous Professor and Rosicrucian I. G. Schwartz: "Following a common sense <...> it is imperative to assume that the true good should be the only one and is common to the entire human races[5]."

Now it is worth touching on the acts of the Order of the Golden-Rose Cross in the Russian Empire that had a significant impact on Russian Freemasonry and Russian society at the end of the 18th century. Yu. E. Kondakov published the

---

[1] The speech was spoken at the opening of the Provincial Lodge in M*** in the presence of His Eminence, Brother K.G.P.G. – M.: The University Printing House of N. Novikov, 1780. - 10 pages.

[2] Ibid. Page 5.

[3] Ibid. Page 8.

[4] A citation was quoted from "Russian Freemasonry in the reign of Catherine II" / G. V Vernadsky. - St. Petersburg. The publishing house named after N. I. Novikov, 1999, page 83; The speech spoken at the opening of the Provincial Lodge in M*** in the presence of His Eminence, Brother K.G.P.G. – M.: The University Printing House of N. Novikov, 1780. Page 10.

[5] Published in Part I of "Evening Dawn," and then, separately printed at the University Printing House of Novikov in 1782. A note by G. V. Vernadsky.

fourth document of “Strong Exhortation”[1]: the “List of the Order of Instructive Provisions Z. R. K. of the ancient system that was established according to the last Main and Reformation General Convention of the Summer of the Lord of 1777 with the consent of the Brothers, introduced for the good preservation of fraternal order in all Circles of the Order, and must be exactly observed from all relatives (associates) belonging to the Order under the oath of fidelity.”

Paragraph 1 of Chapter I established the duty of every Brother to not oppose the “common good”: “All people without this prescription of ours are spiritually and bodily obliged to live a virtuous life to God and Nature. However, the laws of our highly praiseworthy Brotherhood adhere to its worthy members and closely impose and entrust the most excellent fulfillment of Paragraph 1 of the Oath. This paragraph follows the Holy Fear of God, and everyone can feel this Wisdom: *nobody should act against* God, the love of a neighbor, and *the ‘common good’ of the State.* Moreover, everybody as a true Christian being a righteous person and very far from any free thought by religion, should be a peace-loving, quiet, honest, and zealous citizen as much as possible, acquiring all of this from the Creator and His Creatures” (*it was emphasized by the authors of this research*)[2].

The obligation to observe “spiritual and worldly laws” for a person’s own and universal benefit was established in Paragraph 3: “Our Brotherhood's goal is nothing more than gaining the wisdom, science, and virtue to please God and serve our neighbor.

Therefore, following our Order purpose, every Brother should be delighted with it, fulfilling his devoted to God-consecrated Order duties related to the state, religion, land, service, trade, and homebuilding affairs and corresponding with the spiritual and worldly laws for his benefit and satisfaction …[3].” After violating those above-mentioned obligations, any member of the Order had to be expelled from the Order by all means[4].

The matters of the “common good” were put in the first place in an important document relating to the duties of the Russian Rosicrucians (Rozencraitsers in the Russian sources). The name of that paper was “The positions of the R. K. Ancient System in the junior meetings, read by Chryzophiron with the

---

[1]Yu. E. Kondakov “The Secret Instructions of the Russian Rosicrucians of the 18th-19th centuries.” – M.: Ganga, 2018. Pages 436-466.
[2] Ibid. Page 436.
[3] Ibid. Page 437.
[4] Ibid. Page 466.

appendix of the speeches of other Brothers in 1782."[1] The positions were not subject to the secret Masonic requirement. It can be read in "The Ninth Convention of the Reasoning about the sixth position" that no secret regarding the "common good" can be hidden. "The bourgeoisie should first notify a Hetman. If a Hetman cannot or does not dare to solve the matter, he should go to the board, and the board must notify the Emperor![2]." It was further explained that Masonic secrets did not include the state, family, and official matters: "He never demands anything other than what concerns him. He does not want to know about the secrets of the state, home, and service belonging to the Emperor and other authorities. The betrayal of them is incompatible with the requirement …[3]."

The activities of the Masonic Order (including the activities of the lodges) and actions of each Brother of the Order had to serve "the 'common good' and the benefit of each Brother of the Order …[4]." It was emphasized in the "Discourse on the Seventh Office" of the "Tenth Convention" that, according to the meaning of the Order, the righteous person is the one that "serves his neighbor and benefits the State," "staying in humble obedience and being faithful to God and his Sovereign …[5]."

The book "Carl Hubert Labreich von Plumenek, the open influence of True Freemasonry, etc." was very popular among the Russian Rosicrucians and was included in the famous "Library Containing Some Hermetic, Kabbalistic, Magic and, in addition, the writings of the Highly Praised Brothers Z. R. K. of the Ancient System of True Freemasons, and other Books. This book was composed in Russian with modern explicable translation with detailed explanations for

---

[1]RGB. NIOR. Fund 14. # 1657 "The positions of the Z. R. K. Ancient System in the junior meetings, read by Chryzophiron with the appendix of the speeches of other Brothers in 1782." Most likely, I. Kh. Wölner, one of the German Brothers, a Prussian Minister of Justice was hiding under the pseudonym "Chrysofiron." This was indicated by Yu. E. Kondakov. See Kondakov "The Secret Instructions of the Russian Rosicrucians." Page 57. The document was signed with the name Fidelis. Page 219. It was not indicated who was hiding under the Order Name "Fidelis" in the Dictionary of A. I. Serkov (A. I. Serkov "Russian Freemasonry." 1731-2000: An encyclopedia of words. - M.: ROSSPEN, 2001. Pages 955-957). G. V. Vernadsky suggested that G. K. Ecker and Eckhoffen (1754-1809), Hamburg Lawyer, an Official of the German Duchies, and Chancellor of the Order of St. Iakim was hiding under the name Fidelis. See "Russian Freemasonry in the reign of Catherine II" / G. V. Vernadsky. - St. Petersburg.: The publishing house named after N. I. Novikov, 1999. Page 372.

[2]RGB. NIOR. Fund 14. # 1657 "The positions of the R. K. Ancient System in the junior meetings, read by Chryzophiron with the appendix of the speeches of other Brothers in 1782." Page 178.

[3]Ibid. Page 180.

[4]Ibid. Page 184.

[5]Ibid. Page 208.

exercising the knowledge of God, nature, and themselves and choosing only one true way among many false ones. Part X[1]." The book directly indicated the purpose of the influence of "True Freemasonry": "the 'common good' of the States[2]." A direct answer was given to the following question "What should be the true intention of the True Freemason, and what is his duty and vow?": "...our Brotherhood contributes to *the welfare of society* to a large degree and never teaches *against religion, the state, love of one's neighbor, and good morals...*"[3] (*it was highlighted by C. Plumenek*).

The prosperity and benefit of all mankind became the main task of the life of a Freemason: *"The closest learning of God from the works of Creation, the radical opening of all created things, and the increased benefit to all other Sciences. This is the subject of our exercises. We try to make our work useful for the common benefit of humanity. So, we can be, in all fairness, called cosmopolitans, i.e., such Citizens of the world that have a great concern for the welfare of their fellow citizens ... "*[4] (*it was highlighted by C. Plumenek*).

---

[1]Carl Hubert Labreich von Plumenech "The open influence of True Freemasonry, etc." "A Library Containing Some Hermetic, Kabbalistic, Magical, and other Books and, in addition, the writings of the Highly Praised Brothers Z.R.K. of the Ancient System of True Freemasons. Translated into Russian. Composed with the modern explanatory notes. For the benefit of those that wish to exercise in the knowledge of God, nature, and themselves; for exercising in the knowledge of God, nature, and themselves and choosing only one true way among many false ones." Part X. // RGB. NIOR. Fund 14. # 1588. According to Yu. E. Kondakov, von Levenfeld was hiding under the pseudonym "Plumenek" - see Yu. E. Kondakov "The Secret Instructions of the Russian Rosicrucians." Pages 53-57.
[2]RGB. NIOR. Fund 14. # 1588. Page 16. Compare: B. J. Schleiss von Levenfeld "The influence of True Freemasonry on the 'common good' of states, discovered and proven from the true purpose of its original establishment (foundation)" / Carl Hubert Lobreich von Plumenek. Written at the end of the 18th century, in refutation of the works of Yaakov Moser: On the tolerance of Freemasonry communities, especially regarding the Westphalia Peace. Translated from the second edition in German, printed in Amsterdam in 1779. - Moscow: Printed in the University Printing House, 1816. - [4], VIII, 211, [3] p.
[3]RGB. NIOR. Fund 14. # 1588. Page 17.
[4]Ibid. Page 22.

Picture 26. A vignette from the book of Plumenek, "The Open Influence of True Freemasonry ..." depicts the Greek Sphinx reclining on a book floating in the sea - symbols of trials, wisdom, and chaos.

The book directly refers to the books of the theorists of the "common good," popular in the German lands - J. Bielfeld and J. Justi. The author argues the respect and maintenance of the state religion by referring to the provisions already developed and proven by his predecessors: *"A person that carefully reads the writings of Bel, Walter, Arzhan, and many others of this quality will completely make sure that they want to overthrow the entire religion. However, religion is the most imminent support of the State Thrones (* Bielfeld's Concept of the Doctrine of Politics. Volume I.) and, undeniably, the greatest part of the moral state of the subjects (**) * * Justi. The State. Economic. Volume I"*[1] (*it was highlighted by C. Plumenek*). Part II of the book proves that the institution of Freemasonry was not established against religion or the state[2]. Moreover, it had a positive effect on the welfare of all states. The welfare of society and the state (in which Masonic Lodges exist) are very important: *"We should serve the state and the Authorities that were given to us by God and should be faithful. We should do everything for the welfare of society, sincerely advancing and helping with disregard of all our intentions"*[3] (*all words were highlighted in the original by C. Plumenek*). The deductive analysis of this work should be considered: it can be argued that German political and legal theory influenced German Freemasonry that, in turn, largely shaped the ideology of Russian Freemasonry. When combining this conclusion with the earlier conclusion about the continuity of German and Russian political and legal thought (Paragraph 1 of this Chapter), it can be concluded that German

---

[1]RGB. NIOR. Fund 14. # 1588. Page 27. This refers to the work of J. Bielfeld "The Political Instructions of Baron Bielfeld," translated into many European languages: Institutions Politiques, par Monsieur Le Baron de Bielfeld. Tome premier (1760), and the work of J. Justi "The state economy or a systematic treatise of all economic and cameral sciences": Staatswirtschaft oder systematische Abhandlung aller ökonomischen und Cameralwissenschaft (1755).

[2] RGB. NIOR. Fund 14. # 1588. Page 77

[3] Ibid. Page 103.

(and Russian after German) political and legal thought found a fertile environment for the dissemination of the ideas by German and Russian Freemasonry.

Some images of a socio-political utopia were given in the "New Outline of True Theology[1]," translated from French by N. N. Trubetskoy and published by I. V. Lopukhin in 1784: "… any need will gradually disappear (even mercenarism and slavery) in the new kingdom of believers, poor subjects should be exempt from taxes, the houses for beggars and pilgrims, hospitals and schools for the poor should be built on a grand scale …[2]." Society and the state will take the form of theocracy and the state within the state: the new society "in matters of conscience will have no other leader but Jesus Christ so that all its members will strive to allow themselves to be ruled solely by the Spirit of God, and to love and serve each other as brothers according to the teachings of Christ and His Apostles …[3]." Practical morality will become a guide to action: society "will strive to incessantly fulfill in the best way the good that was taught or will be taught by others …[4]." Some specialization in "departments" (Supreme, State, Church, Cathedral, Council, Zemsky, Educational, Foreign, Scientist, and Economic) should be created for better managing the society[5]. It is clear from this book (this book was very popular among Russian Freemasons) that ideas about an ideal society and the "common good" can lead to the construction of speculative utopias. Some representatives of Freemasonry tried to put those utopias into practice. However, this was not the mainstream in Russian Freemasonry. The speculative concepts of some Freemasons rather demonstrated the religious and political utopianism that had not been accepted by the bulk of Russian Freemasons supporting the existing order.

It can be read in the "Brief outline of the purpose of the Order," being part of "The Rites regarding the Student □": "… keeping and giving some important sacrament (from the very ancient ages and even the first man on the Earth) to

---

[1] A New Outline of True Theology: The doctrine of salvation is presented in a new light to the glory of God and the general edification with a letter attributed to all people: Theological and moral correction / [Translated from French by N.N. Trubetskoy]. - M.: Printed in the printing house of I. Lopukhin with decree permission, 1784. Part 1. - 442, 8 p.; A new outline of True Theology: The doctrine of salvation is presented in a new light to the glory of God and the general edification with a letter attributed to all people: Theological and moral correction / [Translated from French by N. N. Trubetskoy]. - M.: Printed in the printing house of I. Lopukhin with decree permission, 1784. Part 2. - 276.5,[1] p.

[2] A citation was quoted from "Russian Freemasonry in the reign of Catherine II" / G. V. Vernadsky. Page 245.

[3] A citation was quoted from "Russian Freemasonry in the reign of Catherine II" / G. V. Vernadsky. Page 245.

[4] Ibid. Page 246.

[5] Ibid. Page 247-248.

posterity … and, maybe, the fate of the human race depends on this sacrament as long as God is favorably disposed, opening this sacrament *for the good of mankind* and to the whole world …"[1] (*an emphasis was added by the authors of this study.*).

The documents that were widespread among most of the Masonic Systems in the Russian Empire at the end of the 18th – the first quarter of the 19th centuries should be considered further.

An extremely important document circulated among Russian Freemasons (Russian Freemasons used this paper when working in the Masonic Lodges and drawing up the internal Masonic acts) is the Charter of Freemasons[2]. The Charter was attributed by T. O. Sokolovskaya, Yu. Kondakov, and other scientists. It was established that the main provisions of the Charter had been developed at the Wilhelmsbad convention in 1782. However, the final Charter was formulated by Russian Freemasons in 1787[3]. Not all lodges in Europe accepted the provisions of the Wilhelmsbad Convention. The provisions of the Charter as exemplary were duplicated in many Masonic Lodges of the 19th century, being subject to interpretation[4]. The desire for the "common good" among the Freemasons was transformed into love for the Fatherland. The "common good" included the general order, the trust and respect of the Sovereigns, the excellent performance of the state (warrior, judge), public (lord, servant), and family (husband, son) positions. A Freemason voluntarily and freely re-assumed the same duties that civil law and public morality imposed on a citizen[5].

It was stated in Member 3 of the "General Establishments of Freemasons" that was an integral part of the "General Laws of Freemasons": "A man that is not completely devoted to the faith he was born in, that does not obey his Sovereign and Fatherland, and that does not observe good behavior should not be admitted to

---

[1] "A brief outline of the purpose of the Order," "The rites regarding the Student □"// RGB. NIOR. Fund 14. # 65. "The Acts." Page 2.

[2] A Charter of Freemasons that was approved at the General Council of the Convention that was held in Wilhelmsbad in 1787 // The Secret Archives of Russian Freemasons / T. Sokolovskaya, D. Lotareva. - Moscow: Veche, 2007. Pages 344-354. See RGB. NIOR. Fund 14. # 1 "The Charter or Rule of Freemasons". Pages 1-7.

[3] See, for example, "An Interpretation of the Charter of Freemasons" (dated March 18, 1820) // RGB. NIOR. Fund 14. # 12. 1727.

[4] Thus, the Lodge of the Three Globes in Berlin declared independence from the decisions of the Wilhelmsbad Convention. See the answer of the Lodge of the Three Globes in Berlin on independence from the decisions of the Wilhelmsbad Convention // RGB. NIOR. Fund 147. # 5.7. Page 55.

[5] A Charter of Freemasons, approved by the General Council of the Convention that was held in Wilhelmsbad in 1787. Pages 346-347.

the Freemasonry Order[1]." A citizen that had a damaged reputation and experienced civil death because of a civil court conviction for a crime, etc. could not join the Freemasons. In other words, there was no place for "followers" of the "common harm" in the Masonic Lodges. Thus, the approach to the selection of candidates for disciples, demonstrated by the Masonic Lodges, allowed to cut off certain candidates that, after their initiation into the lodge, could oppose the "common good," harming themselves, the state, society, and, finally, the Masonic Lodge itself.

One of the researchers of Freemasonry, an outstanding bibliographer, Augusta Vladimirovna Meziere (1869-1935), noted the desire of Freemasons for the "common good." In her opinion, the main goal of Freemasonry was "erasing the prejudices of castes, conditional differences of origin, opinions, and nationalities among people, destroying fanaticism and superstition, eradicating the international hostility and the scourge of war, by using the free and peaceful progress, achieving the consolidation of the eternal and universal right (every person can realize the free and full development of all his or her abilities by using this right), and advancing for the 'common good' with all efforts[4]." A. V. Meziere said that, of course, not all Freemasons had mastered this understanding of Freemasonry, but "… this characteristic is repeated in many Masonic works in parts …[5]."

[1] "The General Institutions of Freemasons," "The General Laws of Freemasons"// RGB. NIOR. Fund 14. # 4. Pages 1-9. Page 2. See also: "The General Institutions of Freemasons"// RGB. NIOR. Fund 14. # 65. "The Acts." Page 13.

Chapter conclusions

The theory of the "common good" became a universal dogma of Western Europe in modern times, realized in political theory, diplomatic correspondence, legal texts and laws, the opinions of lawyers, and various projects of reforms. This theory became widespread in Russia at the end of the 18th century.

According to this theory, the "common good" as a category began to be considered as a goal (the possession of things, the punishment of a criminal, the restriction of rights, rule, the conclusion and execution of a contract), interest ("open sea," "virtues," "life," "the preservation of faith," "the fulfillment of promises," "the fulfillment of contracts," "well-being," etc.), and method (when making decisions). The opposite of the "common good" was the "common harm" - an extremely negative phenomenon. The "common good" in its value was equal to the good of everyone. They could not contradict each other. The "common good" in the Russian theory of the welfare of all and everyone was understood as general and individual happiness (the greater good), a criterion for making decisions, and a method for reconciling interests. The benefits flowing from an autocratic rule were equal to the benefits that were given by liberty. The laws had to be arranged in such a way that when achieving his or her benefit, everybody would benefit from the general use and vice versa. The theory of the welfare of all and everyone extended its influence on education, politics, and law. The terminology of the theory became part of the official business turnover and bills on settling the government. Catherine II, Paul I, and Alexander I adopted the terms and principles of the theory of the welfare of all and everyone, proclaiming the welfare of all and everyone and the prevention of the "common harm" as the goal of their reign. The "common good" was seen by them as an interest, a balance of interests between the state and citizens, and a method for making decisions. The phrase "We have recognized for the good" became a stable expression to denote the legislative will of the Monarch. The theory of the welfare of all and everyone in the first quarter of the 19th century was replaced by the ideas of speculative morality, unlimited subjective freedom, political consciousness, and new social modernization. Those new notions resulted in the Decembrist uprising of 1825. The vocabulary of the theory of the "common good" was present in the Masonic acts, documents, and speeches that were widespread among Brothers-Freemasons, both "Knightly Systems" and the Rosicrucians (Rozencraitsers in the Russian sources). The welfare of all and everyone was the goal of the Masonic Order.

Chapter III

The welfare of all and everyone and the generations of Russian Freemasons

§3.1. The "common good" in the first generation of Russian Freemasons (1750-1769)

To understand the periodicity of the development of the state and legal ideas of Russian Freemasons, the complex reconstructed picture of ideas was divided into several conditional temporary parts (the generations of the membership of an author-Freemason in the Masonic Lodges) by the author of this scientific work (the 1st generation - membership in Masonic Lodges in 1750-1769, the 2nd generation - in 1770-1789, the 3rd generation - 1790-1809, and the 4th generation - 1810-1822)[1]. The knowledge of the generations, together with the imposition of the chronology of generations on the chronology of Russian history (the reign of the imperial family, war, uprising), allows us to talk about legal succession or, conversely, about the difference in ideologies, including state-legal ones. Therefore, the material was presented by the author of this scientific work by following the generations of Russian Freemasonry. If the investigated person or group of persons belong to several generations, they are listed in the section (mentioning the terms of the theory of the "common good") of the generation the work was written or published in. If there is no such work during the period of interest in membership in Masonic Lodges, then, by default, the author is ranked for the generation that came earlier[2]. It is necessary to move on to the analysis of the works of Russian Freemasons, considering the extent to which the theory of the "common good" has been reflected in them from generation to generation.

---

[1]The first two generations have been studied more extensively than presented in this paper and are presented in Appendix # 3..

[2] So, Peter Ivanovich Melissino belongs to the 1st and 2nd generations of Russian Freemasons but is given only in the first generation.

The first generation of Russian Freemasons (1750-1769)

The first generation of Russian Freemasonry was the generation of "pioneers." Masonic Lodges were just emerging in Russia at that time, and the Russian noble audience began to get acquainted with Masonic Systems and rituals. It should be said that Freemasonry in the countries of Western Europe at that time was already developed (Sweden, the Kingdom of Prussia, and England) and was sending its "emissaries" to the Russian Empire. Freemasonry enjoyed the patronage of the Imperial Family in the Russian Empire: Peter III established a Masonic Lodge in Oranienbaum. The first generation embraced the Seven Years War against Prussia (1756-1761), the palace coup of 1762, the strengthening of the role of the nobility, and the centralization of the state under Catherine II.

The first Freemason worth mentioning was Ivan Nikitich Boltin (1735-1792), a native of the nobility (his father was a steward), writer, historian, and archivist. When joining the Freemasons, he was a young officer. When being in Freemasonry, he was a Prime Major. After his visible departure from Freemasonry, he became a Major General and Prosecutor. He enjoyed the patronage of other Freemasons: I. P. Elagin and A. I. Musin-Pushkin. I. N. Boltin became a Freemason at the age of 21 and got a solid 24-year experience in Freemasonry, belonging to the 1st and 2nd generations: from 1756 to 1779. I. N. Boltin was a member of the Lodge of 1756 in St. Petersburg from 1756-1759. He served as a Grand Master in the Chapter of the Templar System in St. Petersburg in the 1760s. I. N. Boltin also served as the great Rhetorician for the Russian language at the Provincial Grand Lodge in St. Petersburg in 1779 and the secretary of the Phoenix Chapter in St. Petersburg in 1779[1]. I. N. Boltin stopped participating in the lodges at the age of 44. When beginning to serve under G. A. Potemkin, he wrote his main works after 1780. Apparently, I. N. Boltin ceased being active in the lodges at that time. Nevertheless, he continued being friends with some Freemasons and sharing Masonic ideas.

I. N. Boltin was one of those Russian historians that published and commentated on the monuments of Russian Law. I. N. Boltin wrote in a response letter to the remarks of Prince Shcherbatov, published in 1789, describing the life of Prince Vladimir: "He did not appropriate the pride and curiosity for the

---

[1]Russian Freemasons.1721-2019. A Biographical Dictionary. Century XVIII. Volume I / A. I. Serkov, M.: Ganga, 2019. Pages 197-199, Russian Freemasons. 1721-2019. A Biographical Dictionary. Century XVIII. Volume III / A. I. Serkov, M.: Ganga, 2019. Pages 113, 121, 146, 200.

irrelevant activities of Vladimir, did not present Vladimir frivolous, caring about the welfare of his subjects only a little bit ...[1]." I. N. Boltin described the well-being of all, which came into conflict with the well-being of everyone: "... and although some of them got the lands near the city, the lands were allotted to all generally and not to everyone particularly, and not by another right all state peasants now have them by. Those lands were numbered and called the Sovereign's lands, as exactly in the Code: Chapter XVIII, Article 51 ...[2]." I. N. Boltin used the terms of the "common good" theory in his comments to the Russian Truth, published in 1792. He noted the concern of Her Imperial Majesty for "the welfare of the Empire" on page I[3]. I. N. Boltin used the phrase "it is especially useful for the community and everyone" on Pages V and VI[4].

Picture 27. A sign of the secretary of the lodge with the image of a goose feather on the plate. Russia. The first quarter of the 19th century. Published in the book "Collection of the Hermitage." 2013. Page 167.

I. N. Boltin's opinion on the state and legal issues can be considered representative of the entire Russian Freemasonry of the 18th century as he had 24 years of experience of membership in Masonic Lodges, collaborating with I. P. Elagin, A. I. Musin-Pushkin, M. M. Shcherbatov, and other well-known

[1] I. N. Boltin "Major General Boltin's response to a letter from Prince Shcherbatov, writer of Russian history." - St. Petersburg: The printing house of the Mining School, [17]89. Page 22.
[2] I. N. Boltin "Major General Boltin's response to a letter from Prince Shcherbatov, writer of Russian history." - St. Petersburg: The printing house of the Mining School, [17]89. Page 139.
[3] Russian Truth or the Laws of the Grand Dukes Yaroslav Vladimirovich and Vladimir Vsevolodovich Monomakh: With the application of the ancient adverbs and syllables to those in common use today and with an explanation of the words and names that became obsolete / Published by lovers of national history. - St. Petersburg: The printing house of the St. Ruler of Synod, 1792. Page I.
[4] Ibid. Pages V-VI.

Freemasons holding the positions of the Great Rhetorician and Secretary of the Chapter (the highest positions in the Masonic Lodges and the governing bodies of the Masonic Lodges). He published "Pravda Russkaya" together with I. P. Elagin and A. I. Musin-Pushkin, providing it with his comments. The works of M. V. Lomonosov and V. N. Tatishchev deeply influenced I. N. Boltin (I. N. Boltin recognized V. N. Tatishchev as his teacher)[1]. I. N. Boltin was an adherent of the "common good" and a patriot of Russia (those facts were reflected in his works).

It is impossible to ignore the Counts of the Vorontsov family, which left a significant mark on the history of Russia. Some of these Counts became Freemasons. Roman Illarionovich Vorontsov (1717-1783) came from a Russian noble family of the early 16th century. He was born into the family of a Privy Councilor, was the Chairman of the Commissioned Commission for drawing up a New Code, a Senator, and a compiler of a noble program. His membership in the Masonic Lodges was impressive: a Master of the Chair, a Granmeter of the Masonic Lodge of 1756 in St. Petersburg in 1756-1759, a member of the Equality Lodge in Moscow and St. Petersburg, a candidate for the post of a Great Master on 07.06.1775; a Great Provincial-Local Master of the Great (English) Provincial Lodge in St. Petersburg in 1772-1775; a Visitor to the Urania Lodge in St. Petersburg on 02.07.1775 and 02.14.1775, then an honorary member of this lodge from 03.14. 1775, a member of the 4th Degree in 1783[2]. Alexander Romanovich Vorontsov (1741-1805), son of R. I. Vorontsov (an Acting Chamberlain, an Acting Privy Councilor, an Honorary Doctor of Civil Law at the University of Oxford, a Judge, a Senator, a Chancellor of the State, Minister) was a member of the Urania Lodge in St. Petersburg in 1773-1775, was scheduled to join and accept the Degree of a Scottish Master in the Great (English) Provincial Lodge in St. Petersburg in 1776. A. R. Vorontsov patronized A. N. Radishchev, and G. R. Derzhavin[3]. A. R. Vorontsov was considered a Staunch Statesman. So, he did not accept the anti-constitutional coup in France[4]. A. R. Vorontsov was promoted to Chancellor in 1802. He defended the rights of the Senate together with his brother S. R.

[1]The Brilliant Age of Catherine II. The second half of the 18th century: a biographical guide: in 4 parts. Part 4 / A compiler and author: V. N. Nikulin. - Kaliningrad: The Publishing House of the Russian State University named after I. Kant, 2010. Page 26.

[2] Russian Freemasons.1721-2019. A Biographical Dictionary. Century XVIII. Volume I / A. I. Serkov, M.: Ganga, 2019. Pages 310-311; Russian Freemasons.1721-2019. A Biographical Dictionary. Century XVIII. Volume III / A. I. Serkov, M.: Ganga, 2019. Pages 22, 5, 82, 121, 169.

[3] Ibid. Pages 82, 169.

[4] N. E. Dorohova "'Russian Tories' and the socio-political thought of Western European education at the turn of the 18th-19th centuries": An abstract of the thesis of a Candidate in Historical Sciences: 07.00.02 / Tomsk State University. - Tomsk, 2006. Page 17.

Vorontsov and participated in the development of a project for the modernization of the Estate Monarchy in Russia: "The all-merciful Deed granted to the Russian people." A. R. Vorontsov called the Deed in French a "constitution" ("une Constitution qui bornedes on Pouvoir et donne droits ..." - the Constitution that limits Power and grants rights...)[1].

Count A. R. Vorontsov emphasized in his note "On Russia at the beginning of the present century[2]," presented to Emperor Alexander Pavlovich upon assuming the office of State Chancellor in November 1801, that "I had only one desire for the common benefit in all my previous ministry, being alien from all personal views and not looking for benefits for myself[3]." A. R. Vorontsov revealed the essence of the common benefit in his note and argued that it rested on the welfare of everyone. Upon accession to the throne of Alexander I (of course, that was the "common good"), all subjects "came alive," and "… each of them, no matter where he or she lived in Russia, whether he or she found himself or herself in the service or his or her own home, feels that he or she began to have a quiet stay from that very day …[4]." A. R. Vorontsov convinced the Emperor that the common well-being had its law of personal security or private bliss: "A prosperous state, the guarantee of which is personal security we all now use, of course, must be and is precious," and everyone wishes "its steadfastness[5]." "Achieving this goal depends on the concern for the 'common good,' all private benefits are inseparably linked with." Various deficiencies in the state structure affected "the private welfare of everyone[6]."

A. R. Vorontsov mentioned some people opposing the "common good" in his notes "About my life and various events[7]." Thus, he wrote: "I opposed strongly to the opinion of some high-ranking and influential people when they disagreed with the 'common good.' In return, they successfully inflicted on me. I suffered a lot of trouble from their vicious blows. I endured them without changing my rules

---

[1] V. N. Alekseev "Counts of the Vorontsov family in the political and public life of Russia in the 2nd half of the 18th – the 1st half of the 19th centuries": An abstract of the thesis of a Candidate in Historical Sciences. Vladimir, 2010. Page 17, 18.

[2] A note by Count A. R. Vorontsov about Russia at the beginning of this century, presented to Emperor Alexander Pavlovich / / An archive of Prince Vorontsov / Edited by P. I. Bartenev – M.: The printing house of A. I. Mamontov, 1870-1897. Book 29: The letters from foreigners to Counts of the Vorontsov family. 1883. Pages 449-470.

[3] Ibid. Page 451.

[4] Ibid. Page 452.

[5] Ibid. Page 453.

[6] Ibid. Page 453.

[7] A. R. Vorontsov "The notes about my life and various events that took place during this time both in Russia and in Europe." A Russian archive. 1883. Prince. 1. Issue. 2. Pages 227-249.

or my model of action[1]." It is important that A. R. Vorontsov's love for the "common good" was combined with his knowledge (at the age of 12) of the works of Voltaire, Racin, Corneille, Boileau, a penchant for politics and history[2], and a legal education he gained at 12-14 at a boarding house (a Professor of Jurisprudence Strube de Pyrmont taught him there)[3].

Artemy Ivanovich Vorontsov (1748-1813), a member of the Three Banners Lodge in Moscow of the 4th Degree in 1784-1785, who rose to the rank of a Real Chamberlain, a Real Privy Councilor, a Senator[4], and Semyon Romanovich Vorontsov (1744 -1832) that rose to the rank of a General from Infantry and occupied the post of Extraordinary and Plenipotentiary Ambassador in London were the members of the Masonic Lodges. S. R. Vorontsov was noted in Freemasonry for the following: the 2nd Overseer in 1774, a member of the Mars Lodge in Yassy in 1775, planned in September 1776 as a member of the Great (English) Provincial Lodge in St. Petersburg as a Scottish Master; a member of the Lodge of the North Star in Warsaw in 1780; a member of the Lodge of Silence (Modesty) in St. Petersburg, the 6th Degree in 1786[5]. According to N. E. Dorokhova, S. R. Vorontsov learned the concepts of "a citizen," "enlightenment," and "natural rights" for life. When being at the age of 16, he became acquainted with the work of Ch. L. Montesquieu's "The Spirit of the Laws." That work shaped the convictions of Count[6]. It can be assumed that S. R. Vorontsov's rationalism and craving for knowledge brought him to the Masonic Lodges. Moreover, R. I. Vorontsov's Father himself belonged to the Freemasons of high dedication. S. R. Vorontsov created his Moscow notes in the form of "The Highly Philosophical Discourse on Freemasonry[7]" of 1785. He analyzed the works of R. Descartes, Helvetius (Gelvetsy in the Russian sources), and Jung (Yung in the Russian sources), cited some examples from his own life, and recalled his meetings with A.

---

[1] A. R. Vorontsov "The notes about my life and various events that took place during this time both in Russia and in Europe." A Russian archive. 1883. Prince. 1. Issue. 2. Page 228.
[2] Ibid. Page 232.
[3] Ibid. Page 234.
[4] Russian Freemasons. 1721-2019. A Biographical Dictionary. Century XVIII. Volume I / Serkov A.I., M.: Ganga, 2019. Pages 308-309, Russian Freemasons. 1721-2019. A Biographical Dictionary. Century XVIII. Volume III / A. I. Serkov, M.: Ganga, 2019. Page 71.
[5] Russian Freemasons. 1721-2019. A Biographical Dictionary. Century XVIII. Volume I / Serkov A.I., M.: Ganga, 2019. Pages 308-309, Russian Freemasons. 1721-2019. A Biographical Dictionary. Century XVIII. Volume III / A. I. Serkov, M.: Ganga, 2019. Pages 82, 125, 260, 268.
[6] N. E. Dorohova "'Russian Tories' and the socio-political thought of Western European education at the turn of the 18th-19th centuries": An abstract of the thesis of a Candidate in Historical Sciences: 07.00.02 / Tomsk State University - Tomsk, 2006. Page 16.
[7] Highly philosophical reasoning about Freemasonry//RGADA. Fund 1261. List of contents 1. Case # 2951. 84 pages.

I. Vorontsov and V. N. Guryev in his notes. His note about his joining Freemasonry and the subsequent disillusionment with it explains the existing fashion of the nobility for secret societies. S. R. Vorontsov indicated in his note (dated September 22, 1785) that he had been ordained into Freemasonry by I. P. Elagin 13 years ago. "I was attending the Masonic Lodge for several years, but I did not find [anything] for my soul-nourishing [,] and stopped visiting it. There were no meetings in this lodge for a long time already[1]."

It can be noted that Counts from the Vorontsov family belonged to all four generations of Russian Freemasons. "The Notes of I. V. Lopukhin[2]," a note "Some Free thoughts of an elderly citizen and his loving Fatherland[3]," and a note "On the state power (composition)[4]" can be found in Fund 36 ("The Vorontsov family is an ancient noble family: Vorontsov Mikhail Illarionovich (1714 -1767), Count; Vorontsov Roman Illarionovich (1707-1783), Count") of the Scientific and Historical Archives of the St. Petersburg Institute of History of the Russian Academy of Sciences. The selection of these notes testified to a genuine interest in advanced political and legal thought. When looking through the archives of the Vorontsov family and glancing over their documents and materials, it can be noticed that Russian Freemasons developed various projects to modernize the state structure and improve legislation, actively exchanging their thoughts and works of domestic and foreign authors, including an anonymous character in the second half of the 18th and the first quarter of the 19th centuries.

Picture 28. A sign of the Chair Master of one of the Degrees of St. Andrew's Freemasonry. Russia. The XVIII century. The sign depicts a nine-pointed star, an equilateral four-pointed cross with the Apostle Andrew the First-Called crucified on it. Published in the book Collection of the Hermitage. 2013. Page 172.

[1] Highly philosophical reasoning about Freemasonry // RGADA. Fund 1261. List of contents 1. Case # 2951. Page 51.
[2] The notes by I. V. Lopukhin. Book VII, 1802 // NIA II SPB RAN. Fund 36 "The Vorontsov family are an ancient noble family: Vorontsov Mikhail Illarionovich (1714-1767), Count; Vorontsov Roman Illarionovich (1707-1783), Count." List of contents 1. Unit of issue 753.
[3] Some free thoughts of an elderly citizen and his loving Fatherland // NIA II SPB RAS. Fund 36 "The Vorontsov Family ...." List of contents 2. Unit of issue 80.
[4] On state power (an essay) // NIA II SPB RAS. Fund 36 "The Vorontsov Family ...." List of contents 2. Unit of issue 84.

Gavriil Petrovich Gagarin (1745-1808) was a very important figure in Russian Freemasonry. He was a native of the ancient clan of the Starodubskaya Branch of the Rurikovich family, a Senator, a Chief Prosecutor who received home education, a member of the Friendly Scientific Society, a Minister, a member of the Permanent Council and the State Council, a member of the Drafting-Laws Commission. G. P. Gagarin was a friend of Alexander B. Kurakin and Alexey B. Kurakin, being, like them, the nephew of P. I. Panin and N. I. Panin. His Masonic work began with the meetings of the membership in a Chapter of the Templar System (Strict Supervision Chapter) in St. Petersburg between 1760 and 1770, a Chair Master and a member of the 7th Degree of English Freemasonry in the Equality Lodge in Moscow and St. Petersburg in 1775-1777.

He was adopted to the Highest Degree of the Swedish Masonic System in 1776 in Stockholm (when living there in 1776-1777) together with A. B. Kurakin. G. P. Gagarin served as the 2nd Guard in the Great (English) Provincial Lodge in St. Petersburg in 1777. Then, he founded the Phoenix Lodge in St. Petersburg, was a Chair Master in 1777-1779, and signed the constitution of the Elagin-Zinnendorf (Tsinnendorf in the Russian sources) Union on behalf of the lodge.

G. P. Gagarin served as a Governor of the Phoenix Chapter, being the Great Prefect of the Chapter since 1778, received the position of the Grand National Master (Grand Master) in 1779, and had a membership in the Chapter in 1781. G. P. Gagarin served as the Grand National (Provincial) Master in the Provincial Grand Lodge in St. Petersburg from 1778 up to 1780. He moved to Moscow in 1781 when the work of the lodge was suspended. Further activities of G. P. Gagarin were associated with Moscow: he served as a Chair Master in Aspis's Lodge in 1780 and was an Honorary Member of the Harmony Lodge in 1780-1783 and a Chair Master in the Lodge of the Sphinx[1].

G. P. Gagarin noted his commitment to the service of God, his neighbor, and the Tsar in his essay "The fun of my solitude in the village of Bogoslovskoye[2]": "When saying that I should renounce, I do not mean by this that I should run away from everything a person may be called to by his rank in the world. But I mean that if a person is noble, rich, and powerful, then he or she

---

[1] Russian Freemasons. 1721-2019. A Biographical Dictionary. Century XVIII. Volume I / A. I. Serkov, M.: Ganga, 2019. Pages 333-335; Russian Freemasons. 1721-2019. A Biographical Dictionary. Century XVIII. Volume III / A. I. Serkov, M.: Ganga, 2019. Pages 42, 48, 55, 60, 62, 82, 114,147, 199, 200, 269.

[2] G. P. Gagarin "The amusements of my solitude in the village of Bogoslovsky" / / The remaining creation of Prince Gavriil Petrovich Gagarin. - St. Petersburg: Printed in the printing house of the Military Ministry, 1813. – 185 pages.

should use all such advantages for the glory of God and the benefit of his or her neighbor[1]."

The opinion of G. P. Gagarin on the state and legal issues can be considered representative of all Russian Freemasonry at the end of the 18th century as he had a 14-year experience of membership in various Masonic Lodges, held senior positions in different Masonic Lodges and Chapters, was the founder of several Masonic Lodges and the bearer of High Degrees. His few works depicted the Masonic ideology and adherence to the natural-legal picture of the world.

Pyotr Ivanovich Melisissino (1726-1797) was I. N. Boltin's Brother in Freemasonry (the author of this work mentioned I. N. Boltin earlier). P. I. Melissino came from a noble Greek family, was a Director of the Cadet Corps, entered Freemasonry with the rank of Major (1759), and became the Chief of Artillery after the closure of his lodges on behalf of Catherine II. P. I. Melissino was initiated into Freemasonry by A. B. Kurakin, then became the creator of a new system of 4 Higher Degrees, and was a member of the 1956 Lodge in St. Petersburg. He founded the Lodge of Silence (Modesty) in St. Petersburg In 1768, acted as a Chair Master (in 1770-1777 and 1781) and a Local Master, being a member of the 6th Degree Lodge (in 1786-1787). P. I. Melissino signed the constitution of the Elagin-Zinnendorf Union on behalf of the lodge, served as the 1st Grand Overseer of the Great English Provincial Lodge (VaPL) in 1776-1779, was a Delegate of the VaPL to the Provincial Chapter in September 1776 and had a Scottish Master's Degree. Later, P. I. Melissino was a member and a Chair Master of the Mars Lodge in Yassy in 1773-1774 and an Honorary Member of the Urania Lodge in St. Petersburg, starting from 04.12. 1774[2]. P. I. Melissino had extensive experience in Freemasonry from 1759 to 1787: 29 years (the 1st and 2nd generations).

Picture 29. An image of the coat of arms of the Melissino clan // P. P. Winkler "Russian Heraldry: The History and Description of the Russian coats of arms, depicting all the nobles and coats of arms, introduced in the All-Russian general armorial." Issue 2. 1894, page 89.

[1] G. P. Gagarin "The amusements of my solitude in the village of Bogoslovsky" / / The remaining creation of Prince Gavriil Petrovich Gagarin. - St. Petersburg: Printed in the printing house of the Military Ministry, 1813. – pages 137-138.

[2] Russian Freemasons. 1721-2019. Century XVIII. Volume II / A. I. Serkov, M.: Ganga, 2019. Pages 102-103. Russian Freemasons. Century XVIII. Volume III / A. I. Serkov, M., 2019. Pages 83, 122, 129, 183, 260.

P. I. Melissino was a supporter of the good of all and everyone. His ode to the case of a peace treaty with the Swedes can be taken for illustrating:

"Ross rejoices with a thundering glory,
Ross is blessed by CATHERINA."
"I arranged many things,
Creating the good for the Ross:
SHE, raising me,
Surpassed my hopes.
For the well-being of man,
The Creator, prolong! HER days of the century …[1]."

The opinion of P. I. Melissino on the state and legal issues can be considered representative of the entire Russian Freemasonry of the 18th century as he had 29 years of experience in his membership in various Masonic Lodges, was a Leader of many Masonic Lodges, created a new system, founded a new lodge, and had different High Degrees. P. I. Melissino was a supporter of government constitutionalism as he was in solidarity with the politics and ideology of Catherine II. This fact can be understood by reading his works.

Alexander Petrovich Sumarokov (1717-1777) was a major figure in Russian Freemasonry of the 18th century. He was a native of the family of Swedish nobles, coming from the family of a Real Privy Councilor, a Real State Councilor at the peak of his service, a writer, a poet, and a member of the 1756 Lodge in St. Petersburg in 1756-1759. A. P. Sumarokov was a member of the Society of the Lovers of Russian Literature together with I. P. Elagin, P. I. Melissino, A. P. Melgunov, and N. V. Repnin. A. P. Sumarokov enjoyed the patronage of A. G. Razumovsky[2].

A. P. Sumarokov defines the Creator as the source of benefit and prosperity in Word VII "On love for one's neighbor." The prosperity of a neighbor is the glory of the Creator. The viceroys of God are concerned about "the benefits

---

[1] P. I. Melissino "A description of the fireworks at the end of the celebration in case of peace concluded between Her Imperial Majesty Catherine II and His Majesty Gustav the Third, King of Sweden": Presented in St. Petersburg on the Tsaritsyn Meadow on September 1790. - St. Petersburg: Printed at the printing house of I. K. Shnor, 1790. Page 8.

[2]Russian Freemasons. 1721-2019. A Biographical Dictionary. Century XVIII. Volume II / A. I. Serkov, M., 2019. Pages 499-501; Russian Freemasons. Century XVIII. Volume III / A. I. Serkov, M., 2019. Page 122.

of the human race." The "Crown-bearer the Great Catherine"[1] also belongs to the viceroys of God.

When studying the work of A. P. Sumarokov, P. N. Berkov noted the following. According to A. P. Sumarokov, the purpose of human life is the "good." "Something that is based on nature and truth can never be misplaced. If something has other grounds, it can be boasted, deceived, introduced, and withdrawn at the will of everybody and without any reason[2]." Morality takes care of the private good. Politics takes care of the "common good." It is understandable that the "clearer" the "mind" of people, the more correct their "morality" and "politics." P. N. Berkov noted that these provisions were the basis of the entire system of the social and political views of Sumarokov. A. P. Sumarokov shared the theory of the welfare of all and everyone, and his opinion was listened to by the noble elite of the 18th century. Therefore, his opinion on the state and legal issues can be considered representative.

It is worth considering Mikhail Mikhailovich Shcherbatov (1733-1790), that was one of the famous historians of the 18th century. M. M. Shcherbatov was from the Rurik family and was raised in the family of a major general. He rose to the rank of a Real Privy Councilor and a Senator during his life. M. M. Shcherbatov was the author of the project on social reforms. According to the history of Russian legal thought, he gained fame for his works. M. M. Shcherbatov was a Freemason of the first generation (1740-1760): he was a member of the 1756 Lodge in St. Petersburg in 1756-1759 and a member of the Chapter of the Templar System and the Chapter of the Petropolitanum in St. Petersburg, starting from 1760[3].

---

[1] A. P. Sumarokov "A complete collection of all the works (verses and prose) of the late Acting State Councilor, a member of the Order of St. Anna Cavalier and the Leipzig Academic Assembly, Alexander Petrovich Sumarokov." Collected and published for the pleasure of the lovers of Russian scholarship by Nikolai Novikov, a member of the Free Russian Assembly at the Imperial Moscow University. – The 2nd edition - Moscow: The University Printing House of N. Novikov, 1787. Part 2. Pages 276-277.

[2] Quoted from P. N. Berkov's "The life and literary path of A. P. Sumarokov" // A. P. Sumarokov "The selected works." – L.: Soviet writer. 1957. Page 12.

[3] Russian Freemasons. 1721-2019. A Biographical Dictionary. Century XVIII. Volume II / A. I. Serkov, M.: Ganga, 2019. Pages 704-706; Russian Freemasons. 1721-2019. A Biographical Dictionary. Century XVIII. Volume III / A. I. Serkov, M.: Ganga, 2019. Pages 115, 123.

M. M. Shcherbatov used the term "the bliss of the people"[1] in his well-known essay "On the Damage of Morals in Russia[2]."

M. M. Shcherbatov posed the following questions to the theory of the welfare of all and everyone in his essay "On the Methods of Teaching Various Sciences"[3]: to find out "what each particular citizen of the society owes to the society and his or her neighbor, and, on the contrary, what the society itself owes to each particular citizen …[4]."

Prince Shcherbatov used the term "the bliss of the people" in his letter about the nobles[5], putting "a direction of the flow of things towards better accomplishment" in this concept. The nobles are the rulers of the state, "otherwise, there would be no need to have rulers if they were only used for corruption and damage …." [6] A Monarch "… gives part of his or her power" to the rulers that enforce the laws so that "the tokens of his favors spread everywhere, and everyone was safe about his or her life, honor, and estates …"[7]. The nobles must obey the law, realize the paternal power of a Sovereign, set an example of high morality (mercy, condescension, good behavior, etc.), and "fully cognize" the law[8].

M. M. Shcherbatov gave an example of the superiority of the common use over the private one in the Discourse "The consideration of the Vices and Autocracy of Peter the Great"[9]: Peter the Great with patience tolerated the behavior of "Prince Dmitry Mikhailovich Golitsyn that forced to destroy the composition of the Camor-Collegiate Regulations drawn by Peter the Great. In other words, yielding his favor to the benefit of the State and seeing the sincerity of the hearts of

---

[1] M. M. Shcherbatov "'On the damage to morals in Russia' by Prince Shcherbatov and 'A journey from St. Petersburg to Moscow' by A. Radishchev" / A preface by Iskander [a pseudonym of A. I. Herzen]. - London: Trubner & C°, 1858. - XVI, II, 340 pages.

[2] Ibid. Page 16.

[3] M. M. Shcherbatov "The works of Prince M. M. Shcherbatov": Volumes 1-2. - St. Petersburg: Prince B. S. Shcherbatov, 1896-1898. – in 2 volumes; 26. The historical, political, and philosophical articles / Edited by I. P. Khrushchov and A. G. Voronov. - 1898. Pages 439-602.

[4] Ibid. Page 588.

[5] M. M. Shcherbatov "A letter to the nobles of the rulers of the state, the works of Senator and Prince M. M. Shcherbatov" // Russian antiquity. - 1872. - Volume 5. - # 1. - Pages 1-15.

[6] Ibid. Page 4.

[7] Ibid. Page 4.

[8] Ibid. Page 4.

[9] M. M. Shcherbatov "The consideration of the Vices and Autocracy of Peter the Great. Conversation" // Different works of Prince M. M. Shcherbatov / A foreword by O. Bodyansky. – M.: The University Printing House. 1860. Pages 5-22.

his graceful servants, Peter the Great did not punish his subjects. Moreover, he showered them with his favors[1]."

The opinion of Prince M. M. Shcherbatov on the state and legal issues for the Russian Freemasonry of the 18th century cannot be considered representative as the information about his membership in Masonic Lodges after the 1760s was not preserved. M. M. Shcherbatov wrote some manuscripts "into the table" because they contained some criticism of the existing political and legal system. Those manuscripts began being published only in the second half of the 19th century.

One of the key figures in Russian Freemasonry was Mikhail Matveyevich Kheraskov (1733-1807), Actual Privy Councilor, a curator of Moscow University, a writer, a poet, and a playwright. He served with A. P. Sumarokov, Counts of the Orlov family, Counts of the Panin family, Prince N. N. Trubetskoy, and Prince M. M. Shcherbatov. They were his colleagues. M. M. Kheraskov, in turn, patronized N. I. Novikov and I. G. Schwartz (Shvarts in the Russian sources) and wrote some philosophical songs to A. A. Rzhevsky and S. E. Desnitsky. It can be assumed that M. M. Kheraskov was ordained a Freemason in the late 1760s because according to the available information, he had already served in the Apollo Lodge in St. Petersburg as the Local Master in 1771. To obtain this position, it was necessary to have a Master's Degree that cannot be given overnight.

M. M. Kheraskov was a Scottish Master in the Great (English) Provincial Lodge in St. Petersburg in September 1776 and was appointed to the Grand Provincial Lodge and the Provincial Chapter. He was one of the three Orators of the Osiris Lodge in St. Petersburg in 1776, the 3rd Degree Freemason, and an Honorary Member of the Lodge in November 1781.

Kheraskov was also the founder of the Latona Chapter in St. Petersburg and an Honorary Member of the Lodge in 1778. Then, he showed his activity in Moscow as the founder of the Harmony Lodge and was a member of the lodge from 1780 up to 1783; he was an Orator of the Provincial Lodge in the summer of 1782 and 1784; he was admitted to a Theoretical Degree in 1782; during the life of I. G. Schwartz (Shvarts in the Russian sources), he was also admitted to the Internal Rosicrucian Order and was the Rhetorician of the Management of the Theoretical Degree. M. M. Kheraskov was given the Order Name "Tacheroth Salemsky." The pinnacle of M. M. Kheraskov in Moscow manifested in the following positions: a member of the Chapter of the XVIII Province in Moscow, a

---

[1] M. M. Shcherbatov "The consideration of the Vices and Autocracy of Peter the Great. Conversation" // Different works of Prince M. M. Shcherbatov / A foreword by O. Bodyansky. – M.: The University Printing House. 1860. Pages 16-17.

member of the Provincial Chapter in 1782-1784, and a Lord of the 8th Province in 1783 (M. M. Kheraskov already received the Order Name "Michael abarista naturante" at that time)[1].

M. M. Kheraskov put the search for the benefits and goodness that are "more needed than gold and silver" in the first place[2] in one of the first compositions, "To the Highly Esteemed Gentlemen, the members of the Board of Trustees of the Imperial Educational House[3]."

M. M. Kheraskov put the following phrase into the mouth of "Moscow" in the play "Cheering Russia,"[4] composed in October 1776: "Oh! Phoebus to erect these joys, my heart thirsting for the common bliss[5]." The term "new prosperity," "the current and future ages of prosperity"[6] comes from the lips of "Phoebus." Moscow notes the desire of Russians for a "temple of the common prosperity[7]." The short play ends with a choral song of the Muscovites:

"Russia of its bliss
Has reached perfection now,
Our fun should be felt by
Mountains, valleys, and forests,
Tell the universe with us,
How generous the heavens are to the Ross."[8]

It is told in the novel "Cadmus and Harmony"[9] by M. M. Kheraskov that the laws correspond to the "common good" when they are natural: the laws of Cadmus were "considered" with the "general welfare of the Fatherland," the laws

---

[1] Russian Freemasons. 1721-2019. Century XVIII. Volume II / A. I. Serkov, M., 2019. Pages 607-610; Russian Freemasons. Century XVIII. Volume III / A. I. Serkov, M., 2019. Pages 48, 49, 54, 69, 85, 91, 120, 145.
[2] M. M. Kheraskov "To the Highly Esteemed Gentlemen, the members of the Board of Trustees of the Imperial Educational House." - [Moscow]: Printed at the University Printing House before1763. - [4] p. Page 2.
[3] Ibid. 4 pages.
[4] M. M. Kheraskov "Merry Russia": Prologue. - [M.: Printed at the University Printing House, B. g.]. - 4 pages.
[5] Ibid. Page 2.
[6] Ibid. Page 2, 3.
[7] Ibid. Page 3.
[8] Ibid. Page 3.
[9] M. Kheraskov's creations: Newly corrected and supplemented. Part 8: Cadmus and Harmony: An ancient narrative: Part 1 revised and supplemented - 1801. - X, [6], 259, [6] p.

were “meek, reasonable, and consequently natural” and gleaned “from the most spiritual qualities of his subjects …[1].”

M. M. Kheraskov used the terms the “bliss of subjects,” the “common good,” the “common use,” the “common evil,” and the “common harm” in the story “Numa Pompilius or Prosperous Rome.” The story sets out a point of view that considers the question of the fact that the benefit of the subjects and the own benefit of the ruler coincide[2].

Picture 30. An illustration by I. Perelyvkin from the book of M. M. Kheraskova, “Numa Pompilius, or Prosperous Rome.” 1768. Page I.

“Sovereigns must eradicate the common evil,” the Nymph Jaeger tells Numa on the Aventine Mountain: “Owners, Nature itself and the entire human race expect their salvation, tranquility, and prosperity from you; you have been given full power to tame, curb, restrain the riots, root vices, educate, and, through prudence, accompany your subjects by way of prudence …[3].” An example of the eradication of vices is some limitation of the tyrannical power of the parents: the limit of this power must follow from the natural law[4]. The fruits of the “common harm” are visible in the story of a stranger that fled his country: “Everybody thought how to keep their property and steal someone else’s while keeping their own; a neighbor to a neighbor, a relative to a relative, suspicious of each other; no one trying to benefit the Fatherland, caring only for his or her own, and impudence

---

[1] M. Kheraskov's creations: Newly corrected and supplemented. Part 8: Cadmus and Harmony: An ancient narrative: Part 1 revised and supplemented - 1801. - X, [6], 259, [6] p., pages 3, 4.
[2] M. Kheraskov's creations: Newly corrected and supplemented. Part 12: [Numa Pompilius or Prosperous Rome]. - [The 3rd edition. - [1803]. Page 35.
[3] M. Kheraskov's creations: Newly corrected and supplemented. Part 12: [Numa Pompilius or Prosperous Rome]. - [The 3rd edition. - [1803]. Page 53.
[4] Ibid. Page 73.

became the only honor ...[1]." But the peoples are happy and obedient to the Sovereigns that "will turn their will to the 'common good' ...[2]." As a result, Numin's life was arranged in prosperity "until later years." M. M. Kheraskov concludes: "May the 'common good' be accomplished ...[3]." An explanation of true bliss is also given. True bliss follows the "prudent laws," and their execution, in turn, shadows the mores of people: "But the laws are only an outline the happiness and well-being of society is affirmed on. The laws demand some fulfillment, and this fulfillment depends on the enlightened and virtuous people. In other words, the laws cannot act by themselves ...[4]." M. M. Kheraskov transfers the mode of Numa's Government to the Sovereigns of his time, confirming their wisdom and philanthropy[5].

M. M. Kheraskov inserted the following lines into the work "The Temple of Russian Prosperity"[6] issued in 1775:

"Peoples! and Kings! I am portraying you
A true temple of our bliss <...>
She set this glorious palace
For the 'common good' for eternity[7]."

As follows from the work, the prosperity of Russians is built on labor, purity of hearts, virtue among the nobility, in general, and Catherine the Great, in particular[8]. The appeal addressed in the work from the Autocrat to the nobles will be replicated in Masonic literature many times. However, the idea of a call to the "common good" remained in the Russian Empire even after the complete ban of Freemasonry in 1822 until the overthrow of the Autocracy in 1917 (this idea will be transformed into the capacious, widespread formulas "Orthodoxy, Autocracy, nationality" and "For Faith, Tsar, and Fatherland!"):

---

[1] M. Kheraskov's creations: Newly corrected and supplemented. Part 12: [Numa Pompilius or Prosperous Rome]. - [The 3rd edition. - [1803]. Page 112.
[2] Ibid. Page 121.
[3] Ibid. Page 134.
[4] M. Kheraskov's creations: Newly corrected and supplemented. Part 12: [Numa Pompilius or Prosperous Rome]. - [The 3rd edition. - [1803]. Page 135.
[5] Ibid. Page 148.
[6] M. M. Kheraskov "The Temple of Russian Prosperity: Dedicated to the Constructor of the Temple, Her Imperial Majesty, the Most Gracious Empress Ekaterina Alekseevna II, the Autocrat of All Russia: Presented at a joyful celebration of the conclusion of peace with the Ottoman Porte. Moscow, July 1775.": Printed at the Imperial Moscow University, 1775. - 15 pages.
[7] Ibid. Page 4.
[8] Ibid. Page 4.

Here is this call (Catherine has the qualities of a Goddess here):
"O! You are the mediators of the people and the state,
The sons of the Fatherland, born for glory,
Your voice can be heard every day,
I give birth to you for the 'common good'!
But you are respectable by me,
When you are excellent by deed and not by rank.
Who serves the Tsar, the Fatherland, the people,
The nobility is nothing without virtues!
Your zealous spirit shows Russia always,
As before, serve your Fatherland forever.
When I spread my gaze through your hearts,
I see the protectors of the crown in your ancestors.
They neglected their calm,
They laid down themselves for the Kingdom and Kings[1]."

M. M. Kheraskov included the construction of cities, the distribution of bounties, and the peace of the people[2] into the concept of the "common good" and represented the "common good" in the artistic image of the temple in an Ode to Her Imperial Majesty in honor of Her visit to Moscow on June 28, 1787[33]. According to M. M. Kheraskov, the prioritized bliss of the subjects was the key to achieving the "common good." The own good would also be achieved in this case[4]. The "common good" excluded wars:

"The heroes' glory is loud in the world,
But their deeds sing in vain:
Neither laurels nor bloody war
do not give any good to people[5]."

---

[1]M. M. Kheraskov "The Temple of Russian Prosperity: Dedicated to the Constructor of the Temple, Her Imperial Majesty, the Most Gracious Empress Ekaterina Alekseevna II, the Autocrat of All Russia: Presented at a joyful celebration of the conclusion of peace with the Ottoman Porte. Moscow, July 1775.": Printed at the Imperial Moscow University, 1775. – Page 5.

[2] M. M. Kheraskov "An ode to Her Imperial Majesty, the Most Gracious Empress Ekaterina Alekseevna II: Presented from Moscow University during the joyous stay of Her Imperial Majesty in Moscow, upon the longed-for return from the midday outlying districts of Russia: June 1787, 28 days." – M.: The University Printing House of N. Novikov, 1787. - 11 pages.

[3] Ibid. Page 5.

[4] Ibid. Page 6.

[5] Ibid. Page 7.

"YOUR praise thunders,
That the spirit of the Laws[1] is the goal for the good
YOU killed Machiavel[2],
Charming the Godless things[3]."

The "common good" is associated with the distribution of material goods and care for those in need in the song XX "Tranquility," included in the collection of the philosophical odes and songs of M. M. Kheraskov[4]. The people that do not care about the "common good" lose everything:
"But if you despise
The 'common good,'
You transform honor, glory, and money
Into poison[5]."

M. M. Kheraskov used the allusions of the "common good" and other terms of the 18th century, telling readers about the history of the Novgorod Republic in the poetic story "The Tsar, or the Saved Novgorod[6]." However, the author unequivocally declared the purpose of his narration in advance, showing the perniciousness of civil strife, imaginary freedom, and equality in Russian history. All of this had some parallels with the coup in France in 1789. Also, he demonstrated general prosperity: "Russia has enjoyed well-being for many centuries …."

M. M. Kheraskov's character Gostomysl sitting in his reflections on the banks of the Volkhov River respects the "common good[7]." The "common good" is combined with the defense of the Fatherland in the elder's speech:

---

[1] A mention of the "spirit of the Laws" in the ode can be interpreted as Catherine II's inclination to study the book of Ch. L. Montesquieu "A Spirit of the Laws." This fact was regarded by contemporaries, including M. M. Kheraskov, very favorably.
[2] The teachings of N. Machiavelli with an extremely wide arsenal of means for capturing, retaining, and using power were rejected by the most intellectual Russian nobles. M. M. Kheraskov noted this trend in the ode.
[3] Ibid. Page 9.
[4] Song XX "Calmness"// M. M. Kheraskov "The philosophical odes or songs by Mikhail Kheraskov." - [Moscow]: Printed under the Imperial Moscow University, 1769. Pages 41-42.
[5] Song XX "Calmness"// M. M. Kheraskov "The philosophical odes or songs by Mikhail Kheraskov." - [Moscow]: Printed under the Imperial Moscow University, 1769. Page 42.
[6] M. M. Kheraskov "Tsar, or Saved Novgorod": A Poetic Tale. - Moscow: The University Printing House of Ridiger and Claudius, 1800. - [10], 246 pages.
[7] Ibid. Page 25.

"Pour blood for the 'common good.'
To turn away the peruns from the Kingdom,
To unite the families like strings,
That is love for the Fatherland!"[1]

M. M. Kheraskov conveys to the reader the idea through the mouth of another character Izonar that the "common good" does not imply the equality of people. Izonar appeals to the manifestations of nature:

"By terrible equality
He seeks general bliss.
But there is no equality in this world!
Look at the whole universe
Copulated in the bulk of
The cold, heat, dark, or light[2]."

According to M.M. Kheraskov, equality means anarchy that leads to the "common harm." The author put this idea into Varangian's appeal to Ratmir:

"Where people being without supreme power
Live like beasts of prey,
Splitting the 'common harm' into parts,
Mighty Kings are honored in slaves[3]."

Laws are a means of establishing the "common good." The reasoning of people without laws (as when moving a ship without a mast) leads to absurd liberties, anarchy, and atheism.

"Being without a mast as if without a law,
It can be seen as an obstacle for the good everywhere.
Their rudder, the movement of their oars,
The intellect was one.
Such intelligence drove
A clan of mortals along crooked paths.

---

[1] M. M. Kheraskov "Tsar, or Saved Novgorod": A Poetic Tale. - Moscow: The University Printing House of Ridiger and Claudius, 1800. - [10], 246 pages. Page 74.
[2] Ibid. Page 93.
[3] M. M. Kheraskov "Tsar, or Saved Novgorod": A Poetic Tale. - Moscow: The University Printing House of Ridiger and Claudius, 1800. - [10]. Page 145.

She instituted a ludicrous liberty
And erected a temple to freedom.
Forgetting that there is a Ruler in the sky,
A King for them and every Lord
Was a yoke on the earth.
Oh, liberty! Stop and heed to me[1]."

M. M. Kheraskov considered "a night in France" (revolution in France in 1789), the assassination of Socrates, and the construction of a golden calf by the ancient Israelites as examples of "the chimera of liberty." The author concluded that "The truth was hidden by the debauchery smoke[2]." According to M. M. Kheraskov, the "common harm" is the desire to own property to the detriment of others:
"How vicious children are from the inheritance,
Insulting an unhappy Mother unreservedly.
The means for murder are invented
To possess the property ...[3]."

According to Yu. S. Limanskaya[4], the works of M. M. Kheraskov reflect both the elements of the doctrine of the "common good" and the Masonic doctrine itself. L. L. Fedotova believes that the works of M. M. Kheraskov represented the classical ideas of statehood and their spiritual and Christian origins[5].

The opinion of M. M. Kheraskov on the state and legal issues can be considered representative of all Russian Freemasonry at the end of the 18th century as he had 14 years of experience as a member of many Masonic Lodges, held senior positions in many Masonic Lodges, being a member of Chapters and the founder of several lodges. He was the author of many poems, verses, and prose works, combining both political and legal ideas and Masonic images there.

---

[1] M. M. Kheraskov "Tsar, or Saved Novgorod": A Poetic Tale. - Moscow: The University Printing House of Ridiger and Claudius, 1800. - [10]. Pages 148-149.
[2] Ibid. Page 149.
[3] Ibid. Page 219.
[4] Yu. S. Limanskaya "The works of M. M. Kheraskov 'The Golden Rod' and 'Cadmus and Harmony' in the Context of Masonic Prose of the last quarter of the 18th Century": An abstract of the thesis of a Candidate in Philological Sciences. - Surgut, 2007. Page 6.
[5] L. L. Fedotova "A Russian national idea in the heroic epic of M. M. Kheraskov": An abstract of the thesis of a Candidate in Philological Sciences. - Moscow, 2009. Page 5.

§3.2. The welfare of all and everyone in the second generation of Russian Freemasons — Part 1 (1770-1779)

The period of 1770-1789 was the heyday of the reign of Catherine II, Russian Voltaireism, faith in reason, the Russian-Turkish war in 1768-1774, peasant uprisings (Kizhi riot in 1769-1771; Plague riot in 1771, Yaitskoe riot in 1772. , the peasant war under the leadership of E. I. Pugachev in 1773-1775), the provincial reform of 1775, the first partition of the Polish-Lithuanian Commonwealth in 1775, the adoption of the Charter of the Deanery in 1782, the annexation of the Crimean Khanate in 1783, free letters to nobles and cities in 1785, the Russian-Turkish war of 1787-1791, and the Russian-Swedish war of 1788-1790.

The second generation of Russian Freemasonry was the most fruitful in terms of the number of Freemasons that reached the highest degrees and showed themselves in public service in the 18th century. There was a spread of many Masonic Systems, the opening of many lodges, the formation of Masonic Unions, and the translation of many publications of the foreign literature of the religious-mystical, political-legal, and artistic content in Russian Freemasonry in the period of 1770-1789. The second generation refers to the period of Russian Freemasons' visiting the Masonic Lodges in 1770-1789. Due to the vastness of the material and the significance of this period, it was divided into two parts.

It is impossible to ignore the following major scientist. Fyodor Grigoryevich Bauze (1752-1812) came from a Pastor's family, studied at the Faculty of Law at Leipzig University, was a Ph.D. in Law, a Professor of Law, Dean of the Faculty of Law, and the Rector of Moscow University. As a Freemason, he showed himself as a member of the 3rd Degree, an Orator in 1779, the 2nd guard in 1781 in the Apollo Lodge in St. Petersburg (working in German), a Secretary of the Phoenix Chapter in St. Petersburg in February 1779, a member of the Lodge of St. George in St. Petersburg in the early 1780s, and the carrier of the Theoretical Degree in 1782-1786 in Moscow. F. G. Bauze received the Order Name "Uberosus Edasth." Being a member of the Three Banners Lodge in Moscow, he received a certificate on 08.02.1783. F. G. Bause was noted as a 4-Grade-Absent Member in the Lodge of Eleusis that worked in Moscow in German in 1784[1].

---

[1]Russian Freemasons. 1721-2019. A Biographical Dictionary. Century XVIII. Volume I / A. I. Serkov, M.: Ganga, 2019. Pages 130-132; Russian Freemasons. 1721-2019. A Biographical

Picture 31. A chest strap of one of the Rosicrucian Degrees. Russia. The end of the 18th century. Silk, gimp, sequins; gold and silver embroidery. Published by Yu. V. Plotnikova in the catalog Collection of the Hermitage in 2013[1].

F. G. Bause noted in his essay "What has been done in Russia for the enlightenment of the people and the glory of the Fatherland from the time of Rurik to Peter the Great," published in the Europe Bulletin in 1806[2], that people can become educated if only they understand that "there is no security in society and happiness in life without a boss[3]." Sovereigns are concerned about "the glory and happiness of the people[4]." F. G. Bauze believed that the examples of such Sovereigns were Boris Godunov, that did a lot for the glory of the Fatherland and the love of the people, Yaroslav the Wise, Ioann Vasilyevich, Mikhail Romanov, Alexey Mikhailovich, Fedor Alexeevich, and Peter the Great[5]. The content of prosperity includes "good behavior and enlightenment," "saving order," and "blessed peace[6]."

F. G. Bauze's opinion on the state and legal issues can be considered representative of all Russian Freemasonry at the end of the 18th century as he held positions in Masonic Lodges and Chapters (although he had only eight years of

---

Dictionary. Century XVIII. Volume III / A. I. Serkov, M.: Ganga, 2019. Pages 63, 71, 77, 86, 200.

[1] The Wisdom of Astrea: the monuments of the Freemasonry of the 18th - the first third of the 19th century in the Hermitage Collection: an exhibition catalog / The State Hermitage Museum - St. Petersburg: The Publishing House of the State Hermitage Museum, 2013. - 480 pages: Page 212, an illustration.

[2] F. G. Bause "What was done in Russia to educate the people and for the glory of the Fatherland from the time of Rurik to Peter the Great" // Europe Bulletin, part of the 25th century, January 1806, pages 3-20, 81-96.

[3] Ibid. Page 6.

[4] Ibid. Page 10.

[5] Ibid. Page 85.

[6] Ibid. Page 86.

experience as a member of Masonic Lodges). The manuscripts of F. G. Bauze could be used for making several large volumes, but the Moscow fire of 1812 destroyed them, along with a collection of Old Russian manuscripts and books that he had prepared for publication. Various works on a variety of topics from the field of Political Economy, the History of Russia, the History of Diplomacy, Roman Law, Numismatics, and others were destroyed. Tomsinov noted that F. G. Bause was influenced by the works of the German jurist I.-G. Geynektsiy. F. G. Bause believed that "the business of the lawyer is to take care of the health of the public body and all its parts, talking about the state and its citizens[1]."

The next person that should be discussed is Alexey Ivanovich Vasilyev (1742-1807), that graduated from the Cadet School under the Senate with the study of jurisprudence and was a nobleman in the 3rd generation, an Actual Privy Councilor, a Senate Secretary, a drafter of the 1775 Finance Laws and a Minister of Finance of the Russian Empire. A. I. Vasilyev is known for providing patronage to F. A. Golubtsov.

A. I. Vasilyev held various positions in the lodges of St. Petersburg. He was a member of the Lodge of Harpocrates in 1775, received the Degree of Scottish Master, served as Treasurer in the Great (English) Provincial Lodge in 1777 and the Great Rite Leader in the same lodge in 1778, and was an honorary member of the Chapter of Latona in 1778[2].

A. I. Vasilyev used the vocabulary of the "common good" theory to substantiate the draft regulations on the development of mining in the Russian Empire in the report of the Minister of Finance[3]. The minister proposed to give freedom to the "Mining Chiefs," acting "in favor of the factories without hindrance," "in favor of the Bosses," "in favor of the objects themselves," in "favor of the Treasury," and "for the good of the inhabitants," but, at the same time, to define the "rules and boundaries" of this freedom as the crime of the Mountain Chiefs can cause "harm to the factories or their colleagues working together with them at those factories[4]." Recalling that due to their duty and by

---

[1] V. A. Tomsinov "The Russian jurists of the XVIII-XX centuries. The essays on life and work": 2 volumes. Volume 1. - M.: Zertsalo, 2007. Pages 178-186.

[2] Russian Freemasons. 1721-2019. A Biographical Dictionary. Century XVIII. Volume I / A. I. Serkov, M.: Ganga, 2019. Pages 251-254; Russian Freemasons. 1721-2019. A Biographical Dictionary. Century XVIII. Volume III / A. I. Serkov, M.: Ganga, 2019. Pages 82, 108, 117.

[3] A. I. Vasilyev "The highest approved report of the Minister of Finance, with the Staffs and other applications on the new formation of the mining authorities and the management of mining plants": [Approved on July 13, 1806]. St. Petersburg: The medical printing house, 1806. Pages 1-254, 249-256, 255-258.

[4] Ibid. Pages 8, 9, 23.

virtue of their oath, Officials were obliged to have "equal care of the benefits of the Treasury," regardless of whether they received their own benefits from the service, A. I. Vasiliev argued that "it cannot be denied that there are some Officials that, when not seeing their own benefit, do not think so much about the benefits of the Treasury …[1]." A. I. Vasilyev argued that "... a person entering any kind of service by his own desire is always more useful in it than the one that is assigned to it by compulsion …[2]." He believed that when recruiting, it was necessary to allow artisans and workers to join the soldiers so that "instead of them, the same number of people could enter the factories from recruits by their own agreement among themselves …[3]." The benefits of this are obvious: "... the peasant, burdened by the family, being forced in turn to introduce himself as recruits," will work harder at the factory and stay with his family, "while another of the artisans not having a wife or children, willingly occupies the place of that peasant in the soldiers with an equal benefit to the State …[4]." A. I. Vasilyev suggested giving some maintenance to the employees that were "mutilated when fulfilling their work" or deprived of life, justifying this "by the benefits of the service itself …[5]."

A. I. Vasilyev looked for and found some ways to set up mining schools so that "benefit to the State and factories" (the "common good") and "benefit to the inhabitants" ("the benefit of everyone") would be delivered[6]. The Speaker also used in his rhetoric the terms "the good of the people" and "the good of mankind" as the goals of the activities of the imperial power[7].

A. I. Vasilyev proposed to establish mountain cities according to the Western model, seeing in this the benefit "not only for the factories but also for the State[8]."

A. I. Vasilyev wrote that the runaways of the convicts caused "the greater harm" to the whole region as they "corrupt morality from an example and behavior." And this harm "cannot be compensated with any profits from the factories …[9]."

---

[1] A. I. Vasilyev "The highest approved report of the Minister of Finance, with the Staffs and other applications on the new formation of the mining authorities and the management of mining plants": [Approved on July 13, 1806]. St. Petersburg: The medical printing house, 1806. Page 69.
[2] Ibid. Pages 79.
[3] A. I. Vasilyev "The highest approved report of the Minister of Finance, with the Staffs and other applications on the new formation of the mining authorities and the management of mining plants": [Approved on July 13, 1806]. St. Petersburg: The medical printing house, 1806. Page 80.
[4] Ibid. Page 80.
[5] Ibid. Page 85.
[6] Ibid. Page 94.
[7] Ibid. Pages 101, 102.
[8] Ibid. Page 107.
[9] Ibid. Pages 151-152.

A. I. Vasilyev reported that “all estates have their societies for the benefit of each one[1].” He understood an “every estate” by each one and “the good of the entire State” by the “common good[2].” A. I. Vasilyev noted that manufacturers did not have their society. Therefore, the author of the report proposed the following method for determining the usefulness for all and everyone: “the best government decrees based on information and cases privately collected are often useful for the local and other circumstances for one part of the estate and are disadvantageous for another one in the same kind of industry. But if these decisions were based on the information selected from the society of the entire estate, then they would be equally useful for the whole class, in general. There is no doubt that the Government has the means to select such information and opinions from each Member of any society separately <...> But <...> a long-term and difficult collection of such information removes the necessary assistance”[3] and causes “some difficulty in agreeing on the difference of opinions and bringing them to the same goals[4].” Emperor Alexander adopted the proposals indicated by A. I. Vasilyev in the project[5].

The opinion of A. V. Vasilyev on the state and legal issues cannot be considered representative of all Russian Freemasonry at the end of the 18th century as he had only a 4-year experience as a member of Masonic Lodges, although he held some senior positions in Masonic Lodges. At the same time, A. I. Vasilyev was familiar with jurisprudence, being involved in the codification of financial legislation and the organization of the mining administration. The study of various legislative acts, memoranda, and works showing his intellectual work is very entertaining.

It is worth touching on the personality of Alexander Borisovich Kurakin (1752-1818), that came from an ancient family of the Grand Duke of Lithuania Gediminas. A. B. Kurakin studied at the University of Strasbourg at the Faculty of Law of Leiden University, prepared a treatise on the Peace of Tilsit together with Prince Lobanov-Rostovsky, was a Real Privy Councilor of the 1st Class, a Chief

---

[1] A. I. Vasilyev “The highest approved report of the Minister of Finance, with the Staffs and other applications on the new formation of the mining authorities and the management of mining plants”: [Approved on July 13, 1806]. St. Petersburg: The medical printing house, 1806. Page 173, a note.

[2] Ibid. Page 174.

[3] Ibid. Page 175.

[4] A. I. Vasilyev “The highest approved report of the Minister of Finance, with the Staffs and other applications on the new formation of the mining authorities and the management of mining plants”: [Approved on July 13, 1806]. St. Petersburg: The medical printing house, 1806. Pages 175-176.

[5] Ibid. Pages 181, 255-256.

Prosecutor, a Senator, a participant in the convention on the patronage of the Order of Malta and the 2nd Section of Rzeczpospolita, a member of the Permanent Council and the State Council, and a bibliophile. Alexander B. Kurakin was a grandnephew of N. I. Panin and P. I. Panin.

Alexander B. Kurakin was very successful in Russian Freemasonry. He was a member of the Chapter of the Templar System and the Chapter of the Petropolitanum in St. Petersburg from 1773. Alexander B. Kurakin was elevated to the 3rd Degree in the Lodge of Equality (that operated in St. Petersburg and Moscow) on 07.07.1775. He received the Degree of Scottish Master and was appointed to the Grand Provincial Lodge and the Provincial Chapter in the Great (English) Provincial Lodge in September 1776. Alexander B. Kurakin acted as Chair Master in St. Alexander's Lodge in St. Petersburg in 1777-1779. He was a member of the Chapter of the Phoenix in St. Petersburg in 1781, a Grand Prior and Representative of Solomon's Vicar. Alexander B. Kurakin was also outlined by N. I. Novikov as a member of the Chapter in February 1783[1].

A. B. Kurakin wrote in his letter to Count N. P. Panin (dated March 24, 1798) that "... loving you the way I love, I dare to hope that, in this case, you will obey the only feelings that will instill into your zeal for the good of your Fatherland and the 'common good[2].'"

The collection of documents related to the testamentary dispositions of A. B. Kurakin in the case of his death is very interesting. Alexander B. Kurakin refers to the Decree on Free Farmers and indicates the desire to "make new donations for the 'common good'" and give his peasants freedom[3] in the "All-subject petition to the Sovereign, Emperor" (dated 12.04.1806)[4]. For this purpose, he freed the peasants from the payment for liberation but imposed the obligation to contribute the patrimonial income for 40 years in favor of the "God-pleasing institutions," and subsequently: "everyone would pay 3 rubles forever" for charitable needs.

---

[1] Russian Freemasons. 1721-2019. A Biographical Dictionary. Century XVIII. Volume I / A. I. Serkov, M.: Ganga, 2019. Pages 678-682; Russian Freemasons. 1721-2019. A Biographical Dictionary. Century XVIII. Volume III / A. I. Serkov, M.: Ganga, 2019. Pages 57, 83, 114, 150, 201.

[2] A letter from Prince A. B. Kurakin to Count N. P. Panin (dated March 24, 1798) // Russian Antiquity. An edition of 1874. Volume X. Page 576.

[1]A. B. Kurakin "A copy of the all-subject petition of Prince Alexander Borisovich Kurakin to the Emperor (dated December 4, 1806)" / / An approved position of Prince Alexander Borisovich Kurakin. St. Petersburg: Printed at the printing house of Friedrich Drechsler. 1807. Pages 3-6.

[4] Ibid. Pages 3-4.

Alexander B. Kurakin asked to fulfill his will and prevent "insanity" on the part of his heirs in his letter to the Minister of Internal Affairs, Count Viktor Pavlovich Kochubei (dated December 4, 1806)[1], asking the minister to submit a petition and "relying on the Monarch's patronage of all such donations for the 'common good[2].'"

Helping his peasants "to remain forever in the prosperity that he always tried to bring them," A. B. Kurakin ordered to collect some monetary contributions from the peasants for the mills transferred to them and the liberation granted to them in his letter addressed to the Chief Prosecutor of the Governing Senate Pyotr Stepanovich Molchanov (dated February 13, 1807)[3]. Those contributions could serve "both for their own and for the 'common good[4].'"

A. B. Kurakin explained in his Notes for including into the Act on the emancipation of the peasants[5] (dated February 13, 1807) what motivated him when writing the Notes: "Considering all human desires extending beyond the limits of life, of course, the worthiest craving is being useful to society even after existence itself[6]." A. B. Kurakin wrote about granting eternal freedom to the Nadezhda peasants after his death, giving them "all his vast and abundant economic establishments, forest country houses, and all sorts of land for their only and eternal benefit[7]," mentioning it in Article II of the Notes.

A. B. Kurakin appointed part of the rent paid by the Nadezhda peasants for their "eternal liberation" to the young pupils Vrevsky and various needs "for the 'common good.'" A. B. Kurakin did not demand "any special payment"[8] for himself for the eternal freedom and benefits provided to the peasants. The note contains the signatures of eight witnesses: V. P. Kochubei, P. V. Zavadovsky, P. V.

---

[1] A Copy from the Relation of Prince Alexander Borisovich Kurakin to the Minister of the Interior, Count Viktor Pavlovich Kochubey (dated December 04, 1806) / / An approved position of Prince Alexander Borisovich Kurakin ... - St. Petersburg. Printed at the printing house of Friedrich Drechsler. 1807. Pages 7-8.

[2] Ibid. Page 8.

[3] My Letter of Faith for having the Governing Senate Chief Prosecutor of the Acting State Councilor and Cavalier Pyotr Stepanovich Molchanov / / An approved position of Prince Alexander Borisovich Kurakin. - St. Petersburg. Printed at the printing house of Friedrich Drechsler. 1807. Pages 19-24.

[4] Ibid. Page 19.

[5] My notes to be included word for word in all its articles in the Act performed on my behalf with my Nadezhda peasants liberated by me / / An approved position of Prince Alexander Borisovich Kurakin. St. Petersburg. Printed at the printing house of Friedrich Drechsler. 1807. Pages 25-87.

[6] Ibid. Page 27.

[7] Ibid. Page 29.

[8] My notes to be included word for word in all its articles in the Act performed on my behalf with my Nadezhda peasants liberated by me // An approved position of Prince Alexander Borisovich Kurakin. St. Petersburg. Printed at the printing house of Friedrich Drechsler. 1807. Page 30.

Lopukhin, A. I. Vasiliev, D. P. Troshchinsky, A. A. Sablukov, I. V. Tutolmin, and N. I. Kalinin. The St. Petersburg Civil Chamber certified the note.

It was noted in a letter from Alexander B. Kurakin to Grand Duchess Maria Fyodorovna (dated May 23, 1807)[1] that as the history of all centuries shows us, the "family considerations among Sovereigns have always given way to the good and needs of their states[2]." Alexander B. Kurakin, in his letter to Grand Duchess Maria Fyodorovna (dated May 30, 1807)[3], mentioned Count Calcrate elevated to the rank of Field Marshal to organize the defense of Danzig, characterizing him: "This is a very experienced warrior having a great mind and wholeheartedly caring about the good situation and the welfare of mankind[4]." Alexander B. Kurakin emphasized his commitment to the state good in his letter to Grand Duchess Maria Fyodorovna (dated June 8, 1807)[5]: "My heart overflowing with grief made me tell Your Imperial Majesty about the events related to the state good and only indirectly concerning myself ...[6]." Discussing the foreign policy of the Russian Empire in his letter to Grand Duchess Maria Fyodorovna dated June 10, 1807[7], Alexander B. Kurakin wrote: "... finally, there are some circumstances when you need to think mainly about self-preservation without being guided by any rules other than the thought of the good states: this is also the greatest truth ...[8]." Alexander B. Kurakin announced his unwillingness to go as an Ambassador to Paris in his letter to Grand Duchess Maria Fyodorovna (dated June 18, 1807)[9]: "... I am too old to subject myself to false interpretations that could be given to all my actions by the people of the opposite system in St. Petersburg at once, even if they were inspired by the very pure jealousy of service and striving for the good of Russia ...[10]."

It is clear in a letter from Prince Kurakin to A. A. Nartov (dated December 1805) that A. B. Kurakin thought that the general benefit belonged to the highest

---

[1] The letters from the road from Prince A. B. Kurakin to the Empress Maria Fedorovna // Russian Archive. - 1868. - Book 1. Notebook 1. Pages 52-60.
[2] Ibid. Page 59.
[3] Ibid. Pages 60-63.
[4] Ibid. Page 63.
[5] The letters from the road from Prince A. B. Kurakin to the Empress Maria Fedorovna // Russian Archive. - 1868. - Book 1. Notebook 2. Pages 161-176.
[6] Ibid. Page 173.
[7] Ibid. Pages 176-183.
[8] Ibid. Page 181.
[9] Ibid. Pages 196-208.
[10] Ibid. Page 206.

values. Discussing the Free Economic Society, he remarked: "... I look at the prosperous fruits of His care for the 'common good' with sincere pleasure."[1]

The opinion of Alexander B. Kurakin on the state and legal issues can be considered representative of all Russian Freemasonry at the end of the 18th century as he had 11 years of experience as a member of many Masonic Lodges, holding positions in the Masonic Lodges and participating in the Chapters. The works of Alexander B. Kurakin should be of interest to the researchers of the state and legal ideas of Russian Freemasonry as he received his legal education in Europe, was a participant in many important political processes in Europe, and had the opportunity to express his opinion on many important state issues.

Demonstrating the views of Russian Freemasons, a Freemasonry researcher and jurist, M. M. Kovalevsky cited as an example the letters of Alexei Mikhailovich Kutuzov (1749-1797), who wasa Prime Major, a Translator, the author of Masonic writings, and one of the founders of the Friendship Scientific Society and studied at the Faculty of Law at Leipzig University. A. M. Kutuzov had many friends: G. Ya. Schroeder, A. N. Radishchev (he lived with him in the same room for 14 years), N. I. Novikov, M. I. Golenishchev-Kutuzov, N. M. Karamzin, and I. V. Lopukhin. A. M. Kutuzov on the recommendation of I. G. Schwartz (Shvarts in the Russian sources) left the civil service in 1783, invested all his savings (3000 rubles) in the printing activities of N. I. Novikov, and devoted considerable time to Freemasonry.

A. M. Kutuzov founded Latona's Lodge and Chapter in Moscow and St. Petersburg in 1778 and received the 3rd Degree in the lodge. He founded the Osiris Lodge in Moscow and St. Petersburg in 1780, occupying the position of the Second Beggar for the Poor in November 1781. A. M. Kutuzov acted as a Chair Master in the box of the Lightbringer Triangle in Moscow in the period from 1782 to 1784. But his main occupation was Russian Rosicrucianism. A. M. Kutuzov became a member of the Theoretical Degree in Moscow and St. Petersburg in 1782. He was a member of the Internal Rosicrucian Order from 1783. A. M. Kutuzov was transferred from N. I. Novikov to G. Ya. Schroeder, becoming subordinate to G. Ya. Schroeder at the beginning of 1786, and received the Order Name "Vivus Velox Statuk." He was scheduled to become a member of the Haupt Directory in 1788. Then, he was sent to Berlin and received a "Practitioner"

[1] A release of the letter from Prince Kurakin to A. A. Nartov (dated December 1805) // P. A. Druzhinin "The unknown letters of Russian writers to Prince Alexander Borisovich Kurakin (1752–1818)." - M.: Truten, 2002. Pages 268-269.

Degree in the Order of the Golden-Rose Cross for his studies in alchemy there. A. M. Kutuzov spent the rest of his life in Berlin, being in a debt prison[1].

A. M. Kutuzov wrote the following lines in his letter to Mrs. Pleshcheyeva (dated March 1792): "Unhappy France! This beautiful land is sacrificed to false philosophy and a few turned heads. Give, God! So that this deplorable example would open the eyes of the Monarchs and clearly show them that the Christian religion is the only basis for the people's welfare and their legitimate power ...[2]." A. M. Kutuzov recalled in his letter to Prince Trubetskoy (April 1792) that "... a true Freemason must be the implacable enemy of any indignation against the legitimate power and 'common good'...[3]."

A. M. Kutuzov's opinion on the state and legal issues can be considered representative of all Russian Freemasonry at the end of the 18th century as he had ten years of experience as a member of many Masonic Lodges, held positions in many Masonic Lodges and participated in Chapters, being a prominent Rosicrucian and having a legal education. A. M. Kutuzov was also well-known in the field of literature, translating the works of Western authors into Russian.

A few lines should be mentioned about Alexey Petrovich Melgunov (1722-1788), that was a friend of I. I. Shuvalov came from the family of the Vice-Governor, and rose to the rank of Actual Privy Councilor, Governor-General of the Yaroslavl and Vologda Provinces. Alexey Petrovich founded the lodge of the same name ("The Melgunov Lodge") in Yaroslavl, holding the position of a Chair Master from 1779 to the day of his death[4].

When writing a circular letter to the nobles of the Yaroslavl province on the issue of opening a home for orphans, A. P. Melgunov expressed his gratitude to Empress Catherine II: "... to the wise legislator for her Motherhood about the 'common good' of care. This country now (the Yaroslavl Province) enjoys the desired prosperity due to it[5]." According to Catherine II (and the Governor-General

---

[1] Russian Freemasons. 1721-2019. A Biographical Dictionary. Century XVIII. Volume I / A. I. Serkov, M.: Ganga, 2019. Pages 691-692; Russian Freemasons. 1721-2019. A Biographical Dictionary. Century XVIII. Volume III / A. I. Serkov, M.: Ganga, 2019. Pages 48, 58, 65, 118, 142, 282.

[2] A citation was quoted from M. M. Kovalevsky's "Freemasonry in the time of Catherine" // Europe Bulletin. 1915. # 9. Page 103.

[3] Ibid. Page 103.

[4] Russian Freemasons. 1721-2019. A Biographical Dictionary. Century XVIII. Volume II / A. I. Serkov, M.: Ganga, 2019. Pages 105-107; Russian Freemasons. 1721-2019. A Biographical Dictionary. Century XVIII. Volume III / A. I. Serkov, M.: Ganga, 2019. Page 259.

[5] L. N. Trefolev "Alexey Petrovich Melgunov, Governor-General of Catherine's times" // Russian archive, 1865. – The 2nd edition. - M., 1866. Page 891.

agreed with her), teaching the orphans of God and the state law would contribute to the "common good." When corresponding with Catherine II, A. P. Melgunov recommended the Archbishop of Yaroslavl and Rostov, Samuel as a person that was "… always eager to advance the 'common good'…[1]."

The opinion of A. P. Melgunov, on the state and legal issues, can be considered representative of all Russian Freemasonry at the end of the 18th century as he had ten years of experience in membership in many Masonic Lodges and held positions in many Masonic Lodges, being both the Governor-General of the province and the founder of the lodge created by him in that province. Due to the combination of the posts of Governor-General and Chair Master, the experience of A. P. Melgunov seems to be very interesting.

It is important to mention Alexey Ivanovich Musin-Pushkin (1744-1817), that was a native of an ancient noble family. A. I. Musin-Pushkin rose to the posts of an Actual Privy Councilor, a Chamberlain, and a Senator. According to his scientific interests, he was a historian and collector of various ancient manuscripts. It is important to note that A. I. Musin-Pushkin was a friend of G. G. Orlov and inherited the library of I. P. Elagin and I. N. Boltin. A. I. Musin-Pushkin, as a Freemason, was a member of the Phoenix Chapter in St. Petersburg, starting his activity there in 1778[2]. He introduced the monuments of Russian writing into scientific circulation.

A. I. Musin-Pushkin and I. N. Boltin composed a preface to the "Russian Truth." As noted earlier, the terminology of the "common good" was present there[3]. There is the following explanation of the instruction of St. Vasiliy (the Great) mentioned in the footnote to "The Spiritual of Vladimir Monomakh"[4] (that instruction was included in "The Spiritual of Vladimir Monomakh"): "The teaching is praiseworthy as it admonishes the Chiefs being the oldest in rank and dignity to be obedient and dutiful towards both their peers and subordinates that are much lower in rank, being courteous, condescending, and affable. Thus, the mutual union of society can be established. *Many private and public benefits* can

---

[1] Ibid. Page 894.

[2] Russian Freemasons. 1721-2019. A Biographical Dictionary. Century XVIII. Volume II / A. I. Serkov, M.: Ganga, 2019. Pages 149-151; Russian Freemasons. 1721-2019. A Biographical Dictionary. Century XVIII. Volume III / A. I. Serkov, M.: Ganga, 2019. Page 202.

[3] Russian True or the Laws of the Grand Dukes Yaroslav Vladimirovich and Vladimir Vsevolodovich Monomakh: With the application of the ancient adverbs and syllables to those that are in common use today and with an explanation of the words and names that became obsolete / Published by lovers of National History. SPb.: The Printing House of the St. Ruling Synod, 1792. Pages I, V-VI.

[4] Vladimir Monomakh "The Spiritual of Grand Duke Vladimir Vsevolodovich Monomakh to his children, named 'Teaching in the annals of Suzdal.'" - St. Petersburg: The Printing House of the Corps of foreign co-religionists, 1793. - X, 61 p.

result from that union. The firmness and *well-being of the State* are based on that union as well"[1] (*it was emphasized by the authors of this scientific work*).

Undoubtedly, Nikita Ivanovich Panin (1718-1783) was one of the key figures in the Russian state. He came from an old noble clan from the family of a Lieutenant-General. He received an excellent education at home, was a Real Privy Councilor of the 1st Class, a Chief Chamberlain, a Chief Hofmeister, a Field Marshal, a Plenipotentiary Minister, a Senator, and an educator of Grand Duke Pavel Petrovich. N. I. Panin attracted Pavel Petrovich to Public Administration. In terms of law and politics, N. I. Panin advocated the limitation of a Monarchy by law, the introduction of a constitution (as a guarantee "against the arbitrariness of strong people and seizure people"), and the rule of the enlightened Monarch on the "firm foundations of the law." He was the author of the state projects and the project of the union of the northern powers.

The activity of the famous "second person" in the state apparatus was not as significant in Freemasonry as it might seem. N. I. Panin was a member of the Muse Lodge in St. Petersburg in 1774. He served as a Great Local Master in the Great (English) Provincial Lodge in St. Petersburg from 1776 up to1777. N. I. Panin was nominated for the membership of the Provincial Chapter with the Degree of Scottish Master in September 1776[2].

At the same time, he abandoned the "common good" reasoning that is of interest. N. I. Panin assured in his letter to Primate Podossky (dated December 22, 1767)[3] that the true good of Poland consisted in a return to the previous constitution and liberty: "... the main point that should be taken care of is to return the republic to its old constitution and former liberties. Also, it is essential to not move away from that main point even if the change and the benefits expected from it would appear in the most seductive form. True good is only for those people that, like you, know how to judge it and equally well weigh the ways to achieve it. As

---

[1] A. I. Musin-Pushkin "A note" // Vladimir Monomakh "The Spiritual of Grand Duke Vladimir Vsevolodovich Monomakh to his children, named 'Teaching in the annals of Suzdal.'" - St. Petersburg: The Printing House of the Corps of foreign co-religionists, 1793. Page 8.
[2] Russian Freemasons. 1721-2019. A Biographical Dictionary. Century XVIII. Volume II / A. I. Serkov, M.: Ganga, 2019. Pages 247-249; Russian Freemasons. 1721-2019. A Biographical Dictionary. Century XVIII. Volume III / A. I. Serkov, M.: Ganga, 2019. Pages 84, 138.
[3] A letter of Count N. I. Panin to the Primate of Podossky // Catherine II "The political correspondence of Empress Catherine II." SPb., 1885-1914. A collection of the Imperial Russian Historical Society. Volume 67: 1766-1767 - 1889. Pages 561-563.

for the lower class of people, everything that is new is never carefully studied, but is discarded for the sole reason that it was not so in the old days[1]."

It was noted in a Dispatch of Count N. I. Panin to the Ambassador, Prince N. V. Repnin (dated December 23, 1767) that the welfare of Gdansk consisted of the slipway right: "... if this slipway right is taken away from Gdansk (this slipway right constitutes all its welfare and wealth) then, seeing the inevitable death in front of itself, this city can easily be let go to extremes. If the city does not rush out of despair into the citizenship of the King of Prussia (that is its closest and strongest neighbor), then, at least, refusing everything, it will clearly oppose new institutions and force the republic through the following: either to the use of force or to the unpleasant need to see their legalization despicable[2]."
It can be read in a letter to Resident Obrezkov to Constantinople (dated August 11, 1768)[3] that Her Imperial Majesty set "herself the well-being of the peoples subject to the state and the well-being of the entire human race, in general, as the first and main subject of justice for the entire time of her statehood ...[4]."

The opinion of N. I. Panin on the state and legal issues cannot be considered representative of all Russian Freemasonry at the end of the 18th century because he had only three years of experience as a member of Masonic Lodges, although holding senior positions in the Union of Masonic Lodges. A. N. Lushin in his monograph popularly presented N. I. Panin's views on the state and law. At the same time, N. I. Panin was a key figure in Russian Freemasonry as he was a Chancellor of the Russian Empire, an Actual Privy Councilor of the 1st class, and a Field Marshal, and his participation in the Masonic Lodges was significant. Obviously, the authority of N. I. Panin gave the Masonic Lodges influence and popularity in Russia. Therefore, many acquaintances, relatives, and subordinates of N. I. Panin subsequently became Freemasons (M. M. Alopeus, A. I. Bibikov, S. A. Kolychev, S. I. Pleshcheev, N. V. Repnin, L. I. Talyzin, etc.). At the same time, N. I. Panin's political ideas, such as the creation of the State Council and sympathy for Swedish constitutionalism,[5] were not and could not be shared by other

---

[1] Ibid. Pages 562-563.
[2] A Dispatch of Count N. I. Panin to the Ambassador, Prince Repnin // Catherine II "The political correspondence of Empress Catherine II." SPb., 1885-1914. A collection of the Imperial Russian Historical Society. Volume 67: 1766-1767 - 1889. Page 569.
[3] A letter of Count Panin to Resident Obrezkov in Constantinople // Catherine II "The political correspondence of Empress Catherine II." SPb., 1885-1914. A collection of the Imperial Russian Historical Society. Volume 87: 1768-1769 - 1893. Pages 138-146.
[4] Ibid. Page 144.
[1]See, for example, A. N. Lushin's "The state-legal ideas of Russian Freemasons…"; N. D. Chechulin "A project of the Imperial Council in the first year of the reign of Catherine II." M.: A book on Demand, 2011. - 26 p.

Freemasons because the issues of politics and religion in any Masonic Lodges were strictly prohibited. So, N. I. Panin communicated his convictions only to a narrow circle of confidants, including D. I. Fonvizin.

A few words should be said about Pyotr Ivanovich Panin (1721-1789), that was N. I. Panin's brother. P. I. Panin was a Field Marshal General. He worked together with D. I. Fonvizin on a constitutional project for Grand Duke Pavel Petrovich. P. I. Panin gained fame as the winner in the civil war over E. Pugachev. According to A. I. Serkov, P. I. Panin was a member of the Lodges of Elagin's System in the 1770s[1].

P. I. Panin used the phrase "the good of the Fatherland" three times in his letter to Grand Duke Pavel Petrovich (dated May 6, 1778), emphasizing that taking care of the welfare of the Fatherland was the goal of all his life[2].

The name, Alexander Nikolaevich Radishchev (1749-1802), gained fame. Alexander Nikolaevich Radishchev was a writer and the Head of the St. Petersburg Customs. A. N. Radishchev rose to the rank of Collegiate Counselor and was brought up in the Corps of Pages together with A. M. Kutuzov studied law in Leipzig and served as a member of the Commission for Drafting Laws. He was arrested, prosecuted, and served a sentence during his life.

A. N. Radishchev was ordained a disciple at the Urania Lodge in St. Petersburg in 1773. He visited it in 1773, on March 29, 1774, and on April 12, 1774. His Masonic "career" stopped at the degree of a student or apprentice (comrade)[3]. A. N. Radishchev's unwillingness or unreadiness to receive the following Freemasonic degrees and initiations manifested itself in the activities that were incompatible with the principles of Freemasonry: he published his radical work "A Journey from St. Petersburg to Moscow" in 1790.

---

[1] Russian Freemasons. 1721-2019. A Biographical Dictionary. Century XVIII. Volume II / A. I. Serkov, M.: Ganga, 2019. Pages 249-251.

[2] Pavel I, P. I. Panin "The correspondence of Grand Duke Pavel Petrovich with Count Peter Panin" // Russian antiquity, 1882. - Volume 33. - # 2. - Page 409-410.

[3] Russian Freemasons. 1721-2019. Century XVIII. Volume II / A. I. Serkov, M., 2019. Pages 329-332; Russian Freemasons. 1721-2019. Century XVIII. Volume III / A. I. Serkov, M., 2019. Page 187.

The following lines can be read in the Ode "Liberty[1]," written by A. N. Radishchev in 1781-1783, giving an idea of the "common good" as an individual and common will:

"But what hates my freedom?
I look through my desires everywhere to the limit
A common power appeared among the people,
The cathedral of all powers is destiny!
Society is obedient to this power in everything,
Being unanimous with it everywhere.
There are no obstacles to the 'common good':
I see my share in the power of all,
I create my own will, making everyone's will:
That's what the law is in society!"[2]

By using his book "Journey from St. Petersburg to Moscow," A. N. Radishchev turned the theory of the "common good" into evidence against serfdom. It can be read in the chapter "Khotilov. Project in the future"[3]: "A driven by self-interest person in his or her endeavors fulfills the activities that can serve his or her own near or far benefit and stops carrying out the actions that do not give him or her his or her own near or far benefit. Following this natural impulse, when doing everything for ourselves, we qualitatively do everything with diligence and assiduity without any compulsion. On the contrary, when not doing everything for our benefit, we do it in error, lazily, obliquely, and crookedly. We find such land makers in our state." A. N. Radishchev knew the theory of the welfare of all and everyone well enough, giving it his interpretation: "People that would like to now confirm their message from above will use more outward appearance of usefulness and then, everyone will be pleased. On the contrary, directing all our forces for the benefit of all and everyone, why should we shine in appearance? The usefulness of

---

[1] A. N. Radishchev's Ode "Liberty" // A. N. Radishchev "The complete works of A. N. Radishchev": in 2 volumes. Volumes 1-2 / Edited by Professor A. K. Borozdin, Professor I. I. Lapshin, and P. E. Shchegolev. - St. Petersburg: M. I. Akinfiev, 1907-1909. – in 2 volumes - 1907. Pages 318-330.

[2] A. N. Radishchev's Ode "Liberty" // A. N. Radishchev "The complete works of A. N. Radishchev": in 2 volumes. Volumes 1-2 / Edited by Professor A. K. Borozdin, Professor I. I. Lapshin, and P. E. Shchegolev. - St. Petersburg: M. I. Akinfiev, 1907-1909. – in 2 volumes - 1907. Page 318.

[3] A. N. Radishchev "A journey from St. Petersburg to Moscow" // A. N. Radishchev "The complete works of A. N. Radishchev": in 2 volumes. Volumes 1-2 / Edited by Professor A. K. Borozdin, Professor I. I. Lapshin, and P. E. Shchegolev. - St. Petersburg: M. I. Akinfiev. In 2 volumes, 1907. Page 152.

our decrees for the good of the state should not shine on our face. Everyone that looks at us will see our prudence, seeing his or her benefit in our feat. Therefore, then everybody will bow down to us, not as if walking in terror, but sitting in goodness[1]." A. N. Radishchev instructed: "Let us be as an example to our later posterity, showing how power and freedom should be combined for our mutual benefit ...[2]."

When answering the question points during the investigation[3] (such as "Why did you write about Bliss in a mocking manner?"), A. N. Radishchev answered: "... I wrote with a mockery, having the intention to take away all the peasants from their landowners and make them free ...[4]."

The political and legal ideas of A. N. Radishchev were alien to Russian Freemasonry. Obviously, for this reason, he did not stay in the Masonic Lodges. However, his thoughts served as a sharp background in contrast to the interpretations of the "common good" by the "real" Russian Freemasons.

---

[1]A. N. Radishchev "A journey from St. Petersburg to Moscow" // A. N. Radishchev "The complete works of A. N. Radishchev": in 2 volumes. Volumes 1-2 / Edited by Professor A. K. Borozdin, Professor I. I. Lapshin, and P. E. Shchegolev. - St. Petersburg: M. I. Akinfiev. In 2 volumes, 1907. Page 165.

[2] Ibid. Page 165.

[3] The question points to Collegiate Counselor and Chevalier Radishchev // A. N. Radishchev "The complete works of A. N. Radishchev": in 2 volumes. Volumes 1-2 / Edited by Professor A. K. Borozdin, Professor I. I. Lapshin, and P. E. Shchegolev. - St. Petersburg: M. I. Akinfiev. 2 v. [1909]. Pages 309-316.

[4] Ibid. Page 315.

§3.3. The welfare of all and everyone in the second generation of Russian Freemasons — Part 2 (1780-1789)

It is worth telling about Ivan Ivanovich Betskoy (1704-1795). I. I. Betskoy was the personal secretary of Catherine II, studied abroad at the universities of Abo, Leipzig, and Copenhagen, and rose to the rank of Actual Privy Councilor[1]. There is some information about the membership of I. I. Betskoy in the 4th Degree in the Lodge of Charity to the Pelican in St. Petersburg in 1783[2].

I. I. Betskoy referred to the "common good" in his letter about the purpose of the Orphanage's activities, addressed to the Board of Trustees on May 1, 1775: "... When having the 'common good' or cruelty in their mind and not getting the certain pass marks, some balloting people started <...>, to talk about the vices of others in public, being not ashamed of any common beneficiaries in the benevolence and the beneficiaries that care for the 'common good' ...[3]." On the contrary, the author believes that it is necessary to serve humanity, "to serve the whole society out of love for that and not out of any predilection," "as the Educational House is a place of beneficence, peacefulness, and peace, and not a site of hatred, strife, and anger[4]." I. I. Betskoy wished "all prosperity and success for the 'common good'"[5] in his letter to the members of the Board of Trustees (dated January 3, 1776). I. I. Betsky did not hold significant posts in any Masonic Lodges. However, his mentioning the "common good" deserves some attention.

An undoubted role in Russian historiography was played by Nikolai Mikhailovich Karamzin (1766-1826), that was a famous historian and writer. He rose to the rank of a Real State Councilor, being an honorary member of various societies and universities. N. I. Novikov, A. M. Kutuzov, S. I. Gamaleya, and Yu. N. Trubetskoy were N. M. Karamzin's friends. N. M. Karamzin became a State Historiographer with the mediation of N. M. Muravyov. He was under the influence

---

[1]Russian Freemasons. 1721-2019. A Biographical Dictionary. Century XVIII. Volume I / A. I. Serkov, M.: Ganga, 2019. Pages 167-169.
[2]Russian Freemasons. 1721-2019. A Biographical Dictionary. Century XVIII. Volume III / A. I. Serkov, M.: Ganga, 2019. Page 97.
[3]A letter (dated May 1, 1775) // The companions of Catherine II: Ivan Ivanovich Betskoy / Russian antiquity. Volume VIII. 1873. Issues 7-12. SPb. The printing house of V. S. Balashev, 1873. Pages 900-903.
[4]Ibid. Page 900.
[5]A letter (dated January 3, 1776) // The companions of Catherine II: Ivan Ivanovich Betskoy / Russian antiquity. Volume VIII. 1873. Issues 7-12. SPb. The printing house of V. S. Balashev, 1873. Pages 711-713.

of I. G. Herder and A. I. Vyazemsky.

N. M. Karamzin was a member of the 2nd Degree in the Lodge of the Golden Crown in Simbirsk from 1885 up to1889[1]. Therefore, his membership in Masonic Lodges cannot be considered serious: N. M. Karamzin never received a Master's Degree, which was the highest degree of the Noannovskiye Lodges. However, N. M. Karamzin was influenced by Masonic ideology.

Picture 32. An image of the coat of arms of the Karamzin Family // P. P. Winkler "Russian Heraldry: History and Description of the Russian coats of arms, depicting all the nobles, coats of arms, introduced in the general armorial of All-Russian Imp." Issue 3. 1894. Page 133.

N. M. Karamzin noted the importance of the Sovereigns of Moscow (these Sovereigns have "a goal of the welfare of the people only"[2]) in his Note "On the Ancient and New Russia[3]," written in 1811. When arguing about the inadmissibility of punishing innocent people along with the guilty ones, N. M. Karamzin noted: "The slightest but useless punishment is closer to tyranny. Nevertheless, the cruelest penalty, but based on justice, has the only goal: the 'common good' …[4]." N. M. Karamzin thought that using punishment and encouragement was necessary for achieving the "common good": "People should be curbed in evil and encouraged to do good with a prudent system of punishments and rewards. But we will repeat that the first action is even more important than the second one …[5]." The "common good" can be achieved through "… the art of choosing people and treating them …[6]." Stating the population of Russia at the beginning of the 19th century at 40 million people, N.

---

[1]Russian Freemasons. 1721-2019. A Biographical Dictionary. Century XVIII. Volume I / A. I. Serkov, M.: Ganga, 2019. Pages 573-577; Russian Freemasons. 1721-2019. A Biographical Dictionary. Century XVIII. Volume III / A. I. Serkov, M.: Ganga, 2019. Page 257.
[2]A note by N. M. Karamzin on the ancient and new Russia//Russian Archive. 1870. #12. Page 2340.
[3]Ibid. Pages 2230-2350.
[4]Ibid. Page 2340.
[5]Ibid. Page 2340.
[6]Ibid. Page 2343.

M. Karamzin argued that the ruling Sovereign, Alexander I, was "zealous for the 'common good' ...[1]."

Regarding criminal punishment in the United States of America, N. M. Karamzin said in his note on the conversation of N. M. Karamzin with M. A. Zhukovsky and Prince A. I. Vyazemsky (dated July 24, 1825) that some "lenient measures in the United States had multiplied the number of criminals. The legislator must keep in mind the 'common good' ...[2]."

The opinion of N. M. Karamzin on issues of the "common good" cannot be considered representative of Russian Freemasonry as N. M. Karamzin parted with Freemasonry after five years of joining the lodge. But the influence of Freemasonry left an imprint on the work of a talented writer.

Another writer that received initiation in the lodge was Vasiliy Alekseevich Lyovshin (1746-1826), that was the author of many works and a member of many scientific and literary societies. He reached the rank of State Councilor through the State Civil Service. V. A. Lyovshin began as a member of the Theoretical Degree of Solomon Sciences in Moscow (where his work started in 1782) in Russian Freemasonry. V. A. Lyovshin became the Order Chief and Director of the Internal Rosicrucian Order in the 19th century, performing these duties until 1824[3].

V. A. Lyovshin's work "The newest journey composed in the Belev city" was published in the magazine "An Interlocutor of the Lovers of Russian Words" in 1984[4]. V. A. Lyovshin, in this work, cited the reasoning of the earthling Narsim about an autocratic ruler that, according to the social laws, "... must act for the good of everyone ...[5]." The speech of the inhabitant of the Moon in V. A. Lyovshin's work also contained a passage about a principle of the "common

---

[1] A note by N. M. Karamzin on the ancient and new Russia// Russian Archive. 1870. #12. Page 2348.

[2] K. S. Serbinovich "Nikolai Mikhailovich Karamzin. The memoirs of K. S. Serbinovich" // Russian antiquity, 1874. - Volume 11. - # 10. Page 246.

[3] Russian Freemasons. 1721-2019. A Biographical Dictionary. Century XIX. Volume IV / A. I. Serkov, M.: Ganga, 2020. Page 169.; Russian Freemasons. 1721-2019. Century XVIII. Volume II / A. I. Serkov, M., 2019 ... Pages 32-34; Russian Freemasons. 1721-2019. A Biographical Dictionary. Century XVIII. Volume III / A. I. Serkov, M.: Ganga, 2019. Page 66.

[4] The newest journey // An interlocutor of the lovers of Russian words. 1784. Part XIII. Pages 138-166. Part XIV. Pages 5-14. Part XVI. Pages 38-45, 49-53.

[5] L. V. Omelko "Masonic ideas in the prose of V. A. Lyovshin in the 1780s" // The Freemasonry and Russian literature of the XVIII and the beginning of the 19th century / Edited by V. I. Sakharov. M., 2000. Page 57.

[6] Vasily Lyovshin "The newest journey composed in the Belev city" //http://lib.ru/RUFANT/LEWSHIN/journey.txt (Accessed: 11/17/2020, free access).

good": about the desire for the well-being of all and everyone: "It is more reasonable for a large light to illuminate a small body than for a smaller light to light up a big body. The only wise arrangement of the connection of all worlds established by the Creator of everything for mutual benefit can be derived from this …[6]." The inhabitant of the Moon reported about "a chain of the mutual benefit" and the "common harm" (war of all against all): "It would be strange to keep the chain linking society to mutual benefit if those (to whom the members of society impose the burden of their freedom, instead of guaranteeing their love for them) delivered villainy, disturbing their peace and encouraging everyone to be at enmity with each other. Who could assure me that my previous bliss will depend on the fact that I entrust my safety to a restless person?[1]" The reader learns that the laws of the inhabitants of the Moon are reduced to the main Christian commandment: "Our law is very short and easy to fulfill as everyone understands that he or she must love God as a benefactor and his or her neighbor as himself or herself and he or she will also acquire a love for himself or herself through this. Thus, he or she will get rid of many annoyances that inevitably occur after breaking this commandment. It can be affirmed that any other opposite law is harmful to society and disgusting before God because everyone will curse the doctrine that is against the feelings of everybody, and everyone does not agree with this tenet, and the general tranquility is violated![2]" Studying the work of V. A. Lyovshin, L. V. Omelko supposed that the above idea was Masonic[3].

It is worth considering the Notes[4] of Ivan Vladimirovich Lopukhin (1756-1816), that came from a noble family, was a Real Secret Councilor, a Senator, the author of many works, including the works translated into many foreign languages, a member of the Friendly Scientific Society, a friend of N. P. Turgenev and Z. Ya. Karneev. I. V. Lopukhin served as a Vice-President of the VIII Provincial

---

[1]Vasily Lyovshin "The newest journey composed in the Belev city" //http://lib.ru/RUFANT/LEWSHIN/journey.txt (Accessed: 11/17/2020, free access).
[2]Ibid.
[3]L. V. Omelko "Masonic ideas in the prose of V. A. Lyovshin in the 1780s" // The Freemasonry and Russian literature of the XVIII and the beginning of the 19th century / Edited by V. I. Sakharov. M., 2000. Page 58.
[4]The notes of Ivan Vladimirovich Lopukhin existed in the form of the numerous lists of the manuscript in the Russian Empire of the 19th century. See "The Notes by I. V. Lopukhin," book VII, 1802 // NIA II SPB RAN. Fund 36 "The Vorontsov family is an ancient noble family: Vorontsov Mikhail Illarionovich (1714-1767), count; Vorontsov Roman Illarionovich (1707-1783), Count." List of contents 1. Unit of issue 753. The first edition of the Notes was issued in 1860 in London. See "The Notes from some circumstances of the life and service of the Active Privy Councilor and Senator I. V. Lopukhin, compiled by himself" / A preface by Iskander. - London: Trübner & C°, 1860. - [2], VIII, 212 p.

Directory in Moscow in 1782. He was ordained to the 3rd Degree in the Secret Siencific Eclectic Lodge of Harmony by I. G. Schwartz (Shvarts in the Russian sources) on June 20, 1783. I. V. Lopukhin served as a Chair Master and a Great Master in the Shining Star Lodge, holding its meetings in Moscow and St. Petersburg in 1784-1785.

I. V. Lopukhin received a Theoretical Degree and supervised the work of the entire Theoretical Degree, being the Overseer of the Russian Brothers of the Theoretical Degree Directory in the Rosicrucian Order in Moscow. I. V. Lopukhin became the Head of the Directory of the Rosicrucian Order in October 1785 and received the name "Philus" there. He was a Representative of the Lodge of the Rising Eagle in Oryol and a member of the Latona Chapter in St. Petersburg in 1785, representing the Subsidiary Lodge of the Rising Eagle in it and holding the position of the Chapter's Commissar[1].

Picture 33. An image of the motto of the Princes of the Lopukhin family // P. P. Winkler "Russian Heraldry: The History and Description of the Russian coats of arms, depicting all the nobles, coats of arms, introduced in the general armorial of All-Russian imp." Issue 3. 1894, page 169.

I. V. Lopukhin expressed the purpose of legislation on the issue of criminal punishment: "This seems to be an undeniable rule of philanthropy in legislation when one subject should be the benefit of mankind on the Earth and all the possible preparation for it in eternity[2]."

Commenting on the reply to the Tsar's letter of February 7, 1802, I. V. Lopukhin used the terms of the theory of the welfare of all and everyone: "... but whenever He wants to know my opinion, I can honestly say that all of this is inconvenient when *coordinating the direct local benefit with the general benefit of*

---

[1]Russian Freemasons. 1721-2019. A Biographical Dictionary. Century XVIII. Volume II / A. I. Serkov, M.: Ganga, 2019. Pages 54-57; Russian Freemasons. 1721-2019. A Biographical Dictionary. Century XVIII. Volume III / A. I. Serkov, M.: Ganga, 2019. Pages 45, 46, 48, 66, 80.
[2]See also: I. V. Lopukhin "The Notes from some of the circumstances of the life and service of the Active Privy Councilor and Senator I. V. Lopukhin, compiled by himself" / A preface by Iskander. - London: Trübner & C°, 1860. Page 10.
[3]The Notes by I. V. Lopukhin, book VII, 1802 // NIA II SPB RAN. Fund 36 "The Vorontsovs ..." List of contents 1. Unite of issue 753. Page 14.

the state. I do not agree with it and submitted my objection on paper to everything ..."[3] (*it was highlighted by the authors of this scientific work*). "I think that not presenting the truth about the 'common good' of the state to the Sovereign is stealing the Sovereign's true glory and the property of the general and necessary welfare and strictly punishable by laws[1]." I. V. Lopukhin declared about the "common good" as a goal on Page 20: "However, the establishment of These Notes is very useful if there would always be its direct goals. Like the establishment of a congregation, it does honor to the enterprising, the 'common good', the diligent Minister, and the great Genius - the Poet That represented these institutions[2]." I. V. Lopukhin, in the entry (dated March 20, 1808), raised an issue of the appeal examination of the cases of the peasants seeking freedom from the landowners in the 8th Department of the Senate. I. V. Lopukhin referred to the "common good" and the "general harm" to substantiate his principled position in defense of the principles of legality and justice: "... to liberate from the Fortresses by selection under the Laws is the destruction of the strength of the Laws, leading to the 'common harm.' And, besides this harm, what is the fruit of such decisions? Several dozen or hundreds of peasants will not be under the rule of the landowners. As a result, most of them may become alcoholics or will wander the streets and along the roads, being hungry and naked <...> if so, who will be the serfs there? And so, you will only excite people with the smallest number of such decisions. Of course, you will not allow liberating many serfs due to the common benefit. The whole villages, many thousands of serfs, will begin to make claims of liberty. The case will start in a small way and end with cannons, or, at least, whips and internal exiles, and, maybe, even gallows that also took place. I have only the public benefit as a subject in this case[2]." According to I. V. Lopukhin, serfdom was justified by the common benefit: "I will also say that I am perhaps the first to wish to have only free persons on the Russian land if only that would be possible without any harm to it. But the people should be curbed for their benefit. In effect, there is no more reliable police for the preservation of the general improvement than the administration of landowners. The tyrants among them must be curbed. But this must be arranged properly: when curbing tyranny, the Governors of the

[1] The Notes by I. V. Lopukhin, book VII, 1802 // NIA II SPB RAN. Fund 36 "The Vorontsovs ..." List of contents 1. Unite of issue 753. Page 14.

[2] The Notes by I. V. Lopukhin, book VII, 1802 // NIA II SPB RAN. Fund 36 "The Vorontsovs ..." List of contents 1. Unite of issue 753. Page 20.

[2] The Notes by I. V. Lopukhin, book VII, 1802 // NIA II SPB RAN. Fund 36 "The Vorontsovs ..." List of contents 1. Unite of issue 753. Pages 69-71. See also: I. V. Lopukhin "The Notes from some of the circumstances of the life and service of the active Privy Councilor and Senator I. V. Lopukhin, compiled by himself" / A preface by Iskander. - London: Trübner & C°, 1860. Pages 194-195.

provinces should fear punishment for their slightest excess or addiction, being sure not to avoid the punishment as tyrants for tyranny. And I will also say that nowadays, the weakening of the ties of subordination to the landowners in Russia is more dangerous than the invasion of the enemy. It is also a characteristic of kind-heartedness to regret that those that have not yet completely recovered from their illnesses can only walk in the hospital garden, drinking and eating only what the doctors tell them. In other words, it is a characteristic of a good Heart to wish that they would use full freedom in everything as soon as possible. But giving freedom to them ahead of time would destroy them[1]." Regarding the issue of extending the ten years' prescription to the affairs of the peasants seeking freedom, I. V. Lopukhin wrote a review in the General Meeting of Moscow Departments, calling for the extension of the ten-year prescription to the affairs of the peasants seeking freedom. I. V. Lopukhin argued his opinion in the following way: "If stop extending the ten years' prescription to such cases and end restricting the rights of those peasants that seek liberty in any way, then, perhaps, an unlimited number of serfs will move away from their landowners by a general undermining of the State of the nobleman and the fundamental laws of its approved advantages. As a result, many ways and means can be opened for the encroachment of various malicious people led by ignorance to embarrass innocence, often against the true benefit of those that want this freedom, and many lawsuits can arise, weakening the ties of subordination that are indescribably useful for the social welfare and improvement![2]."

I. V. Lopukhin understood that the change in laws could result in a "hesitation of minds." That, in turn, could lead to the "common good" or the "common harm": "Of course, the Laws can also be worse and better. According to the time and age of the peoples, it is necessary to change the Laws sometimes. I think it is more convenient to do this change privately, gradually acquainting people with every new legalization. But a sudden change in a whole circle of Legislation in the State by Thunder that could accompany it can produce hesitation in the minds of people, and the consequences of harm or benefit could be difficult to guess[3]." This passage characterized him as a man that was either a liberal-conservative or a cautious liberal.

---

[1] The Notes by I. V. Lopukhin, book VII, 1802 // NIA II SPB RAN. Fund 36 "The Vorontsovs ..." List of contents 1. Unite of issue 753. Pages 69-71. See also: I. V. Lopukhin "The Notes from some of the circumstances of the life and service of the active Privy Councilor and Senator I. V. Lopukhin, compiled by himself" / A preface by Iskander. - London: Trübner & C°, 1860. Pages 195-196.

[2] The Notes by I. V. Lopukhin, book VII, 1802 // NIA II SPB RAN. Fund 36 "The Vorontsovs ..." List of contents 1. Unite of issue 753. Pages 73-74.

[3] Ibid. Page 85.

I. V. Lopukhin wrote in his letter to A. M. Kutuzov (dated November 7, 1790) in response to the denunciation of Freemasons with accusations of "anarchy": "They shout about loyalty and love for the 'common good'. Enough! They only have their farms, ranks, and salaries on their minds. And if asking these fellows well what loyalty, love, and blessing are, they would become speechless at once."[1] It is clear from this commentary that the "common good" among the public was often understood superficially, becoming a persistent cliche of speech circulation while emasculating the content. At the same time, it is false to consider that the "common good" had no content and denotation in Russia in the 18th and 19th centuries. On the contrary, the widespread use of the term testifies to the depth and popularity of the theory of the "common good." And that theory was well absorbed by the elite of society and very superficially absorbed by the broad masses.

The opinion of I. V. Lopukhin on the state and legal issues can be considered representative of all Russian Freemasonry at the end of the 18th and the first quarter of the 19th centuries as he held some positions in many Masonic Lodges, being a member of the Chapter and Overseer of a Theoretical Degree and having only 4 years of experience in membership in Masonic Lodges. I. V. Lopukhin wrote many works. In addition, I. V. Lopukhin influenced the opinion of many people (M. M. Speransky, M. I. Nevzorov, V. Ya. Kolokolnikov, A. M. Kutuzov, and A. I. Kovalkov), introducing them to the Masonic worldview.

P. I. Melissino (it was written about him earlier) was a brother of Ivan Ivanovich Melissino (1718-1795). I. I. Melissino rose to the rank of a Privy Councilor, served as a Chief Prosecutor of the Holy Synod, and a Curator of Moscow University. He created the following two societies: the Free Russian Assembly and the Society of Lovers of Russian Science. I. I. Melissino was a member of the Friendly Scientific Society for some time[2]. I. I. Shuvalov, M. M. Kheraskov, and N. I. Novikov were friends and patrons of I. I. Melissino. It should be noted that I. I. Melissino pursued I. G. Schwartz (Shvarts in the Russian sources), starting in 1783, but at the same time, he patronized H. A. Chebotarev. Leaving a rather modest mark in Freemasonry, I. I. Melissino was a member of the

---

[1] A citation was quoted from M. M. Kovalevsky's "Freemasonry in the time of Catherine" // Europe Bulletin. 1915, # 9. Page 105; M. M. Kovalevsky "Freemasonry in the time of Catherine (On the history of German influence in Russia)" / / M. M. Kovalevsky "The selected works": Bipartite. Part 2. M.: ROSSPEN, 2010. Pages 64-84.

[2] Russian Freemasons. 1721-2019. A Biographical Dictionary. Century XVIII. Volume II / A. I. Serkov, M.: Ganga, 2019. Pages 100-102; Russian Freemasons. 1721-2019. A Biographical Dictionary. Century XVIII. Volume III / A. I. Serkov, M.: Ganga, 2019. Page 129.

6th-Degree Lodge in 1786-1787. At the same time, it should be mentioned that he was not indifferent to the terms of the theory of the "common good."

There is an interesting document in the Russian State Archive of Ancient Acts (Fund 146 "Investigative Files," Unit 23 "Matters of a secret expedition"). This is a denunciation to the Commander-in-Chief in Moscow, Prince Alexander Alexandrovich Prozorovsky, about the need to ban Martinism at Moscow University. This denunciation was made by a Curator of the Imperial Moscow University, Privy Councilor I. I. Melissino, on June 13, 1790. This denunciation precedes the persecution of N. I. Novikov, which was started in 1792[1]. The denunciation appeals to the "common good": "... I must sincerely confess to your Excellency that it would be highly desirable for me if the very root of it could be exterminated from the university in order not only to establish *the prosperity of this school but also to save the well-minded* from innocent criticism by getting rid of the so-called Martinists ..."[2] (*it was emphasized by the authors of this scientific work*).

It is worth mentioning Iosif Alekseevich Pozdeev (1742-1820) that grew up in a Captain's noble family and was the largest representative of the Freemasons of the 2nd, 3rd, and 4th generations. As for his career, I. A. Pozdeev rose to the rank of Colonel, served as a Chief of the Chancellery, and enjoyed the patronage of P. I. Panin and Z. G. Chernyshev. Thanks to Freemasonry, by recruiting personnel for civil service positions from among the Freemasons, I. A. Pozdeev could influence the Ministers of the Russian Empire in the first quarter of the 19th century[3]. I. A. Pozdeev had an impressive 39 years of experience in many Masonic Lodges.

I. A. Pozdeev had the following track record in the Masonic Lodges of the 18th century: a founder of the Latona Chapter in St. Petersburg in 1780 and, then, he became its member, a Great Local Master of the Provincial Grand Lodge in St. Petersburg in 1780, a Local Master of the Provincial Lodge in Moscow that began working no later than December 1781, a founder of the Orpheus Lodge in the Ryazan Regiment and, after that, in St. Petersburg, the Head of Meetings from 1782, a Chair Master from 11/7/1784 up to 12/26/1785, the Actual Head of the St. Catherine's Lodge of the North Star in Vologda that was opened in 1783, a member

[1] See the denunciation in Appendix # 4.

[2] RGADA. Fund 146. Search cases. Unit of issue # 23 (The Reports of the Curator of the Imperial Moscow University, Privy Councilor Ivan Ivanovich Melissino to the Commander-in-Chief in Moscow, Prince Alexander Alexandrovich Prozorovsky, with the appendix of his correspondence with Ober Kamerger Shuvalov and other persons about the known Friendly Scientific Society, now known colloquially under the name "Martinists"). Page 1.

[3] See the previously cited studies of A. I. Serkov and Yu. E. Kondakov.

of the Chapter XVIII Province in Moscow in 1784, an Honorary Member of the Three Banners Lodge in Moscow in the middle of 1784, a Freemason of the 4th Degree, served as the 2nd Overseer in 1785 and a Representative of the Lodge in Dorpat in the Lodge of the Morning Star in 1786, was a holder of the Theoretical Degree in Moscow in the Rosicrucian Order, a Ritual Leader of the Theoretical Degree in 1784-1789, was accepted to the Internal Order of the Rosicrucians (Rozencraitsers in the Russian sources) in 1785, had a Degree in Practice, led his own Theoretical Circle in Moscow, curated the works in Vologda in 1791-1792, had the Order Name "Pius" and the Motto "Sophus Pius de Eove," was a Ritual Leader, a Chair Master, and a Scottish Great Master in Scottish (Old Ecos) Lodge in Moscow around 1789[1]. When visiting the Masonic Lodges of the 19th century, I. A. Pozdeev attended dining meetings at the Neptune Lodge in Moscow on June 24, 1809, and June 24, 1810, being a member of the lodge until 1814. He also founded the Manna Seekers Lodge in Moscow on December 7, 1817[2].

Picture 34. A sign of the Manna Seekers Lodge. Russia. Moscow. The beginning of the 19th century. Bronze, silk; sewing, chasing, gilding, mounting. Published in the catalog "A Collection of the Hermitage" by L. I. Dobrovolskaya in 2013. Page 270.

The following lines can be read in a letter of I. A. Pozdeev, addressed to the Lodge of the North Star, dated March 5, 1784[3]. Talking about late I. G. Schwartz (Shvarts in the Russian sources), I. A. Pozdeev described him as "a person of an

[1] Russian Freemasons. 1721-2019. A Biographical Dictionary. Century XVIII. Volume II / A. I. Serkov, M.: Ganga, 2019. Pages 283-284; Russian Freemasons. 1721-2019. A Biographical Dictionary. Century XVIII. Volume III / A. I. Serkov, M.: Ganga, 2019. Pages 22, 23, 26, 47, 54, 67, 73, 76, 119, 147, 256.
[2] Russian Freemasons. 1721-2019. Century XIX. Volume IV / A. I. Serkov, M.: Ganga, 2020. Pages 146, 159.
[3] A letter of I. A. Pozdeev to the Lodge of the Northern Star (dated March 5, 1784) // From the History of Russian Rosicrucianism / N. P. Kiselev. - St. Petersburg: Printed at the publishing house named after N. I. Novikov, 2005. Pages 376-378.

excellent spirit that has labored for the Good of the Russian Brotherhood ..."[1] I. A. Pozdeev said in his letter that the Good is "the only and most successful": "... Knowing the Order and the usual care of those that are sincerely committed to it, it remains to bless Providence arranging everything according to its wise providence towards our only and most successful good ..."[2]

Picture 35. An image of the coat of arms of the Pozdeev family // P. P. Winkler "Russian Heraldry: History and Description Russian coats of arms, depicting all the nobles, coats of arms, introduced in the general armorial of all-Russian imp." Issue 1. 1892, page 46.

I. A. Pozdeev used the already known to us formula "I recognize for the good" in his letter to V. I. Ostolopov (dated February 6, 1797): "... confirming with a guide <...> over Brothers <...> and over those that will be entrusted to you for the good ...[3]."

The opinion of I. A. Pozdeev on the state and legal issues can be considered representative of all Russian Freemasonry at the end of the 18th and the first quarter of the 19th centuries, as he had 39 years of experience in membership in many Masonic Lodges, held senior positions in many Masonic Lodges and the Unions of Lodges was a carrier of high degrees, the founder of Lodges and Chapters. I. A. Pozdeev was one of the most famous Russian Freemasons. Yu. E. Kondakov wrote that I. A. Pozdeev had influenced the Minister of Public Education A. K. Razumovsky, M. Yu. Vielgorsky and other Freemasons at the beginning of the 19th century.

Alexander Vasilyevich Khrapovitsky (1749-1802), coming from an old noble family from the family of the General-In-Chief, belonged to the second

---

[1] A letter of I. A. Pozdeev to the Lodge of the Northern Star (dated March 5, 1784) // From the History of Russian Rosicrucianism / N. P. Kiselev. - St. Petersburg: Printed at the publishing house named after N. I. Novikov, 2005. Page 376.

[2] Ibid. Page 377.

[3] See "A letter of I. A. Pozdeev to V. I. Ostolopov" (dated February 6, 1797) // From the History of Russian Rosicrucianism / N. P. Kiselev. - St. Petersburg: Printed at the publishing house named after N. I. Novikov, 2005. Page 320.

generation of Freemasonry. He rose to the rank of an Actual Privy Councilor, the position of a State Secretary of Catherine II, and a Senator. A. V. Khrapovitsky enjoyed the patronage of the Grand Duke Peter Fyodorovich (Peter III) and K. G. Razumovsky. In turn, A. V. Khrapovitsky provided his patronage to A. N. Radishchev.

A. V. Khrapovitsky showed himself quite active both in Freemasonry and in public service. He served in many positions in the St. Petersburg Lodges: he was a member of the Muses Lodge in 1770-1774, an Orator in the Harpocrates Lodge in 1773-1775, was listed as a Scottish Master in the Great (English) Provincial Lodge in September 1776, served as a Chair Master in the Astrea Lodge in 1776, acted as a Chair Master in the Lodge of Nemesis in 1776-1777, and served as a Chair Master in the Chapter of Latona, starting in 1780[1].

One interesting entry (dated February 2, 1793) can be read in the diary of A. V. Khrapovitsky[2]. That note describes a dialogue between A. V. Khrapovitsky and Catherine II on "the villainous killing of the King of France" and the subsequent reaction in France: "There was a turn to her reign. And I had a question about the observance of the rights of everyone. I replied that nothing had been taken away from anyone under the new orders necessary for the benefit of the state. Moreover, the rights and privileges were granted to us by Her Majesty."[3]

The opinion of A. V. Khrapovitsky on the state and legal issues can be considered representative of all Russian Freemasonry at the end of the 18th century as he had 11 years of experience as a member of some Masonic Lodges, holding senior positions there.

Khariton Andreevich Chebotarev (1745-1815), coming from a Sergeant's family, can be considered a major figure in the 2nd generation of Freemasonry. He rose to the rank of a State Councilor and received the posts of a Professor, a Dean, the Rector of Moscow University, the Censor, and Secretary of the Friendship Scientific Society.

Kh. A. Chebotarev achieved great success in the Masonic Lodges: he was initiated in the Equality Lodge in Moscow and St. Petersburg on July 25, 1775, was elevated to the 2nd Degree on September 7, 1775, received the 3rd Degree on

---

[1]Russian Freemasons. 1721-2019. A Biographical Dictionary. Century XVIII. Volume II / A. I. Serkov, M.: Ganga, 2019. Pages 615-617; Russian Freemasons. 1721-2019. A Biographical Dictionary. Century XVIII. Volume III / A. I. Serkov, M.: Ganga, 2019. Pages 85, 93, 109, 120, 139, 140.

[2]A. V. Khrapovitsky "A Diary of A. V. Khrapovitsky." 1782-1793: From January 18, 1782 to September 17, 1793 / From his original manuscripts, with a biographical article and explanatory indications by Nikolay Barsukov, a member of the Archaeological Commission - Moscow: Russian archive, 1901 (1902). - XXII, 404 pages.

[3]Ibid. Page 246.

September 12, 1775, was appointed as a Secretary on September 12, 1775, was appointed as the 2nd Overseer for Dining Lodges, was secretly ordained to all remaining Degrees in 1775. In St. Petersburg, Kh. A. Chebotarev founded the Osiris Lodge, acting as its Secretary in 1776 and as the 2nd Overseer in November 1781 (while the lodge was already operating in Moscow).

Picture 36. An image of the coat of arms of the Chebotarev family // P. P. Winkler "Russian Heraldry: History and Description of the Russian coats of arms, depicting all the nobles, coats of arms, introduced in the general armorial of All-Russian imp." Issue 3. 1894. Page 128.

Kh. A. Chebotarev continued his Masonic work in Moscow: he was joined to the Lodge of the Three Banners around November 1781, performing the duties of the 2nd Overseer in 1785-1786 and, then, the duties of the 1st Overseer there; he acted as a Chair Master in the Lodge of the Sphinx from February 10, 1782 up to June 24, 1785, was the 4th Degree Freemason, then served as a Local Master; was accepted into a Theoretical Degree around 1782 and initiated into the Internal Rosicrucian Order of I. V. Lopukhin around 1785[1], had the Order Name "Thitanus a terruca"[2] and the Knighthood Name "Chariton eques a terruca."[3]

There are some references to the "common good" in the translation of "A Brief General History" by I. Freyer[4], edited by Kh. A. Chebotarev in 1769: the main object of the care of Yekaterina Alekseevna II "… is the true well-being of her vast state"[5] that includes "… the well-being of her lands …" and "… the population of them …."[6] The establishment of the upbringing of noble maidens in

[1]Russian Freemasons. 1721-2019. A Biographical Dictionary. Century XVIII. Volume II / A. I. Serkov, M.: Ganga, 2019. Pages 633-635; Russian Freemasons. 1721-2019. A Biographical Dictionary. Century XVIII. Volume III / A. I. Serkov, M.: Ganga, 2019. Pages 57, 62, 70, 75.
[2]Can be translated from Latin as "A Titan of the Earth."
[3]Translated from Latin as "Khariton, equal to the earth."
[4]I. Freyer Hieronymus Freyer "A Brief General History with its continuation to the very present times and the addition of Russian History to it: Translated from German into Russian, corrected, and multiplied at the Imperial Moscow University for the use of studying youth." Translated by Chebotarev. - [Moscow]: Printed at the same University, 1769. - [18], XLVIII, 500, [76] p.
[5]Ibid. Page 451.
[6]Ibid.

St. Petersburg was also a manifestation of the desire for "… the bliss of the subjects of every state …"[1]

Kh. A. Chebotarev used the term "the bliss of the human race"[2] in the "Word on the Invention of the Art of Writing"[3] in 1776.

It can be read in the "A Word on the Methods and Ways Leading to Enlightenment"[4] of 1779 that enlightenment was part of the "general welfare" and "general saving benefit,"[5] contributing to the achievement of them. The general welfare manifested itself in the form of material and non-material benefits: "… sciences open the way for us to the perfect temporary and eternal bliss; they create the general security, judgment, and truth for us; they keep us healthy and provide us with all the needs, abilities, and benefits in life …."[6]

According to Kh. A. Chebotarev, the whole humanity was an example of the "common good," and the Fatherland was an example of the private good: a wise person was adorned with "... a zealous desire to promote the good of the entire human race in general and, especially, his or her Fatherland …."[7] To accomplish this task, he or she had to exercise in the sciences: "... the 'common good' requires that every citizen loving his or her Fatherland should exercise in useful sciences in the same way, and through enlightenment and sciences,

---

[1] I. Freyer Hieronymus Freyer "A Brief General History with its continuation to the very present times and the addition of Russian History to it: Translated from German into Russian, corrected, and multiplied at the Imperial Moscow University for the use of studying youth." Translated by Chebotarev. - [Moscow]: Printed at the same University, 1769. - [18], XLVIII, 500. Pages 452, 454.

[2] A Convolute. A word about an invention of the art of writing. Did this discovery serve to the detriment of the human mind and good morals? On the joyous day of the accession of the August Monarch, Empress Catherine II the Great, All-Russian Empress and Autocrat, and so on to the All-Russian Imperial Throne. That day was solemnly celebrated with the deepest reverence at the Imperial Moscow University on June 30, 1776; Spoken by Khariton Chebotarev, a Public Extraordinary Professor of Reasoning and Moralizing, a University Sub-Librarian, and a member of the Free Russian Assembly at the same University. - [Moscow]: Printed at the University Printing House, [1776]. - 23, [1] p.

[3] Ibid. Page 20.

[4] A Convolute. A word on the Methods and Ways Leading to Enlightenment: On the highly solemn birthday of Her Majesty, the All-Russian Empress and Autocrat, Catherine II, the Wisest Legislator and True Mother of the Fatherland, at the public meeting of the Imperial Moscow University (dated April 22, 1779) / Spoken by Khariton Chebotarev, a Public Ordinary Professor of History, Reasoning, and Moralizing, a University Librarian and Conference Secretary, and a member of the Moscow Russian Assembly. - M.: Printed at the University Printing House, [1779]. - 28 pages.

[5] Ibid. Page 4.

[6] Ibid. Page 6.

[7] Ibid. Page 12.

improving his or her mind, trying to bring his or her talents to greater perfection, and becoming most capable of advancing the 'common good' of his or her Fatherland by using all of this ...."[1]

The opinion of Kh. A. Chebotarev on the state and legal issues can be considered representative of all Russian Freemasonry at the end of the 18th century as he had 12 years of experience as a member of many Masonic Lodges, holding some senior positions there. He also founded the Osiris Lodge in St. Petersburg and was the author of some works and a translator of some works about the "common good."

---

[1] A Convolute. A word on the Methods and Ways Leading to Enlightenment: On the highly solemn birthday of Her Majesty, the All-Russian Empress and Autocrat, Catherine II, the Wisest Legislator and True Mother of the Fatherland, at the public meeting of the Imperial Moscow University (dated April 22, 1779) / Spoken by Khariton Chebotarev, a Public Ordinary Professor of History, Reasoning, and Moralizing, a University Librarian and Conference Secretary, and a member of the Moscow Russian Assembly. - M.: Printed at the University Printing House, [1779]. - 28 pages. Page 24.

§3.4. The welfare of all and everyone in the third and fourth generations of Russian Freemasons (1790-1822)

The third generation of Russian Freemasons (1790-1809)

Several events took place at that time at once, preventing the massive spread of Freemasonry.

Firstly, it was banning the meetings, declared by the Order of the Golden-Rose Cross in response to the grandiose scandal and the subsequent prohibition of the Illuminati Order by the Bavarian Kurfüst in 1784-1787.

Secondly, Catherine II initiated an investigative case against N. I. Novikov and the banning of the meetings of Swedish Freemasons and the publishing activities of the Russian Rosicrucians (Rozencraitsers in the Russian sources) to reduce the influence of Prussian and Swedish Freemasonry in the Russian Empire.

Thirdly, Paul I's ban on holding lodge meetings because of the coup in France in 1789 and the subsequent growth of nationalist and revolutionary sentiments in some provinces of the Russian Empire (modern territories of the Baltic states, eastern Poland, and Ukraine).

Therefore, the number of representatives of this generation was extremely small.

That period was marked in the history of Russia by the military campaigns of A. V. Suvorov, the coup d'état of 1801, and the Russian-Swedish war (1808-1809).

Considering this time, it is worth touching on the life and work of A. F. Labzin. Alexander Fedorovich Labzin (1766-1825) came from a poor noble family. He rose to the rank of an Actual State Councilor, was one of the Directors of the Bible Society, a writer, publisher, a Censor, and a Vice-President of the Academy of Arts. A. F. Labzin was a pupil of I. G. Schwartz (Shvarts in the Russian sources), collaborated with N. I. Novikov, and served under F. P. Klyucharev. He was a friend of G. R. Derzhavin and enjoyed the patronage of A. N. Golitsyn and P. P. Turgenev.

A. F. Labzin became a Freemason on April 23, 1783. He founded the "Dying Sphinx" Lodge on January 15, 1800. The meetings of this lodge were first held in the apartment of A. F. Labzin, and then, they were arranged in the house of a merchant A. V. Glushkova until 1822. A. F. Labzin performed the duties of a Chair Master in the lodge. As for Russian Rosicrucianism, he served as a Chief Primate of the Theoretical Degree of Solomon Sciences in St. Petersburg in 1809-1810, using the pseudonym "A." A. F. Labzin also founded the Bethlehem Lodge in St. Petersburg until 1809, being a Chief-Master of the Lodge in 1815-1822. He was an honorary member of the lodges in St. Petersburg: the Pelican Lodge in 1810 and later, starting in December 28, 1816, and the Russian Eagle Lodge that started working on 03/12/1818. A. F. Labzin performed the duties of an Assistant Guard in the Lodge of Neptune in Moscow on March 19, 1819[1]. Thus, A. F. Labzin was a Freemason for about 40 years.

A. F. Labzin shared the general political and legal attitude of the nobles in Russia in the first quarter of the 19th century and supported the theory of the "common good." So, A. F. Labzin spoke about some cases of beneficence with pathos on the pages of the journal "Sionskiy Vestnik": "The heart rejoices even more in its ecstasy of joy for the good as all these benefactors are Russians. Russia, our earthly Fatherland, sanctified by the great destinies of God, intended for the testimony and manifestation of the great deeds of the Lord![2]."

The opinion of A. F. Labzin on the state and legal issues can be considered representative of all Russian Freemasonry at the end of the 18th and 19th centuries as he had 40 years of experience as a member of many Masonic Lodges, held positions in many Masonic Lodges, founded his lodge and managed it for many years in the first quarter of the 19th century. A. F. Labzin wrote and issued many printed works and translations of Western literature. Yu. S. Vasilyeva researched the biography of his public life.

The next person to be discussed was Novosiltsev Nikolai Nikolaevich (1768-1838). N. N. Novosiltsev rose to the ranks of a Real Privy Councilor and a Real Chamberlain, was an active member of the Secret Committee, the author of many legal and state projects, an Assistant Minister of Justice, and a member of the Law Drafting Commission in the first quarter of the 19th century. There are the following storage units, among others, in fund 176 "Novosiltsev (Novosiltsev) Nikolai Nikolaevich (1768-1838), statesman; President of the St. Petersburg Academy of Sciences (1803-1810)" of the Scientific and Historical Archives of the St. Petersburg Institute of History of the Russian Academy of Sciences: 1) 235 "March 24, 1803. Yakov Markevich's letter to Alexander I with the attachment of projects on the improvement of the state"; 2) 236 "October 1, 1803. Demyan Polyansky's Letter to Alexander I with the attachment of 3 projects on the improvement of the 'common good.'"

---

[1]Russian Freemasons. 1721-2019. A Biographical Dictionary. Century XVIII. Volume I / A. I. Serkov, M.: Ganga, 2019. Pages 5-8; Russian Freemasons. 1721-2019. A Biographical Dictionary. Century XIX. Volume IV / A. I. Serkov, M.: Ganga, 2020. Pages 157, 252, 324, 357, 485, 489.

[2]A citation was quoted from P. Bessonov's "A. F. Labzin. A literary and biographical essay" / / Russian archive, 1866. - Issue 6. - SPb. Pages 817-836.

It can be assumed that the letters of Y. Markevich and D. Polyansky about the state improvement and the improvement of the "common good" were in the possession of N. N. Novosiltsev due to his position. Considering that N. N. Novosiltsev was a member of one of many Masonic Lodges in St. Petersburg (the lodge of the United Friends (Amis Réunis) that operated from June 10, 1802, first according to the French System, then according to the Swedish System[1]), it becomes clear that the Masonic striving for the "common good" did not interfere with the work on the "common good." On the contrary, N. N. Novosiltsev got an increased desire for working on the "common good," and not only figuratively and indirectly, but literally, intensively working on the projects of the state improvement and the "common good." N. N. Novosiltsev in one of his letters to A. R. Vorontsov, written in French (dated August 30, 1804) referred to the fact that the ideas of the "common good" guided the Sovereign: "Cet envoi sera suivi dans peu de jours des rapports que la commission a présentés a S.M.I. à la fin de chaque mois: votre excellence y trouvera plusieurs choses qui doivent être décidés par le Souverain lui-même; mais comme S.M. n'a jamais d'outre sentiments sur tous de objets que celui qui porte sur soi le caractère de convenir de la manière la plus propre *au bien-être général* et a l'ordre de choses le plus solide et stable, il n'est pas douteux que les opinions de votre excellence sur ces sujets, guidées par l'experience et la réunion des lumières, ne pourraient être que très-agréables a l'Empereur et infinimeut utiles a la chose"[2] (*an emphasis was added by the authors of this work – Fred Y. Ford and Alexey V. Dmitriev*).

---

[1] Russian Freemasons. 1721-2019. A Biographical Dictionary. Century XIX. Volume II / A. I. Serkov, M.: Ganga, 2020. Pages 723-727; Russian Freemasons. 1721-2019. A Biographical Dictionary. Century XIX. Volume IV / A. I. Serkov, M.: Ganga, 2020. Pages 423, 443.

[2] A letter of N. N. Novosiltsev to Count Alexander Romanovich // An archive of Prince Vorontsov / Edited by P. I. Bartenev – M.: The printing house of A. I. Mamontov, 1870-1897. Book 30: The letters from Rogerson, N. N. Novosiltsov, historians Miller and Bantysh-Kamensky, Pozzo di Borgo, Prince Kurakin, and others. - 1884. Pages 303-304. The author's translation: "In a few days, this dispatch will be followed by the reports presented by the commission to the Sovereign at the end of each month: Your Excellency will find several things to be decided by His Majesty the Emperor himself there; but as His Excellency never has other feelings on all subjects, except those that are of such a nature as to reconcile the general welfare and the firmest and stablest order of things in the most proper way, then there is no doubt that the opinions of Your Excellency on these subjects, guided by the experience and commonwealth of enlighteners, can only be very pleasing to the Emperor and infinitely useful for the cause."

Picture 37. An image of the coat of arms of the Novosiltsev family // P. P. Winkler "Russian Heraldry: History and Description of the Russian coats of arms, depicting all the nobles, coats of arms, introduced in the general armorial of All-Russian imp." Issue 3. 1894. Page 143.

The next figure to be mentioned was Ivan Petrovich Turgenev (1752-1807). He was a native of the Tatar Murza clan, from the family of a Major Seconds that rose to the rank of a Privy Councilor. I. P. Turgenev enjoyed the patronage of A. A. Prozorovsky and Z. G. Chernyshev. Also, he was a friend of M. N. Muravyov. I. P. Turgenev experienced some opposition from P. I. Golenishchev-Kutuzov and M. I. Kovalinsky. He was returned from exile (he had been in banishment since 1792) after the accession to the throne of Paul I and received the rank of an Actual Councilor of State (1796). Also, he was appointed Director of Moscow University.

I. P. Turgenev's Masonic life was in full swing. I. P. Turgenev was a member of the Lodge of Harpocrates in St. Petersburg from 1773 up to1776. There is a record that I. P. Turgenev was ordained a Freemason in October 1776 at the Alexander Fortress in the Crimea, serving as an Orator of the Lodge in 1778 in the Crimea. Then, I. P. Turgenev expanded his activities in St. Petersburg, being an honorary member in the Chapter of Latona in 1778 and acting as the 1st Alms Collector in the Lodge of Osiris in November 1781. I. P. Turgenev spent the main Freemasonry work in Moscow, being a Rosicrucian: he became a member of the Harmony Lodge, which worked from 1780 up to 1783, became a member of the Directory of the VIII Province from 1782 up to February 1783, received the Order Name "Jannes eques ab aurora boreale[1]," was a member of the Deucalion Lodge that operated from October 20, 1782, was admitted to a Theoretical Degree in 1782 and into the Internal Rosicrucian Order during the life of I. G. Schwartz (Shvarts in the Russian sources), had the Order Name "Vegetus" ("Blooming"), his Motto was "Vegetus Turnuper" ("Vegetus Enion Rhuan"), then he was transferred from the

[1]It can be translated from Latin as an Ioannov Horseman of the Northern Lights.

subordination of N. I. Novikov under the leadership of G. Ya. Schroeder, was a member and a Registrar of the Haupt Directory in Moscow in September 1788, was transferred from the circle of N. I. Novikov into the circle of I. V. Lopukhin in October 1788 and was appointed Senior there, was a Chief Overseer of the Theoretical Degree in 1792, and worked under the command of N. I. Novikov. He founded two lodges: the Astrea Lodge in Moscow until 1783 (the exact date of foundation is unknown) and the Golden Crown Lodge in Simbirsk, which had been operating since 1784[1].

I. P. Turgenev talked about the "common good" in his work "Who can be a good citizen and loyal subject?[2]." " … The essential welfare of society (taking into consideration its welfare in various respects) depends on the zealous and diligent performance of public positions. The stronger the encouragement for this performance, the more reliably the welfare of society is acquired[3]." I. P. Turgenev strove to show in his work that "… providing the good to people" is an enduring value[4], but serving the good "is full of toil, grief, failure, and sorrow for a sensitive soul …[5]." Religion was capable of helping in serving the "common good" with its slogan "… when serving the Emperor, you serve God …[6]." I. P. Turgenev believed that the main point of "public service" was the service of "all, in general, and everyone, in particular, and the uncomplaining performance of the positions connected with the good of society depends on this service …[7]."

This service is spiritual and "presupposes and requires obedience of a person's own will to the will of laws[8]," depriving of a person's precious freedom in favor of the will of a Sovereign and the demands of laws[9]. I. P. Turgenev likened the state of the "true and divine social bliss" to the Golden Age - the ideas of Russian Freemasons, as well as Christian mystics about the Kingdom of God, the

---

[1] Russian Freemasons. 1721-2019. A Biographical Dictionary. Century XVIII. Volume II / A. I. Serkov, M.: Ganga, 2019. Pages 554-556; Russian Freemasons. 1721-2019. A Biographical Dictionary. Century XVIII. Volume III / A. I. Serkov, M.: Ganga, 2019. Pages 45, 46, 48, 49, 69, 108, 120, 144, 257.

[2] I. P. Turgenev "Who can be a good citizen and a faithful subject?" / Translated from French into Russian by Serpukhov Protopop Vasily Protopopov. - M.: Printed in the University Printing House of Ridiger and Claudius, 1796.- [4], 39, [1] p.

[3] Ibid. Page 5.

[4] I. P. Turgenev "Who can be a good citizen and a faithful subject?" / Translated from French into Russian by Serpukhov Protopop Vasily Protopopov. - M.: Printed in the University Printing House of Ridiger and Claudius, 1796.- [4], 39, [1] p. Page 24.

[5] Ibid. Page 25.

[6] Ibid. Pages 26-27.

[7] Ibid. Page 27.

[8] Ibid. Page 28.

[9] Ibid. Page 32.

utopia of a happy society. The more bliss in society, "… the more prosperous this society is. The less bliss in society, the more unhappy this society is[1]." A far-reaching conclusion can be drawn from the teachings of I. P. Turgenev: the level of bliss in society is measured by general happiness.

The opinion of I. P. Turgenev, on the state and legal issues, can be considered representative of all Russian Freemasonry at the end of the 18th century as he had 16 years of experience as a member of many Masonic Lodges, holding some senior positions there. He was also a member of Chapters, a founder of several lodges, and translated Western literature into Russian. According to A. N. Pypin[2], Turgenev was the author of the discourse in French (published in the translation of V. Protopopov) "Who can be a good citizen and loyal subject." Another original work of his, "Some imitation of the songs of David," should be noted. He also translated some mystical treatises: John Mason's "Know thyself"; Johann Arndt's "On True Christianity"; "An Apology, or Defense of the Order of the Freemasons." I. P. Turgenev, along with Laharpe and Protasov, was an educator of the Grand Duke Alexander Pavlovich.

It is worth mentioning the personality of Adam Adamovich Czartoryski[3] (1770-1861), that came from the Lithuanian princely family of the Gediminids, rose to the rank of a Privy Councilor and the position of a Senator, was a member of the Secret Committee, the Permanent Council, and the State Council, and defended the interests of the Kingdom of Poland. He completed the third Freemasonry generation. A. A. Czartoryski enjoyed the patronage of N. V. Repnin and State Chancellor A. R. Vorontsov in 1803. N. N. Novosiltsev became an opponent of the views of A. A. Czartoryski in 1820.

Picture 38. An image of the coat of arms of the Czartoryski Family // P. P. Winkler "Russian Heraldry: History and Description of the Russian coats of arms, depicting all the nobles, coats of arms, introduced in the general armorial of All-Russian imp." Issue 2. 1894. Page 50.

[1] I. P. Turgenev "Who can be a good citizen and a faithful subject?" / Translated from French into Russian by Serpukhov Protopop Vasily Protopopov. - M.: Printed in the University Printing House of Ridiger and Claudius, 1796.- [4], 39, [1] p. Page 39.
[2] A. N. Pypin "Russian Freemasonry: the 18th and the first quarter of the 19th centuries." Petrograd: Lights, 1916. Page 254.
[3] The surname "Czartoryski" was sometimes written as "Chartorizhski" in Russian.

A. A. Czartoryski was consecrated in Freemasonry at the beginning of 1790 in the Lodge of the Shrine of Isis (Great East of the Kingdom of Poland and the Grand Duchy of Lithuania) in Warsaw. He served as a Judge in 1811 in the Northern Shield Lodge in Warsaw, being a member and an Officer of the Lodge in 1815 and an honorary member of the Lodge later. A. A. Czartoryski was an Honorary Member of the Isis Shrine Lodge in Warsaw, starting on November 23, 1814. He became a member of the 4th Degree of the Grand Capitular Lodge in Warsaw on August 17, 1815. A. A. Czartoryski received the 7th Degree in the System of the Greater East of Poland in February 1816. He founded the Casimir the Grand Lodge in Warsaw in 1816, being its member until 1821. A. A. Czartoryski was also an Honorary Member of the Lodge of Dispersed Gloom in Zhytomyr from September 26, 1818up to 1821[1].

A. A. Czartoryski, like A. R. Vorontsov, strove for the "common good" and the protection of the rights of everyone. So, he pointed out in his memoirs: "... I firmly believed that I would be able to reconcile the aspirations inherent in Russians with humane ideas, directing the Russians' thirst for primacy and glory to serve the 'common good'... I wanted Alexander to become, in a way, the supreme judge and mediator for all civilized peoples of the world, being the protector of the weak and the oppressed, the guardian of justice among the peoples. Finally, I would like his reign to serve as the beginning of a new era in European politics *based on the 'common good' and respect for the rights of everyone"*[2] (*it was emphasized by the authors of this scientific work: Fred Y. Ford and Alexey V. Dmitriev*).

---

[1]Russian Freemasons. 1721-2019. A Biographical Dictionary. Century XVIII. Volume II / A. I. Serkov, M.: Ganga, 2019. Pages 628-633; Russian Freemasons. 1721-2019. A Biographical Dictionary. Century XVIII. Volume III / A. I. Serkov, M.: Ganga, 2019. Page 304; Russian Freemasons. 1721-2019. A Biographical Dictionary. Century XIX. Volume IV / A. I. Serkov, M.: Ganga, 2020. Pages 79, 643.

[2]A citation was quoted from A. N. Arkhangelsky's "Alexander I." - M.: Young Guard, 2005. Page 61. See also: A. Czartorysky "The memoirs and correspondence with Emperor Alexander I" / Edited by A. Kizevetter. Volume 1. St. Petersburg, 1912-1913. Page 170.

The fourth generation of Russian Freemasons (1810-1822)

There was a real heyday of Russian Freemasonry in the 19th century in this period. The number of lodges and Brothers grew. Two great alliances were formed: the Grand Lodge of Astrea and the Great Provincial Lodge. The activities of the lodges were regulated by the state, starting from 1810. The military campaign lodges were created in Russia and abroad in 1812-1815. Many Russian nobles and the Tsar himself shared mystical and religious ideas. Alexander I banned Masonic Lodges and other secret societies by Decree in the Russian Empire in 1822. The history of Russia of this period is replete with wars: the Russian-Turkish war (1806-1812), the Patriotic war of 1812, the foreign campaigns of the Russian army (1813-1815), the creation of the Kingdom of Poland and the Principality of Finland, and the granting of constitutions to them. The formation of the Holy Alliance took place in 1815. The growth of the national liberation movement occurred in Europe (Italy, Greece, and Spain).

Mikhail Yurievich Vielgorsky (1788-1856), one of the famous Freemasons of the XIX century, left a note saying that the "common good" was the goal of the Masonic Order. M. Yu. Vielgorsky served in the Collegium of Foreign Affairs from 1804 up to 1812 and, later, in the Department of the Minister of Public Education A. K. Razumovsky. He was in the service of the Ministry of the Interior from 1813 up to 1824. M. Yu. Vielgorsky rose to the rank of the Chief of the Imperial Court (an Official of the 2nd Class). He became known to the public as a musician and a friend of the writers N. M. Karamzin, V. A. Zhukovsky, P. A. Vyazemsky, and A. S. Pushkin[1].

The activity of M. Yu. Vielgorsky in Freemasonry was extensive. He was consecrated in the Palestine Lodge in St. Petersburg in the spring of 1810, being Chair Master there from the summer of 1810 up to 1814. M. Yu. Vielgorsky was an Honorary Member of the Lodge, starting in 1817. He served as the 1st Great Overseer in the Chapter of Mount Tabor (the Governing Body of the highest degrees of the French system) in 1812. M. Yu. Vielgorsky was a member of the Lodge of the United Friends (Amis Réunis) in the 7th Degree in St. Petersburg in 1812. He served as an Honorary Member of the Lodge, starting in 1817.

M. Yu. Vielgorsky was attached to the Lodge of Elizabeth to Virtue in 1815, received the 9th Degree in it, acted as a Chair Master in 1815-1817, and was an Honorary Member of the Lodge starting from December 15, 1817. He was also

[1] Russian Freemasons. 1721-2019. Century XIX. Volume I / A. I. Serkov, M.: Ganga, 2020. Pages 398-403.

a member of the Three Virtues Lodge in St. Petersburg and a Chair Master of the Lodge in 1815-1819. Being a member of the Great (Directory) Provincial Lodge, M. Yu. Vielgorsky held the following positions there: a Vice-Chancellor in 1815, the 1st Great Local Master from November 10, 1815 up to 1816, a Representative of the Lodge of Elizabeth to Virtue in 1816, a Great Master from May 24, 1817 up to 1820. He founded the Lodge of the Golden Lion Alexander in St. Petersburg in 1816, holding the position of a Chair Master until November 8, 1818. He was an Honorary Member of this Lodge, starting from November 30, 1818. M. Yu. Vielgorsky became an Honorary Member of the following lodges in St. Petersburg: the White Eagle Lodge, which had been operating since 1818, and the Three Luminaries Lodge, starting on December 4, 1816. He installed the Manna Seekers Lodge in Moscow in 1817, performing the function of a Grand Master on December 7, 1817. M. Yu. Vielgorsky was President and Grand Sub-Prefect of the Phoenix Chapter in St. Petersburg in 1817, a Prefect of the Chapter starting on October 7, 1818, having an Order Name "Eques a Cygno Argento (Alba)," which means, "A Knight of the Silver (White) Swan"; his Motto was "Candore" – "Purity (purity)." M. Yu. Vielgorsky attended the Lodge of the Golden Key to Virtue as an Honorary Member of the Lodge in Simbirsk, starting on April 12, 1818. He acted as a Chair Master in the Sphinx Lodge in St. Petersburg from November 12, 1818 up to 1819. M. Yu. Vielgorsky was an Honorary Member of the Lodge of the Oak Valley to Allegiance, starting on June 20, 1820. Then he opened the Lodge of St. Theologian Ioann in St. Petersburg on April 7, 1821, and was a member of that lodge[1].

Picture 39. A sign of the Lodge of the United Friends. Russia. St. Petersburg. The beginning of the 19th century Bronze; stamping, gilding, engraving. The triangle contains two hands connected in a handshake. Published by L. I. Dobrovolskaya in the catalog "A Collection of the Hermitage" in 2013. Page 265.

[1]Russian Freemasons. 1721-2019. A Biographical Dictionary. Century XIX. Volume IV / A. I. Serkov, M.: Ganga, 2020. Pages 141, 220, 238, 247, 253, 256, 268, 322, 334, 416, 429, 457, 469, 477, 496.

M. Yu. Vielgorsky wrote in his note to the chosen Brothers: "The motivation to form a secret harmonious fraternal bond has the following main goals:

1. To actively engage in the teachings of the Order according to the given instructions, directions, and drawings of the beneficent leader. To establish general meetings for fulfilling this.
2. To unite with the closest ties of sincerity and unhypocritical mutual participation for the 'common good' through the Order, and vigilantly try to protect communication from temptations, lures, and infidelities, spreading this intention in favor of two lodges."[1] It should be noted that the desire for the "common good" was characteristic of the activities of Masonic Lodges and for Russian Freemasons, and the Order acted as a means of achieving the "common good."

Of course, the central figure in the history of the theory of the "common good" in Russia in the first quarter of the 19th century was a Professor, Dean of the Faculty of Philosophy and Law of St. Petersburg University, Pyotr Dmitrievich Lodiy (1764-1829) that served on the Commission for Drafting Laws and rose to the rank of an Actual State Councilor.

P. D. Lodiy showed violent activity in Freemasonry: he was elevated to the 2nd Degree in the Lodge of Elizabeth to Virtue in St. Petersburg on September 26, 1810, and the 3rd Degree on January 16, 1811; he was a member of the Polar Star Lodge in St. Petersburg (the Lodge worked in 1807-1810); he was listed as a member of the Lodge of Peter to Truth in St. Petersburg in 1810 and a member of the Lodge of Alexander to the Triple Salvation in Moscow in 1818-1819[2].

P. D. Lodiy was one of the few Russian Freemasons that theoretically developed the category of the "common good."[3] P. D. Lodiy used the formula "all

---

[1] RGIA. Fund 938. List of contents 1. Case # 440. "The Masonic notes written by Count M. Yu. Vielgorsky," Page 1.

[2] Russian Freemasons. 1721-2019. Century XIX. Volume II / A. I. Serkov, M., 2020. S. 488-489; Russian Freemasons. 1721-2019. Century XIX. Volume IV / A. I. Serkov, M., 2020. Page 128, 283, 383, 411.

[3] As the publication of the book was carried out in 1828 (after the prohibition of Masonic Lodges) and P. D. Lodiy did not occupy any serious position in Russian Freemasonry according to the available data, P. D. Lodius was not included in the list of Freemasons that used the category of the "common good," according to Appendix 4.

and everyone"[1] in his Theory of General Rights in 1828. Substantiating the theoretical provisions, P. D. Lodiy referred to the Natural Public Law of S. Pufendorf. He dealt with the historiography of the Theory of Natural Law and also mentioned the names of H. Wolf, Frederick II, J. Justi, and D. Nettelbladt[2]. P. D. Lodiy defined general welfare (salus publica) as "... such a state of the state when it can make its state the most perfect, in other words, easily succeeding in achieving its goal ...[3]," and private welfare - as "... such a state of citizens when each of them can make his or her internal and external states the most perfect <...> receiving everything that is required by the needs, benefits, and pleasures of life ...[4]."

Sovereigns had to fulfill their main duty: "the achievement of the goal and prosperity of the State"[5] without losing their duties, regarding God, themselves, their neighbors, and their religion. To do this, they had to have "some sufficient knowledge of their state, both in legal and political terms," and also have "a good and constant will to advance the 'common good'[6]." The aim of a Monarchy was "the welfare of all citizens, in general, and everyone, in particular." The goal of the despotic state was "the prosperity of the Despot." All citizens under monarchical rule had complete freedom "in actions that were civilly indifferent." All actions under despotic rule (both attributable to the "common good" and "civilly indifferent") "depend on the arbitrariness of the Despot[7]."

P. D. Lodiy was criticized and attacked in the 1820s, but his "The Theory of Common Rights)" (1828) demonstrates that the theory of the "common good" continued existing after the banning of Masonic Lodges in the Russian Empire in 1822.

Another evidence of the spread of the categories of the "common good" among Russian Freemasons was the speech of Andrey Petrovich Rimsky-Korsakov (1778-1862) "Reflection on the Difference of Systems in Freemasonry" on August

---

[1] P. D. Lodiy "The theory of common rights, containing the philosophical doctrine of natural universal state law" / The works of Peter Lodiy, Doctor of Free Arts and Philosophy - St. Petersburg: the printing house of the Department of External Trade. 1828. Page 27.
[2] Ibid. Pages 443-445.
[3] Ibid. Page 2.
[4] Ibid. Page 2.
[5] P. D. Lodiy "The theory of common rights, containing the philosophical doctrine of natural universal state law" / The works of Peter Lodiy, Doctor of Free Arts and Philosophy - St. Petersburg: the printing house of the Department of External Trade. 1828. Pages 224-225.
[6] Ibid. Page 227.
[7] Ibid. Page 327.

19, 1816[1] (he served as the 1st Overseer in the Lodge of Elizabeth to Virtue). This is evidenced by the following lines: "… Freemasonry established and so graceful for the good of the universe …"; "… Gratitude to the good providence that cares so wonderfully about us …"; "Blessed is the man that has the opportunity to remove himself from any worldly vanities and impose some Chains on his feelings, stirring up the excitement of passions, to gather in himself and become the source of his bliss in the source of His Life in the heart. Leaving all his prejudices about his Knowledge and gifts behind the doors of our temple, for this reason, he will cleanse his heart to accept the true Masonic teaching and learn it."[2] It can be seen from the speech that the source of bliss was the man himself, that knew how to curb his passions and abandoned prejudices. It should be recalled that A. P. Rimsky-Korsakov rose to the rank of a Full State Councilor. He was appointed an Official in the Department of the Ministry of Justice on March 28, 1806, served as the Head of the 1st Department of the Office of the Minister of Internal Affairs in 1812-1820, became an Official at Special Assignments in the Special Chancellery of the Ministry of Internal Affairs on August 29, 1821, and was appointed Volyn Civil Governor. The Masonic career of A. P. Rimsky-Korsakov was equally impressive. A. P. Rimsky-Korsakov was consecrated in the Lodge of Elizabeth to Virtue in St. Petersburg in 1810 and elevated to the 3rd Degree on October 12, 1811. He served as a Secretary in this lodge in 1811-1812, fulfilling the duties of the 1st Overseer in 1816 -1817 and a Local Master in 1817-1818. Subsequently, he became an Honorary Member of this Lodge, and the 7th Degree Freemason. A. P. Rimsky-Korsakov was a member of four more lodges in St. Petersburg for the period from 1812 up to 1816: a member of the Lodge of the United Friends (Amis Réunis), starting on April 2, 1812; a member of the Lodge of the Sphinx, 5th Degree, on June 25, 1815; a member of the Palestine Lodge until mid-1815; a member of the Lodge of Golden Lion Alexander, starting on 1816 and serving as the 1st Overseer and the Governor in it. A. P. Rimsky-Korsakov received membership in the Supreme Governing Bodies of Masonic Lodges in St. Petersburg, starting in 1816: performing the positions of a Grand Secretary in the Great (Directory) Provincial Lodge, starting on March 9, 1817, he was the 2nd Grand Stewart, starting on January 14, 1818, and a Grand Chancellor from April 1818 up to 1820; being the bearer of the 8th Degree in the Chapter of the Phoenix, he served as a Secretary of the Chapter from October 5, 1817 up to January 1818, receiving the Order Name "Eques ab api" ("A Knight of the Bee") and having the Motto "Eligit Optimum" ("Labor best combines"); he served as a Secretary in

[1] A reflection on the difference of Freemasonry Systems by Andrey Rimsky Korsakov // GA RF. Fund 48. List of contents 1. Unit of issue # 499. Part 3. The documents of Masonic Lodges: poems, songs, and cantata in honor of the accession to the throne of Alexander I. Pages 69-78.
[2] Ibid. Pages 69, 77-78.

1817 and a Curator of the archives in the Scottish Directory in 1818. A. P. Rimsky-Korsakov founded and installed the lodges, occupying some leading positions in them. He also attended some lodges as an honorary member in Odessa (he was a member of the Euxin Pontus Lodge starting on October 29, 1817, acting as a Representative of the Lodge in the Great Provincial Lodge and being an Honorary Member of the Lodge. A. P. Rimsky-Korsakov founded the Scottish Lodge of the Three Kingdoms of Nature (the Friends of Nature) on August 14, 1818). He founded the Orpheus Lodge (Orpheus to Perfect Harmony) in St. Petersburg on November 28, 1818, and was a Local Master, starting on December 3, 1818, a Chair Master in 1818-1819, and an Honorary Member of the Lodge, starting on December 8, 1819. A. P. Rimsky-Korsakov was an Honorary Member of the Lodge of the Three Luminaries, starting on November 27, 1818. He was a Chair Master of the Lodge of the Three Virtues, starting on October 20, 1819. A. P. Rimsky-Korsakov was an Honorary Member of the Russian Eagle Lodge, starting in March 1820. He was the 6th Degree Freemason and an Honorary Member of the Friends of Humanity Lodge that worked in the union of the Great East of Poland in Grodno, starting on May 20, 1817. A. P. Rimsky-Korsakov installed[1] the Manna Seekers Lodge in Moscow on December 7, 1817, performing the function of the 1st Overseer in it and being an Honorary Member of the Lodge, a member of the Circle, and Holder of a Theoretical Degree in the Rosicrucian Order[2].

Picture 40. A sign of the Lodge of the Three Virtues. Russia. The beginning of the 19th century. Brass, silk; casting, chasing. The sign contains a crossed anchor, a cross, and a sword. Published by I. N. Ukhanova in the catalog "A Collection of the Hermitage" in 2013. Page 282.

[1]Installation in Freemasonry was the procedure for checking and approving a newly opened lodge. After verifying, the lodge could work without hindrance.

[2] Russian Freemasons. 1721-2019. Century XIX. Volume III / A. I. Serkov, M., 2020. Pages 256-258; Russian Freemasons. 1721-2019. A Biographical Dictionary. Century XIX. Volume IV / A. I. Serkov, M., 2020. Pages 67,147, 171, 203, 215, 223, 250-251, 293, 326, 330, 341, 447, 465, 474, 503-504, 508.

Mikhail Mikhailovich Speransky (1772-1839) came from the clergy, was a Knight of the Order of St. Ioann of Jerusalem, a well-known Statesman, Lawyer, and a Compiler of many Decrees and Manifestos, systematized Russian Legislation, enjoyed the patronage of Prince Alexey B. Kurakin, Grand Duke Alexander Pavlovich, I. V. Lopukhin, and V. P. Kochubey. M. M. Speransky rose to the rank of Director of the Law Drafting Commission, the Deputy Minister of Justice, a State Secretary of the State Chancellery, and Chairman of the Law Department of the State Council. M. M. Speransky experienced some opposition from N. M. Karamzin, A. D. Balashov, and D. A. Guryev during his career. It should also be noted that M. M. Speransky was an honorary member of many scientific societies and universities.

M. M. Speransky was initiated into Freemasonry by F. P. Klyucharev and I. V. Lopukhin in 1810. He acted as a Chair Master in the Lodge of the Pole Star (1807-1810) in St. Petersburg in 1810[1]. According to some scientists, M. M. Speransky planned to subordinate Freemasonry to state control and make it a forge of personnel for the benefit of the state service. However, he faced very strong opposition, and the event stopped halfway[2].

Emphasizing the conventionality of the division of the rights to private and public by the Romans in his note "On the system of laws, in general," M. M. Speransky pointed to the belonging of laws to the "common good" as the laws serve the interests of both the state and every inhabitant: "It is impossible to imagine the state without ordinary people and, consequently, to imagine the laws that could be useful to the state, but useless for private people. Nevertheless, there are private property and the property of the state (res publica et res privata). But, in this respect, the privacy laws should be opposed only by the laws of the state economy and not by all laws, in general, that do not belong to private property."[3]

Using the terms of the theory of the "common good" in his notes, M. M. Speransky considered the separation of powers as "the first guarantee of the 'common good'"[4]: "the disadvantages of complex management," "positive harm,"

---

[1]A. I. Serkov "Russian Freemasonry. 1731-2000." - M.: ROSSPEN, 2001. Pages 764, 1088, 1089.

[2] See the studies of V. Yu. Zakharov, E. A. Vishlenkova, A. I. Serkov, E. Yu. Kondakov, and A. V. Dmitriev.

[1]The thoughts of Count M. M. Speransky. On the system of laws, in general. // An archive of the historical and practical information relating to Russia, published by Nikolai Kalachov [Text]. - St. Petersburg: Printed at the Printing House of the 2nd Department of His Own Imperial Majesty Chancellery, 1858. Page 6.

[4] Speransky // F. M. Dmitriev "Speransky" / The works of F. Dmitriev. – M.: [without publishers], 1862. §3. Page 3.

"harm to the people themselves," "social harm,"[1] "public good," "idea of benefit," and "the well-organized state."[2] M. M. Speransky noted the inadmissibility of maximizing the "common good" to the detriment of everyone's good: "... if a public good is sometimes built on a private sacrifice, then, this beginning being unconditional in exceptional cases should not be the rule of everyday life. The administration can violate the law because of the idea of benefit, and this is not tolerated by the well-organized state. Moreover, the very habit of acting in the interests of society and not individuals gives the administration a tendency to invade the sphere of private interests, subordinate them to its goals, and hinder the free development of those elements it is composed of according to the very desire for the 'common good' ..."[3]

F. Dmitriev, in his article "Speransky and his state activities," assessed the activities of young reformers (A. R. Vorontsov, M. M. Speransky, and others): "... they wanted the institutions less prone to arbitrariness, designed to uphold the law and *ensure the rights of all and everyone* ..."[4] (*it was highlighted by the authors of this work: Fred Y. Ford and Alexey V. Dmitriev*).

The opinion of M. M. Speransky on the state and legal issues cannot be considered representative of Russian Freemasonry in the 19th century as he had only 2 years of experience of membership in Masonic Lodges, and the reform of Freemasonry he had conceived was stopped. However, the scientific research of M. M. Speransky about the "common good" and his approaches to the "common good" were ahead of their time and are of undoubted research interest.

Thus, the terms of the "common good" appeared in the 1st generation and survived until the 4th generation in the written heritage of Russian Freemasons. This fact indicates the presence of a theory of the "common good" in the worldview of Russian Freemasons. For some Freemasons, the theory poured into philosophical and theoretical reasoning, while for other Freemasons, the vocabulary of the theory was used when discussing some socio-political and legal topics[5]. At the same time, some authors used the terminology of the "common good" before they entered the Masonic Lodges (6 works of N. I. Panin, M. M. Kheraskov, and Kh. A. Chebotarev). The generation of 1770-1789 (the 2nd generation of Russian Freemasons) was the most fruitful for publication. The

---

[1] Speransky // F. M. Dmitriev "Speransky" / The works of F. Dmitriev. – M.: [without publishers], 1862. §3. Pages 3, 6, 7.
[2] Ibid. §3. Page 9.
[3] Ibid. §3. Pages 9-10. See also: F. Dmitriev "Speransky and his state activity" // Russian archive, 1868. - The 2nd edition. - M., 1869. Page 1599.
[4] Ibid. §3. Pages 9-10. See also: F. Dmitriev "Speransky and his state activity" // Russian archive, 1868. - The 2nd edition. - M., 1869. Page 1583.
[5] See Appendix 5 for more details.

publications mentioning the "common good" (common use) were made in 1790-1809 (the 3rd generation of Russian Freemasons). In total, only 18 works related to the vocabulary of the "common good" were written at a time when the author was a member of some Masonic Lodge. The largest number of works (33) were written or published after the author left the Masonic Lodges or stopped appearing at the meetings of Brothers. This indicates that the vocabulary of the "common good" was perceived by the authors from the general political and legal, cultural environment, regardless of their membership in Masonic Lodges. However, the factor of their membership in Masonic Lodges increased the use of the vocabulary of the "common good" in the writings of the authors, even when the authors stopped attending Masonic meetings.

A modern researcher of Freemasonry, Malgorzata Abassy, notes that Russian Freemasonry strived for the "common good." She notes that Russian Freemasonry (especially that which was centered around I. G. Schwartz and N. I. Novikov) can be called the beginning of the civil society of that time. In other words, Russian Freemasonry can be called a socio-political system that approved any initiative at the grassroots level, and a Tsar was perceived as a person that implemented the will of the majority and defended common prosperity[1].

Taking into account the influence of Western Freemasonry (first of all, German and Swedish Freemasonry with their concepts of the "common good" and "common use"), taking into consideration the dominance of the theory of the welfare of all and everyone in the Russian Empire in the 18th – the first quarter of the 19th centuries, and considering the requirements of the normative documents of Russians Freemasons to strive for the "common good" and prevent the "common harm," it can be assumed that Russian Freemasons shared the theory of the welfare of all and everyone. That theory was reflected in the texts of Freemasons' writings, letters, speeches, and projects.

[1] Malgorzata Abassy "A Russian Mason on the Paths of his Native Culture." Krakow. 2014. P. 63.

Chapter Conclusions

The terms of the "common good" appeared in the vocabulary of Russian Freemasons in the 1750s and survived until the prohibition of Russian Freemasonry in 1822. Russian Freemasonry encouraged and inspired the Brothers to use the vocabulary of the "common good" in their works. This influence manifested itself even when the author of the work stopped attending Masonic meetings. Considering the decisive influence of German and Swedish Freemasonry and the spread of the theory of the welfare of all and everyone in the Russian Empire in the second half – the first quarter of the 19th century, as well as the requirements of the normative documents of Masonic Lodges and Unions to strive for the "common good" and prevent the "common harm," it can be concluded that Russian Freemasons shared and supported the theory of the welfare of all and everyone (this was the root of their political and legal ideas). Russian Freemasons rejected any violent methods of overthrowing the government as incompatible with the principles of the "common good," ruled out any radicalism, and condemned any actions leading to the "common harm," prolonged wars, and civil disasters.

Conclusion

The Russian Freemasonry of the second half of the 18th – the first quarter of the 19th centuries is a significant historical phenomenon that revealed itself in the peculiarities of the organization of Masonic Lodges, in the relationships between a Freemason and his Masonic Lodge, the carriers of higher and lower degrees in Freemasonry, and Masonic Lodges and the state institutions, in the organization of lodges as an institution of civil society, and in characterizing the activities of Freemasons as a social movement with its attitudes, symbols, and stages of development, as well as through teaching and, more broadly, culture (some literature, regulatory documents, and documents of personal origin). After finishing this research, Freemasonry was emphasized as an organization with a clear framework. The disclosure of the state and legal ideas of Russian Freemasons was carried out through the theory of the "common good" and its interpretations in the political, legal, and general cultural life of the Russian Empire. The doctrine of the "common good" is a theory as its terms, concepts, and points were included in the texts of many political and legal documents, correspondence, and works of art. In other words, they were tested and implemented in the Russian Empire. Russian Freemasons used the vocabulary and ideas of the theory of the "common good," developing these ideas and actively participating in the state, political, and legal life of the country.

The historiography given in the book confirms the novelty of this research: approaches, terminology, and conclusions. Previously, Russian Freemasonry was not considered as its relation to the theory of the "common good." Some pre-revolutionary authors created an empirical basis for research on the history of Freemasonry. They published and introduced new sources on the history of Russian Freemasonry in the 18th century. They also made some attempts to present the history of Russian Freemasonry in its chronological order. Some pre-revolutionary historians and literary scholars attempted to theoretically comprehend Masonic Doctrine and heritage. Freemasonry was researched in three of its aspects at once: as a social movement, teaching, and organization. Some source studies were carried out, and the socio-political activities of the Freemasons of the 18th century were studied as well. An assessment of the influence of Freemasonry on the policy of the state and the development of social and political thought was made.

The issues of source study on Freemasonry were poorly developed during the Soviet period, and research was mainly based on the Masonic documents and books that were published during the tsarist era.

The scientists of the Soviet period concluded that:

1. Freemasonry was a progressive phenomenon in public life, assuming a moral ideal and the general rights of a human person and having certain features: a combination of mysticism and rationalism, Orthodox Christianity and moral improvement, ethical individualism, a combination of cosmopolitanism and patriotism.
2. Even though the origins of Russian Freemasonry are taken from Western moral-mystical and political-legal ideas, Russian Freemasonry was distinguished by its moral philosophy, apolitical features, and lack of protectionism.
3. The centers of Russian Freemasonry were the cities of St. Petersburg and Moscow; 4. The authors recorded the following changes in the worldview: from "Voltaire" to "Masonic" (I. P. Elagin, I. V. Lopukhin, N. I. Novikov, and D. I. Fonvisin), from "Masonic" to "Rational" (A. N. Radishchev), and from "Masonic" to "Sentimental" (N. M. Karamzin).
5. It was established that some Freemasons interfered in the foreign policy issues of the Russian Empire (relations with Prussia), as well as in the issue of succession to the throne (some Freemasons were preparing Pavel Petrovich for the occupation of the highest position in the Masonic hierarchy).
6. Masonic ideas influenced the state policy (reforms of Paul I and Alexander I), the Decembrists, Slavophiles, and Pochvenniki (the Pochvennichestvo).
7. The incompatibility of Freemasonry and Decembrism was established.

The Masonic ethics, rituals, and socio-political views began to be studied from the beginning of the 90s of the XX century. In the post-Soviet period, a breakthrough was made in the field of history (A. I. Serkov and S. P. Karpachev published some reference books on the Freemasons, some dissertations were defended, and fundamental monographic publications on the history of Freemasonry (A. I. Serkov, Yu. Kondakov, and S. P. Karpachev) were issued) and in the field of philosophy (S. V. Arzhanukhin defended and published several fundamental works and Yu. L. Khalturin and E. L. Kuzmishin made a serious contribution to the development of the philosophy of Russian Freemasonry). The contribution to the development of "Freemasonry" was made by V. V. Kuchurin, E. A. Vishlenkova, A. Yu. Minakov, O. P. Vedmin, D. E. Kharitonovich, V. Yu. Zakharov, P. D. Nikolaenko, S. V. Belykh, and A. Yu. Palyulin. An interest in the topic of Russian Freemasonry in the scientific community has not subsided yet, continuing. The dissertation of A. N. Lushin was the only fundamental work in the field of the history of political and legal doctrines after 1990. He investigated the

Masonic activities of two Order directions and introduced some new sources into scientific circulation. A. N. Lushin proved that Freemasons remained the consistent supporters of a Monarchy with the preservation and harmonization of the estate system and serfdom and that the representatives of the Masonic Community stood at the origins of Russian Law in the late 18th and the early 19th centuries. Yu. E. Kondakov, E. L. Kuzmishin, A. I. Serkov, and some other authors (the scientists of the XXI century) disclosed some questions about the history of Russian Freemasonry in the XVIII and the first quarter of the XIX century, as well as the ideology and views of the Russian Freemasonry of that period. V. A. Tomsinov, in his studies, developed the political and legal worldview of the Russian Monarchs – Paul I and Alexander I.

The study is characterized by the presence of many archival, unpublished materials in the funds of NIA SPB II RAN (1 fund), RGB (3 funds), RGADA (4 funds), GA RF (5 funds), and RGIA (7 funds). The exceptions are the notes of I. V. Lopukhin, published in London, and the Charter of Freemasons, published by T. O. Sokolovskaya. All the studied materials (the legislative projects and legislation, the acts of Masonic Lodges, the compositions of a different nature, notes, memoirs, dictionaries, and the collections of various materials) gave an objective picture of the spread of the theory of the "common good" as the main idea of Russian Freemasons about the state and law.

The scientific literature underlying the study consists of a significant block of primary sources (F. G. Bauze, J. F. Bielfeld, Z. A. Goryushkin, S. Pufendorf, M. M. Speransky, V. N. Tatishchev, I. A. Stark, and J. G. Justi); a block of the literature of the second half of the 19th century – the first half of the 20th century (G. V. Vernadsky, M. M.Kovalevsky, S. A. Korf, B. E. Nolde, M. N. Pokrovsky, M. A. Reisner, V. I. Semevsky, T. O. Sokolovskaya, B. I. Syromyatnikov, B. Fey, etc.), and a block of the literature of the second half of the XX century – the first quarter of the XXI century (M. Abassy, T. V. Andreeva, S. V. Arzhanukhin, T. V. Artemieva, K. D. Bugrov, E. A. Vishlenkova, K. Gerlakh, V. Yu. Zakharov, S. V. Kodan, Yu. E. Kondakov, A. N. Lushin, A. Y. Minakov, V. S. Nersesyants, O. A. Omelchenko, A. P. Semitko, A. I. Serkov, V. A. Tomsinov, and others). The number of primary sources and other sources was evenly distributed. When researching, an attempt was made to overcome the problem of determining the membership in Masonic Lodges (the lodge protocols and protocol-based handbooks were used), the problem of the preservation of documents and materials (the archival materials reliably confirm the research hypothesis), a problem of the proper selection of sources (some materials using the same vocabulary were selected).

The research began with the selection and study of the dissertation research, pre-revolutionary sources, sources published from 1917 to 1990, archival materials, and literature in foreign languages (English and French). The main provisions of foreign literature confirmed the theses about rejecting the French political and legal doctrine and French Freemasonry in Russia as Russian Freemasonry was apolitical, did not think of itself outside the institutions of the state and Church, had a conservative color, and showed its loyalty to the Russian Government. On the other hand, French Freemasonry was political in nature, setting the stage for and taking part in the French Revolution of 1789. Russian Freemasons cleansed Russia of revolutionary ideas, preventing radical political and social changes in Russia.

Because of the lack of evidence of the existence of political and legal projects in Masonic Lodges in the archives, the absence of such projects in the materials of investigative cases and opinions different from the existing official ideology, the sources of the official political and legal doctrine of the Russian Empire in the second half of the XVIII and the first quarter XIX centuries were studied instead. By using observation, the theoretical construction of the "common good" was discovered in the documents, speeches, and writings of Russian Freemasons, and a corresponding selection was made. The same construction was found in some political and legal documents, including the legislation of the corresponding period of Russian history. The etymology of the terms led to some doctrinal sources: the works of the foreign and domestic jurists that can be united by a common theory of the "common good," known in Russia as the theory of the welfare of all and everyone. The comprehensive analysis of various sources allowed us to conclude their reliability, consistency, and semantic unity.

The main ideas, concepts, and approaches to the state and law on the part of Russian Freemasons in the studied period were rooted in the theory of the "common good" (the well-being of all and everyone) that was shared by some Officials of the Russian Empire, implanted in education, dominant in Western European scientific thought and the political and legal practice of the Western European world. The theory of the "common good" had its conceptual apparatus (the "common good," the "common harm," and the benefit of "all and everyone"), principles, and natural-legal rationale.

The theory of the "common good" became widespread in Russia by the end of the 18th century thanks to the translations of the works of G. Grotius, S. F. Pufendorf, J. G. Justi, and J. F. Bielfeld into Russian. This theory took root in

Russian legal thought by the efforts of F. Prokopovich and V. N. Tatishchev. This theory was called the theory of the welfare of all and everyone in the Russian Empire. The "common good" in political and legal discourse began to be considered as a goal (the possession of things, the punishment of a criminal, the restriction of rights, rule, the conclusion and execution of a contract), interest ("open sea," "virtues," "life," "the preservation of faith," "the fulfillment of promises," "the fulfillment of contracts," "well-being," "the greatest benefit," "justice," "silence," "peace," "the faith and fear of God," "building bridges, roads," "general and individual happiness," etc.), and method (when making decisions). The opposite of the "common good" was the "common harm." A person guided by the theory of the "common good" had to direct his or her actions towards his or her good for the benefit of "all citizenship" and other citizens. To do this, he or she had to coordinate his or her will with the will of others and, if necessary, limit it. The same principle applied to the activities of a ruler (Sovereign). The "common good" was possible only if the good of everyone was realized (Ch. L. Montesquieu). The "common good" in its value was equal to the good of everyone, and they did not contradict each other (J. G. Justi and C. Beccaria). The legislation that considered the good of all and everyone was good. On the contrary, the legislation that did not consider the good of all and everyone was bad, "torture" (C. Bekkaria and J. G. Justi). These provisions of the theory in Russia were implemented in the state and legal policy and legislation. The principles of the theory of the welfare of all and everyone sounded like this: the "common good" was inextricably linked with the rights (privileges) and freedom of a Monarch and all classes, the "common good" served as a balance of interests between the state and citizens, the well-being of all and everyone required a good knowledge of the "state, titles, and exercises" of citizens and the world around them to organize life for the "common good," as well as to know their rights and responsibilities.

The Russian theory of the welfare of all and everyone was developed thanks to I. G. Reichel, Catherine II, Z. A. Goryushkin, and other scientists and thinkers. The "common good" was understood as general and individual happiness (the greater good), a criterion for making any decisions, and a method for reconciling any interests. The good of all was rooted in the Common Law (the State Law), and the good of everyone - in the Special Law (Civil Law). The benefits that flowed from autocratic rule were equal to the benefits that liberty gave. The laws had to be arranged in such a way that everyone, when achieving his or her benefit, would benefit the common one and vice versa.

The theory of the welfare of all and everyone extended its influence on education and politics. The "common good" was presented in the lightweight and censored form in the textbooks. It was mixed with the good of the state and manifested itself in the duties of citizens regarding God, parents, the Supreme Power, and the bosses determined by this Power, relatives, teachers, etc. The theory of the "common good" was very important in political thought, either. The terminology of the theory became part of the official business turnover. The "common good" became the basis of bills on the state structure. Catherine II made the bliss of all and everyone the goal of her reign and adapted the theory of the welfare of all and everyone for the legislation of the Russian Empire, building it under the provisions of the theory. Paul I believed that the "common good" could be achieved through the establishment of morals among citizens. In turn, those morals would be formed through laws. Alexander I believed that everyone had to see their own obvious benefits (use) in obedience to the laws.

The theory of the welfare of all and everyone in the first quarter of the 19th century was replaced by the ideas of speculative morality, unlimited subjective freedom, political consciousness, and new social modernization. All of this resulted in the Decembrist uprising of 1825.

The terms of the "common good" appeared in the vocabulary of Russian Freemasons in the 1750s and survived until the prohibition of Russian Freemasonry in 1822. They were present in Masonic acts, documents, and speeches among both the "knightly systems" and the Rosicrucians (Rozencraitsers in the Russian sources). The well-being of all and everyone was the goal of the Masonic Order. Russian Freemasonry encouraged and inspired Brothers to use the vocabulary of the "common good" in their works. This influence was manifested even when the authors of the works stopped attending Masonic meetings. As a result of the decisive influence of German and Swedish Freemasonry and the spread of the theory of the welfare of all and everyone in the Russian Empire in the second half of the 18th – the first quarter of the 19th century, as well as due to the requirements of the normative documents of Masonic Lodges and Unions to strive for the "common good" and prevent the "common harm," it can be concluded that Russian Freemasons shared and supported the theory of the welfare of all and everyone (that was the root of their political and legal ideas). Russian Freemasons rejected any violent methods of overthrowing the government as incompatible with the principles of the "common good," ruled out any radicalism, condemned any action leading to the "common harm," prolonged wars, and civil disasters.

To sum up, the authors of this scientific work would like to quote the words of one of the leaders of Freemasonry in Russia I. A. Pozdeev, addressed a narrow circle of Brothers-Masons about the need (for the "common good") to maintain the existing political and social system with its connections and dependencies: *"And therefore, each of us must desire the One-Man Power, especially, in such a vast state so that it could contain all the states depending. This One-Man Power has been habitually strengthened for many centuries. The habitualness is naturally applied. Then, if relaxed, all these [connections] that have supported a whole circle for so many centuries will be destroyed. And all external neighbors have desired this destruction through envy for a long time. So, everyone that loves his Fatherland should not wish to weaken these ties, diminishing the power of the Sovereigns. And the duty of every loyal subject consists of it and the laws oblige as well ...*[1]."

[1] A discourse on the support of the Freemasons of Monarchical Power in Russia // RGB. NIOR. Fund 014. # 455. Pages 2-3.

Source List and Citation

Archival Sources

1. The conversation with Brothers, read by I. A. Pozdeev // The Research Department of the Manuscripts of the Russian State Library. Fund 014 ("Arsenyev Vasily Sergeevich: a collection, XVIII-XIX centuries"). # 607. 8 pages.
2. The questions of A. A. Nartov (1783) and the answers of I. E. Schwartz (Shvarts in the Russian sources) // Fund 14 # 694. 6 pages.
3. The questions answered by I. E. Sh. NIOR RGB Fund 14. Unit of issue # 681.
4. An extract from the acts of the General Convention held in Wilhelmsbad in July and August 1782. Member XII // NIORG RGB. Fund 147 # 6. Pages 67-74.
5. The extracts from the archives of the Police Department and the State Council on Masonic Societies for 1810-1826 // GA RF. Fund 137. List of contents 1. Case # 127. 31 pages.
6. The extracts from the protocols of the Union of the Great Provincial Lodge, compiled for the Government // RGB. NIOR. Fund 147. Case # 32. 277 pages.
7. The highly philosophical reasoning about Freemasonry // RGADA. Fund 1261. List of contents 1. Case # 2951. 84 pages.
8. The cases of the Manna Seekers Lodge // RGB. NIOR. Fund 014. Case # 370. 311 pages.
9. The case of the papers concerning Freemasonry, left after the death of the Tsar Tsarevich // GA RF. Fund 109. List of contents 62. Case # 54. 5 pages.
10. The case of the consideration of the documents found in the office of Alexander I after his death by the Investigative Commission: the notes and letters of F. Bulgarin, N. Koltovskaya, M. K. Gribovsky, K. Batyushkov, E. Kushelev, D. Zavalishin, and others about the situation regarding Masonic Lodges in Russia, the mood in different classes of Russian society, the mood of the Poles, in the soldier's environment // GA RF. Fund 48. List of contents 1. Case # 12. 90 pages.
11. The positions of R.K. of the ancient system in the junior meetings, read by Chrysophiron with the appendix of the speeches of other Brothers of 1782 // RGB. NIOR. Fund 14. Case # 1657.
12. The reports of the "Great" Master of the "Masonic" Lodge of Astraeus to the Ministry of Internal Affairs on the activities of the lodge with the attachment of reports, minutes of meetings, and correspondence on the admission of new

members and the organization of new lodges in Moscow and Chisinau // GA RF. Fund 1165. List of contents 3. Case # 56.104 pages.

13. The dispatches of the Curator of the Imperial Moscow University, Privy Councilor Ivan Ivanovich Melissino to the Commander-in-Chief in Moscow, Prince Alexander Alexandrovich Prozorovsky, with the attachment of his correspondence with Ober Kamerger Shuvalov and other persons about the reputed Friendly Scientific Society, now colloquially known under the name "Martinists" // RGADA. Fund 146. Unit of issue # 23. 59 pages.
14. The laws of the state all-Russian Grand Lodge, created on January 05, 1780. The laws of the State Grand Lodge // RGB. NIOR. Fund 14. Case # 34. Page 2.
15. A note about the Freemasons, drawn up after the report of Rosenkampf and Fessler // RGB. NIOR. Form 147. Case # 6. Pages 108-129.
16. The notes (unsigned) "On Masonic Lodges and other secret societies" from 1811-1826 (from the Secret Department of the Military Scientific Archive. Copies) // GA RF. Fund 1137. List of contents 1. Case # 126. 69 pages.
17. The notes of I. V. Lopukhin, book VII, 1802 // NIA II SPB RAN. Fund 36. List of contents 1. Unit of issue # 753. Pages 69-85.
18. The notes on Masonic Lodges, a copy of the ancient German manuscript "Woodcutters" and the excerpts from the criminal code stolen from the Seim in 1818 (about secret societies), found in the office of Alexander I after his death, with the report of the Chief of the General Staff of "His Imperial Majesty" Dibich to Tsarevich Konstantin // GA RF. Fund 1165. List of contents 3. Case # 61. 23 pages.
19. An extract from the instruction to the Theoretical Brothers for worthy Brothers, Supervisors of the Theoretical Degree of Solomon Sciences // RGB. NIOR. Fund 014. Case # 224. 22 pages.
20. Karl Hubert Labreich von Plumenek, the open influence of the True Freemasonry, etc." "A Library Containing Some Hermetic, Kabbalistic Magic and other Books; there are also the writings of the Highly Praised Brothers Z. R. K. True Freemasons of the Ancient System. In Russian. Composed by modern explicable Translation. For the benefit of those that wish to exercise in the knowledge of God, nature, and themselves and choose one true path among many false ones. Part X. // RGB. NIOR. Fund 14. Case # 1588. Pages 16-103.
21. The copies and extracts from the documents of the fund of the Chief of the General Staff of the First Army, the correspondence of I. N. Dibich with Grand Duke Konstantin Pavlovich, and other sources, made by an unidentified person and containing some information about the first Decembrist organizations, the

activities of Masonic Lodges, the United Slavs Society, the Northern and Southern Societies, the uprising on December 14, and the Chernigov Regiment uprising // GA RF. Fund 1463. List of contents 3. Case # 2321. 43 pages.

22. “A brief outline of the purpose of the Order,” “The Rites concerning the Student Degree □”// RGB. NIOR. Fund 14. Case # 65 “Acts.” Page 2.

23. The Masonic notes written by Count M. Yu. Vielgorsky // RGIA. Fund 938. List of contents 1. Case # 440. Page 1.

24. Something written under the dictation of Iosif Alekseevich Pozdeev in February 1817 [manuscript] / [Compiled by Sergei Stepanovich Lanskoy] // RGB. NIOR. Fund 147. Case # 147.5. 10 pages.

25. On the state power (composition) // NIA II SPB RAN. Fund 36. List of contents 2. Unit of issue 84.

26. The general institutions of Freemasons // RGB. NIOR. Fund 14. Case # 65. Page 13.

27. From the Chief of Police to the Chiefs of Masonic Societies in St. Petersburg. 1810 // RGB. NIOR. Fund 147. Case # 6. Pages 81-84.

28. The answer of the Three Globes Lodge in Berlin about its independence from the decisions of the Wilhelmsbad convention // RGB. NIOR. Fund 147.Case # 5.7. Page 55.

29. The official correspondence of Freemasons with the authorities, including the official correspondence on the closure of the lodges in 1822 and 1826 from 1816 to 1826 / RGB. NIOR. Fund 147. Case # 75. 184 pages.

30. The correspondence with the Minister of War on the application of the resolution of the Committee of Ministers on granting the Governors of Border Provinces the broader powers to monitor the population // GA RF. Fund 1165. List of contents 1. Case # 151. 8 pages.

31. The correspondence with the St. Petersburg Military Governor-General and the Riga Military Governor on the opening of the Masonic Lodge of Freemasons in Mitava // GA RF. Fund 1165. List of contents 1. Case # 34. 6 pages.

32. A letter of Alexander I to Count Viktor Pavlovich on the closure of Masonic Lodges in Russia // RGADA. Fund 8. List of contents 1. Unit of issue 261. 2 pages.

33. I. A. Pozdeev “The instructions and orders” // RGB. NIOR. Fund 013. Case # 33 24. 2 pages.

34. A. Pozdeev "The speeches in the Lodge of Orpheus." 1818 // RGB. NIOR. Fund 147. Case # 94. 103 pages.

35. The regulations on the state structure // RGIA. Fund 938. List of contents 1. Case # 661. Page 10.

36. The rules for free and accepted Freemasons // RGB. NIOR. Fund 014. Case # 160. 4 pages.

37. The draft of the conditions of the existence of societies, partnerships, brotherhoods, and other organizations, including the government-authorized Masonic Lodge "Vladimir to Truth" // GA RF. Fund 109. List of contents 1a. Case # 2246. 3 pages.

38. The minutes of the meetings of the Manna Seekers Lodge (Comradely and Master's Degrees) // RGB. NIOR. Fund 014. Case # 368. 96 pages.

39. The reflection on the difference of systems in Freemasonry by Andrei Rimsky Korsakov // GA RF. Fund 48. List of contents 1. Unit of issue # 499, part 3. The documents of Masonic Lodges: poems, songs, cantata in honor of the accession to the throne of Alexander I ... Pages 69-78.

40. The reasoning on the support of monarchical power by Freemasons in Russia // RGB. NIOR. Fund 014. Case # 455. Pages 2-3.

41. The reports of the Masters of the "Great Provincial Lodge" A. A. Zherebtsov, Count M. Yu. Vielgorskiy, and other Commander-In-Chief of St. Petersburg on the activities of this and other lodges with the attachment of the minutes of the meetings, the lists of members of the lodges, and other materials // GA RF. Fund 1165. List of contents 3. Case # 54. 265 pages.

42. The reports, minutes of meetings, lists of members, correspondence, and other materials about the activities of the "Grand Lodge of Astrea" and other Masonic Lodges // GA RF. Fund 1165. List of contents 3. Case # 55. 548 pages.

43. The discourses on the Masonic Oath // RGB. NIOR. Fund 014. Case # 429. 36 pages.

44. The collection. The instructions of I. A. Pozdeev to Brother Fonvizin // RGB. NIOR. Fund 147. Case # 564. Pages 12-13.

45. The free thoughts of an elderly citizen loving his Fatherland // NIA II SPB RAN. Fund 36. List of contents 2. Unit of issue 80.

46. The list of cases about the Moscow Societies of the Military Scientific Archive of the General Staff according to the catalog compiled by Bender // GA RF. Fund 1137. List of contents 1. Case # 111. 5 pages.

47. A list of the members of the Union of the Grand Provincial Lodge 5820 // RGB. NIOR. Fund 147. Case # 38. Page 69.

48. A list of the members of the Manna Seekers Lodge made on January 1, 1821 // RGB. NIOR. Fund 013. Case # 24.34. 2 pages.

49. The Statute of the Masonic Order (the System of the Highly Respectable, Strong, and Wise Order of the Cavaliers and Brothers of Light, from the Seven Wise Fathers, Heads of Seven Churches in Asia) // RGIA. Fund 1101. List of contents 1. Case # 230. Pages 1-169.

50. The Theoretical Degree of Solomon's Sciences // RGB. NIOR. Fund 014. Case # 232. 28 pages.

51. An Interpretation of the Charter of the Holy Kingdom of March 18, 1820 // RGB. NIOR. Fund 14. Case # 12 1727.

52. A Charter or a Rule of Freemasons // RGB. NIOR. Fund 14. Case # 1. Pages 1-7.

53. S. P. Fonvizin “The extracts from Masonic and mystical writings from 1811 to 1818” // RGB. NIOR. Fund 013. Case # 43.3. 21 pages.

Legislative Acts

54. The act of approval for the Imperial University in Vilna dated April 04, 1803 // The Legislation of Emperor Alexander I, 1801-1811 [Text]: [the collection of legislative acts] / a compiler and the author of the entry V. A. Tomsinov. - Moscow: Zertsalo, 2011. - XXVIII, 562 pages. Page 128.
55. The All-Merciful Manifesto “On the establishment of the crosses for the Clergy and the medals and various benefits and favors for the army, nobility, and merchants” (dated August 30, 1814) // The Legislation of Emperor Alexander I, 1812-1825 [Text]: [the collection of legislative acts] / [a compiler and the author of the entry V. A. Tomsinov]. - Moscow: Zertsalo, 2011. – XVI. 288 pages. Pages 61-66.
56. The Highly Approved Instruction to Senators appointed to inspect the Provinces of August 1, 1805. // The Legislation of Emperor Alexander I, 1801-1811 [Text]: [the collection of legislative acts] / a compiler and the author of the entry V. A. Tomsinov. - Moscow: Zertsalo, 2011. - XXVIII, 562 pages. Pages 320-322.
57. The Highest Approved Project “On the establishment of widows' houses, public houses, and hospitals” (dated February 01, 1803) // The Legislation of Emperor Alexander I, 1801-1811 [Text]: [the collection of legislative acts] / a compiler and the author of the entry V. A. Tomsinov. - Moscow: Zertsalo, 2011. - XXVIII, 562 pages. Page 115.
58. The Imperially Approved Charter of the Academy of Sciences (dated July 25, 1803) // The Legislation of Emperor Alexander I, 1801-1811 [Text]: [the collection of legislative acts] / a compiler and the author of the entry V. A. Tomsinov. - Moscow: Zertsalo, 2011. - XXVIII, 562 pages. Pages 150-170.
59. The Charter for the rights and benefits of the cities of the Russian Empire (dated April 21, 1785) // The Legislation of Empress Catherine II, 1783-1796 [Text] / Moscow State University named after M. V. Lomonosov, Legal Faculty, The Department of History of the State and Law; a compiler and the author of the entry V. A. Tomsinov. - Moscow: Zertsalo, 2011. - 272 p.
60. The Declarations on behalf of Her Imperial Majesty the All-Russian, made by her Extraordinary and Plenipotentiary Ambassador, Prince Repnin to the Polish Republic collected at the Seim of 1766 // Catherine II (Her Imperial Majesty; 1729-1796). The political correspondence of Empress Catherine II. - [St. Petersburg: b. i.], 1885-1914. - 26 cm. - (A Collection of the Imperial Russian

Historical Society / Russian Historical Society). Volume 67: 1766-1767 [Text]. - 1889. - XXI, 578 pages, [1] p. Pages 84-94.

61. The Declaration, honored by the Highest Name of Her Imperial Majesty the All-Russian to the noble knighthood and zemstvo, and, especially, located in Courland and Semigalia // Catherine II (Her Imperial Majesty; 1729-1796). The political correspondence of Empress Catherine II. - [St. Petersburg: b. i.], 1885-1914. - 26 cm. - (A Collection of the Imperial Russian Historical Society / Russian Historical Society). Volume 67: 1766-1767 [Text]. - 1889. - XXI, 578 pages, [1] p. Pages 37-41.

62. Catherine II. The Order for the Commission on drawing up a draft of a new Code // Catherine II (Her Imperial Majesty; 1729-1796). The works of Empress Catherine II: Volumes 1-3. - St. Petersburg: A. Smirdin, 1849-1850. - 3 volumes; 17. - (The Complete Works of Russian Authors). Volume 1. - 1849. – 666 pages, II p.

63. The Legislation of Empress Catherine II, 1783-1796 [Text] / Moscow State University named after M. V. Lomonosov, Legal Faculty, The Department of History of the State and Law; a compiler and the author of the entry V. A. Tomsinov. - Moscow: Zertsalo, 2011. - 272 pages.

64. A personal decree "On the transformation of the Commission for Drafting Laws," given to the Senate on February 28, 1804 // The Legislation of Emperor Alexander I, 1801-1811 [Text]: [the collection of legislative acts] / a compiler and the author of the entry V. A. Tomsinov. - Moscow: Zertsalo, 2011. - XXVIII, 562 pages. Pages 171-189.

65. A Nominal Decree "On the inviolability of the rights granted to the Nobility," given to the Senate on March 21, 1803 // The Legislation of Emperor Alexander I, 1801-1811 [Text]: [the collection of legislative acts] / a compiler and the author of the entry V. A. Tomsinov. - Moscow: Zertsalo, 2011. - XXVIII, 562 pages. Page 126.

66. A Nominal Decree "On the non-conferring of any rank, either military or civilian, to the titles of Chamberlains and Kamer-Junkers, and on the obligation of persons in these ranks to enter the active service and continue this under the established procedure, starting from the initial ranks," given to the Senate on April 03, 1809 // The Legislation of Emperor Alexander I, 1801-1811 [Text]: [the collection of legislative acts] / a compiler and the author of the entry V. A. Tomsinov. - Moscow: Zertsalo, 2011. - XXVIII, 562 pages. Pages 375-377.

67. A Nominal Decree "On the establishment of a special Council under the Commission for Drafting Laws," given to the Senate on March 7, 1809 // The

Legislation of Emperor Alexander I, 1801-1811 [Text]: [the collection of legislative acts] / a compiler and the author of the entry V. A. Tomsinov. - Moscow: Zertsalo, 2011. - XXVIII, 562 pages. Pages 365-366.

68. A Nominal Decree "On the destruction of Masonic Lodges and any secret societies," given to the Governor of the Ministry of Internal Affairs, Count Kochubei on August 01, 1822 // The Legislation of Emperor Alexander I, 1812-1825 [Text]: [the collection of legislative acts] / a compiler and the author of the entry V. A. Tomsinov. - Moscow: Zertsalo, 2011. - XVI, 288 pages. Pages 265-266.

69. A Nominal Decree given to Lieutenant General Melissino "On the necessary corrections in the teaching of Sciences in the Artillery and Engineering Cadet Corps" (dated February 21) // The Legislation of Empress Catherine II, 1783-1796 [Text] / Moscow State University named after M. V. Lomonosov, Legal Faculty, The Department of History of the State and Law; / a compiler and the author of the entry V. A. Tomsinov. - Moscow: Zertsalo, 2011. - 272 pages. Pages 15-30.

70. A Nominal Decree given to the Governor-General of Livonia, Estonia, and Lithuania to Prince Repnin "On the division of the Grand Duchy of Lithuania into three parts and on the way of managing them" (dated October 30, 1794) // The Legislation of Empress Catherine II, 1783-1796 [Text] / Moscow State University named after M. V. Lomonosov, Legal Faculty, The Department of History of the State and Law; / a compiler and the author of the entry V. A. Tomsinov. - Moscow: Zertsalo, 2011. - 272 pages. Pages 204-221.

71. A Nominal Decree "On the structure of schools," given to the Senate on January 24, 1803 // The Legislation of Emperor Alexander I, 1801-1811 [Text]: [the collection of legislative acts] / / a compiler and the author of the entry V. A. Tomsinov. - Moscow: Zertsalo, 2011. - XXVIII, 562 pages. Page 109.

72. The Convention concluded between the Emperor of Russia and the Government of the American United States in St. Petersburg "On the unshakable preservation of the friendly relationship between them" (dated April 17, 1824) // The Legislation of Emperor Alexander I, 1812-1825 [Text]: [the collection of legislative acts] / a compiler and the author of the entry V. A. Tomsinov. - Moscow: Zertsalo, 2011. - XVI, 288 pages. Pages 274-276.

73. A Convolute. The Decrees of the All-Blessed Great Sovereign Empress Catherine Alekseevna the All-Russian Autocrat: Held from July 01, 1765 to January 01, 1766. / Printed by Her Highest Imperial Majesty command. - In St. Petersburg: At the Senate, 1779. - [6], 379 pages, Page [9].

74. A Convolute. The Decrees of Emperor Paul I, the Autocrat of all Russia: [From January 17 to December 30, 1799]. - Moscow: In the Senate printing house, 1799. - [328] pages.

75. A Manifesto "On contracts concluded for the benefit of the State; on the accession to the Russian Empire of the most extensive part of the Duchy of Warsaw, under the name of the Kingdom of Poland on raising arms again against Napoleon Bonaparte that left the Island of Elba" (dated May 09, 1815) // The Legislation of Emperor Alexander I, 1812-1825 [Text]: [the collection of legislative acts] / a compiler and the author of the entry V. A. Tomsinov. - Moscow: Zertsalo, 2011. - XVI, 288 pages. Pages 70-73.

76. A Manifesto "On the conclusion of peace between Russia and Sweden" (dated October 01, 1809) // The Legislation of Emperor Alexander I, 1801-1811 [Text]: [the collection of legislative acts] / a compiler and the author of the entry V. A. Tomsinov. - Moscow: Zertsalo, 2011. - XXVIII, 562 pages. Pages 384-395.

77. A Manifesto "On the non-recovery of salary income to the treasury from the newly acquired regions from Poland until 795" (dated April 13, 1793) // The Legislation of Empress Catherine II, 1783-1796 [Text] / Moscow State University named after M. V. Lomonosov, Legal Faculty, The Department of History of the State and law; a compiler and the author of the entry V. A. Tomsinov. - Moscow: Zertsalo, 2011. - 272 pages. Pages 190-191.

78. A Manifesto "On Duels" (dated April 21, 1787) // The Legislation of Empress Catherine II, 1783-1796 [Text] / Moscow State University named after M. V. Lomonosov, Legal Faculty, The Department of History of the State and law; a compiler and the author of the entry V. A. Tomsinov. - Moscow: Zertsalo, 2011. - 272 pages. Pages 136-144.

79. A Manifesto "On privileges for various inventions and discoveries in arts and crafts" (dated June 17, 1812) // The Legislation of Emperor Alexander I, 1812-1825 [Text]: [the collection of legislative acts] / a compiler and the author of the entry V. A. Tomsinov. - Moscow: Zertsalo, 2011. - XVI, 288 pages. Pages 3-6.

80. A Manifesto "On the dissolution of the marriage of Tsarevich and Grand Duke Konstantin Pavlovich with the Grand Duchess Anna Fedorovna and on an additional Decree on the Imperial Family" (dated March 20, 1820) // The Legislation of Emperor Alexander I, 1812-1825 [Text]: [the collection of legislative acts] / a compiler and the author of the entry V. A. Tomsinov. - Moscow: Zertsalo, 2011. - XVI, 288 pages. Pages 153-154.

81. A Manifesto “On the collection of the zemstvo militia within the state” (dated July 6, 1812) // The Legislation of Emperor Alexander I, 1812-1825 [Text]: [the collection of legislative acts] / a compiler and the author of the entry V. A. Tomsinov. - Moscow: Zertsalo, 2011. - XVI, 288 pages. Pages 6-7.

82. A Manifesto “On the establishment of the State Loan Bank” (dated June 28, 1786) // The Legislation of Empress Catherine II, 1783-1796 [Text] / Moscow State University named after M. V. Lomonosov, Legal Faculty, The Department of History of the State and Law; a compiler and the author of the entry V. A. Tomsinov. - Moscow: Zertsalo, 2011. - 272 pages. Pages 98-113.

83. A Manifesto of January 1, 1807 “On the new benefits, differences, advantages, and new ways to spread and strengthen the commercial enterprises granted to the merchants” // The Legislation of Emperor Alexander I, 1801-1811 [Text]: [the collection of legislative acts] / a compiler and the author of the entry V. A. Tomsinov. - Moscow: Zertsalo, 2011. - XXVIII, 562 pages. Pages 327-338.

84. A Manifesto to the Slavic peoples of the Balkan Peninsula // Catherine II (Her Imperial Majesty; 1729-1796). The political correspondence of Empress Catherine II. - [St. Petersburg: without publishers], 1885-1914. - 26 cm. - (A Collection of the Imperial Russian Historical Society / Russian Historical Society). Volume 87: 1768-1769 [Text]. - 1893. - XVIII, 555 pages. Pages 322-326.

85. Manifesto of September 12, 1801 // The Legislation of Emperor Alexander I, 1801-1811 [Text]: [the collection of legislative acts] / a compiler and the author of the entry V. A. Tomsinov. - Moscow: Zertsalo, 2011. - XXVIII, 562 pages. Pages 51-53.

86. A Manifesto of August 9, 1807 “On the conclusion of peace with the French Empire” // The Legislation of Emperor Alexander I, 1801-1811 [Text]: [the collection of legislative acts] / a compiler and the author of the entry V. A. Tomsinov. - Moscow: Zertsalo, 2011. - XXVIII, 562 pages. Pages 338-346.

87. A Manifesto on the “General establishment of Ministries” (dated June 25, 1811). The Russian Legislation of the X-XX centuries: in 9 volumes. Volume 6. The Legislation of the first half of the 19th century. Editor-In-Chief O. I. Chistyakov. M., Legal Literature, 1988. Pages 92-134.

88. On the prohibition of the sale of household people and peasants separately and without land // An Archive of the State Council. - St. Petersburg: printed in the Second Branch of His Imperial Majesty Own Chancellery, 1869-. - 28 cm. Volume 4: The reign of Emperor Alexander I (from 1810 to November 19, 1825). The journals for the Department of Laws. Part 2: Drafting, reviewing, and approving the statutes, regulations, and articles for various parts of the Legislation. - 1874 (a

foretitle of 1875). - XII, [16] p., 1020 pages, page XXVI by 2 columns. Pages 323-348.

89. Paul I. Order // M. N. Semevsky “The materials for Russian History of the 18th century” // Europe Bulletin. Volume 1. March 1867. Pages 316-322.

90. Russia. Empress (1762-1796; Catherine II). About the nobility.: [Certificate of honor. Approved on April 21, 1785]. - [St. Petersburg]: Printed in the Senate on April 24, 1785. - [4], 24 pages, VIII p.

91. Russia. Empress (1762-1796; Catherine II). The Decrees of the All-Blessed Great Sovereign Empress Catherine Alekseevna, the All-Russian Autocrat: Held from July 01, 1765 to January 01, 1766. / Printed at the behest of Her Imperial Majesty. - St. Petersburg: At the Senate, 1779. - [2], 169 pages, page [3].

92. The Decree of His Imperial Majesty. Printed in the printing house of St. Petersburg on August 3, 1798, issued in Moscow on August 19, 1798 // The Decrees of Emperor Paul I, the All-Russian Autocrat: [from January 1 to December 16, 1798]. - Moscow: The Senate printing house, 1798. - [272] pages. Pages 145-146.

93. The Decrees of the All-Blessed Sovereign, Great Empress Catherine Alekseevna, the All-Russian Autocrat: Held from January 1768 to 1769. / Printed at the behest of Her Imperial Majesty. - In St. Petersburg: At the Senate, 1786. - [2], 92 pages, IV p.

94. The Decrees of Emperor Paul I, the Autocrat of all Russia: [from January 1 to December 16, 1798]. - Moscow: The Senate printing house, 1798. - [272] pages. Pages 11-13.

Dissertations and Abstracts

95. V. N. Alekseev "Counts of the Vorontsov family in the political and social life of Russia in the 2nd half of the 18th – the 1st half of the 19th centuries": an abstract of the thesis of a Candidate in Historical Sciences: 07.00.02. - Vladimir, 2010. - 23 pages.
96. T. V. Andreeva "Secret societies in Russia in the first third of the 19th century: the government policy and public opinion": a thesis of a Ph.D. in Historical Sciences. - St. Petersburg, 2010. – 1,101 pages.
97. V. M. Bokova "Liberal-constitutional ideas in Russia at the beginning of the XIX century (1801-1812)": an abstract of the thesis of a Candidate in Historical Sciences. - Moscow, 1991. - 21 pages.
98. K. D. Bugrov "The Formation of Republicanism Ideas in the Russian Socio-Political Thought of the 18th Century": an abstract of the thesis of a Ph.D. in Historical Sciences: 07.00.02 / Konstantin Dmitrievich Bugrov; [The location of defending the thesis: Ural Federal University named after the first President of Russia B. N. Yeltsin]. - Yekaterinburg, 2018. - 45 pages.
99. A. A. Vasilyev "The conservative legal ideology of Russia: the essence and forms of manifestation": an abstract of the thesis of a Ph.D. in Legal Sciences. - Yekaterinburg, 2015. - 55 pages.
100. E. A. Vishlenkova "Religious policy in Russia, the first quarter of the XIX century": a thesis of a Ph.D. in Historical Sciences: 07.00.02. - Kazan, 1998. Pages 122-133.
101. L. S. Gimishyan "The state legal views of A. P. Kunitsyn": an abstract of the thesis of a Candidate in Legal Sciences: 12.00.01 / The Saratov State Academy of Law. - Saratov, 2004. - 22 pages.
102. D. V. Gorbachev "The social and political views of I. A. Fessler": an abstract of the thesis of a Candidate in Historical Sciences: 07.00.03 / Dmitry Viktorovich Gorbachev; [The location of defending the thesis: The Saratov State University named after N. G. Chernyshevsky]. - Saratov, 2012. Page 15.
103. N. Ye. Dorokhova "'Russian Tories' and the socio-political thought of Western European education at the turn of the 18th-19th centuries": an abstract of the thesis of a Candidate in Historical Sciences: 07.00.02 / Tomsk State University. - Tomsk, 2006. - 26 pages.
104. A. V. Zavrazhin "The historical experience of the development of the political outlook of Russian society": 1721-1917: an abstract of the thesis of a Ph.D. in Historical Sciences: 07.00.02 / Anatoly Vladimirovich Zavrazhin; [The location of defending a thesis: The Russian Economic Academy named after G. V. Plekhanov]. - Moscow, 2010. - 58 pages.

105. V. Yu. Zakharov "The Russian constitutionalism of the 2nd half of the 18th - 1st quarter of the 19th centuries in the context of the development of Western European legal thought": A thesis of a Ph.D. in Historical Sciences: 07.00.02. Moscow, 2010. Page 146.

106. S. V. Kodan "The legal policy of the Russian state": 1800-the 1850s: an abstract of the thesis of a Ph.D. in Legal Sciences: 12.00.01 / The Institute of the State and Law of the Russian Academy of Sciences. - Moscow, 2004. - 60 pages.

107. Yu. V. Kostin "The ideas of the correlation among the state, law, and morality in the history of political and legal thought in pre-revolutionary Russia in the second half of the 19th and early 20th centuries": an abstract of the thesis of a Ph.D. in Legal Sciences. - Moscow, 2008. - 46 pages.

108. Yu. S. Limanskaya "The works of M. M. Kheraskov 'Golden Rod' and 'Cadmus and Harmony' in the context of Masonic prose of the last quarter of the 18th century": an abstract of the thesis of a Candidate in Philological Sciences: 10.01.01 / Yulia Sergeevna Limanskaya; [The location of defending the thesis: The Surgut State Pedagogic University]. - Surgut, 2007. - 18 pages.

109. A. N. Lushin "The state and legal views of Russian Freemasons at the turn of the XVIII-XIX centuries": A thesis of a Candidate in Legal Sciences: 12.00.01. - Nizhny Novgorod, 2004. - 161 pages.

110. I. Mikheeva "The law-making activities of the Ministries of the Russian Empire in the 19th - early 20th centuries": an abstract of the thesis of a Ph.D. in Legal Sciences: 12.00.01 / Irina Vyacheslavovna Mikheeva; [The location of defending the thesis: Vladimir Juridical Institute of the Federal Services of Execution of Punishments]. - Vladimir, 2011. - 45 pages.

111. O. A. Omelchenko "The Monarchy of enlightened absolutism in Russia: Political doctrine, legal policy, and state reforms": A thesis of a Ph.D. in Legal Sciences: 12.00.01.-Moscow, 2001. - 389 p.

112. A. N. Ostroukh "Bentham's doctrine about the law": A thesis of a Candidate in Legal Sciences: 12.00.01. - Moscow, 2002. - 240 pages.

113. A. A. Pavlov "The legal concept of Hugo Grotius": an abstract of the thesis of a Candidate in Legal Sciences: 12.00.01 / North-South Academy of the State Service. - St. Petersburg, 2002. - 20 pages.

114. D. V. Timofeev "European Ideas in the Public Consciousness and Communicative Practice of an Educated Russian Citizen of the First Quarter of the 19th Century: an experience of studying the basic socio-political concepts": an abstract of the

thesis of a Ph.D. in Historical Sciences: 07.00.02 / Dmitry Vladimirovich Timofeev; [The location of defending the thesis: Chelyabinsk State University]. - Chelyabinsk, 2011. - 34 pages.

115. L. L. Fedotova "The Russian national idea in the heroic epic of M. M. Kheraskov": an abstract of the thesis of a Candidate in Philological Sciences: 10.01.01 Luiza Leonidovna Fedotova; [The location of defending the thesis: The Moscow State Humanitarian University named after M. A. Sholokhov]. - Moscow, 2009. - 29 pages.

116. Yu. L. Khalturin "The philosophy of the Russian Freemasons of the late 18th - early 19th centuries: critical reconstruction": A thesis of a Candidate in Philosophical Sciences: 09.00.03 - Yekaterinburg, 2010. Page 32.

Literature in a Foreign Language

117. T. Bakounine "La repertoire biographique des francs - masons russes (XVIII et XIX - e siecles)." - Paris, 1967. - 655 pages.
118. Dante Alihieri "Monarchia" R. IMBACH & C. FLÜELER (ed. Andtr.), L. II, v, 2, Stuttgart, 1989.
119. Eberhard Isenmann "The notion of the Common Good, the concept of politics, and practical policies in Late Medieval and Early Modern German cities" // De Bono Communi. The Discourse and Practice of the Common Good in the European City (13th-16th p.) / Edited by Elodie Lecuppre-Desjardin & Anne-Laure Van Bruaene. 2010, Brepols Publishers n.v., Turnhout, Belgium. P. 107-148. - 290 p.
120. I. A. Fessler "Resultate seines Denkens und Erfahrens als Anhang zu seinen Rückblicken auf seine 70-jaerige Pilgerschaft." Breslau, 1826.
121. Fessler´ssämmtliche Schriften über Freymaurerey. "Wirklich als Manuckript für Brüder." Berlin. 1801.- 499 p.
122. Fessler´ssämmtliche Schriften über Freymaurerey. "Wirklich als Manuckript für Brüder." Bd. 1. Zweite verbesserte und mit einem Anhange versehene Auflage. Freyberg, 1805.
123. "Freemasonry: its aims and ideals" by J.S.M. Ward B.A>, F.S> S., F.R. Econ. Soc. London. William Rider & Son limited 8-II Paternoster Row, E.C. 4 1923. - 232 p.
124. Friedrichs "Geschichte der einstigen Maurerei in Russland." B., 1904.
125. Grunwald (Constantin de) "Histoire de la Franc-Maconnerie en Russie" // Traveau Villard de Honnecourt. T. 5. 1969. 424 p.
126. Hass Ludwik "WolnomularstwowEuropieSrodkowo - WschodniejwXVIII – XIXwieku." - WroclawZakladN10 Wydawnictwo, 1982. - 572 pages.
127. Karlheinz Gerlach "Die Freimaurer im Alten Preussen 1738-1806: die Loge in Berlin." Teil 1. Publisher, Studien Verlag, Innsbruck, Wien, Bozen 2014. - 1254 p.
128. "La Franc-maconnerie et la Revolution intellectuelle Du XVIII siècle Par Bernard Fay Profeseurau Collere de France." - PARIS VI, 1935. - 286 p.
129. Malgorzata Abassy "A Russian Mason on the Paths of his Native Culture. The Case Study of Nicolas Novikov." Krakow. 2014. - 195 p.
130. "Revolution and Freemasonry 1680-1800" Bernard Faÿ. Boston. Little, Brown, and Company. 1935. - 349p.
131. "The Rosicrucians in Russia" by Frater Boris Telepneff. Privately printed by Dr. W. Wynn Westcoit, 1924. 17 p.
132. Russian Masons by Bro. B. Telepneff, 1925. 32 p.
133. "A Few Pages from the History of Swedish Freemasonry in Russia." By Bro. Boris Telepneff, 1928. 23 p.

134. The principles of Masonic law: a treatise on the constitutional laws, usages, and landmarks of Freemasonry / by Albert Mackey [Luton; England]: Andrews U.K. Ltd., 2010. - 235 p.
135. Uber arbeiteteun der weiterte Neuauflageü (StandFebruar 2000) der Ausgabe von 19322000 by F. A. Herbig Verlags buchhandlung GmbH, München, 951 p.
136. An extract from the Acts of the Wilhelmsbad Convention of 1782 // http: //triple-point.xooit.com/t1249-RER-%3A-Recès-du-Convent-de-Wilhelmsbad-%281782%29.htm (date of access: 10/11/2019).
137. An extract from the Acts of the Wilhelmsbad Convention of 1782 // https: //www.le-ritdefrance.com/wp-content/uploads/1782-Wilhelmsbad.pdf (date of access: 17.10.2020).

Bibliographies

138. N. M. Azarkin "The history of legal thought in Russia": A course of lectures. - M.: Juridical literature, 1999. - 526 pages.

139. S. V. Kodan "Alexander I and reforms: between absolutism and constitutionalism" // Official. - 2005. - # 6 (40). http://chinovnik.uapa.ru/ru/issue/2005/06/09/.

140. M. V. Antonov "The history of legal thought in Russia": lecture notes; - Moscow; St. Petersburg: NIU VSHE, 2012. - 210 pages.

141. S. V. Arzhanukhin "From the lectures of I.G. Schwartz (Shvarts in the Russian sources) 'On three knowledge: curious, useful, and pleasant.'" The excerpts from the philosophical conversations of the late Professor I. G. Schwartz (Shvarts in the Russian sources) [a preface, the preparation for publication by S. V. Arzhanukhin (Yekaterinburg)]. Philosophical sciences. Scientific and theoretical journal. M.: "High school," 1992. # 1. Pages 78-91.

142. S. V. Arzhanukhin "Philosophical views of Russian Freemasonry: Based on the materials from the magazine 'Freemasonry shop'" / S. V. Arzhanukhin; Ural State University named after A. M. Gorky, The Research Institute of Russian Culture under Ural State University. - Yekaterinburg: UrSU, 1995. - 223 pages.

143. Aristotle "Politics." The works in 4 volumes / Aristotle. - M.: Mysl (Thought), 1983. - Volume 4. - 619 pages.

144. A. N. Arkhangelsky "Alexander I." - Moscow: Young Guard, 2005. - 444 [4] p.

145. An archive of the historical and practical information relating to Russia, published by Nikolai Kalachov [Text]. - St. Petersburg: Printed in the 2nd branch of His Own Imperial Majesty Chancellery, 1858. Pages 3-20.

146. Grandmother's alphabet to Grand Duke Alexander Pavlovich / Catherine II. - M.: MGI named after E. R. Dashkova, 2004. - 92, [3] p.

147. M. A. Balugiansky "National wealth. An image of various economic systems" // Statistical journal. SPb., 1806. Volume 1. Part two. Page 62.

148. F. G. Bauze "What was done in Russia for the enlightenment of the people and the glory of the Fatherland from the time of Rurik to Peter the Great" // Europe Bulletin, part of the XXV century, January 1806, pages 3-20, 81-96.

149. N. P. Bedzir "Lectures on the methodology of literary research" / http://nataliabedzir.com/2013/12/11/ (access: 05.24.2016).

150. Beccaria on the crimes and punishments in comparison with Chapter X of the Order of Catherine II and modern Russian Laws: Materials for the development of the comparative study of the theory and practice of criminal legislation. / [The works] of S. Zarudny. - St. Petersburg: printed in the 2nd branch of Her Own Imperial Majesty Chancellery, 1879. - [6], II, XXIV, 196 p.

151. Beccaria "Reasoning about crimes and punishments." / Translated from Italian into French by Andrey Morellet, and from French into Russian by Dmitry Yazykov. With the addition of Diderot's notes and the correspondence between the writer and Morellet.; Printed by Order of His Highest Imperial Majesty. - In St. Petersburg: Under the Provincial Government, 1803. - XLIV, 268 p.

152. P. N. Berkov "The life and literary path of A. P. Sumarokov" // A. P. Sumarokov. Selected works. - L.: Soviet writer. 1957. - 609 pages. Pages 5-46.

153. P. Bessonov "A. F. Labzin. A literary and biographical sketch" // Russian archive, 1866. - Issue 6. - SPb. Pages 817-836.

154. J. F. Bielfeld "The instructions of the political Baron Bielfeld" / Translated from French by Collegiate Counselor and Eloquence Professor Anton Barsov. Part 2. - M.: Printed at the Imperial Moscow University, 1775. - 498 p.

155. The Brilliant Age of Catherine II. The second half of the 18th century: biographical reference: in 4 parts, Part 4 / the author-compiler V. N. Nikulin. - Kaliningrad: The publishing house of the RGU named after I. Kant, 2010. - 196 p.

156. K. D. Bugrov "Natural Law and Virtue: The Integration of European Influence into the Russian Political Culture of the Eighteenth Century." A monograph / K. D. Bugrov, M. A. Kiselev. Yekaterinburg: The Publishing House of the Ural University, the University's Publishing House, 2016. - 480 p.

157. A. I. Vasilyev "The highest approved report by the Minister of Finance, with the staffs and other annexes on the new formation of the mining authorities and management of mining factories": [Approved on July 13, 1806]. - In St. Petersburg: Printed in the Medical Printing House, 1806. - 1-254, 249-256, 255-258, [2] p.

158. A. A. Vasilchikov "The Razumovsky family" / The works of A. A. Vasilchikov. - St. Petersburg: The printing house of M. M. Stasyulevich, 1880-1894. - 25 cm. Volume 2. - 1880. - IV, 557 pages, XXI p.

159. G. V. Vernadsky "Russian Freemasonry during the reign of Catherine II." SPb., 1999. S. V.

160. Vladimir Monomakh "The Spiritual of Great Prince Vladimir Vsevolodovich Monomakh to his children, mentioned as Precept in the chronicle of Suzdal." - St. Petersburg: The printing house of the Corps of foreign co-religionists, 1793. - X, 61 p.

161. The influence of true Freemasonry on the "common good" of the states, discovered and proven from the true purpose of its original establishment (foundation). [Text] / Karl Hubert Lobreich von Plumenek.; Written at the end of the 18th century in refutation of the work of Yak. Moser: On the tolerance of Freemasonry communities, especially, regarding the Peace of Westphalia. Translated from the second edition in German, printed in Amsterdam in 1779. - Moscow: Printed in the University Printing House, 1816. - [4], VIII, 211, [3] p.

162. A. R. Vorontsov "The notes about my life and about various events that took place during this time both in Russia and in Europe. Russian archive. 1883. Book 1. Issue 2. Pages 227 -249.

163. G. P. Gagarin "The amusements of my solitude in the village of Bogoslovskoye" // The remaining creation of Prince Gabriel Petrovich Gagarin. - St. Petersburg: Printed in the printing house of the Ministry of War, 1813. - [12], 185, [1] p.

164. K. G. Gayking "The days of Emperor Paul: the notes of Courlandsky nobleman": (translated from German into Russian / [Barron Karl Heinrich Geyking]. - St. Petersburg: F. I. Bulgakov, 1907. - 70 p.

165. Z. A. Goryushkin "The description of judicial actions, or the Easiest way to quickly obtain the proper knowledge for the administration of positions in judicial places, especially those that, having no opportunity to exercise in domestic laws, will be used in the civil service." - Moscow: Printed in the University Printing House of Lyubiy, Gariy, and Popov. M., 1807. Page 34.

166. Z. A. Goryushkin "A guide to the knowledge of Russian Art of Law, containing the State Law, People's Law, and, finally, the Laws on Animals. Binding 4. Moscow: printed in the University printing house. 1816. 1427-2214 p.

167. H. Grotius "True Christian piety: Proved against the atheists, pagans, Jews, and Mahometans" / Translated by the Ecclesiarch of the Moscow Great Dormition Cathedral Peter Alexiev. - [Moscow]: Printed at Imperial Moscow University, 1768. - [20], 220 p.

168. H. Grotius "Reasoning against atheists and neutralists" / Translated from Latin into Russian by Amvrosy (A. S. Zertis-Kamensky). - Moscow: The Senate printing house 1765. - [2], 66 p.

169. Hugo Grotius "On the law of war and peace": Reprint, with the edition of 1956 - M.: Ladomir, 1994. - 868 p.

170. Dante Alighieri "A Monarchy" / Translated from Italian by V. P. Zubov. Comments by I. N. Golenishchev-Kutuzov. - M.: "Kanon-press-Ts" - "Kuchkovo field," 1999. - 192 p.

171. A despatch of Count N. I. Panin to the Ambassador, Prince Repnin // Catherine II (Empress; 1729-1796). The political correspondence of Empress Catherine II. - [St. Petersburg: b. i.], 1885-1914. - 26 cm. - (A Collection of the Imperial Russian Historical Society / Russian Historical Society). Volume 67: 1766-1767 [Text]. - 1889. - XXI, 578 pages, [1] p. Page 569.

172. F. Dmitriev "Speransky and his state activity" // Russian archive, 1868. – The 2nd Edition. - M., 1869. - SPb. 1527-1656.

173. A. Dmitriev-Mamonov "A note on the meetings of the Masonic Lodge called the Manna Seekers Lodge in Moscow from its opening to January 1, 1818" // Russian Archives: The History of the Fatherland in evidence and documents of the XVIII-XX centuries.: Almanac. - M.: Studio TRITE: Russian Archive, 1999. - Pages 73-74.

174. Spirit of Laws: A creation of the famous French writer de Montesquieu: in 3 parts / Translated by E. Karneev, a foreword by E. Karneev. Parts 1-3. - St. Petersburg: The printing house of N. Grech, 1839. – in 3 volumes (Yegor Vasilyevich Karneev - Freemason according to Serkov's dictionary of the 18th century, p. 579). - 371 p. P. 46.

175. The note of Count A. R. Vorontsov about Russia at the beginning of this century, presented to Emperor Alexander Pavlovich // The archive of Prince Vorontsov / Edited by P. I. Bartenev. - Moscow: The printing house of A. I. Mamontov, 1870-1897. Book 29: Letters from foreigners to the Counts of the Vorontsov family. - 1883. - XI, 492 p. Pages 449-470.

176. My notes for introduction from word to word in all her articles into the Act performed on my behalf with my Nadezhda peasants freed by me // The approved document of Prince Alexander Borisovich Kurakin. - St. Petersburg: Printed in the printing house of Friedrich Drechsler, 1807. - [2], 107, [1] p. Pages 25-87.

177. S. I. Zarudny "Beccaria on crimes and punishments in comparison with Chapter X of the Order of Catherine II and with modern Russian Laws: The materials for the development of the comparative study of the theory and practice of criminal legislation" / The works of S. Zarudny. - St. Petersburg: The printing house of the Second Branch of the Her Imperial Majesty Own Chancellery, 1879. - [6], II, XXIV, 196 pages.

178. P. M. Zakharyin "The path to good behavior, or an Abbreviated instruction to learning youth: Containing the useful and moralizing rules for every rank and state

of people." / The composition of Peter Zakharyin. By supporting a Moscow merchant Semyon Nikiforov. - Moscow: The printing house of A. Reshetnikov, 1796. - [2], VI, 1-64, 69-104 [= 100] p.

179. The name-day of Mrs. Vorchalkina // Catherine II (Empress; 1729-1796). The works of Empress Catherine II: Volumes 1-3. - St. Petersburg: A. Smirdin, 1849-1850. – in 3 volumes. 17. - The complete works of Russian Authors. Volume 2. - 1849. - 612 pages.
180. The history of Freemasonry in documents / E. L. Kuzmishin. - M.: The printing house of the publishing house "Ars Tectonica." 2010. - 404 pages.
181. The history of political and legal doctrines. A textbook for universities. The 3rd edition supplemented / Edited by a Ph.D. in Legal Sciences, Professor O. E. Leist and a Ph.D. in Legal Sciences, Professor V. A. Tomsinov. M.: The publishing house "Zertsalo," 2009. - 584 pages.
182. The history of political and legal doctrines: A textbook for universities / Edited by an Academician of RAN, a Ph.D. in Legal Sciences, Professor V. S. Nersesyants. - 4th edition reviewed and supplemented. - M.: Norma, 2004. - 944 pages.
183. S. P. Karpachev "The art of Freemasons" [Text]: a scientific reference monograph / S. P. Karpachev. - Moscow, 2015. Page 460.
184. S. P. Karpachev "M. M. Kovalevsky // Freemasonry and Freemasons." A digest of articles. Issue I. "Era," Moscow, 1994 – 123 pages. - Pages 76-90.
185. Franqois Quesnay (Kene in the Russian sources) "Natural law" // F. Quesnay, A. R. J. Turgot (Tyurgo in the Russian sources), P. S. Dupont de Nemours (Dyupon de Nemur in the Russian sources). K 33 Physiocrats. The selected economic works / F. Quesnay, A. R. J. Turgot, P. S. Dupont de Nemours; a foreword by P. N. Klyukin; translated from French, English, and German into Russian - M.: Eksmo, 2008. - 1200 pages. Pages 327-339. Pages 334-335.
186. M. S. Kiseleva "The intellectual choice of Russia in the second half of the 17th-the early 18th centuries: from the ancient Russian book-learning to European scholarship." - Moscow: Progress-Tradition, 2011. - 471 pages.
187. M. M. Kovalevsky "The struggle of German influence with the French one at the end of the 18th and in the first half of the 19th centuries" // M. M. Kovalevsky "The selected works": in 2 parts - Part 2. - M.: a Russian Political Encyclopedia (ROSSPEN), 2010. - 448 pages. Pages 85-126.
188. M. M. Kovalevsky "From the history of the state power in Russia" // M. M. Kovalevsky "The selected works": in 2 parts - Part 1. - M.: a Russian Political Encyclopedia (ROSSPEN), 2010. - 576 pages. Pages 55-156. Page 122.
189. M. M. Kovalevsky "Freemasonry in the time of Catherine (On the history of German influence in Russia)" // M. M. Kovalevsky "The selected works": in 2 parts - Part 2. - M.: a Russian Political Encyclopedia (ROSSPEN), 2010. - 448 pages. Pages 64-84.

190. M. M. Kovalevsky "Freemasonry in the time of Catherine" // Europe Bulletin. 1915, # 9. Pages 95-115.
191. S. V. Kodan "The political and legal approach in the study of the state and legal development of Russia (the XIX – the early XX centuries)" // Sociodynamics. - 2012. - # 2. - Pages 88-117. DOI: 10.7256 / 2306-0158.2012.2.177.
1. URL: http://e-notabene.ru/pr/article_177.html.

192. A convolute. A word about the invention of the art of writing. Did it serve to the detriment of the human mind and good manners? On the all-joyous day of the accession of the August Monarch of the Great Empress Catherine II, the Empress and Autocrat of All Russia, and so on to the All-Russian Imperial Throne, solemnly celebrated with the deepest reverence at the Imperial Moscow University on June 30, 1776. Spoken by Khariton Chebotarev, an Extraordinary Public Professor, Professor of Rhetoric and Moralizing, a university Sub-Librarian, and a member of the Free Russian Assembly at the same University. - [Moscow]: Published at the University Printing House, [1776]. - 23, [1] p.

193. A convolute. A word about the methods and ways leading to enlightenment. On the highly solemn birthday of Her Majesty, the Empress and Autocrat of All Russia Catherine II, the wise Legislator and True Mother of the Fatherland, at a public meeting of the Imperial Moscow University, held on April 22, 1779 / Spoken by Khariton Chebotarev, a Public Professor of History, Rhetoric, and Moralizing, a University Librarian, a Conference Secretary, and a member of the Moscow Russian Meeting. - Moscow: Published at the University Printing House, 1779. - 28 pages.
194. Yu. E. Kondakov "The 'Knightly' Systems of Freemasonry in Russia: 1772-1822." [Text]: [16+] / Yuri Kondakov. A foreword by R. Collis, an afterword by A. I. Serkov, an article by R. A. Gorodnitsky. - Moscow: Ganga, 2017. - 595 pages.
195. Yu. E. Kondakov "The Order of the Gold and Rose Cross in Russia. The Theoretical Degree of Solomon Sciences." [Text]: a monograph / Yu. E. Kondakov. - St. Petersburg: Asterion, 2012. - 615 pages.
196. Yu. E. Kondakov "The secret instructions of the Russian Rosicrucians (Rozencraitsers in the Russian sources) of the 18th-19th centuries." [Text]: [16+] / Yuri Kondakov. A preface by E. L. Kuzmishin, an afterword by A. I. Serkov. - Moscow: Ganga, 2018. - 561, [1] p. Pages 436-466.
197. Yu. E. Kondakov "Esoteric movement in Russia at the end of the 18th – the first half of the 19th centuries." - M.: Kastalia Club. 2018. - 670 pages. Page 637.
198. M. A. Korf "The life of Count Speransky." [Text]: [volumes 1-2]. - St. Petersburg, 1861. - 24 cm. Volume 1, parts 1 and 2.- 1861. - XVIII, 283 pages, [2] p.

199. S. A. Korf “The Russian state law” / Barron S. A. Korf, an Ordinary Professor of Helsingfors Imperial Alexander University. Part 1-. - Moscow: A quick printing house of A. A. Levenson, 1915. - 25. Part 1. - 1915. - IV, [2], 315 pages.
200. E. L. Kuzmishin “Freemasonry” / Evgeny Kuzmishin. A foreword by A. I. Serkov and Yu. E. Kondakov, an article by R. A. Gorodnitsky and E. L. Kuzmishin. – The 2nd edition revised and supplemented - Moscow: Ganga, 2019. – 547 pages, [3] p.
201. A. B. Kurakin “A copy from the document revealing the Relationship of Prince Alexander Borisovich Kurakin to the Minister of Internal Affairs, Count Viktor Pavlovich Kochubei (dated December 4, 1806)” // An approved position of Prince Alexander Borisovich Kurakin. - St. Petersburg: Printed in the printing house of Friedrich Drechsler, 1807. - [2], 107, [1] p. Pages 7-8.
202. A. B. Kurakin “A copy of the most submissive petition of Prince Alexander Borisovich Kurakin to the State Emperor of 4th December 1806” // An approved position of Prince Alexander Borisovich Kurakin. - St. Petersburg: Printed in the printing house Friedrich Drechsler, 1807. - [2], 107, [1] p. Pages 3-6.
203. V. V. Kuchurin “From the history of political struggle at the beginning of the 19th century: an unrealized project of the Masonic Reform of M. M. Speransky” // St. Petersburg Historical Magazine. St. Petersburg Institute of History of the Russian Academy of Sciences. # 3 (11), 2016. – Pages 6-18.
204. V. V. Lapaeva “The types of legal thinking: legal theory and practice.” [Text]: a monograph / V. V. Lapaeva. - Moscow: RAP, 2012. – 577, [1] p.
205. M. V. Lomonosov “From the words of the praiseworthy Peter the Great” // The selected philosophical works / M. V. Lomonosov; edited by G. S. Vasetsky, a foreword by G. S. Vasetsky; Moscow State University named after M. V. Lomonosov, The Department of History of Russian Philosophy. - [Moscow]: Gospolitizdat, 1950. - 759 p. Pages 493-511.
206. M. V. Lomonosov “On the reproduction and preservation of the Russian people” // The selected philosophical works / M. V. Lomonosov; edited by G. S. Vasetsky, a foreword by G. S. Vasetsky; Moscow State University named after M. V. Lomonosov, The Department of History of Russian Philosophy. - [Moscow]: Gospolitizdat, 1950. - 759 p. Pages 598-614. Page 598.
207. M. V. Lomonosov “A letter about the benefits of glass to I. I. Shuvalov” // The works of M. V. Lomonosov. - Petrograd: Kopeyka, [1916]. - 88 pages. Pages 33-43.
208. M. V. Lomonosov “A letter of the late Mikhail Vasilyevich Lomonosov to Ivan Ivanovich Shuvalov.” From the Magazine of Ancient and New Literature, published by Mr. Olin. - St. Petersburg: The printing House of the Department of Public Education, 1819. - 38 pages.

209. M. N. Longinov "Novikov and the Moscow Martinists": The research of. M. N. Longinov. - Moscow: The printing house of Grachev and K °, 1867. - [4], IV, 384, 0176 pages.
210. I. V. Lopukhin "The notes from some circumstances of the life and service of Actual Privy Councilor and Senator I. V. Lopukhin, compiled by himself" / A foreword by Iskander. - London: Trübner & C °, 1860. - [2], VIII, 212 pages.
211. M. N. Marchenko, I. F. Machin "The history of political and legal doctrines": A textbook. - M.: Higher Education, 2005. - 495 pages.
212. Ch. F. Masson "The secret notes on Russia. And in the part about the end of the reign of Catherine II and the reign of Paul I." Volume I. Translation from the 2nd edition of N. Na-go. Moscow, 1918. An edition of I. I. Casanov. The printing house "KULTURA" A. K. Mieserova. - 94 pages.
213. A. Mezyer "In search of truth and the meaning of life (an Essay from the History of Russian Freemasonry)" // History and Social Issues. # 112. The publishing house of O. N. Popova, 1906. S. Petersburg. - 142 pages.
214. P. I. Melissino "The description of the fireworks at the end of the celebration in case of the concluded peace between Her Imperial Majesty Catherine II and His Majesty Gustav the Third King of Sweden": [Text]: Presented on the Tsaritsyno Meadow in St. Petersburg in September 1790. - St. Petersburg: The printing house of Shnor, 1790. - [10] p. P. 8.
215. A. Yu. Minakov "Russian conservatism in the first quarter of the 19th century." [Text]: a monograph / A. Yu. Minakov. - Moscow: Direct-Media, 2011. - 558, [1] p.
216. I. V. Mikheeva "The legislative process in the Russian Empire: on the question of the ministerial initiative // The traditions and innovation of Russian legal thought: history and modernity: (to the 100th anniversary of the death of S. A. Muromtsev)": The materials of the IV International Scientific-Practical Conference, Ivanovo, September 30 - October 2, 2010: in 3 parts - Ivanovo: Ivanovo State University, 2010, Part 2. - Pages 230-249.
217. I. V. Mikheeva "The originality of the legislative initiative in the Russian Empire" // The bulletin of the Nizhny Novgorod Academy of the Ministry of Internal Affairs of Russia, 2011, # 1 (14). Pages 54-57.
218. My letter of faith to the Governing Senate, the Ober of the Prosecutor of an Actual State Councilor, a Cavalier Peter Stepanovich Molchanov // An approved position of Prince Alexander Borisovich Kurakin. - St. Petersburg: Printed in the printing house Friedrich Drechsler, 1807. - [2], 107, [1] p. Pages 19-24.
219. Ch. L. Montesquieu "On the essence of laws": Part 1: The creation of Montesquieu / Translated from French into Russian by Dmitry Yazykov. - Moscow: Sopikov, 1809. - XLVI, 310 pages.

220. A. I. Musin-Pushkin "A note // Vladimir Monomakh (Grand Duke; 1053-1125). The Spiritual of Grand Duke Vladimir Vsevolodovich Monomakh to his children, named a Doctrine in the chronicle of Suzdal." - St. Petersburg: The printing house of the Corps of Foreign Co-Religionists, 1793. - X, 61 pages. Page 8.
221. The thoughts of Count M. M. Speransky. On the system of laws, in general. // Nikolai Vasilievich Kalachov (1819-1885). An archive of the historical and practical information relating to Russia, published by Nikolai Kalachov. [Text]. - St. Petersburg: The printing house of the 2nd Branch of His Imperial Majesty's Own Chancellery, 1858. Pages 3-20.
222. The guidance to the Supreme Police Committee. 1805 / Gendarmes of Russia / [Compiler V. S. Izmozik]. - SPb.: Neva; M.: OLMA-Press, 2002.-638, [1] p.
223. V. S. Nersesyants "Plato" / V. S. Nersesyants. - Moscow: Legal Literature, 1984. - 104 pages.
224. V. S. Nersesyants "Socrates." [Text] / V. S. Nersesyants. The Academy of Sciences of the USSR. - Moscow: Nauka, 1977. - 152 pages.
225. V. S. Nersesyants "The philosophy of law." A textbook for universities. - M.: The publishing group INFRA • M - NORMA, 1997. - 652 pages.
226. A new outline of true theology: The doctrine of salvation is presented in a new light for the glory of God and universal edification, with a letter attributed to all people: The theological and moral correction / Translated from French by N. N. Trubetskoy. - Moscow: Printed in the printing house of I. Lopukhin with the indicated permission, 1784. - 8 ° (19 cm). Part 2. - 276.5, [1] p.
227. B. E. Nolde "A legislative initiative on Russian Law" // Law. - 1911. - # 44. – An article 2418.
228. On crimes and punishments / Translated from Italian into Russian with the sketch "The Significance of Beccaria in Science and the History of Russian Criminal Law" [S. Belikov]. - [Kharkov]: S. Ya. Belikov, 1889. - XIV, 232 pages.
229. On crimes and punishments. Translated from Italian into Russian / C. Beccaria. Compiled by M. Yu. Yumashev. Translated by Yu. M. Marinin and G. V. Cherdantsev – the 5th edition revised and increased. - M.: Stels, 1995. - 304 pages.
230. On the reason of laws / The composition of Mr. Montesquia. Translated from French into Russian by Vasily Kramarenkov. - St. Petersburg: Under the Imperial Academy of Sciences, 1775. - 4 °. Volume 1. - 1775. - [2], XXXIV, 424 pages.
231. Social thought in Russia in the 18th century: in 2 volumes. - Volume 1: Philosophia rationalis / Compiled by T. V. Artemyeva, a preface by T. V. Artemyeva. M.: ROSSPEN, 2010.-760 pages.
232. From the Empress to Mr. Real Privy Counselor Panin // The correspondence of Empress Catherine II with different persons // Catherine II. The correspondence of Empress Catherine II with different ... - St. Petersburg, 1807. - 156 p. Pages 15-17.

233. The answer of Major General Boltin to the letter of Prince Shcherbatov, the author of Russian History. - St. Petersburg: The printing house of the Mountain School, [17] 89. - 183 pages.
234. A letter of Prince Kurakin to A. A. Nartov (dated December 1805) // P. A. Druzhinin "The unknown letters of Russian writers to Prince Alexander Borisovich Kurakin (1752-1818)." - M.: Truten, 2002. - 504 pages. Pages 268-269.
235. A report on the Moscow Public Museum from the time of its foundation to January 1, 1864, presented by the former Director of the Museum of the Retinue of His Imperial Majesty, Major General N. V. Isakov for ... [Text]. - St. Petersburg: Printed in the printing house of Rogalsky and Co., 1864- [1922]. - 26 cm. 1864 - 1865. - 50 pages.
236. Pavel I, P. I. Panin "The correspondence of Pavel Petrovich with Count Peter Panin" // Russian antiquity, 1882. - Volume 33. - # 2. - Pages 403-418.
237. Song XX Tranquility // M. M. Kheraskov "The philosophical ode or song of Mikhail Kheraskov." - [Moscow]: Printed under the Imperial Moscow University, 1769. - [2], 72 p. Pages 41-42.
238. The letters of Empress Catherine II to Count Rumyantsov 1773 // Catherine II (Empress; 1729-1796). The works of Empress Catherine II: Volumes 1-3. - St. Petersburg: A. Smirdin, 1849-1850. – in 3 volumes; 17. - (The complete works of Russian Authors).
239. The letters of O. A. Pozdeev to Count A. K. Razumovsky // A. A. Vasilchikov "The Razumovsky family." Volume 2. SPb., 1880. pages 448-518.
240. The letters from the road from Prince A. B. Kurakin to the Monarch Empress Maria Feodorovna // Russian Archive. - 1868. - Book 1, Notebook 1. - Pages 23-86; Notebook 2. - Pages 161-240.
241. A letter of Count N. I. Panin to Primate Podossky // Catherine II (Empress; 1729-1796). The political correspondence of Empress Catherine II. - [St. Petersburg: b. i.], 1885-1914. - 26 cm. - (A Collection of the Imperial Russian Historical Society / Russian Historical Society). Volume 67: 1766-1767 [Text]. - 1889. - XXI, 578, [1] p. Pages 561-563.
242. A letter from Count Panin to the Resident Obrezkov to Constantinople // Catherine II (Empress; 1729-1796). The political correspondence of Empress Catherine II. - [St. Petersburg: without publishers], 1885-1914. - 26 cm. - (A Collection of the Imperial Russian Historical Society / Russian Historical Society). Volume 87: 1768-1769 [Text]. - 1893. - XVIII, 555 pages. Pages 138-146.
243. A letter of I. A. Pozdeev to V. I. Ostolopov (dated February 6, 1797) // From the history of Russian Rosicrucianism / N. P. Kiselev; compiling and preparing the text and comments by M. V. Reizin and A. I. Serkov. - St. Petersburg: The publishing house named after N. I. Novikov, 2005. - 420, [2] p. Page 320.

244. A letter of I. A. Pozdeev to the Lodge of the North Star (dated March 5, 1784) // From the history of Russian Rosicrucianism / N. P. Kiselev; compiling and preparing the text and comments by M. V. Reizin and A. I. Serkov. - St. Petersburg: The publishing house named after N. I. Novikov, 2005. - 420, [2] p. Pages 376-378.
245. A letter of the Empress to the Pomerelsky Governor Count Fleming // Catherine II (Empress; 1729-1796). The political correspondence of Empress Catherine II. - [St. Petersburg: b. i.], 1885-1914. - 26 cm. - (A Collection of the Imperial Russian Historical Society / Russian Historical Society). Volume 97: 1769-1771 [Text]. - 1896. - [2], XXI, 543 p. Pages 1-2.
246. A letter from Prince A. B. Kurakin to Count N. P. Panin on March 24, 1798 // Russian Starina, edition of 1874, volume X, pages 575-579.
247. The Russian truth or the Laws of Grand Dukes Yaroslav Vladimirovich and Vladimir Vsevolodovich Monomakh: With the application of these ancient dialects and syllables to those used today and an explanation of the words and names that came out of use / Published by lovers of Russian history. - [Saint Petersburg]: The printing house of St. Ruler of Synod, 1792. - [2], VIII, [13], 100, XVI p.
248. N. S. Prozorova "The Political and Legal Views of John Lilberne." M.: The State Publishing House of Legal Literature. 1960. - 53 pages.
249. S. M. Propper "Freemasonry and its importance for cultural success." SPb. 1907. - 60 pages.
250. S. Pufendorf "On the position of a person and a citizen according to the law of nature": Translated into Russian in 1726 / V. M. Kruglov: in 2 volumes. Volume I. - St. Petersburg: Nestor-History, 2011. - 214 pages.
251. A. N. Pypin "Social movement in Russia under Alexander I": The historical essays of A. N. Pypin. – the 3rd edition supplemented. - St. Petersburg: The printing house of M. M. Stasyulevich, 1900.-XIV, 587 pages.
252. A. N. Pypin "Russian Freemasonry: the XVIII and first quarter of XIX centuries / A. N. Pypin. Edited by G. V. Vernadsky, a foreword and the notes by G. V. Vernadsky. - Petrograd: Lights, 1916. - VIII, 571, [4] p.
253. Reflections on the reasons for the majesty of the Roman people and their decline / Translated from French into Russian by Alexei Polenov. - St. Petersburg: Under the Imperial Academy of Sciences, 1769. - [8], 315, [2] p.
254. Reasoning on the inconveniences to give freedom to peasants and servants in Russia or to make the property of estates // The readings of the Society of Russian History and Antiquities. M.: The University printing house. 1861. Book 3, - 796 pages. Pages 98-134.
255. M. M. Rassolov "The history of political and legal doctrines": a tutorial for the university students studying in the specialty 021100 "Jurisprudence." – The 2nd edition revised and supplemented - M.: UNITY-DANA, - 271 pages.

256. M. A. Reisner "The 'common good' and the absolute state" // A bulletin of Law: A Magazine of the Legal Society at the Imperial St. Petersburg University. - St. Petersburg, 1871-1906. Volume XXXII. 1902, # 9/10 (Nov.-Dec.). Pages 1-128.
257. L. P. Repina "Historical science at the turn of the XX-XXI centuries: social theories and historiographic practice." - M.: Krug, 2011. - 559 pages.
258. The speech was spoken at the opening of the Provincial [Lodge] in M *** in the presence of His Majesty. - [Moscow]: [The University printing house of N. Novikov], [1780]. - 10 pages.
259. Russian Freemasons. 1721-2019. A Biographical Dictionary. XIX century. Volume II / A. I. Serkov, M.: Ganga, 2020. - 748 pages.
260. Russian Freemasons. 1721-2019. A Biographical Dictionary. The XIX century. Volume IV / A. I. Serkov, M.: Ganga, 2020. - 662 pages.
261. Russian Freemasons. 1721-2019. A Biographical Dictionary. The XIX century. Volume I / A. I. Serkov, M.: Ganga, 2020. - 704 pages.
262. Russian Freemasons. 1721-2019. A Biographical Dictionary. The XIX century. Volume III / A. I. Serkov, M.: Ganga, 2020 - 820 pages.
263. Russian Freemasons. 1721-2019. A Biographical Dictionary. The XVIII century. Volume I / A. I. Serkov, M.: Ganga, 2019 - 710 pages.
264. Russian Freemasons. 1721-2019. A Biographical Dictionary. The XVIII century. Volume III / A. I. Serkov, M.: Ganga, 2019 - 320 pages.
265. Russian Freemasons. 1721-2019. A Biographical Dictionary. The XVIII century. Volume II / A. I. Serkov, M.: Ganga, 2019 - 748 pages.
266. The Russian legislation of the X-XX centuries: [Texts and comments.]. In 9 volumes. / Edited by O. I. Chistyakov, a foreword by O. I. Chistyakov. - M.: Legal literature, 1984-. - 22 cm. Volume 6. The Legislation of the first half of the XIX century [Text]. - M., 1988. - 431 pages.
267. Russian Freemasonry during the reign of Catherine II / G. V. Vernadsky. - SPb.: The publishing house named after N. I. Novikov, 1999. - 567, [2] p.
268. A Collection of the Imperial Russian Historical Society. - SPb., 1867-1916. – in 148 volumes. Volume 32: The historical information about the Catherine Legislative Commission for composing a draft of the New Code. Part 4 / Collected and published under the supervision of Professor V. I. Sergeevich. - SPb.: The printing house of N. A. Lebedev, 1881. - XXI, 638 pages.
269. A Collection of the Imperial Russian Historical Society. - SPb., 1867-1916. - in 148 volumes. Volume 45: The financial documents of the reign of Emperor Alexander I / Collected and published by A. N. Kulomzin. - SPb.: The printing house of V. Bezobrazov and Company, 1885. - [6], VI, 623 pages.
270. A Collection of the Historical Materials recovered from the Archives of His Imperial Majesty's Own Chancellery / Edited by N. Dubrovin. - SPb.: The state

printing house, 1876-1915. Issue 1: The decrees and rescripts of 1812. - 1876. - XXXVI, 466, XIII p.

271. A Collection of the Historical Materials recovered from the Archives of His Imperial Majesty's Own Chancellery / Edited by N. Dubrovin. - SPb.: The state printing house, 1876-1915. Issue 3. - 1890. - XIX, 512, [1] p.
272. A Collection of the Historical Materials extracted from the Archives of His Imperial Majesty's Own Chancellery / Edited by N. Dubrovin. - SPb.: The state printing house, 1876-1915. Issue 4. - 1891. - XXIII, 493 pages.
273. A Collection of the Historical Materials extracted from the Archives of His Imperial Majesty's Own Chancellery. Issue 11. - 1902 (reg. 1901). - XIII, 510 pages.
274. F. Sevastyanov "The development of the 'higher police' under Alexander I / The gendarmes of Russia" / [Compiled by V. S. Izmozik]. - SPb.: Neva; M.: OLMA-Press, 2002.-638, [1] p.
275. L. F. Segur "The notes of Count Segur on his stay in Russia during the reign of Catherine II. (1785-1789)": Translated from French into Russian with comments - St. Petersburg: The printing house of V. N. Maikov, 1865. - 386 pages.
276. V. I. Semevsky "The questions about the transformation of the state system in Russia in the 18th and the first quarter of the 19th centuries." An essay on the history of political and social ideas // Byloe, 1906. # 1.
277. V. I. Semevsky "Decembrists-Masons" // The past years. 1908." # 2. Pages 1-50.
278. V. I. Semevsky "The political and social ideas of the Decembrists" / The works of V. I. Semevsky. - St. Petersburg: The printing house # 1 of the SPb. Work Artel, 1909. - XII, 694, [4] p.
279. A. P. Semitko "The culture of law and the 'common good'" // The legal state: theory and practice. # 2 (52). 2018. Pages 25-33.
280. A. I. Serkov "The History of Russian Freemasonry of the XIX century" / Russian Freemasonry: Materials and studies / Edited by M. V. Reizin and A. I. Serkov. - The 2nd edition revised and extended. Russian Freemasonry: Materials and studies Volume 4. - SPb.: The publishing house named after N. I. Novikov, 2000. - 390, [3] p.
281. A. I. Serkov "Russian Freemasonry. 1731-2000": An Encyclopaedical Dictionary / A. I. Serkov. - M.: ROSSPEN, 2001. – 1,222 pages.
282. A. I. Serkov "The fate of Masonic meetings in Russia. 500 years of gnosis in Europe. Gnostic tradition in printed and handwritten books: Moscow – Petersburg" / An exhibition catalog in the All-Russian State Library of Foreign Literature, Moscow and the All-Russian Museum of A. S. Pushkin, Petersburg. - Amsterdam, 1993. - Pages 27-34.
283. A word about the way arousing love for the Fatherland in the ancient citizens: On the highly solemn birthday of the August Monarch of the Great Empress Catherine

II, Empress and Autocrat of all Russia, and so on, celebrated with the deepest reverence at the Imperial Moscow University on April 22, 1775 / Spoken by Johann Gottfried Reichel, a Public Ordinary Professor of History. Translated from Latin into Russian by University Sub-Librarian Khariton Chebotarev. - [Moscow]: Published at the University Printing House, [1775]. - 23, [1] p.

284. T. O. Sokolovskaya "Early Alexander Freemasonry. The Revival of Freemasonry" / Freemasonry in its past and present: in 2 volumes. / Edited by S. P. Melgunov and N. P. Sidorov. - A reprint. Volume 2. - M.: IKPA, 1991. - 266 pages.
285. T. O. Sokolovskaya "From materials on the history of Freemasonry (The secret attitude of the Minister of Internal Affairs to the Chief of the General Staff, January 9, 1826, # 13.)" // Russian antiquity. 1907. February. Pages 344-346.
286. T. O. Sokolovskaya "The secret archives of Russian Freemasons" / T. Sokolovskaya, D. Lotareva. - Moscow: Veche, 2007.-477, [1] p.
287. The works of Empress Catherine II: Volumes 1-3. - St. Petersburg: A. Smirdin, 1849-1850. – in 3 volumes; 17. - (The Complete Works of Russian Authors). Volume 1. - 1849. - 666, II p.
288. The works of Empress Catherine II: Volumes 1-3. - St. Petersburg: A. Smirdin, 1849-1850. – in 3 volumes; 17. - (The Complete Works of Russian Authors). Volume 3. - 1850. - [4], 504 pages.
289. Speransky // F. M. Dmitriev, Speransky [Text] / The works of F. Dmitriev. - Moscow: without publishers, 1862. - 190 pages. Paragraph 3. Page 3.
290. A. P. Sumarokov "The complete collection of all works in poetry and prose" / A late Actual State Councilor, a Holder of the Order of St. Anna and a member of the Leipzig Scientific Meeting Alexander Petrovich Sumarokov. Collected and published for the pleasure of the lovers of Russian scholarship by Nikolai Novikov, a member of the Free Russian Assembly at the Imperial Moscow University. – The 2nd edition - Moscow: The University printing house of N. Novikov, 1787. - 8 °. Part 2. - 290 pages.
291. M. I. Sukhomlinov "The history of the Russian Academy" / The works of M. I. Sukhomlinov. - St. Petersburg: The printing house of Imperial Academy of Sciences, 1874-1888. - 23 cm. Issue 5. - 1880. - IV, 432 pages.
292. M. I. Sukhomlinov "Boltin's judgments on the issues of the state and public life; his view of serfdom and the liberation of the peasants" // The history of the Russian Academy / The works of M. I. Sukhomlinov. - St. Petersburg: The printing house of Imperial Academy of Sciences, 1874-1888. - 23 cm. Issue 5. - 1880. - IV, 432 pages.
293. V. M. Syrykh "The logical foundations of the general theory of law." Volume 2. The logic of legal research (How to write a thesis). - M., 2004. - 560 pages.
294. V. N. Tatishchev "The Spiritual of Vasily Nikitich Tatishchev." - Leipzig: Wolfgang Gergard, 1862. - 40 pages.

295. V. N. Tatishchev "The Spiritual to my son. The contents of the conversation about the benefits of sciences and other works. The Explanatory Articles: The Texts of the Spiritual and Exhortation" /. 1685-1750. - St. Petersburg: I. Glazunov, 1896. - [2], II, 84 pages. Pages 49-56.
296. V. N. Tatishchev "The arbitrary and concordant reasoning and opinion of the assembled Russian gentry about the state rule" // V. Tatishchev. The collected works: in 8 volumes. Volume 8. - M.: Ladomir, 1996. Pages 146-152.
297. V. N. Tatishchev "The conversation of two friends about the benefits of science and schools" // V. Tatishchev. The collected works: in 8 volumes (in 5 books): Book 5 / Volume 7. Russian History. Volume 8. The Selected Works: A reprint from 1968, 1979 - M.: Ladomir, 1996. Pages 51-132.
298. The Creations of M. Kheraskov: Corrected and supplemented again. Part 12: [NumaPompilius or Prosperous Rome]. - The 3rd edition. - 1803. - [2], VIII, 165 pages.
299. The Creations of M. Kheraskov: Corrected and supplemented again. Part 8: Cadmus and Harmony: An Ancient Narrative: Part 1 revised and supplemented - 1801. - X, [6], 259, [6] p.
300. V. A. Tomsinov "Emperor Paul I (1754-1801): a Statesman and a Legislator // The Legislation of Emperor Paul I" / Compiled by V. A. Tomsinov, a foreword and a biographical sketch by V. A. Tomsinov. - M.: Zertsalo, 2008. Pages XV – LXIV.
301. V. A. Tomsinov "A Diploma for the rights, liberties, and advantages of the noble Russian nobility." Published in the publication: The Legislation of Empress Catherine II. 1783-1796" / Compiled V. A. Tomsinov, an introductory article by V. A. Tomsinov. M.: Zertsalo, 2011. Pages XI – XL.
302. V. A. Tomsinov "The history of the Russian political and legal thought of the X-XVIII centuries" / V. A. Tomsinov. Moscow State University named after M. V. Lomonosov. Legal Faculty - M.: Zertsalo, 2003. - 255 pages.
303. V. A. Tomsinov "The Russian jurists of the 18th - 20th centuries. The essays on life and work": in 2 volumes. Volume 1. - M.: Zertsalo, 2007. - 672 pages.
304. V. A. Tomsinov "Speransky" / Vladimir Tomsinov. - Moscow: Young Guard, 2006. - 451 pages.
305. L. N. Trefolev "Alexey Petrovich Melgunov, the Governor-General of Catherine's times" // Russian Archives, 1865. – The 2nd edition - M., 1866. - Pages 873-952 by 2 columns.
306. I. P. Turgenev "Who can be a good citizen and loyal subject?" / Translated from French into Russian by Serpukhov Protopop Vasily Protopopov. - Moscow: The University Printing House of Ridiger and Claudia, 1796. - [4], 39, [1] p.
307. The Code of the Great Masonic Lodge of Astrea in the East of St. Petersburg; The Laws of the Grand Masonic Lodge of Astrea in the East of St. Petersburg or Under

the Constitution of the Grand Lodge of Astrea of the constituted Masonic Union. In 2 parts. 1815. Parts 1-2. SPb., 1816. - 345 pages.

308. The destruction of Masonic Lodges in Russia in 1822: the rediscovered secret notes and reports of Senator Ye. A. Kushelev // Russian antiquity. -1877. - Volume 18. – Pages 455-480.
309. The Charter of Freemasons, approved at the General Council of the Convention that was held in Wilhelmsbad in 1787 // T. O. Sokolovskaya "The secret archives of Russian Freemasons" / T. Sokolovskaya, D. Lotareva. - Moscow: Veche, 2007.- 477, [1] p. Pages 344-354.
310. The Charter of Freemasons was approved by the General Council of the Convention that was held in Wilhelmsbad in 5787 (XVIII-XIXb.b.). From the history of Russian Freemasonry. SPb.: Economic Type Literature. 1907. - 16 pages.
311. I. I. Felbiger "On the positions of a person and a citizen, a book for reading determined in the people's city schools of the Russian Empire, published at the highest command of the reigning Empress Catherine II." St. Petersburg, 1783 - 180 pages.
312. Feofan Prokopovich "The truth of the Monarch will." - [Moscow]: Published in the Moscow Printing House, August 07, 1722. - 59 pages.
313. I. G. Findel "The history of Frank-Freemasonry from its inception to the present": The translation from the 2nd German edition. Volumes 1-2 / The works of I. G. Findel. - St. Petersburg, 1872-1874. – in 2 volumes. Volume 1. - 1872. Page 58.
314. I. G. Findel "The history of Frank-Freemasonry from its inception to the present": The translation from the 2nd German edition. Volumes 1-2 / The works of I. G. Findel. An edition of the Freemasonic magazine "DieBauhütte." - St. Petersburg: The printing house of N. Skaryatin, 1872-1874. – in 2 volumes. Volume 2. - 1874. Pages 59, 138, 310.
315. Thomas Aquinas "The sum of theology" / Translated by S. I. Eremeev and A. A. Yudin. Parts I-II. Questions 90-114. - Kiev: Nika-Center, 2010. - 432 pages.
316. O. Fortunatov "The memorable notes of Vologzhanin" // Russian Archive. 1867. Volume 12. Pages 1646-1707. Pages 1651, 1652. An annotation.
317. I. Freyer "Jerome Freyer's Brief General History with its continuation to the very present times and the addition of Russian History to it": Translated from German into Russian for the use of students, corrected and multiplied at the Imperial Moscow University / [Translated by Kh. A. Chebotarev]. - [Moscow]: Published at the same University, 1769. - [18], XLVIII, 500, [76] pages.
318. M. M. Kheraskov "Tsar or Saved Novgorod": A Poem. - Moscow: The University printing house of Ridiger and Claudia, 1800. - [10], 246 pages.
319. M. M. Kheraskov "Merry Russia: Prologue." - [M.: The University printing house, B.g.]. - [4] p.

320. M. M. Kheraskov “To the highly esteemed gentlemen and members of the Board of Trustees of the Imperial Educational House.” - [Moscow]: [The University printing house], [not earlier than 1763]. - [4] p.
321. M. M. Kheraskov “An Ode to her Imperial Majesty, the most merciful Empress Ekaterina Alekseevna II: Presented from the Moscow University during the all-joyful stay of Her Imperial Majesty in Moscow after Her Imperial Majesty’s returning from Russia's midday outlying districts”: June 28, 1787. - Moscow: The University printing house of N. Novikov, 1787. - 11 pages.
322. M. M. Kheraskov “The Temple of Russian Prosperity: Dedicated to the builder of it, Her Imperial Majesty, the most merciful Empress Ekaterina Alekseevna II; the All-Russian Autocrat: Presented at the joyous celebration of the conclusion of peace with the Ottoman Port in Moscow, in July 1775.” - [Moscow]: Published at the Imperial Moscow University, [1775]. - [15] pages.
323. A. V. Khrapovitskiy “The diary of A. V. Khrapovitsky. 1782-1793: From January 18, 1782 to September 17, 1793” / From the original of his manuscripts, with the biographical article and explanatory directions. Nikolay Barsukov, a member of the Archeographical Commission. - Moscow: Russian archives, 1901 (region 1902). - XXII, 404 pages.
324. The flourishing state and glory of Russia from the heroic virtues of Her Autocrat: At the ten-year triumph of the prosperous reign of the August Monarch, the Great Empress Catherine II, the Empress and Autocrat of all Russia, and so on, celebrated at the public meeting of the Imperial Moscow University on June 30, 1772 / With the deepest zeal, a Professor of History John Gottfried Reichel, an Orator elected to this event, a Public Ordinary Librarian, a University Conference Secretary and a member of Leipzig Scholar Society. Translated from Latin into Russian by a History Teacher Khariton Chebotarev. - [Moscow]: Printed under the Imperial Moscow University, [1772]. - 24 pages.
325. A. Czartoryski “Memoirs and Correspondence with Emperor Alexander I” / Edited by A. Kizevetter. Volume 1. SPb., 1912-1913. Page 170.
326. N. D. Chechulin “The Project of the Imperial Council in the first year of the reign of Catherine II.” - M.: Book on Demand, 2011. - 26 pages.
327. I. G. Schwartz (Shvarts in the Russian sources) “Lectures” / Compiled by A. D. Tyurikov. Donetsk: “Veber” (Donetsk branch), 2008. - 172 pages.
328. G. F. Shershenevich “The philosophy of law” / G. F. Shershenevich. - Moscow: The Brothers of The Bashmakov family, 1910-1912. - 24 cm. Volume 1, # 1: The theoretical part. Issue # 1. The General Theory of Law. - 1910. - VI, 320 pages.
329. N. K. Shilder “Emperor Alexander I: His life and reign: With 450 illustrations”: in 4 volumes. / The works of N. K. Schilder. – The 2nd edition. - SPb.: The printing house of A. S. Suvorin, 1904-1905, Volume 2. - 1904. - 408 pages.

330. N. K. Shilder “Emperor Alexander I: His life and reign: With 450 illustrations”: in 4 volumes. / The works of N. K. Schilder. – The 2nd edition -SPb.: The printing house of A. S. Suvorin, 1904-1905, Volume 4. - 1905. - 651 pages.
331. Schleiss von Levenfeld, Bernhard Josef “The influence of the true Freemasonry on the ‘common good’ of states, discovered and proven from the true purpose of its original establishment (foundation).” [Text] / Karl Hubert Lobreich von Plumenek. Written at the end of the 18th century in refutation of the works of Yakov Moser: On the tolerance of Freemasonry communities, especially, regarding the Peace of Westphalia. Translated from the second edition in German, printed in Amsterdam in 1779. - Moscow: Printed in the University Printing House, 1816. - [4], VIII, 211, [3] p.
332. I. A. Stark (Shtark in the Russian sources) “The Apology or Defense of the Order of Freemasons” / Written by a Brother ****, a member of the Scottish ** Lodge, in P **.; Translated from German into Russian by I. P. Turgenev. - M.: The printing house of Lopukhin, 1784. - 224 pages.
333. V. G. Shcheglov “The State Council in Russia, especially during the reign of Emperor Alexander the First: a historical and legal study” / The works of V. G. Shcheglov. - Yaroslavl: The printing house of M. H. Falge, 1892-1895. – in 2 volumes – The general title of the 2nd volume: The state Council in Russia. Volume 2. Issue. 1: The Council of State in the reign of Emperor Alexander the First. - 1895. - [6], V, 501, [1] p.
334. M. M. Shcherbatov “A letter to the nobles, the rulers of the state, the works of Senator Prince M. M. Shcherbatov” // Russian antiquity. - 1872. - Volume 5. – Issue # 1. - Pages 1-15.
335. M. M. Shcherbatov “‘On the damage to the mores in Russia’ by Prince Shcherbatov and ‘The Journey from St. Petersburg to Moscow’ by A. Radishchev” / A foreword by Iskander [pseudonym of A. I. Gertsen]. - London: Trubner & C °, 1858. - XVI, II, 340 pages.
336. M. M. Shcherbatov “The consideration of the vices and autocracy of Peter the Great. A conversation.” // Mikhail Mikhailovich Shcherbatov (1733-1790). Various works of Prince M. M. Shcherbatov / A foreword by O. Bodyansky. - Moscow: The University printing house, 1860. - [2], 140 p. Pages 5-22.
337. M. M. Shcherbatov “The works of Prince M. M. Shcherbatov: Volumes 1-2. - St. Petersburg: book. B. S. Shcherbatov, 1896-1898. – in 2 volumes; 26. The historical, political, and philosophical articles / Edited by I. P. Khrushchov and A. G. Voronov. - 1898. - [2], X p., page 630 by 2 columns.
338. J. G. Justi “The essential image of the nature of people's societies and all kinds of laws” / Composed by Mr. Justi. Translated from German into Russian by Avraam Volkov. - M.: Printed under the Imperial Moscow University, 1770. –384 pages.

Illustrations

— Picture 1. A view of Mount Ararat was gained from the territory of the Republic of Armenia in May 2016 (a photo was made by the author of this research).
— Picture 2. A masonic sign is in the form of an owl, acacia, and wild stone. The late 18th century - the early quarter of the 19th century. Metal, engraving. Published in the catalog of the exhibition of the State Hermitage Museum in 2013 // G. A. Mirolyubova, I. N. Ukhanova "Everybody was a Mason at that time." The Wisdom of Astrea: The Monuments of Freemasonry of the 18th – the first third of the 19th centuries in the Hermitage Collection: An Exhibition Catalog / State Hermitage - St. Petersburg: The Publishing House of the State Hermitage Museum, 2013. - 480 p.: ill. Pages 9-26. P. 20.
— Picture 3. The white husky puff with blue silk piping. Russia. The end of the 18th century. Published by Yu. V. Plotnikova in the catalog of the exhibition of the State Hermitage in 2013 // The Wisdom of Astrea: the monuments of Freemasonry of the 18th – the first third of the 19th centuries in the collection of the Hermitage: a catalog of the exhibition / The state Hermitage - St. Petersburg: The Publishing House of the State Hermitage. Hermitage Museum, 2013. - 480 pages: ill. Page 184.
— Picture 4. The Russian State Historical Archives in St. Petersburg. The front entrance. September 2018. A photo by the author of this research.
— Picture 5. A sign is in the form of a bone Master Key on a blue moire neck ribbon. Russia. The late 18th – the early 19th centuries. Published by I. N. Ukhanova // The Wisdom of Astrea: The Monuments of Freemasonry of the 18th - the first third of the 19th centuries in the Hermitage collection: an Exhibition Catalog / State Hermitage - St. Petersburg: The Publishing House of the State Hermitage Museum, 2013. - 480 p.: ill. Page 141.
— Picture 6. Alexander Nikolaevich Pypin (1833-1904). A photo of a young scientist. From open sources
— Picture 7. Vladimir Vasilievich Semevsky (1848-1916). A photo of a young scientist. From open sources.
— Picture 8. Ivanov-Razumnik, Razumnik Vasilievich (1878-1946). A photo. From open sources
— Picture 9. Vasily Osipovich Klyuchevsky (1841-1911). A photo of a young scientist. From open sources.
— Picture 10. The cover of the magazine "GENESIS": The Historical Research by the printing house of Nota Bene at https://www.nbpublish.com/e_hr/ (accessed: March 29, 2021: open access).

— Picture 11. A photo of one of the globular nodules in the Torysh Hole on the Mangistau Peninsula, Kazakhstan. From open sources.
— Picture 12. A gang of French peasants in revolt in 1789. The reproduction of P. A. Svedomsky's painting of the early 20th century // An album of the Historical Painting [Text]: in engravings taken from the paintings of Russian and foreign artists. - [St. Petersburg]: the publication of the magazine "World Illustration," [1891]. - [53] p.: ill. Page VII. Color processing by A. N. Makarov.
— Picture 13. A photo of Maxim Maksimovich Kovalevsky (1851-1916). From open sources.
— Picture 14. A photo of Mikhail Andreevich Reisner (1868-1928). From open sources.
— Picture 15. A Frontispiece // J. F. Bielfeld "The political instructions of Baron Bielfeld" / Translated from French by Prince Fyodor Shakhovsky. - [Moscow]: Printed under the Imperial Moscow University, 1768-1775. - 4 °. Part 1 [Text]. - 1768. - [12], 462, [9] p.
— Picture 16. A Vignette // J. F. Bielfeld "The political instructions of Baron Bielfeld" / Translated from French into Russian by Prince Fyodor Shakhovsky. - [Moscow]: Printed under the Imperial Moscow University, 1768-1775. - 4 °. Part 2 [Text]. - 1775. - [4], 494, [6] p., 4 p.
— Picture 17. Charles Louis de Montesquieu (1689-1755). A Frontispiece // Ch. L. Montesquieu "On the essence of laws." Published by Vasily Sopikov. - Moscow, 1809 - 1814. Part 1. - XLVI, 310 pages.
— Picture 18. An Engraving ["Prayer"] // P. M. Zakharyin "A path to good behavior, or an Abbreviated instruction to the learning youth," Moscow: The printing house of A. Reshetnikov, 1796. VI, 1-64, 69-104 pages.
— Picture 19. The illumination of the St. Petersburg Academy of Sciences, presented on September 06, 1750: Prosperity pours the flowers and fruits on the free sciences and shows those practicing in these sciences a new way to zealous diligence about them. Moreover, it protects them with the name of Her Imperial Majesty: [print] / G. I. Sokolov under the Academy of Sciences and Art. - [St. Petersburg, 1750]. - 1 p.
— Picture 20. Action 1 of the wick fire of the entertainment lights, presented at the end of the wedding celebration of their imperial highnesses, in St. Petersburg, in October 1773: Russia before the altar in the temple of bliss erected by the Great Catherine begs heaven for the continuation of its prosperity. As a result of the prayer heard, the good geniuses fly down, wearing the signs of a marriage union, two flaming hearts, and the fiery marriage candles / Gravé par S. M. Roth; I. de Stehlin inv [eni] t; performance by M. Nemov. – SPb. 1773. - 1 page.
— Picture 21. Emperor Alexander I. An engraving from a portrait painted by Veil in 1802 // "The regicide on March 11, 1801: the notes of participants and

contemporaries (Sablukov, Count Bennigsen, Count Langeron, Fonvizin, Princess Lieven, Prince Czartoryski, Baron Geyking, Kotzebue)": With 17 portraits, views, and plans. - St. Petersburg: Edited by A. S. Suvorin, 1907. - XLVIII, 375, [4] p., [17] p. Color processing by A. Makarov.

— Picture 22. Nikolai Semenovich Mordvinov (1754-1845). A portrait of an unknown artist of the 1920s. The XIX century. From open sources.
— Picture 23. Johann August von Stark (Shtark in the Russian sources) (1741-1816). Painting by a German artist. From open sources.
— Picture 24. A vignette // I. A. Stark (Shtark in the Russian sources) "An Apology, or Defense of the Order of the Free Stones / Written by a Brother ****, a member of the Scottish ** Lodge, in P **"; Translated from German into Russian by I. P. Turgenev. - M.: The printing house of Lopukhin, 1784. - 224 pages.
— Picture 25. A sign of the Lodge "To Three Globes." Prussia. The mid-18th century. Published by M. A. Dobrovolskaya // The Wisdom of Astrea: The Monuments of the Freemasonry of the 18th – the first third of the 19th centuries in the Hermitage collection: an Exhibition Catalog / The State Hermitage - St. Petersburg: The Publishing House of the State Hermitage Museum, 2013. - 480 p.: ill. Page 238.
— Picture 26. A vignette // B. Y. Schleiss von Levenfeld "The influence of the true Freemasonry on the 'common good' of states, discovered and proven from the true purpose of its original establishment (foundation)" / Karl Hubert Lobreich von Plumenek. Written at the end of the 18th century in refutation of the works of Yakov Moser "On the tolerance of Freemasonry communities, especially, regarding the Peace of Westphalia." Translated from the second edition in German, printed in Amsterdam in 1779. - Moscow: Printed in the University Printing House, 1816. - [4], VIII, 211, [3] p.
— Picture 27. A sign of the secretary of the lodge with the image of a goose feather on the plate. Russia. The first quarter of the 19th century. Published by I. N. Ukhanova // The Wisdom of Astrea: The Monuments of the Freemasonry of the 18th – the first third of the 19th centuries in the Hermitage Collection: an Exhibition Catalog / The State Hermitage - St. Petersburg: The Publishing House of the State Hermitage Museum, 2013. - 480 p.: ill. Page 167.
— Picture 28. A sign of the Chair Master of one of the Degrees of St. Andrew's Freemasonry. Russia. The XVIII century. Published by L. I. Dobrovolskaya // The Wisdom of Astrea: The Monuments of the Freemasonry of the 18th – the first third of the 19th centuries in the Hermitage Collection: an Exhibition Catalog / The State Hermitage - St. Petersburg: The Publishing House of the State Hermitage Museum, 2013. - 480 p.: ill. Page 172.
— Picture 29. An image of the coat of arms of the Melissino family // P. P. Winkler "The Russian Heraldry: The History and Description of the Russian coats of arms,

depicting all the coats of arms of the nobles, introduced in the general armorial of All-Russian imp." Issue 2. 1894, page 89.

— Picture 30. An illustration by I. Perelyvkin / | M. Kheraskov's creations: Corrected and supplemented again. Part 12: [NumaPompilius or Prosperous Rome]. – The 3rd edition. - 1803. Page I.
— Picture 31. A chest strap of one of the Rosicrucian Degrees. Russia. The end of the 18th century. Silk, gimp, sequins; gold and silver embroidery. Published by Yu. V. Plotnikova // The Wisdom of Astrea: The Monuments of the Freemasonry of the 18th – the first third of the 19th centuries in the Hermitage Collection: an Exhibition Catalog / The State Hermitage - St. Petersburg: The Publishing House of the State Hermitage Museum, 2013. - 480 p.: ill. Page 212.
— Picture 32. An image of the coat of arms of the Karamzin family // P. P. Winkler "The Russian Heraldry: The History and Description of the Russian coats of arms, depicting all the coats of arms of the nobles, introduced in the general armorial of All-Russian imp." Issue 3. 1894, page 133.
— Picture 33. An image of the Motto of the book. Lopukhin // P. P. Winkler "The Russian Heraldry: The History and Description of the Russian coats of arms, depicting all the coats of arms of the nobles, introduced in the general armorial of All-Russian imp." Issue 3.1894, p. 169.
— Picture 34. A sign of the Lodge of the Manna Seekers. Russia. Moscow. The beginning of the 19th century. Bronze, silk; sewing, chasing, gilding, mounting. Published by L. I. Dobrovolskoy // The Wisdom of Astrea: The Monuments of the Freemasonry of the 18th – the first third of the 19th centuries in the Hermitage Collection: An Exhibition Catalog / The State Hermitage - St. Petersburg: The Publishing House of the State Hermitage Museum, 2013. - 480 p.: ill. Page 270.
— Picture 35. An image of the coat of arms of the Pozdeev family // P. P. Winkler "The Russian Heraldry: The History and Description of the Russian coats of arms, depicting all the coats of arms of the nobles, introduced in the general armorial of All-Russian imp." Issue 1. 1892, page 46.
— Picture 36. An image of the coat of arms of the Chebotarev family // P. P. Winkler "The Russian Heraldry: The History and Description of the Russian coats of arms, depicting all the coats of arms of the nobles, introduced in the general armorial of All-Russian imp." Issue 3. 1894, page 128.
— Picture 37. An image of the coat of arms of the Novosiltsev family // P. P. Winkler "The Russian Heraldry: The History and Description of the Russian coats of arms, depicting all the coats of arms of the nobles, introduced in the general armorial of All-Russian imp." Issue 3. 1894, page 143.
— Picture 38. An image of the coat of arms of the Czartorisk family // P. P. Winkler "The Russian Heraldry: The History and Description of the Russian coats of arms,

depicting all the coats of arms of the nobles, introduced in the general armorial of All-Russian imp." Issue 2. 1894, p. 50.

— Picture 39. A Sign of the Lodge of the United Friends. Russia. St. Petersburg. The beginning of the 19th century. Bronze, stamping, gilding, engraving. The triangle contains two hands connected in a handshake. Published by L. I. Dobrovolskoy // The Wisdom of Astrea: The Monuments of the Freemasonry of the 18th – the first third of the 19th centuries in the Hermitage Collection: An Exhibition Catalog / The State Hermitage - St. Petersburg: The Publishing House of the State Hermitage Museum, 2013. - 480 p.: ill. Page 265.

— Picture 40. A sign of the lodge of the Three Virtues. Russia. The beginning of the 19th century. Brass, silk; casting, chasing. The sign contains a crossed anchor, a cross, and a sword. Published by I. N. Ukhanova // The Wisdom of Astrea: The Monuments of the Freemasonry of the 18th – the first third of the 19th centuries in the Hermitage Collection: An Exhibition Catalog / The State Hermitage - St. Petersburg: The Publishing House of the State Hermitage Museum, 2013. - 480 p.: ill. Page 282.

FRED Y. FORD
ALEXEY V. DMITRIEV

As a manuscript

The Theory of the "Common Good" and Russian Freemasonry in the Second Half of the 18th Century – the First Quarter of the 19th Century

Annex

2021

Table Of Contents

Chapter I – The Generations of Great-Master Freemasons in the Russian Empire of the 18th century and some conclusions 310

Chapter II – I. Iabalone shells. Melissino's Denunciation 374

Chapter III – A table of the chronology of the works of authors, testifying to the attitude toward the "common good" and membership in Masonic Lodges. 376

Conclusions 396

A review of the book "The Theory of the 'Common Good' and Russian Freemasonry in the Second Half of the 18th Century – the First Quarter of the 19th Century"

Looking for any magical means to jump into ancient times and escape from day-to-day reality? Plunging deep into the breathtaking pages of books about the glorious past is a wonderful method to go about it. Considering history in all respects from different angles, it could be concluded that it is quite messy and complex, however, a large amount of it is not ugly at all, and skilled specialists can successfully process it. The more the reader knows about it, the more the disorder makes sense, both in an up-to-date and historical setting. In Fred Ford and Alexey Dmitriev's book *The Theory of the 'Common Good' and Russian Freemasonry in the Second Half of the 18th Century – the First Quarter of the 19th Century,* the authors eloquently cover the best historical themes in detail: Freemasonry as a very Old Secret mystical Organization and everything that has surrounded it (its origin, Freemasons, the emergence of Masonic Lodges, the processes running inside various Masonic Lodges, the participation of Masonic Lodges in the life of the States, etc.). This book about Freemasonry gave me a piece of extensive knowledge of history and historical events cloaked in mystery. Of course, they say that tastes differ, and that is true. For example, some people consider it advantageous to be born and raised in New York. Others probably have a very different opinion about being born and raised in Paris. Nevertheless, nearly everyone in the world has heard of Freemasonry and Freemasons, so this was a very interesting historical topic to extensively read about.

The authors of the book carefully and systematically described many events regarding Freemasonry in Russia in this historical book using research from the second half of the 18th century and the very beginning of the 19th century. In addition, this historical research embraced and acknowledged the "common good" that profoundly influenced many people in the past and in current times continues to influence many people, Also, many photos throughout the book depicted famous Masonic Signs and Relics.

Many aspects were thoroughly researched in the book: the national history, the history of philosophy, the state and law, and the Russian political and legal doctrines of that time. Many issues were revealed from a legal science point of view, including the state and legal ideas of Russian Freemasons. After reading the book, it is clear that the research used was gained from many genuine Russian and foreign archives, including secret documents.

An enormous scientific work was comprehensively fulfilled when creating this historical book, disclosing many unknown facts and events connected with Freemasonry in Russia and Russian Freemasons. It was demonstrated throughout the book that European Freemasonry (German, French, and British) came to Russia and was firmly rooted there, deeply influencing Russian high society, comprising Russian Sovereigns, and the state as a whole. The research showed the socio-political and philosophical views Of Russian Freemasons and gave a historical analysis of the normative documents of Freemasons. The book demonstrated the process of reforming Russian Freemasonry at the very beginning of the 19th century. The problem of the legalization of Freemasonry and the theme of enlightened absolutism in Russia was mentioned as well. Many biographical sources and collections of various historical materials were used in the book. The authors identified and analyzed the basic state and legal ideas of Russian Freemasons in correlation with the theory of the "common good."

The study of Freemasonry as an established organization and having a charter with minutes of meetings was thoroughly presented in the work. It should also be noted that this undoubtedly merited the study. The doctrine of the "common good" was examined in the book in the form of a theory that is better known to many western readers as utilitarianism. l. Bentham, D Locke, S. Montesquieu, C, Beccaria, and other famous scientists successfully developed the doctrine of utilitarianism. In many sections of the book, the authors validated that the abovementioned doctrine was comprehensively developed in Russia. Russian Freemasons were the carriers of this doctrine, receiving and developing Western ideas all over Russia. Following some leading European scientists, Russian Monarchs, Russian scientists, and Russian Freemasons defined the "common good" as common and individual happiness. In effect. it is very important to know that the interests of any individual were not excluded or suppressed in the Russian theory of the "common good." That was a quite progressive idea at that time. In addition, the terms and semantic concepts of the theory ("the common good," "the welfare of all and everyone," etc.) spread to the sphere of education and politics in the Russian Empire, becoming widespread throughout Russia. It was evidenced in the research that

Russian Freemasons used the term "common good" from the 1750s to 1822.

At the same time, unfortunately, no comparative analysis of utilitarianism and the theory of the "common good" (widespread in Russia) was carried out in the work. It is a well-known fact that freedom was an integral part of utilitarianism. Nevertheless, freedom was not considered in the book as well. Overall, demonstrated the theory of the "common good" in Russia (shown by the points of view of Russian Emperors and Russian Freemasons) which was a completely different view of the terms and phenomena that were potentially unknown in the United States at that time.

In conclusion, I would highly recommend this book to learn more about an unknown part of the history of Russia and Russian Freemasonry, uncovering the mystic mist of Freemasonry as a whole. I am confident that it would interest many categories of readers: Freemasons, various types of scholars and researchers, students involved in studying history, and people who are interested in learning about history and enjoy mysteries.

Amy Walker Miller, Ed.D.

Assistant Director to the Provost's Office
almiller@tntech.edu
(931) 372-3659
Tennessee Tech University
Derryberry Hall 434
1 William L Jones Dr Cookeville, TN 38505

Chapter I

The Generations of Great-Master Freemasons in the Russian Empire of the 18th century and some conclusions

To understand the periodicity of the development of the state and legal ideas of Russian Freemasons, those that can be considered as "Great Masters" (considering the duration and degree of participation in Masonic Lodges) were singled out from the total number of Russian Freemasons and the Freemasons that carried out work on the territory of the Russian Empire and cannot be classified as Russian Freemasons. The degree of participation of these "Great Masters" in the formation of Russian political and legal thought was analyzed. The generations of the membership of a certain person in Masonic Lodges (the 1st generation - membership in Masonic Lodges in the 1750-1760s, the 2nd generation - in the 1770-1780s, the 3rd generation - 1790-1800s, and the 4th generation - 1810-1820s[1]) were singled out. Some knowledge of generations, together with the imposition of the chronology of generations on the chronology of Russian history (the reign of the Imperial Family, wars, uprisings, etc.), allowed us to discuss succession or, conversely, the difference or variety of ideologies, including the state-legal world views. *The list was structured by generations (from the 1st generation to the 2nd generation). Freemasons within each generation were structured alphabetically. The Freemasons whose literary heritage could not be found (V. I. Bibikov, V. A. Vsevolozhsky, P. I. Golenishchev-Kutuzov, and O. G. K. Hoven) were included in the separate list.*

Sources:

1. Russian Freemasons. 1721-2019. Biographical Dictionary. Century XVIII. Volume I / A. I. Serkov, M.: Ganga, 2019 - 710 p. (in the table - Vol. 1).
2. Russian Freemasons. 1721-2019. Biographical Dictionary. Century XVIII. Volume II / A. I. Serkov, M.: Ganga, 2019 - 748 p. (in the table - Vol. 2).
3. Russian Freemasons. 1721-2019. Biographical Dictionary. Century XVIII. Volume III / A. I. Serkov, M.: Ganga, 2019 - 320 p. (in the table - Vol. 3).
4. A. I. Serkov "Russian Freemasonry." 1731-2000: Encyclopedic Dictionary. / A. I. Serkov. - M.: ROSSPEN, 2001. - 1222 p. (in the table - Serkov, 2001).
5. L. Mukhovitskaya "Trubetskoy. Aristocrats in spirit." - M.: Entrast Trading, 2015. - 256 p. (in the table - Mukhovitskaya, 2015).
6. K. G. Geiking "The days of Emperor Paul: Notes of Courland nobleman": (translated from German) / [Barron Carl Heinrich Geiking]. - St. Petersburg: F. I. Bulgakov, 1907. - 70 p. (in the table - Geiking, 1907).
7. V. Yu. Zakharov "The Russian constitutionalism of the 2nd half of the 18th – the 1st quarter of the 19th centuries in the context of the development of Western European legal thought": A thesis of a Ph.D. in Historical Sciences: 07.00.02. Moscow, 2010. - 1142 p. (in the table - Zakharov, 2010)
8. Yu. E. Kondakov "Esoteric movement in Russia at the end of the 18th - the first half of the 19th centuries." – M.: Club Castalia. 2018. - 670 p. (in the table - Kondakov, 2018).

[1]The 3rd and 4th generations were not included in this application due to the limited text size. However, there are some indications of the 3rd and 4th generations if a Freemason belonged to the 3rd and 4th generations.

Abbreviations:
"P." – Petersburg (St. Petersburg)
"M." - Moscow
"PGL" – The Provincial Grand Lodge in St. Petersburg
"GEPL" - The Grand English Provincial Lodge in St. Petersburg

Note:

The use of the phrase "Great Master" only means that, according to our classification, considering the time of visiting Masonic meetings in the lodges, the performance of duties in Masonic Lodges can be called a "Great Master." The name "Great Masters" is not identical to the name of the Masonic positions of the XVIII century. The "Great Master" under this classification should not be confused with the position of a "Great Master" used to perform duties in the Masonic Lodge Unions. The use of term "length of service" refers to the length of time that a person has attended Masonic Lodges, meetings, and participation in rituals. The selection of "Great Masters" was made by the following criteria: founding new lodges, holding some officer positions in the lodge, having membership in the leading lodges (Chapters), creating new Masonic Systems, the duration of membership in Masonic Lodges in the degree of Master and above. Compliance with two or more criteria allowed a Freemason to be included in the list of "Great Masters."

The 1st generation - 1750-1769 (before the palace coup, the assassination of Peter III, and the accession of Catherine II)

Full name, years of life, place of birth (if any)	**Rank, positions, origin**	**The number of lodges according to the study of A. I. Serkov (the first number in the lines), the name of the lodges, who was listed and when**	**Patronage**	**Relatives**	**Influence on**	**Sources**
Ivan Nikitich Boltin January 12, 1735, village Zhdamirovo, Nizhny Novgorod Province - October 6 [17], 1792	A Major-General, a Prosecutor, writer, Historian, Archivist, from the nobility, his father was a Steward (Stolnik), he was a young Officer at the time of joining the Freemasons, and he was a Prime Major when being in Freemasonry. *He became a General and Prosecutor after leaving the Masonic Lodges.*	86 The Chapter of the Templar System in P., 1760s, a Great Master of the Templar Chapter. 89 The Lodge of 1756 in P., 1756-1759. 97 The PGL in P., a Great Rhetorician of Russian in 1779. 107 The Phoenix Chapter in P., a Chapter Secretary in 1779. *A Great Master, the length of service: 1756-1779 - 24 years (the 1st and the 2nd generations), became a Freemason at 21, stopped participating in lodges at 44, the main works were*	I. P. Yelagin, A. I. Musin-Pushkin			Vol. 1. P. 197-199. Vol. 3. P. 113, 121, 146, 200.

		written after 1780, when he began to serve under G.A. Potemkin and, apparently, became inactive in the lodges, but continued to be friends with Freemasons and share Masonic ideas – the length of service, positions in Freemasonry, Masonic connections cannot be suddenly forgotten.				

An opinion of I. N. Boltin, on the state and legal issues, can be considered representative of all Russian Freemasonry of the 18th century as he had a 24-year membership in Masonic Lodges, collaborated with other well-known Freemasons (I. P. Yelagin, A. I. Musin-Pushkin, and M. M. Shcherbatov), held the positions of a Great Rhetorician, Secretary of the Chapter - the highest positions in Masonic Lodges and in the governing bodies of Masonic Lodges. He published "Pravda Russkaya" together with I. P. Yelagin and A. I. Musin-Pushkin, providing it with his comments. A huge influence on I. N. Boltin was provided by the works of V. N. Tatishchev (recognizing him as his teacher[1]) and M. V. Lomonosov. I. N. Boltin was an adherent of the "common good" and a patriot of Russia. This was reflected in his works (for example, in "Russian Truth or the Laws of the Grand Dukes Yaroslav Vladimirovich and Vladimir Vsevolodovich Monomakh[2]," in "Major General Boltin's response to the letter of Prince Shcherbatov, a writer of Russian history"[3]).

---

[1]The Brilliant Age of Catherine II. The second half of the 18th century: a biographical guide: in 4 Parts, Part 4 / Compiled by V. N. Nikulin. - Kaliningrad: The Publishing House of the Russian State University. I. Kant, 2010. - 196 p. Page 26.

[2]I. N. Boltin "Russian Truth or the Laws of the Grand Dukes Yaroslav Vladimirovich and Vladimir Vsevolodovich Monomakh: With the application of the ancient adverbs and syllables to those in common use today, and with an explanation of words and names that became obsolete" / Published by lovers of national history. - [St. Petersburg]: The printing House of the Saint Ruler of Synod, 1792. - [2], VIII, [13], 100, XVI p.

[3]I. N. Boltin "Major General Boltin's response to a letter from Prince Shcherbatov, a writer of Russian history." - St. Petersburg: The Printing House of the Mining School, [17]89. - 183 p.

Yakov Alexandrovich Bruce (1732 - November 30 (December 11), 1791)	A Governor-General, a Commander-in-Chief, from an ancient Scottish noble clan, *he became a Governor-General of St. Petersburg (1786-1791) and, at the same time, a Commander-in-Chief in Moscow (1784-1786) after leaving the Masonic Lodges, he received patronage from his wife - a friend of Catherine II.*	86 The Chapter of the Templar System in P., a member of the Chapter of the Petropolitanum (St. Petersburg Chapter of Strict Observation) in 1765-1768. 100 A member of the Perfect Union (Consent) in P., visitor in 1771-1772. 107 The Chapter of the Phoenix in P., 1778-1783, a member of the Chapter. *A Great Master,* length of service 1765-1783 - 29 years (the 1st and the 2nd generations), entered Freemasonry at 33, became inactive - at 51.	Closed the Printing House of N. I. Novikov in the second half of the 1780s	Spouse: Praskovya, sister of Field Marshal P.A. Rumyantsev and wife of Yu. N. Trubetskoy, a friend of Catherine II	Closed the printing house of N. I. Novikov in the second half of the 1780s.	Vol. 1. P. 218-220. Vol. 3. P. 114, 153, 200.

An opinion of Ya. A. Bruce, on the state and legal issues, can be considered representative of all Russian Freemasonry of the 18th century as he had 29 years of membership in Masonic Lodges, wife Praskovya was a sister of the famous Freemason P. A. Rumyantsev and the wife of another Freemason Yu. N. Trubetskoy was a member of the governing bodies of Masonic Lodges, which also included I. N. Boltin (86, 107). He was a supporter of government constitutionalism as he was associated with the Imperial Family, receiving different ranks and positions from the Empress.

Roman Illario novich Vorontsov (1717-1783)	A Chairman of the Code Commission for drawing up a New Code, a Senator, a compiler of the noble program freedom of orders from cultivators, from the family of a Privy Councilor, a Senator, a Real Chamberlain (1746), a General-in-Chief (1761), Senator (1760), a Governor-General of Vladimir, Penza, and Tambov (1778-1783), *was already a Real Chamberlain upon joining Freemasonry.*	14 The Lodge of "P. I. Berg" in Vladimir, probably a member of the lodge. 55 The Lodge of Equality in M. and P., a candidate for the post of a Great Master on 07.06.1775. 73 GEPL in P., a Great Provincial Local Master in 1772-1775. 89 The Masonic Lodge of 1756 in P., 1756-1759, a Chair Master, a Granmetr. 105 The Lodge of Urania in P., a visitor on 02.07.1775 and 02.14.1775, an Honorary Member from 03.14.1775, a member of the 4th Degree in 1783. *A Great Master, length of service: 1756-1783 - 28 years (the 1st and the 2nd generations), he was devoted to Freemasonry until his death.*				Vol. 1. P. 310-311. Vol. 3. P. 22, 5, 82, 121, 169.

An opinion of R. I. Vorontsov, on the state and legal issues, can be considered representative of all Russian Freemasonry of the 18th century as he had a 28-year membership in Masonic Lodges, was the Head of Masonic Lodges, had high degrees, was a supporter of government constitutionalism as he was in solidarity with the ideology of Peter III, Catherine II on granting guarantees of liberty to the Nobles and mitigation of the morals of the peasants. There are few printed works left, so a thorough study of his biography and written heritage can be neglected or dealt with later.

Theodor Gottlieb Gippel (Senior) January 31, 1741, Gerdauen, East Prussia - April 23, 1796, Königsberg, East Prussia	A Privy Councilor, *graduated from the Faculty of Law of the University of Königsberg, a Lawyer, Legal Adviser, Judge, Police Chief,* philosopher, *an author of the Prussian General Land Law, wrote many books on jurisprudence, anti-corruption fighter, a son of a rural schoolteacher. German origin, mother tongue – German.*	137 Foreign lodges, consecrated on 01.28.1762 in the lodge of *the Three Crowns in Königsberg. An Orator from 01.31.1762, a Chair Master from 04.08.1768, a member of Strict Obedience, Clericat, Cleric (a member of the 6th Degree), an Honorary Member of some lodges from October 21, 1764, a member of the Order of the Golden-Pink Cross from May 1781, holding some administrative posts there. A Great Master, length of service from 1762 to 1781 - 30 years (the 1st and the 2nd generations), became a Freemason at the age of 21, and was in contact with Russian lodges only from 1781.*				Vol. 1. P. 378 - 380. Vol. 3. P. 272.

An opinion of T. G. Gippel on the state-legal issues cannot be considered representative of all Russian Freemasonry of the 18th century, although he had a 30-year membership in Masonic Lodges, held positions in Masonic Lodges, and had high degrees. He accepted the state-legal ideas of German Freemasons. His influence on the state-legal ideas of Russian Freemasons was minimal. Most likely, he represented a typical German Legal School. He was known in Königsberg and Prussia but not in St. Petersburg and Moscow.

Johann-Albrecht Korf (1697-1766)	A Full Privy Councilor, an Envoy, a bibliophile, an author of the defensive alliance of the northern states. *German origin, mother tongue – German.*		137 Foreign lodges, consecrated in the lodge of St. Martin in Copenhagen in December 1743 (Munnich was a Chair Master there). Raised to the 3rd Degree in this lodge. 03.05.1744. Following this, the lodge worked in his house, and his employees and servants were accepted into the lodge as Servant Brothers. *An Honorable Master of the Lodge from 06/29/1746 to 07/06/1746. In 1749 he became one of the founders of the Grand Provincial Lodge of Denmark and Norway (he served as the Great Local Provincial Master there).* His Order Name was “Equesde Cocagne.” He was a member of the “Scottish” Lodge in Copenhagen in 1753. *A Great Master, length of service; 1743-1753 - 11 years (the 1st generation), he became a Freemason at 46.*	He was an acquaintance of N. I. Panin			Vol. 1. P. 646 - 647. Vol. 3. P. 281.

An opinion of I. A. Korf cannot be considered representative of all Russian

Freemasonry of the 18th century on the state and legal issues, although he had 11 years of membership in Masonic Lodges, held senior positions in Masonic Lodges, and founded lodges in Denmark and Norway. He accepted the state-legal ideas of Danish and Swedish Freemasons. His influence on the state-legal ideas of Russian Freemasons was indirect through N. I. Panin.

Pyotr Petrovich Lefort (1719-1796)	A Major General, *studied at the law faculty of the un-ty in Halle*, a participant in the palace coup, he was appointed the 2nd Ambassador to Beijing in 1762.	13 The Old Scottish Lodge in Vyshnevets, 1742, a founding member of the lodge (A. I. Serkov does not indicate his middle name). 35a The Adoptive Lodge in Mitava, a member of the lodge in 1782. 137 He founded the lodge of the Three Brothers in Warsaw together with A. Mokronovsky in 1744. *A Great Master, length of service: 1742-1782 - 41 years (the 1st and the 2nd generations).*				Vol. 2. P. 41. Vol. 3. P. 21, 40, 284.

An opinion of P. P. Lefort on the state-legal issues cannot be considered representative of all Russian Freemasonry of the 18th century, although he had 41 years of membership in Masonic Lodges, founded some lodges in Vishnevets, Warsaw, and Mitau. He accepted the state-legal ideas of German Freemasons. His influence on the state-legal ideas of Russian Freemasons was minimal.

Bernhard Johann Meyer (1745-1805)	*A Lawyer, studied law in Jena and Leipzig*, from a merchant family. *German origin, mother tongue – German.*	99a The Andrey Lodge of St. George's Lodge in P., a Deputy Chief Meister in 1780 and 1784, a Freemason of the 8th and 9th Degrees. 107 *The Phoenix Chapter in P., a Diploma of the 8th Degree of "The Secret Brother of Salomon" received on 04/12/1779.* Then he became a missing member of the Phoenix Chapter. 115 The Three Pole Axes in Revel, *a founding member of the lodge in 1778* (he unsuccessfully ran for joining the Revel Lodge of Isis on 09.28.1776), *a Chair Master from 1779 to 1785.* 137 Foreign lodges, dedicated on the recommendation of Teden in the Lodge of Minerva to the Caliper (Minerva to The Three Palm Trees from 1766) in Leipzig. Entered the VII Province of the System of Strict Obedience and *the Prefecture in Leipzig* under the Order Name "Bernardus Armigera Minerva." *A Great Master, length of service: 1766-1784 - 19 years (the 1st and the 2nd generations).*				Vol. 2. P. 95-96. Vol. 3. P. 152, 201, 223, 286.

An opinion of B. J. Meyer cannot be considered representative of all Russian Freemasonry of the 18th century on the state and legal issues, although he had 19 years of membership in Masonic Lodges, founded lodges in Revel, held positions in Masonic Lodges and their governing bodies, and accepted the state-legal ideas of German Freemasons. His influence on the state-legal ideas of Russian Freemasons was minimal.

Pyotr Ivanovich Melissino (1726 - December 26, 1797)	A Lieutenant General, a Chief of Artillery, a Director of the Cadet Corps, from a noble Greek clan. *He entered Freemasonry with the rank of Major (1759), became a Chief of Artillery after closing his lodges on behalf of Catherine II.*	He was dedicated by Kurakin. Also, he was a creator of the New System of 4 Higher Degrees. 31 The Lodge of Minerva in Kremenchug and Nemirov, not on the list. 73 GEPL in P., the 1st Grand Overseer in 1776-1779, scheduled for Provincial Chapter in September 1776, a Scottish Master. 89 A 1956 Lodge in P., Freemasons and Great Masters in 1756-1759, a member of the lodge. 90 The Lodge of Silence (Modesty) in P., from 1768, a founding member of the lodge, a Chair Master in 1770-1777 and 1781, a Local Master, a member of the lodge of the 6th Degree in 1786-1787. He signed the constitution of the Yelagin-Zinnendorf Union on behalf of the lodge. 105 The Lodge of Urania in P. He attended the lodge from 04.12.1774, an Honorary Member of the lodge. 134 The Lodge of Mars in Yassy, he was a member of the lodge in 1773, a Chair Master in December 1773-1774. *A Great Master, length of service: 1759-1787 - 29 years (the 1st and the 2nd generations).*				Vol. 2. P. 102-103. Vol. 3 P. 83, 122, 129, 183, 260.

An opinion of P.I. Melissino, on the state and legal issues, can be considered representative of all Russian Freemasonry of the 18th century as he had a 29-year membership in Masonic Lodges, was the Head of Masonic Lodges, created a new system, founded a Lodge of Silence, had high degrees, was a supporter of government constitutionalism because he was in solidarity with the policy and ideology of Catherine II according to his works (see, for example, "The description of fireworks at the end of the celebration in case of a peace concluded between Her Imperial Majesty Catherine II ... and His Majesty Gustav the Third, King of Sweden"[1]).

Alexey Semyonovich Musin-Pushkin (1730-1817)	A Full Privy Councilor, Minister, Envoy, from the family of a Court Adviser, he lived abroad at the Russian Embassies in European countries from 1765.	137 Foreign lodges, dedicated in Hamburg in 1765. He was a member of the Strict Surveillance Lodge in Hamburg in 1766. A member of the Tempelburg chapter. His Order Name was "Eq. Ab Elephante" ("Elephant Knight"). Founded a colony of the Templars among the Germans in Saratov. *A Great Master, length of service: 1765-1766 - 2 years (the 1st generation).*				Vol. 2. P. 151-152. Vol. 3. P. 289.

An opinion of A.S. Musin-Pushkin, on the state and legal issues, cannot be considered representative of all Russian Freemasonry of the 18th century as he had a 2-year membership in Masonic Lodges, although he founded the Templar Colony in Saratov, held positions in the governing bodies of Masonic Lodges. His influence on the state-legal ideas of Russian Freemasons was minimal.

[1]P. I. Melissino "The description of fireworks at the end of the celebration in case of a peace concluded between Her Imperial Majesty Catherine II ... and His Majesty Gustav the Third, King of Sweden": [Text]: Presented in St. Petersburg on the Tsaritsyn Meadow on September 1790. - St. Petersburg: Printed by I. K. Shnor, 1790. - [10] p.

Stepan Vasilyevich Perfilyev (1734-1793)	A Lieutenant General, a Deputy of the Commission for drafting up a New Code, St. Petersburg Governor (September 22, 1773 - September 10, 1774).	73 GEPL in P., a Great Provincial Keeper of Treasure (Treasurer) from 12/18/1773 to 1774. 89 The Lodge of 1756 in P. 1756-1759, a member of the lodge. 90 The Lodge of Silence (Modesty), a 6th-Degree member of the lodge in 1786-1787. 95 The Prefecture of M. in P., a member in 1783, a Vice Prefect in 1789. 100 The Lodge of the Perfect Union (Consent), a member or a visitor of the lodge in 1771-1772. 107 The Phoenix Chapter in P., recommended by N. I. Novikov in February 1783 as a member of the Chapter, became a member, he was allowed by the Vicariate to make him a Pro-Prefect of the Chapter in August 1783. *A Great Master, length of service: 1756-1789 - 35 years (the 1st and 2nd generations).*	A friend of A. I. Meshchersky and G. R. Derzhavin			Vol. 2. P. 263 - 264. Vol. 3. P. 84, 122, 131, 146, 155, 202.

An opinion of S.V. Perfilyev, on the state and legal issues, can be considered representative of all Russian Freemasonry of the 18th century as he had a 35-year membership in Masonic Lodges, was the Head of Masonic Lodges (a Vice-Prefect), and had high degrees. However, the written heritage of S. V. Perfilyev is unknown to the public. Therefore, considering the time for biographical and literary analysis, his works can be neglected or dealt with later.

Ivan Karlovich Reichel (1729-1791)	A Councilor of State, from the family of a Major, graduated from the University of Göttingen. A Director of Sciences in the Land Gentry Cadet Corps until 1778. *German origin, mother tongue – German.*	*A founder of the Freemasonry System of 7 Degrees.* 73 GEPL in P., a Representative of the Revel Lodge of Isis from 09.28.1776, *a Scottish Master in September 1776*, scheduled to be a member of the Grand Provincial Lodge and the Provincial Chapter. 74 *The Lodge of Apollo in P., a founding member of the lodge from 1771*, a Chair Master in 1771-1773, a former Chair Master in 1775. 78 *The Lodge of Harpocrates in P. from 1773, a founding member of the lodge*, was absent in the 3rd Degree in 1775, a member of the lodge in 1776-1778. 88 The Chapter of Latona in P, an Honorary Member of the lodge in 1778. 113 *The Revel Lodge of Isis in Revel, 1773-1794, a founding member of the lodge* (this lodge was not indicated in the biography given by A. I. Serkov). 137 Foreign lodges,				Vol. 2. P. 354-355. Vol. 3 P. 84, 90, 108, 119, 216, 295.

		consecrated by General W. Kingsley in the English Lodge in the Allied Army and elevated to the 6th Degree, *a member of the Brunswick Chapter from 1762,* he was a member of a number of Brunswick Lohe in 1765-1767 (these organizations worked according to a System of Strict Surveillance), he worked under the leadership of Zinnendorf from September 1766, he broke with him because of Zinnendorf's monetary demands approximately in 1776, was absent in 3rd Degree at the Pilgrim Lodge in London 1785-1788. *A Great Master, length of service: 1762-1788 - 17 years (the 1st and the 2nd generations).*				

An opinion of I. K. Reichel, on the state and legal issues, can be considered representative of all Russian Freemasonry of the 18th century as he had 17 years of membership in Masonic Lodges, created a new Masonic System, was a founder and leader of Masonic Lodges, and had high degrees. However, his written heritage is inaccessible to Russian-speaking readers, and his views on the state and law are still terra incognito.

Alexander Sergeevich Stroganov (January 3 (14), 1733, Moscow - September 27 (October 9), 1811)	*A Full Privy Councilor of the 1st Grade,* Senator, studied at the universities of Geneva, Bologna, and Paris, from an old family of Russian merchants and manufacturers.	61 The Theoretical Degree in M., not in the lists. 88 The Chapter of Latona in P., received *an offer to become an Honorary Member of the Chapter* in 1783. 103 *The Lodge of Happy Agreement in P., a Local Master in 1762, his Order Name was "Mecenas," a Chair Master from 1765.* 107 The Phoenix Chapter in P., not listed 137 Foreign lodges, 08.27.1771 joined the Lodge of the Three Crowns in Königsberg, *became the founder of the Lodge "LesAmisReunis" (United Friends) in Paris in 1771 (12.24.1773), its member until 1778, in March 1775, at the founding of the Grand Orient of France, was a Deputy of the Lodge "La Parfait Egalite" in Besançon and all associated lodges in the Franche-Comte region. A Treasurer of the Chamber of Administration from the date of foundation on 06.21(26).1773, the 1st Expert from 07.20.1773 and in 1777, a Great Keeper of the Seal from 12.27.1773, the 1st Great Overseer and a member of the Commission for degrees in 1775, the 2nd Overseer of the Grand Orient of France from the end of 1777, the 2nd Guardian of St. Jean de la Candeur (Honest Hearts) in Paris from the day of foundation (03.21.1775), a member until 1779, then an Honorary Member until 1782. A member of the Adoptive Lodge of the same name in 1779, a member of the Neuf Sceurs (Nine Sisters)*	Mother - Sofya Kirillovna, a sister of S. K. Naryshkin, a relative of K. G. Razumovsky. A sister Maria - mother of N. N. Novosiltsev. The 1st Wife - Anna Mikhailovna Vorontsova, a daughter of the State Chancellor, a niece of R. I. Vorontsov, the 2nd wife – a daughter of P. N. Trubetskoy			Vol. 2. P. 487-490. Vol. 3. P. 120, 159, 299.

		Lodge in Paris in 1778-1783, a member of the Chapter of the United Friends in 1788. A Grand Master, length of service from 1762 to 1788 - 27 years (the 1st and the 2nd generations).				

An opinion of A. S. Stroganov, on the state and legal issues, cannot be considered representative of all Russian Freemasonry of the 18th century, although he had a 27-year membership in Masonic Lodges, held positions in Masonic Lodges, and founded some of them ("United Friends" in Paris), but his participation was limited in mainly by foreign lodges, chiefly in France. Considering the rejection of the influence of Republican France by Russian Freemasonry, the influence of A. S. Stroganov on the state-legal ideas of Russian Freemasons was minimal. It should be noted that A. S. Strogonov influenced Alexander I. and supported his republican and liberal ideas, but Alexander I practically did not give them any moving forward as the conservative wing of Russian Freemasonry had a greater influence on him[1].

Yuri Nikitich Trubetskoy (1736-1811)	A Full Privy Councilor, a Senator, a founding member of the Friendly Scientific Society from the clan of Princes.	45 The Chapter of the VIII Province in M., a Dean in 1782-1783, his Order Name was "Eques Georgi (Georgiuseques) afortitudine." 46 The Lodge of Harmony in Moscow, a member of the lodge from 1780 (according to other sources, he joined the lodge as an "Old Freemason" in 1780-1781). 61 A Theoretical Degree in M., adopted in the Theoretical Degree in 1782, accepted into the Internal Order of the Rosicrucians during the life of I. E. Schwartz, probably, in 1783, a member of the Haupt Directorate of the Theoretical Degree in fall 1788, his Order Name was "Neastes," then – "Repertus." 90 The Lodge of Silence" (Modesty), a member of the lodge of the 6th Degree in 1786-1787. 103 The Lodge of Happy Agreement in P., the 2nd Steward in 1762, his Order Name was	A friend - N. M. Karamzin, a close friend of N. I. Novikov and Schwartz.	Maternal brother - M. M. Kheraskov		Vol. 2. P. 550-551. Vol. 3. P. 48, 49, 69, 132, 159.

[1]See, for example, Minakov A. Yu. "'Right' Freemasonry and Russian conservatism in the first quarter of the 19th century" / A. Yu. Minakov; Voronezh State University // A Scientific Bulletin of BelSU. A Serial "History." Political Science. Economy. Informatics. - 2010. - # 13, issue 15. - Pages 123-130.

		"Alexander." *A Great Master, length of service: from 1762 to 1788 - 27 years (the 1st and the 2nd generations).*				

An opinion of Yu. N. Trubetskoy, on the state and legal issues, can be considered representative of all Russian Freemasonry of the 18th century as he had 27 years of membership in Masonic Lodges, held positions in Masonic Lodges (a Dean, Steward), and had high degrees. However, the works of Yu. N. Trubetskoy, according to which one could judge his political and legal views, is not known to the general public, and his contribution to the history of political and legal doctrines is a matter for the coming years.

Johann August Stark (1741-1816)	A Doctor of Theology, A Professor of Philosophy, from the family of a Lutheran Pastor. *German origin, mother tongue – German.*	A member of the Lodge of the Melissino System. 37 The Lodge of the Three Crowned Swords in Mitava was active in 1775-1794, a member of the lodge. 86 The Chapter of the Templar System in P., *President of the Chapter from 1765, his Order Name was "Archimedes ab Aquilafulva."* *107 The Chapter of Phoenix in P., a founding member of the lodge in 1768.* *107a Capitulum Clericorum Regularium in P., a member of the Chapter*, his Order Name was "Archimedes." 137 Foreign lodges, initiated in the French Military Lodge in Göttingen in 1761, *founded the Lodge of Zudendrei Lowen (Three Lions) in Wismar in February 1767, a founder of the Chapter of Clerics (Weak Observation) in Wismar in 1770 (1768)*, a visitor from 09.03.1769, a member of the Lodge of the Three Crowns in Königsberg from 1770, *the Head of the Chapter of Clerics, including Königsberg.* *A Great Master, length of service: 1765-1794 - 30 years (the 1st, the 2nd, and the 3rd generations).*				Vol. 2. P. 687-688. Vol. 3. P. 40, 115, 203, 204, 306.

An opinion of I. A. Stark, on the state and legal issues, can be considered representative of all Russian Freemasonry of the 18th century as he had a 30-year membership in Masonic Lodges, created several Chapters (Templars, Phoenix, and Clerics Chapters) in St. Petersburg,

Wismar, was the Head and a member of Masonic Lodges and Chapters, possessed high degrees, expressed his thoughts in numerous works on history, theology, philosophy, religious societies and Masonic Lodges (for example, I. A. Stark "The letters to a friend and testament to his son about the Order of St. K." [Text]: Translated from German. - St. Petersburg: Printed in the Marine Printing House, 1816. - [2], VIII, 224, [2] p.; J.A. Stark "An Apologia, or Defense of the Order of Freemasons" / Written by Brother ****, a member of the Scottish ** Lodge, in P **. Translated from German by I. P. Turgenev. - M.: The Printing House of I. Lopukhin, 1784. - 224 p.).

The 2nd generation - 1770s-1780s - the heyday of the reign of Catherine II, Voltairianism, faith in reason, as well as the time of the Russian-Turkish war in 1768-1774, peasant uprisings (Kizhi in 1769-1771; the Plague Riot in 1771, the Yaitski Rebellion in 1772, the peasant war led by E. I. Pugachev in 1773-1775), the Provincial Reform of 1775, the First Division of the Rzeczpospolita in 1775, the adoption of the Charter of the Deanery in 1782, the annexation of the Crimean Khanate in 1783, the Free Charter to Nobles and cities in 1785, the Russian-Turkish war of 1787-1791, the Russian-Swedish war of 1788-1790.

Fyodor Grigoryevich Bause (1752-1812)	*A Doctor of Law, a Professor of Law, a Dean of the Law Faculty of the Moscow University, studied at the Law Faculty of the University of Leipzig*, from the family of a Pastor. *German origin, mother tongue – German.*	61 A Theoretical Degree in M. in 1782-1786, a Rosicrucian, his Order Name was "Uberosus Edasth." 62 The Lodge of the Three Banners in M., received a certificate on 08.02.1783. 66 The Lodge of Eleusis in M, absent in the 4th Degree in 1784, German language. 74 The Lodge of Apollo in P, German language, in 3rd Degree in 1779, an Orator in 1779, the 2nd Guard in 1781. 99a The Lodge of the St. George in P., a member in the beginning of 1780s. 107 *The Chapter of the Phoenix in P., a Secretary of the Chapter in February 1779.* *A Great Master, length of service: from 1779 to 1786 - 8 years (the 2nd generation).*	No	No		Vol. 1. P. 130-132. Vol. 3. P. 63, 71, 77, 86, 200.

An opinion of F. G. Bauze, on the state and legal issues, can be considered representative of all Russian Freemasonry of the late 18th century, although he only had an 8-year membership in Masonic Lodges and held positions in Masonic Lodges and Chapters. The manuscripts of F. G. Bauze could be enough for several large volumes, but the Moscow fire of

1812 destroyed them, along with a collection of the ancient Russian manuscripts and books that were prepared by F. G. Bauze for publication. Many works on a variety of topics, from the field of political economy, the history of Russia, the history of diplomacy, Roman Law, numismatics, etc., were destroyed. He believed that "the business of the jurist is to take care of the health of the public body and all its parts, i.e., the state and its citizens[1]." V.A. Tomsinov noted that F. G. Bause was influenced by the works of the German jurist I. G. Gainection.

Ivan Vasilyevich Byober (1746-1820)	A Full Privy Councilor, a Freemasonry historian, a Director of the Public School and the 2nd Cadet Corps, from the family of a Chimneysweep. *German origin, mother tongue – German.*	*A member of the Order of the Illuminati (his Order Name was "Gregorius") from August 1783.* *74 The Lodge of Apollo in P., dedicated in 1776, the 1st and 2nd Guard in 1779, a Local Master from 11/12/1781.* *77 The Lodge of Charity to the Pelican in P., a Chair Master in 1780, an Honorary Member from 1781, the 4th class in 1783, the 3rd Degree in 1785.* *97 P.G.L. in P., a Great Secretary for German language in 1779-1780, participated in the Wilgelsbad Convention of 1782-1783.* *99 The Lodge of St. Alexander in P., a member of the 3rd Degree in 1784.* *99a The Lodge of St. George in P., the 2nd Guard in 1780.* *107 The Chapter of the Phoenix in P., the 2nd Guard in February 1779, a member of the Chapter in 1779-1781.* *115 The Lodge of the Three Pole Axes in Revel, a founding member of the lodge in 1778-1785.* *A Great Master, length of service: from 1776 to 1785 - 10 years (the 2nd generation).*	P. I. Melissino	Son-in-law E. A.Kushelev		Vol. 1. P. 130-132. Vol. 3. P. 86, 96, 146, 148, 151, 200, 222.

An opinion of I. V. Byober on the state-legal issues can be considered representative of all Russian Freemasonry at the end of the 18th century as he had a 10-year membership in Masonic Lodges, held positions in Masonic Lodges and Chapters, founded Masonic Lodges, and

[1]Tomsinov V.A. "Russian jurists of the XVIII - XX centuries. The essays on life and work.": In 2 volumes. Volume 1. - M.: Zertsalo, 2007. - 672 p. Pages 178-186.

participated in all-Masonic Conventions. However, his works are a bibliographic rarity. Many of them have not been translated into Russian. In this regard, his significance in the history of ideas remains hidden for the time being.

Alexey Ivanovich Vasilyev (1742-1807)	A Full Privy Councilor, a Senate Secretary, *graduated from the Junker School under the Senate with the study of jurisprudence, a compiler of the Finnish Laws of 1775,* the Minister of Finance, a Nobleman in the 3rd generation.	73 GEPL in P., a Treasurer in 1777, a Great Ceremonial Leader in 1778. 78 The Lodge of Harpocrates in P., a member in 1775, a Scottish Master. 88 The Chapter of Latona in P., an Honorary Member in 1778. *A Great Master, length of service: from 1775-1778 - 4 years (the 2nd generation).*			F. A. Golubtsov	Vol. 1. P. 251-254. Vol. 3. P. 82, 108, 117.

An opinion of A. V. Vasilyev, on the state and legal issues, cannot be considered representative of all Russian Freemasonry at the end of the 18th century as he had only 4 years of membership in Masonic Lodges, although he held the highest positions in Masonic Lodges. At the same time, A. I. Vasilyev was familiar with jurisprudence and was engaged in the codification of Financial Legislation and the disposition of the Mining Department. A study of the legislative acts, memorandums, and works that left the stamp of his intellectual work would be quite remarkable. These works correspond with the provisions of government constitutionalism and the Masonic Doctrine. So, some information from them can be cited in this work.

Gavriil Petrovich Gagarin (1745-1808)	A Senator, *a Chief Prosecutor,* educated at home, a member of the Friendly Scientific Society, a Minister, a member of the Indispensable and State Council, *a member of the Commission of Laws,* from an ancient family of the Starodubskiy branch of Rurikovich.	41 The Lodge of Aspis in M., a Chair Master in 1780. 46 The Lodge of Harmony in M., an Honorary Member. 55 The Lodge of Equality in M. and P., a Chair Master in 1775-1777, a member of the 7th Degree of English Freemasonry. 59 The Lodge of Sphinx in M., a Chair Master from 1783. 60 The Lodge of Talii in M. and Polotsk, a visitor on 07.18.1775. 73 GEPL in P., the 2nd Guard in 1777. 86 The Chapter of the Templar System in P., a member of the Chapter of Strict Supervision between 1760 and 1770. 97 The PGL in Petrograd, a Great National (Provincial) Master in 1779-1780 (from 1778), moved to Moscow in 1781, the work of his lodge was suspended. 106 The Lodge of Phoenix in P., initiated into Freemasonry by A. B. Kurakin, a founding member of the lodge, a Chair Master in 1777-1779, signed the constitution of the Yelagin-Zinnendorf Union on behalf of the lodge. 107 The Chapter of Phoenix in P., an Administrator of the Chapter of Phoenix, a Great Prefect of the Chapter from 1778, a Great National Master (Grand Master) in 1779, a member in 1781. 137 Foreign lodges, he was accepted to the highest degrees of the Swedish Masonic System together with A. B. Kurakin in Stockholm in 1776. *A Grand Master, length of service from 1770 to 1783, 14 years (the 2nd generation).*	A. B. Kurakin	He was the nephew of P. I. Panin and N. I. Panin		Vol. 1. P. 333-335. Vol. 3. P. 42, 48, 55, 60, 62, 82, 114, 147, 199, 200, 269.

An opinion of G. P. Gagarin, on the state and legal issues, can be considered representative of all Russian Freemasonry at the end of the 18th century as he had 14 years of membership in Masonic Lodges, held the highest positions in Masonic Lodges and Chapters, a founder of some Masonic Lodges, and a holder of high degrees. The Masonic ideology and commitment to the natural-law picture of the world were revealed in his few works.

Carl (Armand) Alexandrovich Geiking (July 22 (August 2), 1751), the Okseln Estate in Courland [2] - October 18 (October 30), 1809.	A Full Privy Councilor, a Senator, from the Courland Nobles, a member of the Commission for drafting up the laws, loved the works of J. J. Rousseau. *German origin, mother tongue – German.*	8 The Society of the Knights of St. Carl in Vilna and Warsaw, one of the founders, established one of the Commanderships in Warsaw and one in Vilna 1775-1776. 10 The Lodge of the Complete Union (Consent) in Vilna, a founder of the lodge in 1780, a member in 1781. 35a The Adoptive Lodge in Mitava, a member of the lodge, the lodge was founded in 1782. 50 The Lodge of Clio in M. (he was not put on the list of the lodge according to A. I. Serkov). 137 Foreign lodges, he was initiated in Germany or in the lodge of Catherine to the North Star in Warsaw, *he founded a new 3-Degree Masonic System "Les Amies de l'eprueve" in Dresden.* A member of the Lodge of the Friends of Experience in 1770-1780. A founder of the Lodge of Catherine to the North Star in Warsaw. A founder of the Lodge "Freedom" (Petersburg, then Warsaw). A Plenipotentiary Representative of the Lodge of Catherine to the North Star in Warsaw at the Royal York Lodge to Friendship in Berlin in 1780. *A Great Local Master of the Provincial Lodge to the North Star in Warsaw from 11/24/1779. A Great Local Master of Catherine of Poland of the Great East of Poland in 1781.* A Deputy of Poland in the lodge of the United Friends at the Masonic Congress in Paris in 1785. A member of the Lodge of the Goddess Eleusis in Warsaw from 1787. *A member of the Masonic Convention in Berlin in 1787.* A Knight of the Order of Malta during the reign of Paul I. *A Great Master, length of service: 1775-1787, 14 years old (the 2nd generation).*				Vol. 1. P. 354-356. Vol. 3. P. 12, 13, 40, 270-271. Geiking, 1907, P. 46.

An opinion of K. A. Geiking, on the state and legal issues, cannot be considered representative of all Russian Freemasonry of the 18th century, even though he had 14 years of membership in Masonic Lodges, held the highest positions in Masonic Lodges, founded a new Masonic System and Masonic Lodges in Vilna and Warsaw. But his participation was limited mainly to foreign lodges, chiefly in Poland and on the territory of the former Grand Duchy of Lithuania. It is necessary to look at his works to determine the state-legal ideas of Polish Freemasonry and their differences from the state-legal ideas of Russian Freemasonry. K. A. Geiking also left some notes about Courland, Poland. He was a biographer of Paul I and left a number of works about his reign and regicide. These works are valuable. K. A. Geiking published a work (in Latin) on Monarchy as the best form of government. Regimen monarchicum ab ipsa naturaetin corrupta ratione emanatum etc. a K. A. Ruttieniae Nobili (any data on the publication of the book in the library stocks of Russia, Estonia, Germany, and Italy was not found). The masonic activity was abandoned by C. A. Geiking before his appointment to St. Petersburg as a Senator, but Masonic connections and the right to be an Honorary Member certainly remained.

Yegor Yegorovich Gine (1758-1835)	A Full Privy Councilor, a Judge. *German origin, mother tongue – German.*	61 A Theoretical Degree in M., worked in 1792 under the leadership of the Chief Overseer N. V. Repnin. 62 *The Lodge of the Three Banners in M., joined on 04.20.1784, a Freemason of the 4th Degree and the 1st Overseer from the summer of 1784 to 1785. A Presiding Master at the meetings on 10.09.1784, 10.16.1784, and 12.25.1784. A Local Master in 1785, a Chair Master in 1785-1786. Probably, a Managing Master after the departure of G. Ya. Schroeder.* 120 The Lodge of the Small Light in Riga, a member of the lodge until 1802. 123 The Lodge of Orpheus in the Ryazan regiment, a member in 1783, absent in 3rd Degree in November 1784, presided on 01/06/1785. *A Great Master, length of service: 1783-1803 - 21 years (the 2nd and 3rd generations).*	N. V. Repnin		Influenced A. N. Golitsyn, R. A. Koshelev, and Alexander I.	Vol. 1. P. 376-377. Vol. 3. P. 64, 71, 242, 255. Kondakov, 2018.

An opinion of E. E. Gine, on the state and legal issues, can be considered representative of all Russian Freemasonry of the late 18th century and the first quarter of the 19th century as he had 21 years of membership in Masonic Lodges, held the highest positions in Masonic Lodges and Chapters, was a bearer of high degrees. E. E. Gine, according to Yu. E. Kondakov, influenced A. N. Golitsyn, A. R. Koshelev, and Alexander I. His works deserve special attention. They need to be looked for by the researcher in the silence of libraries.

Samuil Carlovich Greig (1735-1788)	A Vice Admiral, a member of the Royal Society in London and the Academy of Sciences in P., *from a Scottish noble family. Scottish origin, mother tongue – English.*	32 The Lodge of Neptune in Kronstadt, a Local Master from 1779. A member of the lodge of the 3rd Degree in 1779-1780. The 1st Warden in 1781. A Chair Master in November 1781. A Chair Master of the works in English approximately in 1786 or from 1786. 105 The Lodge of Urania in P., he was mentioned in the minutes of the lodge in 1788 and 1792. *A Great Master, length of service: 1779-1792 - 14 years (the 2nd and the 3rd generations).*	S. R. Vorontsov			Vol. 1. P. 431 - 433. Vol. 3. P. 36, 172.

An opinion of S. K. Greig, on the state and legal issues, can be considered representative of all Russian Freemasonry of the late 18th century as he had 14 years of membership in Masonic Lodges, held positions in Masonic Lodges. S. K. Greig came from the Scottish Nobility, his manuscripts, stored in the library of the Institute of History of the Russian Academy of Sciences, are of particular interest.

Ludwig Shimon Gutakovsky (1738-1811)	A Judge, a Senator, *a supporter of the Constitution,* educated at the PR school in the Vilna Province and at the Nobilium Collegium in Warsaw with the	10 The Lodge of the Perfect Connection (Consent) in Vilna, 1780-1787, a Local Master from 12/31/1786. 19 The Lodge of the Happy Liberation in Grodno worked in French. Subordinated to the Great East of Poland. He was initiated in 1781, a Chair Master. 137 *Foreign lodges, a Representative of the Warsaw Lodge of the Shrine of Isis in the Great East of Poland in 1783. A Lithuanian Governor from 12/31/1786. In 1786 A founder of the Lodge of the Przesad Zwyciezony in Krakow.* *A Great Master, length of service: from 1781 to 1787 - 7 years (the 2nd generation).*				Vol. 1. P. 451-453. Vol. 3 P. 14, 24, 274-275.

	teaching of Law. *Polish origin, mother tongue – Polish.*					

An opinion of L. Sh. Gutakovsky, on the state and legal issues, cannot be considered representative of all Russian Freemasonry at the end of the 18th century as he had a 7-year membership in Masonic Lodges, held senior positions in Masonic Lodges, founded a Masonic Lodge in Krakow, his participation was limited mainly to foreign lodges, mainly in Poland and on the territory of the former GKL. L. Sh. Gutakovsky received a Degree in Legal Sciences and was a supporter of the Constitution. It is necessary to look at his works to determine the state-legal ideas of Polish Freemasonry and their differences from the state-legal ideas of Russian Freemasonry.

Joseph Friedrich -August Darbis (1747-1810)	Artist. *German origin, mother tongue – German.*	*A Novice of the Order of the Illuminati from July 1785.* A member of lodges of Strict Obedience in P. 113 The Lodge of Isis in Revel, in German, a visitor on 11/18/1782, attached 12/23/1782, he was issued a Master's Certificate on 12/10/1783, absent in 3rd Degree in 1785-1786. 120 The Lodge of the Small Light in Riga, in German and Russian. He was not listed in the lodge, according to A. I. Serkov. 137 Foreign lodges, a visitor from 04.08.1790, an affiliated member of the lodge "RoyalYorkdel'Amitie" in Berlin from 04.29.1794. He held a position of the architect of the temple in the lodge in 1795-1796, an Assistant Master from 09/06/1796, The 1st Great Orator of the Old Scottish Lodge-Mother Royal York to Friendship in 1797-1799, a Freemason of the 7th Degree. He was a Censor and Preparer in the Daughter Lodge of Urania in 1800. A member of the lodge up to 1802. *A Great Master, length of service:*	Friend of I. A. Fessler			Vol. 1. P. 460-461. Vol. 3. P. 213, 275.

		1782 - 1802 - 21 years (the 2nd and the 3rd generations).				

An opinion of I. F. A. Darbis, on the state and legal issues, cannot be considered representative of all Russian Freemasonry at the end of the 18th century, although he had a 21-year membership in Masonic Lodges, held senior positions in Masonic Lodges, founded a Masonic Lodge in Krakow, his participation was limited mainly to foreign lodges, chiefly in Estonia and Prussia. At the same time, an acquaintance and friendship with I. A. Fessler can make the study of his literature (if any) a very entertaining affair.

Ivan Perfilyevich Yelagin (1725-1794)	A Full Privy Councilor, a Chief Chamberlain, from an ancient noble family, from the family of a Collegiate Adviser.	A holder of English and Swedish Degrees, a Great Master of the Supreme Chapter of the 8th Degree. 41 The Lodge of Apis in M., a founding member of the lodge. 73 GEPL in P., a Scottish Master, a Great Provincial Master (a Grand Master) in 1772-1779, a Local Master in 1778. 75 The Lodge of Astrea in P. (according to A. I. Serkov, Yelagin was not on the lists). 77 The Lodge of Charity to the Pelican in P., a Chair Master. 88 The Chapter of Latona in M., P., an Honorary Member in 1778. 90 The Lodge of Silence (Modesty) in P., a founding member in 1775, a Chair Master, a member of the lodge of the 6th Degree in 1786-1787. 91 The Lodge of Muses in P., a founding member, a Chair Master in 1774-1777, a Local Master, signed the constitution of the Yelagin-Zinnendorf Union on behalf of the lodge. 100 The Lodge of the Perfect Union (Consent) in P., attended the lodge in 1770-1772. 105 The Lodge of Urania in P., a visitor 07.10.1773, joined the lodge as a full member on the same day, an Honorary Member from 04.01.1788.	A student of A. P. Sumarokov		A Patron of Fonvizin and Lukin	Vol. 1. P. 517-519. Vol. 3. P. 42, 83, 100, 118, 127, 136, 154, 175, 243.

		120 The Lodge of the Small Light in Riga, an Honorary Member since 1791. *A Great Master, length of service: 1770 - 1791 - 22 years (the 2nd and the 3rd generations).*				

An opinion of I. P. Yelagin, on the state and legal issues, can be considered representative of all Russian Freemasonry at the end of the 18th century as he had a 22-year membership in Masonic Lodges, held senior positions in Masonic Lodges, founded Masonic Lodges, headed the Unions of Masonic Lodges. The works of I. P. Yelagin was analyzed by A. N. Lushin in his thesis on the subject of state-legal ideas. Due to the extensive printed heritage of I. P. Yelagin, both in printed and handwritten versions (for example, "Experience in narrative about Russia"), A. N. Lushin made an initial analysis of the works of I. P. Yelagin. A more detailed and in-depth study of the works of I. P. Yelagin, with the aim of extracting the state and legal ideas and bringing them into a system, has yet to be done by future researchers.

Zakhar Yakovlevich Karneev (1748-1828)	A Full Privy Councilor, a Senator, a Governor, it is not known where he studied, *filed a report on religious tolerance to Paul I, a member of the Commission for Drafting the Laws,* a Commission on the resettlement of Jews, a member of societies, from the family of a Centurion of a Cossack regiment - a Little Russian noble family.	61 The Lodge of the Three Banners in M. (not in the lists, according to A. I. Serkov). 70 The Lodge of the Growing Eagle in Oryol, a founding member of the lodge in 1784 (1785)-1792, a Chair Master in 1785, then a Director of the Internal Council, a Director and Censor of the Society, a Chief Overseer of the Theoretical Degree in 1789-1791. 88 The Chapter of Latona in M., P. 1778, a member of the lodge. *A Great Master, length of service: 1778-1792 - 15 years (the 2nd and the 3rd generations).*	A friend of I. V. Lopukhin			Vol. 1. P. 581-582. Vol. 3. P. 80, 118.

An opinion of Z. Ya. Karneev, on the state and legal issues, can be considered representative of all Russian Freemasonry at the end of the 18th century as he had 15 years of membership in Masonic Lodges, held positions in Masonic Lodges, participated in various Chapters, and founded Masonic Lodges. The proceedings of Z. Ya. Karneev should be of interest to the researcher of the state-legal ideas of Russian Freemasonry because Z. Ya. Karneev had to leave works of a legal nature, was a member of the Commission for Drafting the Laws, which implies some knowledge of laws and Law. However, only 2 works by Z. Ya. Karneev of a religious and philosophical nature in 1814 ("My concepts about the symbol of faith"; "The thoughts poured out while reading the Lord's Prayer: Our Father.: Published in favor of poor L ... U ... S ...").

Stepan Alekseevich Kolychev (1746-1805)	A Full Privy Councilor, an Ambassador, a Minister, a Vice-Chancellor, *studied at the Faculty of Law at Leiden University,* participated in the negotiations on the 3rd partition of Poland and *the Franco-Russian Alliance,* from an ancient noble family, from the family of the President of the College of Justice.	83 The Imperial Scottish Lodge in P., not listed. 137 *Foreign lodges, a founding member of the lodge St. Jean de la Candeur (Honesty) in Paris, joined on 04/10/1775, a member in 1775-1778. A member of the lodge "L'egalite par fait et sincere amitie" ("Equality and Sincere Friendship") in Paris in 1775,* he visited other lodges. *A Great Master, length of service: 1775-1778 - 4 years (the 2nd generation).*	N. I. Panin, I. S. Baryatinsky.			Vol. 1. P. 632-633. Vol. 3. P. 280.

An opinion of S. A. Kolychev, on the state and legal issues, cannot be considered representative of all Russian Freemasonry at the end of the 18th century as he had only 4 years of membership in Masonic Lodges, founded a Masonic Lodge in Paris, his participation was limited to foreign lodges, mainly in Paris. At the same time, he had a legal education, was from the family of the President of the College of Justice, and was a supporter of the Russian-French Alliance. His state-legal ideas are of interest for characterizing the legal ideas of Russian residents in France, French Freemasonry, and French political influence on the Russian Nobility.

Alexander Borisovich Kurakin (1752-1818)	A Full Privy Councilor, *a Chief Prosecutor,* a Senator, studied at the University of Strasbourg, *at the Law Faculty of the Leiden University,* a participant in the convention on the patronage of the Order of Malta, on the 2nd Section of the Rzeczpospolita, a member of the Indispensable Council and the State Council, a bibliophile, concluded the Peace of Tilsit, from an ancient family from Grand Duke Lithuanian Gediminas.	55 The Lodge of Equality in M. and P., raised to the 3rd Degree on 07/07/1775. 73 GEPL in P., a Scottish Master, scheduled for the Provincial Grand Lodge and the Provincial Chapter in September 1776. 86 The Chapter of the Templar System in Petropolitanum, a member of the Chapter of the Petropolitanum from 1773. 99 The Lodge of Saint Alexander in P., 1777-1779, a Chair Master. 107 The Chapter of the Phoenix in P., a member of the Chapter in 1781, a Grand Prior, a Representative of the Vicar of Solomon. Scheduled by N. I. Novikov as a member of the Chapter in February 1783. *A Great Master, length of service: 1773-1783 - 11 years (the 2nd generation).*	N. I. Panin and P. I. Panin, great-nephew.			Vol. 1. P. 678-682. Vol. 3. P. 57, 83, 114, 150, 201.

An opinion of Alexander B. Kurakin, on the state and legal issues, can be considered representative of all Russian Freemasonry at the end of the 18th century as he had 11 years of membership in Masonic Lodges, held positions in Masonic Lodges, and participated in various Chapters. The works of Alexander B. Kurakin should be of interest to a researcher of the state-legal ideas of Russian Freemasonry because Alexander B. Kurakin received a legal education in Europe, was a participant in many important political processes in Europe, and had the opportunity to express his opinion on many important state issues.

Alexey Mikhailovich Kutuzov (1748-1792)	A Prime Major, *studied at the Faculty of Law of the University of Leipzig,* a translator, an author of the Masonic writings, one of the founders of the Friendly Scientific Society from the Nobility, his father was a Capitan of the Life Guards of the Preobrazhensky Regiment.	42 The Lodge of Astrea in M. (according to A. I. Serkov, not listed). 46 The Lodge of Harmony in Moscow, 1780-1783, a founding member of the lodge. 56 The Lodge of the Light-Bearing Triangle in M., a Chair Master from 1784 (1782, early 1783). 61 A Theoretical Degree in M., P., a member of the Theoretical Degree from 1782, a member of the Internal Order of the Rosicrucians from 1783. Transferred from N. I. Novikov under Schroeder at the beginning of 1786. His Order Name was "Vivus Velox Statuk." He was scheduled to become a member of the Haupt Directorate in 1788. 88 The Chapter and the Lodge of Latona in M., P., a founding member, 1776-1785, a member of the lodge of the 3rd Degree in 1778. 93 The Lodge of Osiris in M., P., the 2nd Collector of Alms for the Poor in November 1781, was absent at that time. 137 Foreign lodges received the Degree "Practitioner" in the Order of the Gold-Pink Cross in Berlin. *A Great Master, length of service: 1776-1785 - 10 years (the 2nd generation).*	A friend of G. Ya. Schroeder and A. N. Radishchev (lived in the same room for 14 years). Resigned on the recommendation of I. G. Schwartz; N. I. Novikov, M. I. Golenishchev-Kutuzov.			Vol. 1. P. 691-692. Vol. 3. P. 48, 58, 65, 118, 142, 282.

An opinion of A. M. Kutuzov, on the state and legal issues, can be considered representative of all Russian Freemasonry at the end of the 18th century as he had a 10-year membership in Masonic Lodges, held positions in Masonic Lodges, participated in many Chapters, was a prominent Rosicrucian, and had a legal education. Mostly A. M. Kutuzov translated the works of Western authors into Russian.

Yegor Andreevich Kushelev (1763-1826)	A Lieutenant General, a Senator, from the Nobility of the Pskov Province.	77 Charity to the Pelican, dedicated in the 1780s. *Considering the Masonic experience gained in the Masonic Lodges of the XIX century (for example, acting as a Great Local Master of the Lodge of Astrea in P. until 12/12/1820), he was a Great Master, length of service: about 40 years (the 2nd, the 3rd, and the 4th generations).*				Vol. 1. P. 695-696. Vol. 3. P. 101; Serkov, 2001, P. 1046.

An opinion of Y. A. Kushelev, on the state and legal issues, can be considered representative of all Russian Freemasonry at the end of the 18th and 19th centuries as he had a 40-year membership in Masonic Lodges, held positions in Masonic Lodges, and headed Masonic Unions (for example, the Grand Lodge of Astrea in St. Petersburg). He was a prominent Rosicrucian and had a Legal Education.

Alexander Fyodorovich Labzin (1766-1825)	A Full Privy Councilor, one of the Directors of the Public Library, a writer, a publisher, a Censor, the Vice-President of the Academy of Arts, from a poor noble family.	Dedicated on 04/23/1783. *A Great Master by considering his Masonic experience of the 19th century, length of service: about 40 years, for example, he visited the Lodge of Neptune in M., an Assistant Guard in 1819 (the 2nd, the 3rd, and the 4th generations).*	I. G. Schwartz, N. I. Novikov, F. P. Klyucharev. A friend of G. R. Derzhavin. Enjoyed the patronage of A. N. Golitsyn and P. P. Turgenev.			Vol. 2. P. 5-8. Serkov, 2001, P. 1030.

An opinion of A. F. Labzin, on the state and legal issues, can be considered representative of all Russian Freemasonry of the late 18th and 19th centuries as he had 40 years of membership in Masonic Lodges, held positions in many Masonic Lodges, founded his own lodge and managed it for many years in the first quarter of the 19th century. A. F. Labzin issued many printed works and translations of Western literature. The biography of his public life was studied by Yu. S. Vasilyeva[1].

Ivan Vladimirovich Lopukhin (1756-1816)	A Full Privy Councilor, a Senator, an author of some literary works, a member of the Friendly Scientific Society, from the outstanding noble family.	43 The Lodge of the Shining Star in M. and P., a Chair Master (a Great Master) in 1784-1785. 44 The Directory of the VIII Province in M., the Vice-President in 1782 and in July 1783. His Order Name was "Johanne saluce orta." 46 The Secret Sienzific Eclectic Lodge of Harmony. The 3rd Degree, dedicated by I. E. Schwartz on 06.20.1783. 47 The Hermes University Lodge in M., not in the lists. 61 A Theoretical Degree in M, supervised the work of the entire Theoretical Grade, an Overseer of the Russian Brothers of the Directory of the Theoretical Degree. The Head of the Directory in October 1785, a Rosicrucian, His Order Name was "Philus." 70 The Lodge of the Rising Eagle in Oryol, a Representative of the lodge in 1785 88 The Chapter of Latona in P, a member of the lodge in 1785, a Representative of the Daughter Lodge of the Rising Eagle, a Commissioner of the Chapter. *A Great Master, 1782-1785 - 4 years, there is no length of service in the XIX century. It does not appear in the lists of Serkov's dictionary (the 2nd generation).*	A friend of I. P. Turgenev.		N. I. Novikov, M. M. Speransky, M. I. Nevzorov, V. Ya. Kolokolnikov, A. M. Kutuzov, A. I. Kovalkov.	Vol. 2. P. 54-57. Vol. 3. P. 45, 46, 48, 66, 80.

[1]Yu. S. Vasilyeva "A. F. Labzin in the public life of the capitals and provinces of the late 18th – the first quarter of the 19th centuries": monograph / Yu. S. Vasilyeva. - Samara: Ofort, 2009 (Samara: Ofort). - 141 p.

An opinion of I. V. Lopukhin, on the state and legal issues, can be considered representative of all Russian Freemasonry at the end of the 18th and 19th centuries, although he had a 4-year membership in Masonic Lodges, held positions in some Masonic Lodges, was a member of the Chapter and an Overseer of a Theoretical Degree. I. V. Lopukhin wrote many works. In addition, I. V. Lopukhin influenced many people, introducing them to the Masonic worldview (M. M. Speransky, M. I. Nevzorov, V. Ya. Kolokolnikov, A. M. Kutuzov, and A. I. Kovalkov).

Alexander Mikhailovich Lunin (1745-1816)	A Full Privy Council or, a Senator, from a Privy Council or family.	15 The Lodge of St. Catherine to the North Star in Vologda, visited in 1783. 45 The Chapter of the VIII Province in M. from 1782, a Propraetor. 46 The Lodge of Harmony in M., raised to the 3rd Degree by I. E. Schwarz on 06.20.1783. 61 A Theoretical Degree in M., a Theoretical Grade under the supervision of the Chief Overseer I. A. Pozdeev. His Motto was “Rex Nilande Luna.” 62 The Lodge of the Three Banners in M., the 4th Degree, an Honorary Member in the middle of 1784. 65 The Scottish (Old Ekos) Lodge in M., a Chief Meister in 1783. 88 The Chapter of Latona in P., a Pro-Prefect of the Chapter from 1780. 123 The Lodge of Orpheus in the Ryazan regiment and in Petrograd, a Local Master in 1782-1783. *A Great Master, length of service: 1780-1784, 5 years (the 2nd generation).*	A. I. Bibikov.			Vol. 2. P. 61-62; Vol. 3. P. 22, 47, 48, 66, 73, 76, 118, 256.

An opinion of A. M. Lunin, on the state and legal issues, can be considered representative of all Russian Freemasonry of the late 18th century, although he had a 5-year membership in Masonic Lodges, held positions in Masonic Lodges, was a Pro-Prefect and Propraetor of many Chapters. A. M. Lunin’s written heritage is mainly represented by manuscripts.

Christian Friedrich Mattei (1744-1811)	Doctor of Philology, a Professor, Rector. *Studied Jurisprudence at the University of Leipzig.* An author of many works, from the family of a Court Trumpeter. *German origin, mother tongue – German.*	49 *The Lodge of Druzhba in M., a founding member of the 3rd Degree from 1777, a Chair Master from 06.24.1777, in 1779 and in the early 1780s.* 99a The Andreevskaya Lodge of St. George in P., a member of the lodge in the early 1780s. *A Great Master, length of service: 1777-1780 - 4 years (the 2nd generation).*	M. N. Muravyov.			Vol. 2. P. 89-90. Vol. 3. P. 51, 152.

An opinion of C. F. Mattei, on the state and legal issues, cannot be considered representative of all Russian Freemasonry at the end of the 18th century because he only had a 4-year membership in Masonic Lodges, although he founded a Masonic Lodge in Moscow. At the same time, his works may be of research interest as he held some academic positions and wrote some works.

Alexey Petrovich Melgunov (1722-1788)	A Full Privy Councilor, a Governor General, from the family of the Lieutenant Governor.	133 The Lodge of Melgunov in Yaroslavl, a founding member and a Chair Master from 1779 to the day of Melgunov's death in 1788. *A Great Master, length of service: 1779-1788, 10 years (the 2nd generation).*	A friend of I. I. Shuvalov.			Vol. 2. P. 105-107. Vol. 3. P. 259.

An opinion of A. P. Melgunov, on the state and legal issues, can be considered representative of all Russian Freemasonry at the end of the 18th century, although he had a 10-year membership in Masonic Lodges, held some positions in some Masonic Lodges, was a founder of the lodge and, at the same time, the Governor-General of the Province the lodge was founded in. In connection with the combination of the positions of the Governor-General and a Chair Master, the experience of A. P. Melgunov is interesting in its own way.

Joseph Marie de Maistre (1753-1821)	*Received a legal education at the University of Turin,* was influenced by J. J. Rousseau, an Advocate General, a Senator, became a supporter of absolutism under the influence of the French Revolution, a Plenipotentiary Envoy, the Ruler of the Grand Chancellery of the Sandinsky Kingdom, a memoirist. From a noble family - immigrants from Nice, from the family of the President of the Savoy Senate. *French origin, mother tongue – French.*	137 Foreign lodges, a Great Orator in 1774, *the 1st Overseer of the Lodge of Saint-Jean Trois Mortiers (the Three Mortars) in Chambery in 1778, became a founding member of the La Sincerite Lodge in Chambery on 09/03/1778. He was a Great Prefect and a Censor of the College of Chambéry and the Knights of the Benefactors of the Holy City in 1779.* A Procurator and a Master of Economy in the Prefecture of Freemasons in Chambéry, a member of the Scottish Directory of Auvergne (Lyon), his Order Name was "Josephus Euesafloribus," his Motto was "Spagitodorem." Inscription: Recreat, one of the lodges of the initiatory Martinist Order was named after him. *A Great Master, length of service: 1774-1779 - 6 years (the 2nd generation).*			He influenced Alexander I.	Vol. 2. P. 114-115. Vol. 3. P. 287. Kondakov, 2018. Zakharov, 2010.

An opinion J. M. de Maistre, on the state and legal issues, cannot be considered representative of all Russian Freemasonry at the end of the 18th century because he had a 6-year membership in Masonic Lodges located in France. At the same time, his works may be of research interest as J. M. de Maistre influenced Alexander I approximately in 1810-1814.

Andrey Andreevich Nartov (1737-1813)	A Privy Councilor, a member of many scientific societies in different countries, *headed the Medallion Committee together with M. M. Kheraskov and M. M. Shcherbatov*, from the family of a Turner, a Councilor of State.	73 The GEPL in P., he was scheduled for membership in the Grand Lodge and for raising to the Degree of the Scottish Knight (Master) in September 1776. 74 The Lodge of Apollo in P., the 1st Overseer in 1771. 80 The Lodge of Horus in P., a Chair Master in 1775-1777, signed the Constitution of the Yelagin-Zinnendorf Union on behalf of the lodge. 95 The Prefecture of M. in P., applied for opening it, opened in 1783. 106 The Lodge of Phoenix in St. Petersburg, a Local Master in 1779. *A Great Master, length of service:1771-1783 - 13 years (the 2nd generation).*	P. I. Shuvalov.			Vol. 2. P. 165-167. Vol. 3. P. 83, 89, 110, 146, 199.

An opinion of A. A. Nartov, on the state and legal issues, can be considered representative of all Russian Freemasonry at the end of the 18th century as he had 13 years of membership in Masonic Lodges and held the highest positions in Masonic Lodges. Basically, A. A. Nartov translated many books from a foreign language into Russian. In addition, A. A. Nartov wrote some works. One work, “The Epistle to the Faithful Sons of the Fatherland” (1762), written before the entry of A. A. Nartov to Masonic Lodges, can be noted.

Ivan Vasilyevich Nesvitsky (1740-1806)	A Full Privy Councilor, an Ober-Shenk, from a Princely family, from the family of the Governor.	43 The Lodge of the Shining Star in M. and P., a founding member of the lodge from 1784. 54 The Provincial Lodge, headed the Lodge from December 1781. 61 A Theoretical Degree in M., recommended for admission to the Theoretical Degree in 1784. 73 The GEPL in P., the 2nd Great Overseer in 1773-1774. 91 The Lodge of Muses in P., the 2nd Overseer in 1773. 94 The Lodge of the Flaming Star in P., a Chair Master in 1779. 97 The Provincial Grand Lodge in P., the 1st Great Almsgiver in 1779. 100 The Perfect Union (Consent), attended the lodge in 1771-1772. 105 The Lodge of Urania in P., a Lodge Installer on 03.16.1773, a member of the lodge from 07.10.1773, on this day acted as the 2nd Steward. 107 The Chapter of the Phoenix in P., a member of the Chapter in 1779-1781. *A Great Master, length of service: 1771-1784 - 14 years (the 2nd generation).*				Vol. 2. P. 188-189. Vol. 3. P. 45, 54, 67, 83, 138, 145, 147, 155, 185, 202.

An opinion of I. V. Nesvitsky, on the state and legal issues, can be considered representative of all Russian Freemasonry at the end of the 18th century as he had 14 years of membership in Masonic Lodges, held senior positions in some Masonic Lodges, Lodge Unions, and Chapters founded a Masonic Lodge of the Shining Star in St. Petersburg.

Nikolay Ivanovich Novikov (1744-1818)	A Lieutenant, a publisher.	43 The Lodge of the Shining Star in M., P. from 1784, was present at the installation of the lodge. He gave a speech during that installation. 44 The Directory of the VIII Province in M., a Prior (President) in 1783. 45 The Chapter of the VIII Province in M., a Treasurer of the Priory, a member of the Chapter in 1784-1789, its Treasurer from 1782 to 1783. His Order Name was "Eques Nicolai ab ancora" ("Nicolaus eques ab ancora"). 46 The Secret Siencifi Eclectic Lodge of Harmony in 1780-1783, a founding member. 47 The Hermes University Lodge in M., not in the lists. 61 A Theoretical Degree in M., accepted into the Internal Order by the Rosicrucian in 1782-1783. His Order Name was "Vivax," his Motto was "Vivax Evus Klovion." 73 The GEPL in P., scheduled for membership in the Grand Provincial Lodge in September 1776. 75 The Lodge of Astrea in P., raised to the 3rd Degree immediately in June 1775. 88 The Chapter of Latona in P, petitioned for opening, a Local Master and Installer of the lodge in 1776, a Chair Master and a member of the lodge of the 4th Degree in 1776-1777, signed the Constitution of the Yelagin-Zinnendorf Union on behalf of the lodge. A Great Master in 1778. He was raised to the 7th Degree of the Swedish System in 1778, transferred work to M., a Prefect, a founding member of the Chapter. 93 The Lodge of Osiris in P., a member of the 3rd Degree in November 1781, was an Honorary Member of the lodge. 105 The Lodge of Urania in P., a visitor to the lodge 06.13.1775 and 06.27.1775. *A Great Master, length of service: 1775-1789*		Wife - Alexandra Egorovna Rimskaya-Korsakova - niece of Prince N. N. Trubetskoy.		Vol. 2. P. 197-200. Vol. 3. P. 46, 47, 48, 67, 84, 93, 119, 143, 185.

		- 15 years and in the XIX century (the 2nd, the 3rd, and the 4th generations).				

An opinion of N. I. Novikov, on the state and legal issues, can be considered representative of all Russian Freemasonry at the end of the 18th century as he had 15 years of membership in Masonic Lodges, held the highest positions in the Masonic Lodges of the 18th century, was a Great Master in the 19th century, held the highest positions in the Masonic Lodges of the 19th century, was a bearer of high degrees, a founder of lodges and Chapters. He was one of the most famous Russian Freemasons.

Ivan Ivanovich Panaev (1752-1796)	A Collegiate Adviser, *a Prosecutor, a provincial Solicitor (Lawyer)*, from the family of the Turin Governor.	26 The Lodge of the Rising Sun in Kazan, 1776-1787, a Chair Master from the end of 1783. 61 A Theoretical Degree in Moscow, 1782-1786, a member of the Theoretical Degree in M. and P., worked under the leadership of the Chief Overseer I. P. Turgenev, his Order Motto was "ApianusHeavaneon." 72 The Lodge of the Golden Key in Perm, a founding member of the lodge, a Chair Master from 07.29.1783. 80 The Lodge of Gorus in P., a Chair Master in 1780-1781. *A Great Master, length of service: 1780-1786 - 7 years (the 2nd generation).*	A. Ya. Bruce. He was an acquaintance of N. I. Novikov, his Commission Agent.			Vol. 2. P. 245-246. Vol. 3. P. 32, 67, 81, 110.

An opinion of I. I. Panaev, on the state and legal issues, cannot be considered representative of all Russian Freemasonry of the late 18th century because he only had a 7-year membership in Masonic Lodges, although he founded a Masonic Lodge in Perm and held the highest positions in Masonic Lodges. At the same time, his views on the state and law may be typical of an average and petty Official.

Nikita Ivanovich Panin (1718-1783)	The 1st Class Full Privy Councilor, a Chief Chamberlain, a Steward of the Household (Hofmeister), a Field Marshal, a Minister Plenipotentiary, a Senator, a tutor of Grand Duke Pavel Petrovich, attracted him to the state government, received a home education, *advocated limiting the Monarchy by law, the introduction of a Constitution as a guarantee "from the arbitrariness of strong people and fit people," for ruling on the "solid foundations of the law" and an enlightened Monarch, an author of the state projects,* an author of the Union of Northern Powers, from the old noble family, from the family of a Lieutenant General.	73 The GEPL in P., a Great Local Master in 1776-1777, a Scottish Master in September 1776, slated for a Provincial Chapter. 91 The Lodge of the Muses in P., a member of the lodge in 1774. *A Great Master, length of service: 1774-1776 - 3 years (the 2nd generation).*	An opponent of A. K. Razumovsky under Elizabeth Petrovna.			Vol. 2. P. 247 - 249. Vol. 3. P. 84, 138.

An opinion of N. I. Panin, on the state and legal issues, cannot be considered representative of all Russian Freemasonry at the end of the 18th century because he only had a 3-year membership in Masonic Lodges, although he held the highest positions in the union of Masonic Lodges. His views on the state and law were popularly stated by A. N. Lushin in his monograph[1]. At the same time, N. I. Panin was a key figure in Russian Freemasonry as he was the Chancellor of the Russian Empire, a Full Privy Councilor of the 1st class, and a Field Marshal, and his participation in Masonic Lodges was significant. Most likely, that is why the

[1]A. N. Lushin "The state-legal views of Russian Freemasons at the turn of the XVIII-XIX centuries": A thesis of a PhD in Legal Sciences: 12.00.01. - Nizhny Novgorod, 2004. - 161 p.

authority of N. I. Panin gave Masonic Lodges influence and popularity. Many acquaintances, relatives, and subordinates of N. I. Panin subsequently became Freemasons (M. M. Alopeus, A. I. Bibikov, S. A. Kolychyov, S. I. Pleshcheev, N. V. Repnin, L. I. Talyzin, etc.). At the same time, the ideas of N. I. Panin were not and could not be shared by other Freemasons as the issues of politics and religion were prohibited in the Masonic Lodges, and N. I. Panin communicated his beliefs only to a narrow circle of people close to him (D. I. Fonvizin was among them).

Iosif Aleksevich Pozdeev (1842-1820)	A Colonel, the Head of the Chancellery, a manufacturer, from the nobility, from the family of a Captain.	15 The Lodge of St. Catherine to the North Star in Vologda, the Actual Head of the lodge. 16 A Theoretical Degree in Vologda, a leader of the Theoretical Degree in Vologda in 1791-1792. 21 The Lodge of the Morning Star in Dorpat, a Representative of the lodge in the lodge of the Three Banners in 1786. 45 The Chapter of the VIII Province in M. from 1782, a member of the Chapter in 1784. 54 The Provincial Lodge, a Local Master. 61 A Theoretical Degree in M., a Ceremonial Leader of the Theoretical Degree 1784-1789, accepted into the Internal Order of the Rosicrucians in 1785, had a Degree in Practice, led his own circle in M. and work in Vologda in 1791-1792, his Order Name was "Pius," his Motto was "Sophus Pius de Eove." 62 The Lodge of the Three Banners in M., an Honorary Member in the middle of 1784, the 4th Degree Freemason, the 2nd Overseer in 1785, a Representative of the lodge in Dorpat. 65 The Scottish (Old Ecos) Lodge in M., a Ceremonial Leader, a Chair Master (Scottish Great Master) from 1789. 88 The Chapter of Latona in P., from 1780, a founding member of the Chapter. 97 The Provincial Grand Lodge in P., a Great Local Master in 1780. 123 The Lodge of Orpheus in the Ryazan regiment and Petrograd, a leader of the meetings approximately from December 1781, a founding member of the lodge, a Chair Master from 11/07/1784 to 12/26/1785, was absent from the meetings of the lodge. *A Great Master, length of service: 1780-1792 - 13 years (the 2nd and the 3rd generations).*	P. I. Panin, Z. G. Chernyshev.			Vol. 2. P. 283-284. Vol. 3. P. 22, 23, 26, 47, 54, 67, 73, 76, 119, 147, 256.

An opinion of I. A. Pozdeev, on the state and legal issues, can be considered representative of all Russian Freemasonry of the late 18th and the first quarter of the 19th centuries, as he had 13 years of membership in the Masonic Lodges of the 18th century, held the highest positions in the Masonic Lodges of the 18th century, held the highest positions in Masonic Lodges and the Unions of the Lodges was a bearer of high degrees, a founder of Lodges and Chapters. He was one of the most famous Russian Freemasons. He influenced A. K. Razumovsky, Minister of Public Education at the beginning of the 19th century, M. Yu. Vielgorsky and other Freemasons, according to Yu. E. Kondakov.

Stanislav Kostka Pototski (1755-1821)	A Minister of the Kingdom of Poland, a Senator, an educator, a deist philosopher. *Polish origin, mother tongue – Polish.*	137 Foreign lodges, a member of the Lodge of the Northern Shield from 1780 (1781), a member of the Lodge of the Sanctuary of Isis from 1784, attended the Lodge of the Union of Foreigners in Paris in 1787. A Great Orator of the Grand Orient of Poland from April 1784 to 1790, *a Representative at the Grand Orient of France in 1788-1789, promoted Polish-French Masonic connections. A Great Master, length of service:1780-1790 - 11 years (the 2nd and the 3rd generations).*				Vol. 2. P. 305 - 306. Vol. 3. P. 293.

An opinion of S. K. Pototski, on the state and legal issues, cannot be considered representative of all Russian Freemasonry at the end of the 18th century because, although he had 11 years of membership in Masonic Lodges, he carried out Masonic activities on the territory of Poland and France. However, his work may be of research interest.

Nikolai Vasilyevich Repnin (1734-1801)	A Field Marshal General, a Governor General, a Minister, from an ancient princely family, the XXVI generation from Rurik.	A member of the Lodge of I. V. Lopukhin. 30 The Military Lodge in Kinburn, a founding member of the lodge from 1779, a Chair Master. 61 The Theoretical Degree in M., accepted into the Theoretical Degree in M. by G. Ya. Schroeder in 1785, a petit was taken from Schroeder, received the rights of the Chief Overseer of the Theoretical Degree from I. V. Lopukhin and, probably, opened his own circle at his headquarters. 91 The Lodge of the Muses in P., a member of the lodge in 1776. *A Great Master, length of service: from 1776 to 1785 - 10 years (the 2nd generation).*	Z. G. Chernyshev, N. I. Panin.	Wife - Princess Natalya Alexandrovna Kurakina, niece of N. I. Panin.		Vol. 2. P. 357-361. Vol. 3. P. 34, 67, 138.

An opinion of N. V. Repnin, on the state and legal issues, can be considered representative of all Russian Freemasonry at the end of the 18th century as he had a 10-year membership in Masonic Lodges, held positions in Masonic Lodges, and was a founder of the Military Lodge. N. V. Repnin was the author of the manuscript "Les fruits de la Grace, ou Opuscules spirituels de deux amateurs de la Sagesse" in French. - [S. l.], 1790. - 120 p.

Alexey Andreevich Rzhevsky (1737-1804)	A Full Privy Councilor, a Senator, a Judge, graduated from the Moscow University with the teaching of Jurisprudence, a Deputy of the Commission of the State Council,	61 The Theoretical Degree in M., admitted to the Theoretical Degree in July-August 1783, a Chief Overseer of the Theoretical Degree in Petrograd from August to October 1783, then he was on a long vacation. He returned to the management of the Theoretical Degree in the summer of 1784, then he was raised to the "Practitioner" Degree, his Order Name was "Chrisus." 88 The Chapter of Latona in P., an Honorary Member of the Chapter in January 1783. 91 The Lodge of the Muses in P., a member of the lodge in 1774.	A. P. Sumarokov. A friend of G. R. Derzhavin.			Vol. 2. P. 363-365. Vol. 3. P. 68, 119, 138, 147, 202.

	from the nobility, the XXVII generation from Rurik, from the family of a Midshipman.	97 The Provincial Grand Lodge, a Great Provincial Local Master of Works in Russian in 1779. 107 The Chapter of the Phoenix in P., a member of the Chapter of the Petropolitanum, a Local Master in 1779, a member of the Chapter in 1781, an Overseer of the Prefecture until 1783, the President of the Chapter, his Order Name was "The Knight of Good Hope" ("Alexius equesabona Spe"). The Prefect of the Chapter from January 1783, approved in this position on 04/26/1783, abandoned it at the end of August 1783. *A Great Master, length of service: 1774 - 1783 - 10 years (the 2nd generation).*				

An opinion of A.A. Rzhevsky, on the state and legal issues, can be considered representative of all Russian Freemasonry of the late 18th century as he had a 10-year membership in Masonic Lodges, held senior positions in Masonic Lodges and the Unions of the Lodges.

Osip Mikhailovich De Ribas (1751-1800	An Admiral, an Acting Minister, a *participant in the conspiracy against Paul I,* from a noble Catalan family of nobles, from the family of a Marshal in the	77 The Lodge of the Charity to the Pelican in P., an Honorary Member of the lodge in 1782, a member of the lodge of the 4th Degree in 1783. 88 The Chapter of Latona in P., a member of the lodge of the 3rd Degree in 1778. 107 *The Chapter of the Phoenix in P., a member of the Chapter in 1781.* 108 *The French Lodge in P., a Grand Master in 1782*, bore the Order Name "Gladio" in the amended Scottish Charter. *A Great Master, considering the experience in the 19th century, length of service: 1778 - 1783 - 6 years (the 2nd generation).*	I. I. Betsky, A friend of A. V. Suvorov.	Wife - Anastasia Ivanovna Sokolova, illegitimate daughter of I. I. Betsky.		Vol. 2. P. 366-368. Vol. 3. P. 103, 119, 202, 204.

	Neapolita n service.					

An opinion of O. M. De Ribas, on the state and legal issues, cannot be considered representative of all Russian Freemasonry at the end of the 18th century because he only had a 6-year membership in Masonic Lodges and was an adherent of the "French" Freemasonry System. That "French" System became unpopular and "dangerous" after the events of 1789 in France. Although he headed the lodge in Moscow with the rank of Grand Master and was a member of the Phoenix Chapter. The participation of O. M. De Ribas in the attempt on the life of Paul I also testifies to the retreat of O. M. De Ribas from the principles of Freemasonry (non-participation in conspiracies against the Imperial Family and the state).

Alexey Fedorovich Saburov (1748-1804)	A Full Privy Councilor, a Senator, from the family of a Brigadier.	30 The Military Lodge in Kinburn (according to A. I. Serkov, not in the lists of the lodge). 61 The Theoretical Degree in M., recommended to the Theoretical Degree in 1784. 76 The Lodge of Bellona in P., the 2nd Guard (Overseer) in 1774. 94 The Lodge of the Flaming Star in P., a Local Master in 1779, a Chair Master. 97 The Provincial Grand Lodge, the 2nd Great Overseer in 1779, the 1st Great Overseer in 1781. 105 The Lodge of Urania in P., a visitor to the lodge on 08/03/1773. 107 The Chapter of the Phoenix in P., a member of the Chapter in 1779-1781. *A Great Master, length of service: 1774 - 1784 - 11 years (the 2nd generation).*				Vol. 2. P. 412-413. Vol. 3. P. 68, 95, 145, 147, 189, 202.

An opinion of S. F. Saburov, on the state and legal issues, can be considered representative of all Russian Freemasonry at the end of the 18th century as he had 11 years of membership in Masonic Lodges, held senior positions in Masonic Lodges and the Unions of the Lodges, and was a member of the Phoenix Chapter in St. Petersburg.

Pyotr Alexandrovich Soymonov (1737-1800)	A Full Privy Councilor, a Senator.	97 The Provincial Grand Lodge, a Great Secretary of works in Russian in 1779, a Great Chancellor in 1780. 107 The Chapter of the Phoenix in P., a Chancellor of the Chapter in 1779, its member until 1781. *A Great Master, length of service: 1779 - 1781 - 3 years (the 2nd generation).*	A Director of spectacles and music from 03/03/1789 together with A. V. Khrapovitsky.	Wife - Ekaterina - daughter of I. N. Boltin.		Vol. 2. P. 461-462. Vol. 3. P. 147, 202.

An opinion of P. A. Soymonov, on the state and legal issues, cannot be considered representative of all Russian Freemasonry at the end of the 18th century because he only had a 3-year membership in Masonic Lodges, although he was a Chancellor of the Phoenix Chapter and a Chancellor of the Grand Provincial Lodge. Probably, P. A. Soymonov was involved in the Masonic activities by I. N. Boltin (I. N. Boltin was a Freemason of the 1st generation) but did not stay in Freemasonry.

Alexey Grigoryevich Spiridov (1753-1828)	An Admiral, a Governor, from an old noble family, from the family of an Admiral.	32 The Lodge of Neptune in Kronstadt, a Chair Master of the in 1779-1780, absent in the 3rd Degree in February 1781, a Great Master and a member of the lodge of the 4th Degree in November 1781. 90 The Lodge of Silence (Modesty), a member of the lodge of the 3rd Degree in 1786-1787. 105 The Lodge of Urania in P, a Chair Master in 1780-1781, a Freemason of the 4th Degree. 137 Foreign lodges, a founder of the lodge in Livorno. *A Great Master, length of service: 1779-1787 - 9 years (the 2nd generation).*	S. K. Greig, I. G. Chernyshev, G. G. Orlov.	Brother Matvey, he was married to the daughter of M. M. Shcherbatov.		Vol. 2. P. 467-469. Vol. 3. P. 38, 132, 190, 298.

An opinion of A. G. Sviridov, on the state and legal issues, can be considered representative of all Russian Freemasonry at the end of the 18th century as he had 9 years of membership in Masonic Lodges, held senior positions in Masonic Lodges, and was a founder of the lodge in Livorno.

Alexander Nikolaevich Stroganov (1740-1789)	A Full Privy Councilor, a General-in-Chief, from an old family of Russian merchants and manufacturers.	61 The Theoretical Degree in M., assigned for acceptance into the Theoretical Degree in P. in August 1784. 77 The Lodge of the Charity to the Pelican in P., a member of the lodge in 1781, an Honorary Member of the lodge in 1782, a member of the lodge of the 4th Degree in 1783, a member of the lodge of the 3rd Degree approximately in 1785, a member of the lodge in 1786. 107 The Chapter of the Phoenix in P., a member of the Chapter in 1781, a member of the Chapter of the Phoenix. *A Great Master, length of service: 1781-1786 - 6 years (the 2nd generation).*	Wife - Elizabeth - sister of B. A. Zagryazhsky.			Vol. 2. P. 486 - 487. Vol. 3. P. 68, 105, 202.

An opinion of A. N. Stroganov, on the state and legal issues, can be considered representative of all Russian Freemasonry of the late 18th century as he had a 6-year membership in Masonic Lodges, held the highest positions in Masonic Lodges, and was a member of the Phoenix Chapter.

Nikolai Nikitich Trubetskoy (1744-1820)	A Full Privy Councilor, a Senator, from the family of princes.	45 The Chapter of the VIII Province in M., a general visitor in 1783, a member of the Chapter in 1784, his Order Name was "Nicolaus eques ab aquilla boreali." 46 The Lodge of Harmony in M., a founding member of the lodge (according to other sources, a member from the end of 1780). 50 The Lodge of Clio in M., not on the list. 54 The Provincial Lodge, a Local Master in 1784. 61 The Theoretical Degree in M, admitted to the Theoretical Degree in 1782, a Rosicrucian approximately from 1783, a founding member of the Directory of the Theoretical Degree on 04/30/1784, its 1st Overseer in 1783, supervised the work of	A close friend of N. I. Novikov.	Wife - Varvara, sister A. A. Cherkassky, N. N. Trubetskoy was the uterine brother of the poet M. M. Kheraskov.		Vol. 2. P. 548-549. Vol. 3. P. 48, 54, 69, 84, 91, 108, 120, 144. Mukhovit

		Cherkassky, Yengalychev, Kheraskov, and Y. Trubetskoy. His Order Name was “Porrectus” (“Dedicated to the Gods”), then – “Pinnatus” (“Inspired”) (“Porrectus Pinnatus Calibizork”). 73 The GEPL in P., a Scottish Master in September 1776, scheduled for the GPL and the Provincial Chapter. 74 The Lodge of Apollo in P., a Local Master in 1772. 78 The Lodge of Harpocrates in P., a founding member of the lodge, a Chair Master in 1773-1778. 88 The Chapter of Latona in P., an Honorary Member of the lodge in 1778, a Prefect of the lodge in 1781, a founding member of the Chapter, a Prefect of the Chapter in January 1783. 93 The Lodge of Osiris in P., a founding member of the lodge, a Chair Master in 1776-1781, a Prefect in 1784. 103 The Lodge of the Happy Agreement in P., not in the lists. *A Great Master, length of service: 1772-1784 - 13 years (the 2nd generation).*				skaya, 2015. P. 33-34.

An opinion of N. N. Trubetskoy, on the state and legal issues, can be considered representative of all Russian Freemasonry at the end of the 18th century as he had 13 years of membership in Masonic Lodges, held senior positions in Masonic Lodges, was a member of some Chapters, a founder of several lodges, and translated Western literature into Russian. N. N. Trubetskoy “wrote poetry, composed prose (several poems and prose works were published in ‘Moscow Monthly Works’), created some translations from the encyclopedia, as well as the comedy ‘The Spender,’ and some others. But he preferred to remain incognito and did not sign his name.

At the request of his brother M. M. Kheraskov, he translated some articles of economic nature from the French Encyclopedia”[1] and the essay “The New Inscription of True Theology.” He was exiled by Catherine the Great to his estate in the framework of “the case of N. I. Novikov.” “He lived together with his brothers Alexander Trubetskoy, Yuri Trubetskoy, and Mikhail Kheraskov in the same mansion on Tverskaya Street in Moscow in the 1770s. This house remained in the memory of contemporaries as the center of Russian education. The

[1] L. Mukhovitskaya “Trubetskoy. Aristocrats in spirit.” M.: EntrustTrading, 2015. - 256 p. Page 34.

Brothers had many ardent debates about politics, culture, and the economic transformation of society. They read and translated books by European philosophers and enlighteners[1]." In connection with joining the Freemasons, N. N. Trubetskoy abandoned the views of the encyclopedists (Bell, Helvetius, and Voltaire).

Ivan Petrovich Turgenev (1752-1807)	A Privy Councilor, a Director of the Moscow University, from the family of the Tatar Murza, from the family of a Second Major.	He was consecrated in the Alexander Fortress in the Crimea in October 1776, an Orator of the lodge in the Crimea in 1778. 42 The Lodge of Astrea in M. until 1783, a founding member of the lodge. 44 The Directory of the VIII Province in M., a member from 1782 to February 1783, his Order Name was "Jannes eques ab aurora boreale." 46 The Lodge of Harmony in M., active from 1780 to 1783, a member of the lodge. 48 The Lodge of Deucalion in M., a member of the lodge. 61 The Theoretical Degree in M., admitted to the Theoretical Degree in 1782, admitted to the Internal Order of the Rosicrucians during the life of I. E. Schwartz (approximately in 1783), his Order Name was "Vegetus" ("Blossoming"), his Motto was "Vegetus Turnuper" ("Vegetus Enion Rhuan"), transferred from submission to N. I. Novikov under the direction of G. Ya, Schroeder. A member and a Registrar of the Haupt Directorate in M. in September 1788, transferred from the circle of N. I. Novikov into the circle of I. V. Lopukhin in October 1788 and was appointed a Senior in it, a Chief Overseer of the Theoretical Degree in 1792, worked under the command of N. I. Novikov. 78 The Lodge of Harpocrates in P., 1773-1776, a member of the lodge. 88 The Chapter of Latona in P., an Honorary Member in 1778.	A. A. Prozorovsky, Z. G. Chernyshev. A friend - M. N. Muravyov. The opposition: P. I. Golenishchev-Kutuzov, M. I. Kovalinsky.			Vol. 2. P. 554-556. Vol. 3. P. 45, 46, 48, 49, 69, 108, 120, 144, 257.

[1]L. Mukhovitskaya "Trubetskoy. Aristocrats in spirit." M.: EntrastTreyding, 2015. - 256 p. Page 34.

		91 The Lodge of the Muses in P., not in the lists. 93 The Lodge of Osiris in P., the 1st Alms-Gatherer in November 1781. 125 The Lodge of the Golden Crown in Simbirsk, a founding member of the lodge from 1784. *A Great Master, length of service: from 1773 to 1788 - 16 years (the 2nd generation).*				

An opinion of I. P. Turgenev, on the state and legal issues, can be considered representative of all Russian Freemasonry at the end of the 18th century as he had 16 years of membership in Masonic Lodges, held senior positions in Masonic Lodges, was a member of Chapters, a founder of several lodges, and translated Western literature into Russian. According to A. N. Pypin[1], Turgenev was an author of "Reasoning" in French (published in the translation of V. Protopopov), "Who can be a good citizen and a faithful subject." Another original composition of his was "Some Imitation of David's Songs." He also translated several mystical treatises, such as John Mason's "Know thyself"; Johann Arndt's "On true Christianity"; "An Apology, or Defense of the Order of Freemasons." I. P. Turgenev, along with Laharpe and Protasov, was the tutor of Grand Duke Alexander Pavlovich. After accession to the throne of Paul I, he was returned from exile, being there from 1792, received the rank of a Full Councilor of State (1796) and was appointed Director of the Moscow University.

Ignatius Aurelius Fessler (1756-1839)	A Court Counselor, a Professor of Theology and Eastern Languages, *a Legal Consultant, graduated from the Raab Jesuit Collegium and the University of Vienna with the teaching of Law,* a founder of	137 Foreign lodges, was dedicated on 05.01.1783 (1784) in the Lodge of Phoenix to a Lime Board in Lemberg (Lvov), a member of this lodge of the 1st, the 2nd, and the 3rd Degrees in 1784-1785, an Affiliated Member of the lodge of RoyalYorkzurFreundschaft (Royal York to Friendship) in Berlin from 06.02.1796 (*he reformed it*), *a Local Master of the last of these lodges from 06.05.1797, a Chair Master of the of the Daughter Lodge of Urania in 1797-1802, an Assistant to the Great National Master from 06.24.1798 and 1800,* a member of a number of subsidiary lodges. *A Great Master, length of service:*			A Student - P. D. Lodius.	Vol. 2. P. 581-583. Vol. 3. P. 302-303.

[1]A. N. Pypin "Russian Freemasonry: the 18th and the first quarter of the 19th centuries." / A. N. Pypin; Ed., [An introduction and a note by G. V. Vernadsky. - Petrograd: Lights, 1916. - VIII, 571, [4] p. Page 254.

	the Society of the Friends of Humanity and the Union of Scientific Freemasons, *took part in the Commission for Drafting the Laws from 1810, 1819-1824 – an Official for the special assignments of the Commission for Drafting the Laws,* from the family of a retired Austrian Dragoon. *Austrian origin, mother tongue – German.*	*1783-1802 - 20 years (the 2nd and the 3rd generations).*				

An opinion of I. A. Fessler on the state-legal issues cannot be considered representative of all Russian Freemasonry of the late 18th – the first quarter of the 19th centuries, although he had 20 years of membership in Masonic Lodges and was a Local Master and a Chair Master, his Masonic activity took place in Prussian Lodges. He began his Masonic activity in the 19th century in Russia with the formation of the Lodge of the Polar Star in St. Petersburg together with M. M. Speransky. However, the rejection of the reforms (started by I. A. Fessler and M. M. Speransky) by the Masonic world and its leaders (I. A. Pozdeev, A. K. Razumovsky, and others) made the existence of the lodge short (1810-1812) and led to the exile of I. A. Fessler to the Saratov Province. At the same time, I. A. Fessler wrote many interesting works, including the works on the History and Ideology of Freemasonry (those works have not yet been translated into Russian).

Mikhail Matveyevich Kheraskov (1733-1807)	A Full Privy Councilor, a Curator of the Moscow University.	45 The Chapter of the VIII Province in M., a member of the Provincial Chapter in 1782-1784, a Seigneur of the VIII province in 1783, his Order Name was "Michael ab arista naturante." 46 The Lodge of Harmony in M. from 1780-1783, a founding member of the lodge. 47 The University Lodge of Hermes in M., not in the lists. 54 The Provincial Lodge, an Orator of the lodge in the summer of 1782, in 1784 and, approximately, in 1789. 61 The Theoretical Degree in M., admitted to the Theoretical Degree in 1782, was also accepted into the Internal Order of the Rosicrucians during the life of I. E. Schwartz, approximately in 1783, a Rhetorician of the Administration of the Theoretical Degree. His Order Name was "Tacheroth Salemsky." 73 The GEPL in P., was a Scottish Master in September 1776, scheduled for the Grand Provincial Lodge and the Provincial Chapter. 74 The Lodge of Apollo in P., a Local Master in 1771. 78 The Lodge of Harpocrates in P., not in the lists. 88 The Chapter of Latona in P., an Honorary Member of the lodge in 1778, a founding member of the Chapter. 93 The Lodge of Osiris in P., one of the three Orators of the lodge in 1776, a Freemason of the 3rd Degree, and an Honorary Member of the lodge in November 1781. *A Great Master, length of service; 1771-1784 - 14 years (the 2nd*	Counts of the Orlov family, Counts of the Panin family, N. N. Trubetskoy, A. P. Sumarokov, M. M. Shcherbatov – his colleagues.	Mother was married to N. Yu. Trubetskoy (her second marriage), mother of A. N. Trubetskoy.	N. I. Novikov, I. G. Schwartz. He wrote some philosophical songs for A.A.R. (possibly, to Rzhevsky), S.E.D. (possibly, to Desnitsky).	Vol. 2. P. 607-610. Vol. 3. P. 48, 49, 54, 69, 85, 91, 120, 145.

		generation).				

An opinion of M. M. Kheraskov, on the state and legal issues, can be considered representative of all Russian Freemasonry at the end of the 18th century as he had 14 years of membership in Masonic Lodges, held the highest positions in Masonic Lodges, was a member of some Chapters and a founder of several lodges. He was the author of many poems, verses, and prose writings.

Alexander Vasilyevich Khrapovitsky (1749-1802)	A Full Privy Councilor, a Secretary of State of Catherine II, a Senator, from an old noble family, from the family of a General-Anshef.	A member of the Lodge of A. I. Bibikov. 73 The GEPL in P., a Scottish Master in September 1776, scheduled to join the GPL. 75 The Lodge of Astrea in P., a Chair Master in 1776. 78 The Lodge of Harpocrates in P., an Orator in 1773-1775. 88 The Chapter of Latona in P. from 1780., a Chair Master. 91 The Lodge of the Muses in P. in 1770-1774, a member of the lodge. 92 The Lodge of Nemesis in P., a Chair Master in 1776-1777. *A Great Master, length of service: 1770-1780 - 11 years (the 2nd generation).*	Grand Duke Pyotr Fedorovich (Peter III), K. G. Razumovsky.		A. N. Radishchev.	Vol. 2. P. 615-617. Vol. 3. P. 85, 93, 109, 120, 139, 140.

An opinion of A.V. Khrapovitsky, on the state and legal issues, can be considered representative of all Russian Freemasonry at the end of the 18th century as he had 11 years of membership in Masonic Lodges and held the highest positions in Masonic Lodges. He was the author of some memorandums.

Khariton Andreyevich Chebotarev (1745-1815)	A Councilor of State, a Professor, a Dean, a Rector, a Censor, a Secretary of the Friendly Scientific Society, from the family of a Sergeant.	55 The Lodge of Equality in M. and P., was dedicated on 07.25.1775, raised to the 2nd Degree on 09.07.1775 and to the 3rd Degree on 09.12.1775, appointed Secretary on 09.12.1775 and the 2nd Overseer for the table lodges, secretly dedicated to all the degrees in 1775. 59 The Lodge of the Sphinx in M., appointed Chair Master on 02.10.1782 by the Mother Lodge of the Three Banners, held this post until 06.24.1785, a Freemason of the 4th Degree, then a Local Master of the lodge. 61 The Theoretical Degree in M., accepted to the Theoretical Degree approximately in 1782, into the Internal Order of the Rosicrucians by I. V. Lopukhin approximately in 1785, his Order Name was "Thitanusaterruca," his name in the Knighthood was "Chariton equesaterruca." 62 The Lodge of the Three Banners in M., attached approximately in November 1781, the 2nd Overseer in 1785-1786, then the 1st Overseer. 93 The Lodge of Osiris in M. and P., a founding member of the lodge, a Secretary in the absence of A. Schepotyev in 1776, the 2nd Overseer in November 1781. *A Great Master, length of service: 1775-1786 - 12 years (the 2nd generation).*				Vol. 2. P. 633-635. Vol. 3. P. 57, 62, 70, 75.

An opinion of Kh. A. Chebotarev, on the state and legal issues, can be considered representative of all Russian Freemasonry at the end of the 18th century as he had a 12-year membership in Masonic Lodges, held some senior positions in Masonic Lodges, founded the Lodge of Osiris in St. Petersburg, was an author of some works and a translator of some works about the "common good" (the works of J. G. Reichel that was not a Freemason).

Ivan Grigoryevich Schwartz (1751-1784)	A Collegiate Assessor, *a Candidate of Both Laws at the University of Jena,* a Professor of Philosophy, son of Silesian colonists in Transylvania. *German origin, mother tongue – German.*	36 The Lodge of the Red Eagle in Mitava, admitted to the lodge in the second half of the 1770s and received the 5th Degree of the System of Strict Supervision in that lodge. 38 *The Lodge of Hercules in a Cradle in Mogilev on the Dnieper from 1776-1777, a member and a founder of the lodge, he was elected as a Chair Master* upon his return from Mitava. 41 The Lodge of Aspis in M., not in the lists. 45 *The Chapter of the VIII Province in M., a Chancellor in 1781*, his Order Name was "EquesGeorgi (Georgiuseques) abAquilacrescente." 46 *The Lodge of Harmony in M., a founding member of the lodge*, a member of the lodge until 1783. 49 *The Lodge of Friendship in M., a member of the lodge of the 3rd Degree and its Local Master* from 08.10.1779. 61 *The Theoretical Degree in M., received the Theoretical Grade and authority to arrange it in M. from Teden on 10.01.1781 (1782)*, a member of the Directory of the Theoretical Degree. A Rosicrucian, his Order Name was "Garganus Schoeneus (Garganus, Gorgonus) de Viktoritz." 62 The Lodge of the Three Banners in M., a visitor to the lodge on 5/5/1780 (1781), then attached on the recommendation of I. Toussaint, *a Presiding Master in the Scottish Lodge (during a meeting in 4 Degrees) from 02/10/1782. A Chair Master from 08.02.1783 or 10.02.1783 to 02.17.1784 (until 08.30.1783 or*	I. S. Gagarin, P. A. Tatishchev, M. M. Kheraskov, I. I. Shuvalov, N. I. Novikov.			Vol. 2. P. 658-660. Vol. 3. P. 40, 42, 48, 49, 51,70, 75, 145.

		10.30. 1783). 93 The Lodge of Osiris in P., admitted to the lodge through V. I. Maykov in 1776, was absent in the 3rd Degree in November 1781, at the same time an Honorary Member of the lodge. *A Great Master, length of service: from 1776 to 1783 - 8 years (the 2nd generation).*				

An opinion of I. G. Schwartz, on the state and legal issues, can be considered representative of all Russian Freemasonry at the end of the 18th century as he was the main figure in Russian Rosicrucianism of the 18th century, had 8 years of membership in Masonic Lodges, held some senior positions in Masonic Lodges, was a founder of some lodges and an author of the original works of philosophical-religious content (the lectures "On the three knowledges ... ," "Public lectures," "On prayer," etc.).[1]

Heinrich Jacob Yakovlevich Schroeder (1757-1815)	A Prussian Minister. *German origin, mother tongue – German.*	61 The Theoretical Degree in M., *became a Secretary of P. A. Tatishchev in the Theoretical Grade* on the recommendation of Teden in April 1784, *an Overseer of the Directory of the Theoretical Degree*, a Rosicrucian, his Order Name was "Sacerdos." 62 *The Lodge of the Three Banners in M., the 2nd Overseer from 07.02.1783 or 10.02.1783 to 04.20.1784, a Chair Master from 04.20.1784 to 1785.* 137 Foreign Lodges, dedicated on 09.19.1772, elevated to the 2nd Degree on 02.17.1776, raised to the 3rd Degree on 04.08.1778 in the Lodge of Zudendrei Sternen (Three Stars) in Rostock, *a Leader of the Circle of the Rosicrucians in Marburg from 1779, raised to the 6th degree in Berlin on 07/11/1785, raised to the 7th and the 8th Degrees on 09/12/1785*, his Order Name was "a Bona Fide, a Tigride Insurgente." *A Great Master, length of service: from 1776 to 1785 - 10 years (the 2nd*	I. G. Schwartz. A friend - A. M. Kutuzov.			Vol. 2. P. 681-682. Vol. 3. P. 70, 75, 305.

[1]See the studies of A. V. Arzhanukhin and A. D. Tyurikov.

		generation).				

An opinion of H. Ya. Schroeder, on the state and legal issues, cannot be considered representative of all Russian Freemasonry at the end of the 18th century, although he had a 10-year membership in Masonic Lodges, but his Masonic activity mainly touched upon German Lodges and German Rosicrucianism. His works have not been translated into Russian yet.

Friedrich Ulrich Ludwig Schroeder (1744-1816)	An Actor, a Director, a historian and a Freemasonry reformer, from an Organist family. *German origin, mother tongue – German.*	137 Foreign Lodges, consecrated in the lodge of Emanuelzur Mainblume in Hamburg in 1774, its member of the 3rd Degree from 1775, a Chair Master from 1787, *became an initiator of the Freemasonry Reform and a creator of the New System of Schroeder after 1787, cancelling the highest degrees of Freemasonry*, a member of the Lodge of Einigkeitund Toleranz in 1792-1793. *A Great Master, length of service: from 1774 to 1793 - 20 years (the 2nd and the 3rd generations).*				Vol. 2. P. 683-684. Vol. 3. P. 306.

An opinion of F. L. Schroeder, on the state and legal issues, cannot be considered representative of all Russian Freemasonry at the end of the 18th century, although he had 20 years of membership in Masonic Lodges and founded a new system of Freemasonry rituals, but his Masonic activity mainly touched upon German Lodges. His works have not been translated into Russian yet.

Alexey Loginovich Shcherbachev (1720-1802)	A Full Privy Councilor, a Senator, *a Judge*, from the nobility, from the family of the Oryol Governor and Commandant.	73 The GEPL in P., the 1st Great Overseer in 1773-1774, a Scottish Master and the 2nd Great Provincial Overseer in 1776. 90 The Lodge of Silence (Modesty), a member of the lodge of the 6th Degree in 1786-1787. 91 The Lodge of the Muses in P., the 2nd Performer in 1774. 105 The Lodge of Urania in P., a visitor to the lodge on 08.03.1773 and 12.10.1773. *A Great Master, length of service:*	A Field Marshal Apraksin.			Vol. 2. P. 706-707. Vol. 3. P. 85, 134, 139, 197.

		from 1773 to 1787 - 15 years (the 2nd generation).				

An opinion of A. L. Shcherbachev, on the state-legal issues, can be considered representative of all Russian Freemasonry at the end of the 18th century as he held the highest positions in Masonic Lodges and the Unions of the Lodges, had a 15-year membership in Masonic Lodges. However, his works have not been published yet and have been waiting for the researchers.

Yegor Yegorovich Ellizen (1756-1830)	A Full Councilor of State, a Doctor of Medicine, and a Ph.D. in Philosophy, from the family of a Doctor of Medicine. *German origin, mother tongue – German.*	*29 The Lodge of the Three Columns in Kyiv, a founding member of the lodge, a Chair Master of the lodge in 1788.* 137 Foreign lodges, dedicated in the lodge of zum Widder in Berlin on 03.01.1779, he was issued a certificate from this lodge on 11.11.1779, a member of the Lodge of Ferdinand to the Temple in Gildersheim from 1781, raised to the 2nd and 3rd Degrees in that lodge in 1785. *Considering his Masonic experience of the 19th century (for example, the performance of the duties of a Chair Master in 1815-1820 in the Lodge of Peter to the Verity (to the Truth) in P.) - a Great Master, length of service: from 1779 to 1820 - 42 years (the 2nd, the 3rd, and the 4th generations).*		Sister Carolina - mother of A. V. Lerche and V. V. Lerche.		Vol. 2. P. 713-715. Vol. 3. P. 34, 307. Serkov, 2001, P. 1045.

An opinion of Y. Y. Ellisen, on the state and legal issues, can be considered representative of all Russian Freemasonry of the late 18th and the first quarter of the 19th centuries as he held the highest positions in Masonic Lodges and the Unions of the Lodges, had a 42-year membership in Masonic Lodges. His works were published in Latin, German, and Russian in large numbers and mainly dealt with medical issues. A letter of Y. Y. Ellisen on the illegality of the Chapter of Masonic Lodges (addressed to I. V. Beber in 1814) is of particular interest.

The list below includes V. I. Bibikov, V. A. Vsevolozhsky, P. I. Golenishchev-Kutuzov, and O. G. K. Hoven. Their literary heritage could not be found.

Vasily Ilyich Bibikov (1740-1787)	A Real Chamberlain, a Privy Councilor, a Deputy of the Commission of the composition of the New Code.	80 The Lodge of Gorus in P., a Chair Master in 1779. 97 PGL in P., the Second Great Alms-Gatherer in 1779. 100 The Lodge of the Perfect Union (Consent) in P., visited in 1771-1772. 105 The Lodge of Urania in P., visited in 1775. 107 The Chapter of the Phoenix in P., a member of the Chapter in 1779. *A Great Master, the length of service:* from 1771 to 1779 - 9 years (the 2nd generation).				Vol. 1. P. 172-173. Vol. 3. P. 109, 146, 163, 200.
Vsevolod Alekseevich Vsevolozhsky (1769-1836)	A Full Privy Councilor, a Full Chamberlain, a Deputy, from an ancient noble family, the 30th knee from Rurik.	45 *The Chapter of the VIII Province in M.,* a member of the Priory from 1782, a member of the Chapter from 1783. *A Great Master, the length of service:* 1782-1783 - 2 years (the 2nd generation).				Vol. 1. P. 317-318. Vol. 4. P. 47.
Pavel Ivanovich Golenishchev-Kutuzov (1767-1829)	A Privy Councilor, a Senator, an Honorary Member of the Academy of Sciences, from an old Novgorod family.	17 The Lodge of the North Star in Vyborg (in German), attended the lodge in 1789. 32 The Lodge of Neptune in Kronstadt, a member of the lodge since 1786. A Local Master (in Russian) from 1786. A 5-Degree member of the lodge in 1787. 77 The Lodge of Charity to the Pelican in P., dedicated in 1785. 130 The Camping Lodge of Mars at Friedrichsham, a member from 1789. *A Great Master, length of service: 1786-1789 - 4 years (the 2nd generation).*	S. K. Greig. I. V. Gudovich, married to the sister of A. K. Razumovsky - Minister of Education, close to A. S. Shishkov.			Vol. 1. P. 395-397. Vol. 3. P. 23, 36, 258.
Otto	A Privy	37 The Lodge of the Three Crowned				Vol.

German Karlovich Hoven (1740-1806)	Councilor, a Representative of the Courland nobility, a Senator, from an ancient Baltic family. *Baltic origin, mother tongue – German.*	Swords in Mitava, a Chair Master in 1779. *37a The Lodge of the Three Crowned Hearts in Mitava, a Great Inspector of the Lodge in 1780. A Great Master, length of service: 1779-1780 - 2 years (the 2nd generation).*				2. P. 612-613. Vol. 3. P. 41.

Brief conclusions:

1) 95% of the Russian Freemasons that rose to high ranks were from the representatives of the family nobility (the Rurikovich, Romanov, boyar families, the families of the Rzeczpospolita and the Grand Duchy of Lithuania, Courland, Estonia, Swedish, Danish, German families that received the nobility in the first half of the XVIII century for their services to the Fatherland. The remaining 5% of the Russian Freemasons were from the families of lawyers, scientists, and medical workers living in Europe. This circumstance testifies in favor of the non-acceptance of the ideas of freedom, equality, and fraternity by Freemasons or a narrow interpretation of these ideas, not leaving the limits of Masonic meetings.

2) 24 out of the 64 "Great Masters" were of foreign origin (less than half): 17 were of German, Austrian, and Baltic origin. Their native language was German (about 1/3 of the total and more than 2/3 of the number of foreigners). They were the members of the highest bodies of management of many Russian Masonic Lodges, founding new lodges and new Masonic Systems. For comparison, 5 "Great Masters" (including 1 "Great Master" of Polish-French influence) were the conductors of French influence, 2 "Great Masters" were the conductors of Polish influence (including 1 "Great Master" of Polish-French influence), and only 1 "Great Master" was the conductor of English influence.

3) 19 out of the 64 "Great Masters" received legal education, scientific degrees in law, and/or held the positions of a Lawyer, Judge, or Legal Adviser. 12 of them received legal education at European Universities: mainly in Prussia and in the German principalities (Leiden University, Leipzig University, Galle University, Jena University, Turin University, Königsberg University, Collegium Nobilium in Warsaw, and University of Vienna).

4) 6 out of the 17 “Great Masters” of German origin received legal education, scientific degrees in jurisprudence, and/or held the positions of a Lawyer, Judge, or Legal Adviser. Only 2 out of the 5 “Great Masters” that were the conductors of French influence (including Polish-French influence) received legal education or held the positions of a Lawyer, Judge, or Legal Adviser. Only 1 out of the 2 “Great Masters” of Polish influence (including Polish-French influence) received legal education or held the positions of a Lawyer, Judge, or Legal Adviser.

5) Only 40 out of the 60 “Great Masters” had some influence on the majority of Russian Freemasons and were the conductors of the influence of Russian Freemasonry. This fact indicates the selectivity and limited influence of foreign Freemasons on Russian Freemasonry. Also, this case points out that a little less than half of the Freemasons had various political and legal views that did not become decisive and representative of all Russian Freemasonry.

The above-mentioned circumstances testify to the decisive influence of German jurisprudence and German political and legal doctrine on the political and legal ideology of Russian jurisprudence and Russian political and legal doctrine. Also, these circumstances indicate the conclusive influence of the ideology of German Freemasonry on the ideology and organization of Russian Freemasonry. In addition, it should be noted that those processes took place in parallel but in close interconnection and with mutual influence.

Chapter II

I. I. Melissino's Denunciation

The source: RGADA, Fund 146 ("Search files - (Collection) from the funds of the Ambassadorial Order and the Collegium of Foreign Affairs.") units of issue 23 ("The Reports of the Curator of the Imperial Moscow University, Privy Councilor Ivan Ivanovich Melissino to the Commander-in-Chief in Moscow, Prince Alexander Alexandrovich Prozorovsky, with the attachment of his correspondence with Ober Kamerger Shuvalov and other persons about the known Friendly Scientific Society, now colloquially known under the name of the Martinists - 2 original documents. 30 letters in the appendix; in copies). - 59 pages. Pages 1-2.

"Dear Sir, Prince Alexander Alexandrovich,

When talking to me, your Excellency deigned to declare your desire to see my correspondence about the Friendly Scientific Society, now colloquially known under the name of the Martinists. Dear Sir, I dare not burden you with reading all those letters I had to write. I wrote about it on numerous occasions with the utmost sorrow of spirit, trying to turn the mystical communities away from the university as much as I could. Dear Sir, I am forwarding only part of the correspondence in question to you. But even this one is very big. For this reason, I am afraid to burden your patience.

Your Excellency, when reading these letters, you can clearly see that I had to be tormented and am still tormented in spirit, fearing innocently not to be numbered with this absurd and violent Contagion. Also, while reading, you can notice that I had to fight to turn it away from the university, hearing an all-participatory censure on it and realizing that my Comrade himself was the culprit responsible for it. Thanks to God, by using my efforts coupled with my own suffering I endured from this insidious community, this contagious tree lost most of its branches. Nevertheless, I must frankly confess to your Excellency that it would be very desirable for me that the root of this Contagion be exterminated from the university. By doing this, we could not only establish the prosperity of this school, but also save the well-minded from the innocent reproach. This reproof should be applied to the so-called Martinists only.

I humbly apologize for any inconvenience this may cause you, Your Excellency.

Your humble servant,

Ivan Melissino

June 13, 1790."

Chapter III

A table of the chronology of the works of authors, testifying to the attitude toward the "common good" and membership in Masonic Lodges.

The selection of authors was made according to two criteria that must be fulfilled simultaneously:
1. Belonging to Masonic Lodges.
2. The use of the terminology of the theory of the "common good" in the text works. The membership in Masonic Lodges was determined by using the information that was gleaned from some documentary evidence and published by A. I. Serkov. The sample (selection) does not include I. I. Betsky and N. N. Novosiltsev as I. I. Betsky did not belong to the key figures of Russian Freemasonry, and the works of N. N. Novosiltsev are a bibliographic rarity.

The crosses marked the life span of the author and his belonging to the generations of Russian Freemasons. The works were given according to the publication. If the printing was made outside of the given generations, then the generation the writing of the manuscript belongs to was indicated.

#	Full Name		The 1st generation (1750-1769)	The 2nd generation (1770-1789)	The 3rd generation (1790-1809)	The 4th generation (1810-1822)
1	*Boltin Ivan Nikitich (1735-1792)*	Years of life	X	X	X	
		Membership in Masonic Lodges	X	X		
		The Works		I. N. Boltin "Major General Boltin's response to a letter from Prince Shcherbatov, writer of Russian history." - St. Petersburg: The printing house of the Mining School, [17]89. - 183 p.	Russian Truth or the Laws of the Grand Dukes Yaroslav Vladimirovich and Vladimir Vsevolodovich Monomakh: With the application of the ancient dialects and syllables to those in common use today, and with an explanation of the words and names that became obsolete / Published by lovers of national history. - [St. Petersburg]: The printing house of St. Ruler of Synod, 1792. - [2], VIII, [13], 100, XVI p.	
2	*Pyotr*	Years of life	X	X	X	

	Ivanovich Melissino (1726-1797)	Membership in Masonic Lodges	X	X		
		The Works			P. I. Melissino "A description of the fireworks at the end of the celebration in case of peace concluded between Her Imperial Majesty Catherine II... and His Majesty Gustav the Third, King of Sweden: [Text]: Presented in St. Petersburg on the Tsaritsyn Meadow in September 1790." - St. Petersburg: The printing house of I. K. Shnor, 1790. - [10] p.	
3	*Alexander Petrovich Sumarokov (1717-1777)*	Years of life	X	X		
		Membership in Masonic Lodges	X			
		The Works		Word VII "On love for one's neighbor" // A. P. Sumarokov "The complete collection of all works: in verse and prose" / The deceased Full Councilor of State, a Cavalier of the Order of St. Anna and a member of the Leipzig Academic Assembly, Alexander Petrovich Sumarokov. Collected and published for the pleasure of the lovers of Russian Scholarship by Nikolai Novikov, a member of the Free Russian Assembly at the Imperial Moscow University. – The 2nd edition - Moscow: The University Printing House., N. Novikov, 1787. - 8 °.		

				Part 2. - 290 p.		
4	*Mikhail Mikhailovich Shcherbatov (1733-1790)*	Years of life	X	X	X	
		Membership in Masonic Lodges	X			
		The Works		1. M. M. Shcherbatov "'On the damage to morals in Russia' by Prince Shcherbatov and 'A Journey from St. Petersburg to Moscow' by A. Radishchev" / A preface by Iskander [a pseudonym of A. I. Herzen]. - London: Trubner & C°, 1858. - XVI, II, 340 pages. The manuscript was ready in the late 1780s. 2. M. M. Shcherbatov "On the ways of teaching different sciences" // Mikhail Mikhailovich Shcherbatov (1733-1790). The works of Prince M. M. Shcherbatov: Volumes 1-2. - St. Petersburg: Prince B. S. Shcherbatov, 1896-1898. - 2 volumes; 26 cm. The historical, political, and philosophical articles / Edited by I. P. Khrushchov and A. G. Voronov. - 1898. - [2], X p., page 630 by 2 columns. Pages 439-602. The manuscript was ready in the late 1780s. 3. M. M. Shcherbatov "A letter to the nobles, the rulers of the state. The works of a Senator, Prince M. M. Shcherbatov" // Russian Antiquity. - 1872. - Volume 5. - # 1. - Pages 1-15. The		

				manuscript was ready in the late 1780s. 4. M. M. Shcherbatov "The consideration of the vices and autocracy of Peter the Great. Conversation." // Mikhail Mikhailovich Shcherbatov (1733-1790). Various works of Prince M. M. Shcherbatov / A foreword by O. Bodyansky. - Moscow: The University Printing House, 1860. - [2], 140 p. Pages 5-22. The manuscript was ready in the late 1780s.		
5	*Fyodor Grigoryevich Bause (1752-1812)*	Years of life	X	X	X	X
		Membership in Masonic Lodges		X		
		The Works			F. G. Bause "What has been done in Russia to educate the people and for the glory of the Fatherland from the time of Rurik to Peter the Great" // Europe Bulletin, part XXV, January 1806, Pages 3-20, 81-96.	
6	*Alexey Ivanovich Vasilyev (1742-1807)*	Years of life	X	X	X	
		Membership in Masonic Lodges		X		
		The Works			A. I. Vasilyev "A highly approved report of the Minister of Finance, with the states and other applications on the new formation of the Mining Authorities and Management of the Mining Factories (approved on July 13, 1806)." - St. Petersburg: Printed in the Medical Printing	

					House, 1806. - 1-254, 249-256, 255-258, [2] p.	
7	*Alexander Romanovich Vorontsov (1741-1805)*	Years of life	X	X	X	
		Membership in Masonic Lodges		X		
		The Works			1. A note of Count A. R. Vorontsov about Russia at the beginning of this century, presented to Emperor Alexander Pavlovich in November 1801 / / An archive of Prince Vorontsov / Edited by P. I. Bartenyov - Moscow: The printing house of A. I. Mamontov, 1870-1897. Book 29: The letters from the foreigners to the Counts of the Vorontsov family. - 1883. - XI, 492 p. Pages 449-470. 2. A. R. Vorontsov "The notes about my life and various events that took place during this time both in Russia and Europe." Russian Archive. 1883. Book 1. Issue 2. Pages 227-249.	
8	*Gavriil Petrovich Gagarin (1745-1808)*	Years of life	X	X	X	
		Membership in Masonic Lodges		X		
		The Works				G. P. Gagarin "The amusements of my solitude in the village of Bogoslovsky" / / The remaining creation of Prince Gabriel Petrovich Gagarin. - St. Petersburg: Printed in the printing house of the Military Ministry,

						1813. - [12], 185, [1] p.
9	*Alexander Borisovich Kurakin (1752-1818)*	Years of life	X	X	X	X
		Membership in Masonic Lodges		X		
		The Works			1. A letter from Prince A. B. Kurakin to Count N. P. Panin (dated March 24, 1798). Russian Antiquity, an edition of 1874, Volume X, Pages 575-579. 2. A. B. Kurakin "A copy of the most submissive petition of Prince Alexander Borisovich Kurakin to the Emperor (dated December 4, 1806)" / / An approved position of Prince Alexander Borisovich Kurakin. - St. Petersburg: Printed at the printing house of Friedrich Drechsler, 1807. - [2], 107, [1] p.: Pages 3-6. 3. A copy from the Relationship of Prince Alexander Borisovich Kurakin to the Minister of the Interior, Count Viktor Pavlovich Kochubey (dated December 04, 1806) / / An approved position of Prince Alexander Borisovich Kurakin. - St. Petersburg: Printed at the printing house of Friedrich Drechsler, 1807. - [2], 107, [1] p.: Pages 7-8. 4. My Letter of Faith to the Governing Senate, an Ober Prosecutor, a Full Councilor of State and Cavalier Pyotr Stepanovich	

					Molchanov / / An approved position of Prince Alexander Borisovich Kurakin. - St. Petersburg: Printed at the printing house of Friedrich Drechsler, 1807. - [2], 107, [1] p. Pages 19-24.
					5. My notes to be included word for word in all the articles in the Act performed on my behalf with my Nadezhda peasants liberated by me / / An approved position of Prince Alexander Borisovich Kurakin. - St. Petersburg: Printed at the printing house of Friedrich Drechsler, 1807. - [2], 107, [1] p. Pages 25-87.
					6. A letter from Alexander B. Kurakin to the Grand Duchess Maria Fyodorovna (dated May 23, 1807) // The letters from the road from Prince A. B. Kurakin to the Empress Maria Fyodorovna // Russian Archive. - 1868. - Book 1, Notebook 1. - Pages 23-86; Notebook 2. - Pages 161-240. Pages 52-60.
					7. A letter from Alexander B. Kurakin to Grand Duchess Maria Fyodorovna (dated May 30, 1807) // Russian Archive. - 1868. - Book 1, Notebook 1. - Pages 23-86; Notebook 2. - Pages 161-240. Pages 60-63.	

					8. A letter from Alexander B. Kurakin to Grand Duchess Maria Fyodorovna (dated June 8, 1807) // The letters from the road from Prince A. B. Kurakin to the Empress Maria Fyodorovna // Russian Archive. - 1868. - Book 1. Notebook 1. - Pages 23-86; Notebook 2. - Pages 161-240, 161-176.
					9. A letter from Alexander B. Kurakin to the Grand Duchess Maria Fyodorovna (dated June 10, 1807) // The letters from the road from Prince A. B. Kurakin to the Empress Maria Fyodorovna // Russian Archive. - 1868. - Book 1. Notebook 1. - Pages 23-86; Notebook 2. - Pages 161-240. Pages 176-183.
					10. A letter from Alexander B. Kurakin to Grand Duchess Maria Fyodorovna (dated June 18, 1807) // The letters from the road from Prince A. B. Kurakin to the Empress Maria Fyodorovna // Russian Archive. - 1868. - Book 1. Notebook 1. - Pages 23-86; Notebook 2. - Pages 161-240. Pages 196-208.
					11. A release of a letter from Prince Kurakin to A. A. Nartov (dated December 1805) // P.	

					A. Druzhinin "The unknown letters of Russian writers to Prince Alexander Borisovich Kurakin (1752–1818)." - M.: Truten, 2002. - 504 p. Pages 268-269.	
10	*Alexey Mikhailovich Kutuzov (1749-1792)*	Years of life	X	X	X	
		Membership in Masonic Lodges		X		
		The Works			1. A letter to Mrs. Pleshcheeva (March 1792) // Ya. L. Barskov "The correspondence of the Moscow Freemasons of the 18th century, 1780-1792." [Text] / Ya. L. Barskov. - Petrograd: An edition of the Department of Russian language and literature of the Imperial Academy of Sciences, 1915. - LXII, 335, [6] p. Pages 197-199. 2. A letter to Prince Trubetskoy (April 1792) // Ya. L. Barskov "The correspondence of the Moscow Freemasons of the 18th century, 1780-1792." [Text] / Ya. L. Barskov. - Petrograd: An edition of the Department of Russian language and literature of the Imperial Academy of Sciences, 1915. - LXII, 335, [6] p. Pages 200-201.	
11	*Alexander Fyodorovich Labzin (1766-1825)*	Years of life	X	X	X	X
		Membership in Masonic Lodges		X	X	X
		The Works			A quote from the magazine "Sion Herald." See: P.	

					Bessonov "A. F. Labzin. A literary and biographical essay" / / Russian Archive, 1866. - Issue 6. - Pages 817-836 by 2 columns.	
12	*Vasily Alekseevich Lyovshin (1746-1826)*	Years of life	X	X	X	X
		Membership in Masonic Lodges		X	X	X
		The Works		The latest journey // An interlocutor of the lovers of the Russian word. 1784. Part XIII. Pages138-166. Part XIV. Pages 5-14. Part XVI. Pages 38-45, 49-53.		
13	*Ivan Vladimirovich Lopukhin (1756-1816)*	Years of life	X	X	X	X
		Membership in Masonic Lodges		X		
		The Works			1. The notes of I. V. Lopukhin, book VII, 1802 // NIA II SPB RAN. Fund 36 "The Vorontsov family are an ancient noble family: Mikhail Illarionovich Vorontsov (1714-1767), Count; Roman Illarionovich Vorontsov (1707-1783), Count." List of contents 1. Unit of issue 753. 2. A letter of I. V. Lopukhin to A. M. Kutuzov (dated November 7, 1790) // Ya. L. Barskov "The correspondence of the Moscow Freemasons of the 18th century, 1780-1792." [Text] / Ya. L. Barskov. - Petrograd: An edition of the Department of Russian language and literature of the Imperial Academy of	

					Sciences, 1915. - LXII, 335, [6] p. Pages 23-28.	
14	*Ivan Ivanovich Melissino (1718-1795)*	Years of life	X	X	X	
		Membership in Masonic Lodges		X		
		The Works			A delation of I. I. Melissino to A. A. Prozorovsky (dated June 13, 1790) // RGADA. Fund 146. The search cases. Unit of issue # 23 (The reports of the Curator of the Imperial Moscow University, Privy Councilor Ivan Ivanovich Melissino, to the Commander-in-Chief in Moscow, Prince Alexander Alexandrovich Prozorovsky, together with the annex of his correspondence with Ober Kamerger Shuvalov and other persons about the known Friendly Scientific Society, now colloquially known under the name of the Martinists). 59 pages. Page 1.	
15	*Alexey Petrovich Melgunov (1722-1788)*	Years of life	X	X		
		Membership in Masonic Lodges		X		
		The Works		1. A circular letter from A. P. Melgunov to the nobles of the Yaroslavl Province on the issue of opening a home for orphans // L. N. Trefolev. The 2nd edition. - M., 1866. - Pages 873-952 by 2 columns. Page 891. 2. The correspondence of A.		

				P. Melgunov with Catherine II // Russian Archive, 1865. - The 2nd edition - M., 1866. - Pages 873-952 by 2 columns. Page 894. Both works belong to the period of the 80s of the XVIII century when A. P. Melgunov served as Governor-General of the Yaroslavl Province.		
16	*Alexey Ivanovich Musin-Pushkin (1744-1817)*	Years of life	X	X	X	X
		Membership in Masonic Lodges		X		
		The Works			1. Russian Truth or the Laws of the Grand Dukes Yaroslav Vladimirovich and Vladimir Vsevolodovich Monomakh: With the application of the ancient adverbs and syllables to those in common use today and with an explanation of the words and names that have become obsolete / Published by the lovers of National History. - [St. Petersburg]: The printing house of St. Ruler of Synod, 1792. - [2], VIII, [13], 100, XVI p. 2. A. I. Musin-Pushkin "A note" // Vladimir Monomakh (Grand Prince; 1053-1125). The Spiritual of Grand Duke Vladimir Vsevolodovich Monomakh to his children, named in the annals of Suzdal Teaching. - St. Petersburg: The	

					printing house of the Corps of Foreign Co-Religionists, 1793. - X, 61 p. Page 8.	
17	*Nikita Ivanovich Panin (1718-1783)*	Years of life	X	X		
		Membership in Masonic Lodges		X		
		The Works	1. A letter to the Primate of Podos (dated December 22, 1767) / / Catherine II (Empress; 1729-1796). The political correspondence of Empress Catherine II. - [St. Petersburg: without publishers], 1885-1914. - 26 cm. - (A collection of the Imperial Russian Historical Society / Russian Historical Society). Volume 67: 1766-1767 [Text]. - 1889. - XXI, 578, [1] p. Pages 561-563. 2. A depeche to the Ambassador, Prince N. V. Repnin (dated December 23, 1767) // A depeche of Count N. I. Panin to the Ambassador, Prince Repnin // Catherine II				

			(Empress; 1729-1796). The political corresponden ce of Empress Catherine II. - [St. Petersburg: without publishers], 1885-1914. - 26 cm. - (A collection of the Imperial Russian Historical Society / Russian Historical Society). Volume 67: 1766-1767 [Text]. - 1889. - XXI, 578, [1] p. Page 569. 3. A letter to Resident Obrezkov in Constantinopl e (dated August 11, 1768) // Catherine II (Empress; 1729-1796). The political corresponden ce of Empress Catherine II. - [St. Petersburg: without publishers], 1885-1914. - 26 cm. - (A collection of the Imperial Russian Historical Society / Russian Historical Society). Volume 87: 1768-1769			

			[Text]. - 1893. - XVIII, 555 p. Pages 138-146.			
18	Pyotr *Ivanovich Panin (1721-1789)*	Years of life	X	X		
		Membership in Masonic Lodges		X		
		The Works		A letter to the Grand Duke Pavel Petrovich (dated May 6, 1778) / / Pavel I, P. I. Panin "The correspondence to Grand Duke Pavel Petrovich with Count Pyotr Panin" // Russian Antiquity, 1882. - Volume 33. - No. 2. - Pages 409-410.		
19	*Iosif Alekseevich Pozdeev (1742-1820)*	Years of life	X	X	X	X
		Membership in Masonic Lodges		X	X	X
		The Works		A letter of I. A. Pozdeev to the Lodge of the Northern Star (dated March 5, 1784) // From the history of Russian Rosicrucianism / N. P. Kiselev; compiled by M. V. Reizin and A. I. Serkov. The text and comments by M. V. Reizin and A. I. Serkov. - St. Petersburg: The Publishing House named after N. I. Novikov, 2005. - 420, [2] p. Pages 376-378.	A letter of I. A. Pozdeev to V. I. Ostolopov (dated February 6, 1797) // From the history of Russian Rosicrucianism / N. P. Kiselev; compiled by M. V. Reizin and A. I. Serkov. The text and comments by M. V. Reizin and A. I. Serkov. - St. Petersburg: The Publishing House named after N. I. Novikov, 2005. - 420, [2] p. Page 320.	
20	*Ivan Petrovich Turgenev (1752-1807)*	Years of life	X	X	X	
		Membership in Masonic Lodges		X	X	
		The Works			I. P. Turgenev "Who can be a good citizen and a faithful subject?" / Translated from French into Russian by the	

					Serpuhovsky Protopop Vasily Protopopov. - Moscow: Printed in the University Printing House of Ridiger and Claudius, 1796. - [4], 39, [1] p.	
21	*Mikhail Matveyevich Kheraskov (1733-1807)*	Years of life	X	X	X	
		Membership in Masonic Lodges		X		
		The Works	1. M. M. Kheraskov "To the Honorable Gentlemen, the members of the Board of Trustees of the Imperial Educational Home." - Moscow: The University printing house, before1763. - 4 p. 2. Song XX. Calmness. / / M. M. Kheraskov "The philosophical odes or songs by Mikhail Kheraskov." - Moscow: Printed at the Imperial Moscow University, 1769. - [2], 72 p. Pages 41-42.	1. M. M. Kheraskov "Merry Russia: Prologue." - [M.: The University Printing House, without the year of publishing]. - [4] p. (an approximate year of publishing - 1772). 2. M. M. Kheraskov "The Temple of Russian Prosperity: Dedicated to the Constructor of this Temple, Her Imperial Majesty, an Autocrat of all Russia, the Most Gracious Empress Ekaterina Alekseevna II.: Presented at a joyful celebration of the conclusion of peace with the Ottoman Porte. In Moscow, in July 1775." - [Moscow]: Printed at the Imperial Moscow University, [1775]. - [15] p. 3. M. M. Kheraskov "An ode to Her Imperial Majesty, the most merciful Empress Ekaterina Alekseevna II.: Offered from Moscow University during the joyous stay of Her Imperial Majesty in Moscow, upon her longed-for return from midday	1. M. M. Kheraskov "Tsar, or Saved Novgorod: A Poetic Tale." - Moscow: The University printing House of Ridiger and Claudius, 1800. - [10], 246 p. 2. The creations of M. Kheraskov: Newly corrected and supplemented. Part 8: Cadmus and Harmony: Ancient narrative: Part 1, revised and supplemented. - 1801. - X, [6], 259, [6] p. 3. The creations of M. Kheraskov: Newly corrected and supplemented. Part 12: Numa Pompilius or Prosperous Rome. - The 3rd edition. - [1803]. - [2], VIII, 165 p.	

				Russian outlying districts: June 28, 1787." - Moscow: The University printing House of N. Novikov, 1787. - 11 p.		
22	*Alexander Vasilyevich Khrapovitsky (1749-1802)*	Years of life	X	X	X	
		Membership in Masonic Lodges		X		
		The Works			A. V. Khrapovitsky "A diary of A. V. Khrapovitsky. 1782-1793: From January 18, 1782 to September 17 [or 7], 1793" / According to his original manuscripts, a biographical article and the explanatory directions by Nikolai Barsukov, a member of the Archeographical Commission. - Moscow: Russian Archive, 1901 (reg. 1902). - XXII, 404 p.	
23	*Khariton Andreevich Chebotarev (1745-1815)*	Years of life	X	X	X	X
		Membership in Masonic Lodges		X		
		The Works	*I. Freyer* "The Hieronymus of Freyer. A Brief General History with its continuation to the very present times and the addition of Russian History to it." Translated from German into Russian by Ch. A. *Chebotarev* for the use of student youth.	1. *A Convolute.* A word on the invention of the art of writing. Did it serve to the detriment of the human mind and good morals or not? On the all-joyful day of the accession of the August Monarch, the Great Empress Catherine II, Empress and an Autocrat of all Russia (and so on) to the All-Russian Imperial Throne. On this day, solemnly celebrated with the deepest reverence at the Imperial Moscow University on June		

			Corrected and multiplied at the Imperial Moscow University / - Moscow: Printed at the same University, 1769. - [18], XLVIII, 500, [76] p.	30, 1776; Spoken by Khariton Chebotarev, a Public Extraordinary Professor of Reasoning and Moralizing, a University Sub-Librarian, and a member of the Free Russian Assembly of the same University. - Moscow: Printed at the University Printing House, 1776. - 23, [1] p. 2. *A Convolute*. A word on the means and ways leading to enlightenment: On the highly solemn birthday of Her Majesty the Empress and Autocrat of All Russia Catherine II, the Wise Legislator and True Mother of the Fatherland, at the public meeting of the Imperial Moscow University on April 22, 1779. / Spoken by Khariton Chebotarev, a Public Ordinary Professor of History, Reasoning, and Moralizing, a University Librarian and a Conference Secretary, and a member of the Moscow Russian Assembly. - Moscow: Printed at the University Printing House, 1779. - 28 p.		
24	*Adam Adamovich Czartoryski (1770-1861)*	Years of life		X	X	X
		Membership in Masonic Lodges			X	X
		The Works				A. Czartoryski "The memoirs and correspondence with Emperor Alexander 1."

						Edited by A. Kizevetter. Volume 1. St. Petersburg, 1912-1913. Page 170.
25	*Mikhail Yuryevich Vielgorsky (1788-1856)*	Years of life		X	X	X
		Membership in Masonic Lodges				X
		The Works				RGIA. Fund 938. List of contents 1. Case 440 “The Masonic notes written by Count M. Yu. Vielgorsky.” Page 1.
26	*Andrey Petrovich Rimsky-Korsakov (1778-1862)*	Years of life		X	X	X
		Membership in Masonic Lodges				X
		The Works		.		The reflection on the difference of systems in Freemasonry by Andrei Rimsky-Korsakov // GARF. Fund 48. List of contents 1. Unite of issue # 499. Part 3. The documents of Masonic Lodges: poems, songs, cantata in honor of the accession to the throne of Alexander I... Pages 69-78.
27	*Mikhail Mikhailovich Speransky (1772-1839)*	Years of life		X	X	X
		Membership in Masonic Lodges				X
		The Works				1. Speransky // Dmitriev “F. M. Speransky” [Text] / The works of F. Dmitriev. - Moscow: without publishers, 1862. - [190] p. §3. Pages 3-10. 2. The thoughts of Count M. M. Speransky. On the

						system of laws in general // Nikolai Vasilyevich Kalachov (1819-1885). An archive of historical and practical information relating to Russia, published by Nikolai Kalachov [Text]. - St. Petersburg: Printed in the Printing House of the Department II of His Imperial Majesty's Own Chancellery, 1858. Pages 3-20. The manuscript was presumably written in 1826.
Total		Number of representatives	23, of which mature age (from 21 years old - 9).	27, of which mature age (from 21 years old - 23).	23	12
		Number of members in Masonic Lodges	4	*21*	5	7
		Number of works	6	16	*31*	6

Conclusions

1. The terms of the "common good" among Russian Freemasons appeared in the 1st generation and lived up to the 4th generation. This fact indicates the influence of the theory of the "common good" on the worldview of Russian Freemasons. The theory manifested itself in the form of philosophical and theoretical reasoning for some of the Freemasons. Other Freemasons used the vocabulary of the theory when discussing various social-political and legal topics.

2. The terminology of the "common good" appeared in the vocabulary of some authors before they joined the Masonic Lodges (6 works written by N. I. Panin, M. M. Kheraskov, and Kh. A. Chebotarev - about 10 % of the total number of works).
3. The heyday of the publications mentioning the "common good" ("general benefit") fell on 1790-1809.
4. The most fruitful for publication was the generation of 1770-1789.
5. 19 works related to the vocabulary of the "common good" were written when the authors were the members of some Masonic Lodges (about 32 % of the total number of works).
6. The largest number of works were written or published after the authors left the Masonic Lodges or stopped appearing at the meetings of the brothers (33, i.e., about 56 % of the total number of works).
7. The vocabulary of the "common good" was perceived by the authors regardless of Freemasonry from the general political and legal-cultural environment. However, Russian Freemasonry increased the use of the vocabulary of the "common good" in the works of the authors, even when the authors stopped attending Masonic meetings.

www.ingramcontent.com/pod-product-compliance
Lightning Source LLC
Chambersburg PA
CBHW060111120726
48003CB00009B/2587
9798869263407